A GLOBAL INTRODUCT
BAPTIST CHURCH

Coinciding with the four hundredth anniversary of the birth of the Baptist movement, this book explores and assesses the cultural sources of Baptist beliefs and practices. Although the Baptist movement has been embraced, enriched, and revised by numerous cultural heritages, it has focused on a small group of Anglo exiles in Amsterdam in constructing its history and identity. Robert E. Johnson seeks to recapture the varied cultural and theological sources of Baptist tradition and to give voice to the divergent global elements of the movement that have previously been excluded or marginalized. With an international communion of more than 110 million persons in more than 225,000 congregations, Baptists constitute the world's largest aggregate of evangelical Protestants. This work offers insight into the diversity, breadth, and complexity of the cultural influences that continue to shape Baptist identity today.

ROBERT E. JOHNSON is currently Professor of Christian Heritage and Academic Dean at the Central Baptist Theological Seminary. He has also taught at the Faculdade Teológica Batista de São Paulo, Brazil, and the Midwestern Baptist Theological Seminary. He is the editor of *American Baptist Quarterly* and the author of numerous scholarly articles.

A GLOBAL INTRODUCTION TO BAPTIST CHURCHES

ROBERT E. JOHNSON

Central Baptist Theological Seminary

CAMBRIDGE
UNIVERSITY PRESS

CAMBRIDGE UNIVERSITY PRESS
Cambridge, New York, Melbourne, Madrid, Cape Town, Singapore,
São Paulo, Delhi, Dubai, Tokyo, Mexico City

Cambridge University Press
32 Avenue of the Americas, New York, NY 10013-2473, USA

www.cambridge.org
Information on this title: www.cambridge.org/9780521701709

First published 2010

Printed in the United States of America

A catalog record for this publication is available from the British Library.

Library of Congress Cataloging in Publication data

Johnson, Robert E.
A global introduction to Baptist churches / Robert E. Johnson.
p.   cm. – (Introduction to religion)
Includes bibliographical references and index.
ISBN 978-0-521-87781-7 (hardback)
1. Baptists.   I. Title.   II. Series.
BX6331.3.J64   2010
286.09 – dc22   2010010210

ISBN 978-0-521-87781-7 Hardback
ISBN 978-0-521-70170-9 Paperback

Contents

Illustrations

Acknowledgments

I began my faith pilgrimage in a relatively small Baptist church in the eastern United States, a religious context quite misunderstood and often belittled in today's Western culture (and usually with justifiable cause). Little did I know during my formative years the importance this seemingly insignificant faith community would have in shaping my character over the long term. Not only did I gain my earliest spiritual and theological formation through that church; I also formed my very first peer friendships, learned important lessons about communicating across generational barriers, gave my first public addresses amid the plaudits of encouraging community leaders, grew into an awareness of my social justice responsibilities, and began to develop my own sense of vocation. Moreover, growing up in that church community confronted me with my need to embrace a more enduring set of values than the ones to which I initially had been attracted. That fellowship of saints helped me begin the exploration of who I am as an individual in community and taught me to value education, hard work, and a larger perspective of the world. It was not then, nor is it today, an elite or politically powerful congregation, but I am obliged to that community of the faithful for the foundations it gave me for life.

Because hundreds of other churches like that one had valued education and had united in 1830 to establish a college, I was able to continue my intellectual and spiritual journey of formation at a widely known East Coast university. There my horizons were further broadened, my curiosity was sharpened and deepened, and my desire to serve God and humanity was heightened. The vision of still other churches and church leaders enabled me to do graduate studies, providing me with the knowledge, skills, and credentials needed to enter my life's vocation of scholarship and education. I owe an incredible debt to both a wonderful ecclesiastical heritage and to more people than I will ever know personally, many of whom were and are not Baptists.

I must express gratitude, however, to a few of the people I do know for their assistance in making this project possible. First, I want to acknowledge Andy Beck, my initial editor at Cambridge University Press, who assisted me in designing, refining, and launching this project. Then I affirm my appreciation to Jason Przybylski and Emily Spangler of Cambridge University Press and to Larry Fox, Peter Katsirubas, and Katherine Faydash for later phases in reading, editing, and producing this book. There also were anonymous scholars who evaluated the initial manuscript and offered valuable feedback for improvements that have been incorporated into the finished product. This project could never have been completed without the skilled assistance of these and countless other persons.

In addition, I wish to acknowledge the support of Rev. Dr. Molly Marshall, president of Central Baptist Theological Seminary, for allowing me the time needed to research and write this book. I am also indebted to my faculty colleagues, many of whom read portions of the manuscript and offered valuable suggestions for improvement. Special appreciation is offered to Dr. Deborah Van Broekhoven, executive director of the American Baptist Historical Archives, now located at Mercer University in Atlanta, Georgia, and to the library staff of Central Baptist Theological Seminary for their assistance in locating and obtaining resources and graphics essential to the research and illustrating of this book. I am grateful to many other persons who contributed graphics and photographs besides the ones that were finally selected for inclusion in this volume; among them were Laura Willis, Jeff Faggart, John Carter, Ben Chan, and Francisco Litardo. I am appreciative also of the lifework and scholarship of a host of educators and historians of Baptist heritage who have been formative in my understanding, including Edwin Gaustad, Leon McBeth, William Brackney, Albert Wardin, Bill Leonard, Richard Pierard, and many other like-minded scholars, women and men, Anglo, African, Native, and Asian, some who have long ago passed from this life but whose work continues to influence my thinking today.

Finally, I wish to voice the gratitude I hold for my wife, Rebecca, and for her faithful support and encouragement during the lengthy process required to research, write, and edit this manuscript. She sacrificed many holidays, special events, and evenings together as her contribution to the project. For all this and much more I am affectionately grateful.

Important Baptist Organizations

ABA	American Baptist Association (United States)
ABC	American Baptist Convention (American Baptist, United States)
ABC-USA	American Baptist Churches in the USA
ABES	American Baptist Education Society (United States)
ABFMS	American Baptist Free Mission Society (United States)
ABHMS	American Baptist Home Mission Society (United States)
ABMS	African Baptist Missionary Society (United States)
ABMU	American Baptist Missionary Union (United States)
ABPS	American Baptist Publication Society (United States)
AIC	African Indigenous Churches (Africa)
AUCECB	All-Union Council of Evangelical Christians-Baptists (Russia)
BBFI	Baptist Bible Fellowship International
BEM	Baptism, Eucharist, and Ministry
BGC	Baptist General Conference (United States)
BGAV	Baptist General Association of Virginia (United States)
BGCT	Baptist General Convention of Texas (United States)
BMA	Baptist Missionary Association (United States)
BMS	Baptist Missionary Society (England)
BUS	Baptist Union of Scotland (United Kingdom)
BWA	Baptist World Alliance (global)
BWM	Baptist World Mission (Conservative Baptists, United States)
BZM	Baptist Zenana Mission (India)
CBA	Conservative Baptist Association of America (United States)
CBB	Brazilian Baptist Convention (Convenção Batista Brasileira)
CBF	Cooperative Baptist Fellowship (United States)

CBFMS	Conservative Baptist Foreign Mission Society (United States)
CBM	Canadian Baptist Ministries (Canada)
CBM	Convención Bautista Mexicana (Texas, United States)
CBNB	National Baptists (Convenção Batista Nacional do Brasil)
CCT	Church of Christ of Thailand (Thailand)
CEREA	Centre de Regroupement Africain (Congo)
CNBM	National Convention of Mexico (Mexico)
FBFA	Fundamentalist Baptist Fellowship of America (United States)
HBCT	Hispanic Baptist Convention of Texas (United States)
HMB	Home Mission Board (Southern Baptist, United States)
FCBC	Free Christian Baptist Conference (Canada)
FMBNBC	Foreign Mission Board (National Baptist, Inc., United States)
FMBSBC	Foreign Mission Board (Southern Baptist, United States)
FWBES	Free Will Baptist Education Society (United States)
GARB	General Association of Regular Baptists (United States)
GCSDBC	General Conference of Seventh Day Baptist Churches (United States)
IBFI	Independent Baptist Fellowship International (United States)
IM	International Ministries (ABC-USA)
JBU	Jamaica Baptist Union (Caribbean)
JBMS	Jamaican Baptist Missionary Society (Caribbean)
JLJ	Jacob, Lathrop, Jessey Separatist Church (London)
NAFWB	National Association of Free Will Baptists (United States)
NBC	Northern Baptist Convention (American Baptist, United States)
NBCA	National Baptist Convention of America (United States)
NABC	North American Baptist Conference (United States and Canada)
NBCUSA	National Baptist Convention, USA, Inc. (United States)
NCWW	National Committee on Woman's Work (United States)
NM	National Ministries (ABC-USA)
OFWB	Original Free Will Baptists (United States)
PNBC	Progressive National Baptist Convention, USA, Inc.
SBC	Southern Baptist Convention (United States)
UCBRF	Union of Christians-Baptists of the Russian Federation

UEFCC	Union of Evangelical Free Church Congregations (Germany)
WBF	World Baptist Fellowship (United States)
WBFMS	Woman's Baptist Foreign Mission Society (United States)
WBHMS	Woman's Baptist Home Mission Society (United States)
WEIU	Woman's Educational and Industrial Union (United States)
WMU	Woman's Missionary Union (United States)

Global Baptist Timeline

Global Baptist Timeline

		1550	1575	1600	1610	1620
EUROPE	Cultural Traditioning Sources	Elizabeth I (Eng., reigned 1558–1603)		James I (Eng.) (1603–1625)		
		Separatists (Eng.)				
	Baptist Traditioning Sources		First General Baptist Church 1609 (Eng.)			
			Thomas Helwys (1570–1616) (Eng.)			
		John Smyth (fl. 1586–1612)		JLJ Church org. 1616 (Eng.)		
			Spitalfields Church org. 1611 (Eng.)			
NORTH AMERICA	Cultural Traditioning Sources	Indian Nations	French rule Great Lakes & Mississippi Valley ca. 1534–1713			
			Spanish rule SW regions of USA 1609–1854			
		Ponce de León claims Florida for Spain 1513	Jamestown Colony 1607			
			First African slaves arrive 1619			
	Baptist Traditioning Sources					
ASIA	Cultural Traditioning Sources	Major cultures include Afanasievo (Siberia); Ainu (Japan); Angkor (Cambodia/Thai); Champa (Vietnam); Chengbeixi (China); Ottoman (Middle East); Paekche (Korea); Phu Lon (Mekong River); Phung Nguyen (Vietnam); Qijia (Mongolia); Qinglian'gang (China); Sa Huynh (China); Shilla (Korea) Soan (Pakistan/India); Son Vi (Vietnam); Indus (India/Pakistan)				
	Baptist Traditioning Sources					
AFRICA	Cultural Traditioning Sources	Kingdoms of Axum 5th cent. BCE–12th cent. CE; Zimbabwe 500–1700; Ghana 800–1077; Mali 1200–1500; Mandinka 1235–1645; Songhay 1400–1591 Portuguese colonial trade begins early 1500s Slave trade begins in 1520s				
	Baptist Traditioning Sources					
LATIN AMERICA & CARIBBEAN	Cultural Traditioning Sources	Native cultures include Cañans (Ecuador); Caral Supe (Peru); Norte Chico (Peru coast); Chavin (Peru); Chibchas (Colombia); Amazon (Brazil); Moche (Peru) | Mayan civiliz. Mexico c. 600 BCE; New Mayan Empire c. 900–c. 1191;Aztecs est. Mexico City 1327; Cortéz conquers Aztecs 1519; Pachacutec est. Incas in Peru 1438; Pizarro conquers Incas 1533; | African slaves to Hispanolia 1501				
	Baptist Traditioning Sources					
OCEANIA	Cultural Traditioning Sources	Australian Aboriginal and Torres Strait Islander cultures prior to 56,000 BCE Cultures of Polynesia, Micronesia, & Melanesia New Zealand Maori Culture 500–1300				
	Baptist Traditioning Sources					

	1630	1640	1650	1660
EUROPE	Charles I (Eng.) (1625–1649) Mark Lucar leaves JLJ Church over Parish Baptism 1633 (Eng.)	First Particular Baptist Church 1630s (Eng.) First Welsh Baptists 1630s	Cromwellian Commonwealth First London Confession 1644 Seventh Day Baptists 1653 (Eng.)	First Scottish & Irish Baptits, 1650s Dorothy Hazzard, Bristol 1660s (Eng.)
NORTH AMERICA	Plymouth, MA, Colony 1620 (USA) Roger Williams arrives in Boston 1631 (USA)	First Baptist Providence, RI, 1638 (USA) Williams' *Bloody Tenent of Persecution* 1644 (USA)	Newport, RI, Baptist 1641 (USA) Obediah Holmes whipped on Boston Common 1651 (USA) John Clarke's *Ill Newes from New England* 1652 (USA)	First Baptist Church Boston 1667 (USA) Swansee Baptist Church 1667 (USA)
ASIA	Portuguese arrive in Goa 1510, Canton 1517, & Japan 1540s	Dutch gain foothold in Taiwan 1640	Qing Dynasty 1644 (China)	British in Bombay 1661 Dutch expelled from Taiwan 1662
AFRICA	Char Bouba War 1634–1654	Persian Shahdom gains control of East African Coast	Kanem-Bornu conquered by Songhay Empire 1651–1658	Songhay Empire conquers the Mossi 1670s
LATIN AMERICA & CARIBBEAN	Cabral claims Brazil for Portugal 1500 Santa Fe, NM, founded 1605 (USA)	British colonize Bermuda 1612, Barbados 1625, Antigua 1632, Bahamas 1640, & Jamaica 1655	French colonize Dominica 1832, Martinique 1635, &Tortuga 1659	Dutch colonize Suriname 1667
OCEANIA		Explorer Abel Tasman visits Australia 1642 New Zealand 1642, & Fiji 1643		

Global Baptist Timeline

	1670	1680	1690	1700
EUROPE	Royal Restoration (1660) Venner Rebellion 1661 (Eng.) Conventicle Act 1664 (Eng.)	Grantham's *Christianismus Primitivus* 1678	Bristol Baptist College org. 1679 Delaune's *A Plea for the Non-Conformists* 1683 Act of Toleration 1689	The Particular Baptist Fund org. 1717
NORTH AMERICA	Seventh Day Baptist, Newport, RI, 1671 (USA)	Kittery, ME, Baptist Church 1681 Cold Spring Baptist Church 1684 (USA) Pennepeck Baptist Church 1688	Cohansey Baptist Church org. 1690 (USA) First Baptist Charleston, SC, 1696 (?)	WelshTract Baptist Church, Deleware 1703 (USA)
ASIA	Moghul Empire 1526–1858		Treaty of Nertchinsk between Russia & China 1689 China conquers Mongolia 1691	
AFRICA				Dutch est. Cape Town 1689 (S. Africa)
LATIN AMERICA & CARIBBEAN	Henry Morgan governor of Jamaica 1673–1688		Nijmegen Treaty: Spain cedes Western Hispaniola 1699 (modern Haiti) to France 1697	Scottish attempt to colonize Darien (Panama)
OCEANIA				

	1710	1720	1730	1740
EUROPE	Salters' Hall Meeting 1719	Skepp's *Divine Energy* introduces High Calvinist Tradition 1722	English General Baptists of the Gen. Association and Gen. Assembly reunite on basis of Six Principles in Hebrews 6:1–2	Brine to Cripplegate Baptist, London, strong advocate of High Calvinism 1730
NORTH AMERICA	Philadelphia Baptist Association 1707 (USA) Baptist Church in Great Valley formed 1711	Paul Palmer est. General Baptist Churches in NC 1729–1742 (USA)	First Great Awakening begins 1735 George Whitefield in Colonies 1740 First Separate Baptist Church 1743 (USA)	Schism among New Light Congregationalists over Baptism 1740s & 1750s Philadelphia Confession of Faith 1742
ASIA		End of Safavid Dynasty 1722 (Persia) Chinese gain control over Tibet 1724		Nadir Shah raid Delhi 1739
AFRICA	Sherbo People United 1717 (Sierra Leone) Lomé Kingdom est. 1721 (Togo)		Kansar Kingdom est. 1724 (Guinea) Douala Kingdom est. 1727 (Cameroon)	Ibo Kingdom est. 1732 (Nigeria) Yaoundé Kingdom 1741 (Cameroon)
LATIN AMERICA & CARIBBEAN	Montevideo est. 1717 Viceroyalty of Santa Fe de Bogata est. 1717		Coffee introduced to Brazil 1727	
OCEANIA				

Global Baptist Timeline

	1750	1760	1770	1780
EUROPE	Ann Dutton 1740s (Eng.)	Keiss Church org. (Scot.) 1750	Gill's *A Body of Doctrinal Divinity* 1770 (Eng.) New Connection of General Baptist org. 1770	Andrew Fuller to Kettery Baptist Church 1783 (Eng.) Fuller's *The Gospel Worthy of All Acceptation* 1785
NORTH AMERICA	Indian Baptist Church, RI 1750 (USA) Charleston Baptist Assoc. 1751 (USA) Russian rule extend to NW region USA 1742–1841	Sandy Creek Baptist Church 1755 (USA) Acadians expelled 1755 (Can.) Isaac Eaton's Academy 1756	Ebenezer Moulton to Nova Scotia 1760 (Can.) Horton Baptist 1765 (Can.) Kehuckee Assoc. 1765 (USA) Warren Assoc. 1767 (USA)	Black Baptists Henry Cowan [South] Robert Steven [North] (USA), & David George (USA, Can.) Silver Bluff Church 1773 (USA) Loyalist Migrations 1783–1798 (Can.)
ASIA	British victory at Plassey 1757	Konbaung Dynasty makes Rangoon capital of Burma 1755		Chinese gain control of Xinjiang 1768
AFRICA	Igbira Kingdom est. 1743 (Nigeria) Tiv Kingdom est. 1748 (Nigeria)	Baoule Kingdom est. 1750 (Ivory Coast)		First settlement of freed slaves in Sierra Leone 1787
LATIN AMERICA & CARIBBEAN		Brazil Capital removed from Salvador to Rio de Janeiro 1763 Jesuits expelled from Spanish America 1767	First Spanish mission in California at San Diego est. 1769 Viceroyalty of La Plata est. 1776	Frank Spence, Bahaman Baptists 1780
OCEANIA	Spain claims Hawaiian Islands 1751			First English settlement in Australia 1788

	1790	1800	1810	1820
EUROPE	Strict Baptists begin to form Baptist Missionary Society 1792 (Eng.)	Careys to India 1793	Haldane Revivals (Scot.)	Baptist Union 1813 (Eng.) Baptist Irish Soc. 1813
NORTH AMERICA	First African, Savannah 1779 (USA) Free Will Baptists 1780 (USA) United Baptist Churches of Christ in Virginia 1787 (USA)	Second Awakening 1795–1830 (USA) Gen. Conf. of Seventh Day Baptists 1802 (USA) Harding, Chipman, & Dimock (Can.)	Nova Scotia & New Brunswick Assoc. 1800 Horton Academy 1828 (Can.)	Ann & Adoniram Judson 1813 (USA) Triennial Conven. 1814 (USA) Free Baptist Church Nova Scotia 1821 (Can.)
ASIA	Qajar Dynasty est. 1795 (Persia)	First Baptists in India 1793	First Baptists in Indonesia 1813–1857 Krishna Pal, first Baptist of India 1800	Judsons in Burma 1813
AFRICA	David George, Sierra Leone Baptists, 1792 British seize Cape Colony 1806	Lott Carey, Liberian Baptists, 1822		Baptist immigrants to Grahamstown 1823 (S. Africa)
LATIN AMERICA & CARIBBEAN	George Leile, First Jamaican Baptists 1791 Amos Williams, Bahamas 1788	Bethel Baptist, Bahamas 1790	BMS in Jamaica 1814	Baptists in Trinidad 1816 Baptists in Haiti 1823
OCEANIA	Whale hunters est. settlements in New Zealand 1790s		Unification of Hawaii 1795	

	1830	1840	1850	1860
EUROPE	Britain outlaws slavery 1833 Johann G. Oncken becomes Baptist 1834 (Ger.) First Danish Baptists 1830s	Union of Assoc. Churches Baptized Christians in Germany & Denmark, 1849 Swedish Baptists, A.P. Foster 1848	Memel Baptist Church 1841 (Lith.) Frederik Nilsson exiled from Sweden 1851 Finland Baptists 1856	C.H. Spurgeon, Metropolitan Tabernacle (Eng.) Dublin Revival 1859 Norwegian Baptists 1860
NORTH AMERICA	Primitive Baptist Churches (USA) Landmark Baptists (USA) General Baptists in Midwest 1824 (USA) Richard Preston to Nova Scotia 1816	Trail of Tears 1838 Amherstburg Assoc. 1841 (Can.) Free Baptists 1841 (Can.) American Indian Mission 1842 (USA)	Southern Baptist Conven. 1845 (USA) N. American Baptist Conf. 1851 (USA) Baptist General Conf. America 1856 (USA)	African Baptist Assoc. 1853 (Can.) First Chinese Baptist Sacramento, 1860 (USA) Grant's Indian "Peace Policy" 1869 (USA)
ASIA	Assam Baptists 1830s (Ind.) Telugu Baptists 1836 (Ind.) Maitrichit Chinese Baptist Church, Bangkok 1837	Burmese Bible 1840 Karen Baptist 1852 (Myan.) First Chinese Baptists 1840s	Elizabeth Sale, Zenana Mission 1854 (India) Baptist Assoc. of Assam 1851 (Ind.)	Meghalaya Bapt. 1860s (Ind.) Myanmar Baptist Conv. 1865
AFRICA		Baptists on Island Fernando Po, 1841	Telugu Baptist presence (India) in S. Africa Cameroon Baptist Church 1849 Nigerian Baptist 1853	German Baptist immigrants to S. Africa 1858–1861 Carl Gutsche sent by German Mission to S. Africa 1867
LATIN AMERICA & CARIBBEAN	Sharper Morris, Turks & Caicos 1830	Jamaican Baptist Mission Soc. 1842 Baptists in Dominican Republic 1843	Jamaican Baptist Union 1849 Calabar Theological College 1843 (Jamaica)	Baptists in Mexico 1864
OCEANIA	John McKaeg 1832 (Austr.)	Tasmania Baptists 1835 (Austr.) Bathurst St. Sydney 1836 (Austr.)	First Aboriginal Baptist 1848 (Austr.) Baptists in Nelson, NZ, 1851	Austr. Baptist Mission Soc. 1863 Baptist Unions Victoria 1862, S. Austr. 1863, & New S. Wales 1868 (Austr.)

	1870	1880	1890	1900
EUROPE	Baptists in St. Petersburg 1855, Poland 1860s, Ukraine 1864 Baptist Union Wales, 1866 Scottish Baptist Union 1869 Norwegian Baptist Union 1877 Latvian Baptist Union 1879	Marianne Hearn, hymn writer (Eng.) Tbilisi Baptist Church 1880 (Georgia) Bulgarian Baptists 1880	Union of Baptist Churches of Russia 1887 Austria-Hungary Assoc. of Baptists 1885	Merger of General & Particular Baptists 1891 (Eng.) Baptist Union Ireland 1895 Estonian Baptist Union 1896
NORTH AMERICA	Lucinda Williams, Dallas 1868 Hannah Morris 1870 (Can.) General Assoc. of General Baptists 1870 (USA) Women's Baptist Foreign Mission Soc. 1871 (USA)	Bacone College 1880 (USA) First Chinese Baptist San Francisco 1880 (USA)	Baptist Convention Manitoba & Northwest Terr. 1884 (Can.) Primera Iglesia Bautista Mexicana, San Antonio 1887 (USA)	Baptist Convention Ontario & Quebec 1888 (Can.) WMU of SBC 1888 National Baptist Convention 1895 (USA)
ASIA	Naga Baptists 1870s (Ind.) First Baptists in Japan 1873 First Baptist Tokyo 1876		Garo Baptist Conv. 1890 (Bang.) Samacesam of Telugu Baptist Churches 1897	Baptist Church of Mizoram 1903
AFRICA	Ogbomosho Baptist 1874 (Nig.) Xhosa Baptist 1876 (S. Africa) Baptist Union S. Africa 1877 Baptists in Democ. Republic of Congo 1878	ABMU assumes Livingstone Miss. work 1884 (Congo) Afrikaanse Baptiste Kerk 1886 (S. Africa)	Congo Pentecost 1886 First Congo Baptist Church 1887 Coloured Baptists, 1888 (S. Africa)	S. African Baptist Mission Soc. 1892 Baptists in Malawi 1892 Baptist in Zambia 1905
LATIN AMERICA & CARIBBEAN	Baptists in Brazil, 1871	Baptists in Argentina 1881 First Baptist Church, Bahia 1882 Cuban Baptists 1886	Baptists in Chile 1892 German Baptists in Brazil 1893	Bahamas Baptist Union 1892 Convention of the Baptist Churches of Puerto Rico 1902
OCEANIA	Canterbury Assoc., NZ, 1873 Baptist Union Queensland, 1877 (Austr.)	Baptist Union New Zealand 1882 Baptist Union Tasmania 1884	Maori Baptists 1880s New Zealand Baptist Mission Soc. 1885	Whitley College, Melbourne 1891 J.H. Cole Perth Baptists 1895 (Austr.) Baptist Union West. Austr. 1896

Global Baptist Timeline

	1910	1920	1930	1940
EUROPE	Finnish Baptist Union 1904 Baptist World Alliance 1905 Union of Bulgarian Baptist Churches 1908 Federation of Evangelical Baptists 1911 (Fra)	Baptist Union of Romania 1919 Baptist Unity of Brethren 1919 (Czch.) Baptist Union of Hungary 1920	Convenção Baptist Portuguesa 1920 Union of Christian Baptists 1922 (Pol.) Lithuanian Baptist Union 1923	Bund der Baptisten-Gemeinden 1924 (Swit.) Unión Evangélica Bautista Española 1929
NORTH AMERICA	Lott-Carey Convention 1897 (USA) First Japanese Baptists Seattle, 1899 (USA) Northern Baptist Convention 1907 (USA) Convención Bautista Mexicana 1910 Matthews Controv. 1910 (Can.)	National Baptist Conv. of America 1915 American Baptist Assoc. 1924 (USA) Iowa Indian Baptist Church 1924 Baptist Faith & Message 1925 (SBC)	Fundamentalist Baptist Fellowship 1920 & 1965 (USA) National Assoc. of Free Will Baptists 1932 (USA) World Baptist Fellowship 1932	Baptist Federation of Canada 1944 Conservative Baptist Foreign Mission Society 1943 Conservative Baptist Churches 1947
ASIA	Assam Baptist Convention 1914 (Ind.)	Bangladesh Baptist Fellowship 1920 Conv. Philippines Baptist Chur. 1935 Ceylon Baptist Council 1935	Bengal Baptist Union 1935 (Ind.) Nagaland Baptist Council 1937 (Ind.) Baptist Convention of Hong Kong 1938	Japanese Baptist Convention 1947 Baptist Union of North India 1948 Korean Baptist Convention 1949
AFRICA	Seventh Day Baptists, S. Africa 1906 Baptists in Ghana 1918 Nigerian Baptist Conv. 1919 Églises Baptistes de la République Centrafricaine 1920	Baptists in Zimbabwe 1920 Baptists in Mazambique 1921	Baptists in Ivory Coast 1927 Union of Baptist Churches Burundi 1928 Malagasy Baptist Association 1932	Convenção Baptista de Angola 1940 African Baptist Assembly of Malawi 1945 Communauté Baptista du Zaire Ouest 1946
LATIN AMERICA & CARIBBEAN	Convención Bautista de Cuba Occidental 1905 Convención Bautista de Cuba Oriental 1905 Convenção Batista Brasileira 1907	Asociación Bautista de El Salvador 1934 Convención Bautista de Chile 1908	Bahamas National Baptist Missionary & Edu. Conv. 1935 Unión Bautista Boliviana 1936 Convención Bautista de Nicaragua 1937	Convención Bautista Libre de Cuba 1943 Église Baptiste Indépendante 1946 Convención Batista de Guatamala 1946
OCEANIA	General Baptists in Guam 1911	Baptist Union Australia 1926	Baptists in Northern Mariana Islands 1947	Baptists in Papua New Guinea 1949

	1950	1960	1970	1980
EUROPE	Union of Baptist Churches in Austria 1953 Assoc. de Igrejas Batistas Portugueses 1955 Unione Cristiana Evangelica Battista d'Italia 1956	Federación de Igl. Evangel. Independ. de España 1957	Assoc. of Returned Evangelical-Christ. Baptist 1978 (Ger.) Union of Evangel. Christians-Baptists 1979 (Rus.)	First Baptists of Njardvik 1984 (Iceland) Union of Baptism-Minded Congreg. 1989 (Ger.)
NORTH AMERICA	No. Baptists becomes American Baptist Conv. 1950 (USA) Baptist Woman's Miss. Society Ontario & Quebec 1951 Baptist Missionary Assoc. 1950	Original Free Will Baptists 1961 Progressive National Baptist Conv. 1961 (USA) Baptist Women in Ministry 1985	American Baptist Conv. Becomes ABC-USA 1972 Independent Baptist Fellowship International 1984	Alliance of Baptists 1987 (USA) National Miss. Baptist Convention of America 1988
ASIA	Northeast Council of Baptist Churches 1950 (NE India) Conv. Indonesian Baptist 1951 Malaysia Baptist Conv. 1953 Chinese Baptist Conv. 1954 (Taiwan)	Thailand Karen Baptist Conv. 1955 Bangladesh Baptist Sanfha 1956 Japan Baptist Union 1958	Gabungan Gereja Bap. Indonesia 1971 Sri Lanka Baptist Sangamaya 1974 Singapore Baptist Convention 1975	NW India Bapt. Assoc. 1977 Singh Evangelical Baptist Association 1980 (Pak.) Baptist Conv. Syria 1983
AFRICA	Ghana Baptist Convention 1947 Union des Églises Baptistes du Cameroon 1952 Baptist Evangelical Assoc. Ethiopia 1961	Union de Églises Baptistes du Rwanda 1962 Igreja União Baptist 1968 (Mozam.) Baptist Conv. of Malawi 1970	Baptist Convention of Kenya 1971 Baptist Convention of Tanzania 1971 Baptist Union of Uganda 1974	Baptist Conv. of Sierra Leone 1974 Baptist Union of Zambia 1976 Baptist Conv. of Namibia 1984
LATIN AMERICA & CARIBBEAN	Convención Batista de Costa Rica 1947 Convención Nacional Bautista de Venezuela 1951 Convención Nacional Bautista Colombiana 1952 Convención Bautista Paraguay 1956	Convención Bautista Hondureña 1958 Convención Bautista de Panama 1959 Conv. Baptiste de Haiti 1964	Convenção Batista Nacional do Brasil 1967 Dominican National Baptist Conv. 1968 Convención Bautista del Ecuador 1972	Barbados Baptist Conv. 1974 Antigua Baptist Assoc. 1980 Bermuda Baptist Fellowship 1981
OCEANIA	Marianas Assoc. of General Baptists 1962 (Guam) Baptists in Solomon Islands 1969 Baptist Bible College, Kwinkia 1969 (Papua New Guinea)	Fiji Bapitst Mission 1973 Seventh Day Baptists 1975 Queensland (Austr.)	Baptists in Samoa 1976	Baptist Union of Papua New Guinea 1977

Global Baptist Timeline

		1990	2000	2010
EUROPE		Union of Evangelical Christians-Baptists 1990 (Bela.) Union of Evangelical Christians-Baptists 1990 (Georgia) Union of Evangelical Christians-Baptist 1991 (Moldov.)	Union Evangelical Christians-Baptists Central Asia 1992 Union Evangelical Christians-Baptists Ukraine 1992	
NORTH AMERICA		Cooperative Baptist Fellowship 1990 (USA) American Baptist Women's Ministries 1990	Canadian Baptist Ministries 1995	New Baptist Covenant 2008
ASIA		Nepal Baptist Church Council 1993	Baptist Convention in Vietnam 1989	Samevesam Telugu Baptist factions reconstitute the Baptist Convention of Telugu Baptist Churches 2007 (Ind.)
AFRICA		Baptists in Guinea 1988 Convention Baptiste du Togo 1988 Bras Panon Baptists 1989 (Réunion)	Baptists in Guinea-Bissau 1993	
LATIN AMERICA & CARIBBEAN		Granada Baptist Assoc. 1981 Asociación Nacional de los Bautistas Libres 1986 (Uruguay) St. Vincent Baptist Convention 1987	Union Nacional de Iglesias Bautistas de Costa Rica 1981 United Baptist Organization of Suriname 1981 Fraternidad de Iglesias Bautistas de Cuba 1989	
OCEANIA		Dame V. Boyd becomes first woman president of the New Zealand Baptist Union 1984 Fiji Baptist Convention org. 1987		

Introduction

The year 2009 marked the four hundredth anniversary of the birth of the Baptist movement. In late July, leaders from 214 Baptist conventions and unions representing 36 million members and a community of 105 million persons from more than 120 nations gathered in Amsterdam, Holland, to celebrate the event. This gathering contrasted sharply with the first Baptist meeting in that city in 1609, when a company of about 40 English exiles organized the world's first Baptist church. In that contrast lie the stories, problems, and visions that furnish the content of this book. It is generally the case that the original DNA of a movement establishes its future possibilities and limitations. The initial Amsterdam Baptists were a homogeneous, unicultural, and contentious group. After their first major schism, half of the group moved back to England to take up a Baptist witness there. Thus, an Anglocentric interpretation of what it means to be Baptist was launched.

Unwittingly, the tendency to limit Baptist identity to those cultural parameters has lived on. Most often when the Baptist story is told and contextual exploration is undertaken, the contours are confined to the Anglo Baptist cultural experiences. Where others sometimes are treated, they usually are found in the margins – the by-products of the Anglo story. But, as the foregoing description illustrates, the Baptist movement has evolved beyond those boundaries. As the twenty-first century dawns, Baptists have entered a stage of development that demands new assessments of the movement's origins, expansion, global web of partners, and identity.

At its core, the Baptist movement began as a cause within the Anglo (English) culture. Its initial visionaries, though often well educated, addressed themes that became especially relevant to the Anglo under-classes of post-Reformation English society. Those concerns were focused around matters of faith and theology but also reflected social issues associated with the struggles experienced by those classes in seventeenth-century Britain. But, although Anglo social, political, and religious concerns were the early driving force, fairly quickly others added their cultural DNA to the Baptist movement, especially persons of Native and African cultural roots. Baptists' witness of their Bible-based faith had meaning for many non-Anglo hearers, but obviously for those adherents, being Baptist acquired different emphases and definitions because of their unique cultural sources and particular life situations. Ultimately, theirs was far more than simply an African or Native version of Anglo faith. The distinctives of their experiences created new centers of Baptist life from which new themes, new styles, new theological emphases, and new interpretations of the world emerged.

Because the dominant interpreters of the Baptist story have been Anglo, the history of the movement has tended to develop mostly along lines of Anglo cultural themes. But the Baptist movement long ago spread beyond its Anglo cultural core. Consequently, the need exists to expand interpretations of Baptist identity by exploring the cultural themes of the other groups that constitute the global Baptist family. The obligation to do this is persistently raised in classroom, church, and conference settings where Native, African, Asian, and other Baptists raise the question, Where are we in this story? Nothing here reflects our identity as Baptists. This book attempts to expose and survey some of those lines of development. In most instances, space limitations have not permitted a thorough elaboration, so the intent has been to outline pathways that need further exploration to liberate, empower, and value the travails, achievements, and contributions from the many cultures that make up the global Baptist family today. The desired outcome is that they would become more integral to the ongoing evolution of Baptist identity. This book seeks to introduce the global Baptist movement by acknowledging that this story has always been much larger than Anglo or Anglo American Baptists and has included unrecognized cultural roots that have demanded a much larger context. This means that Baptist identity continues in formation and must include a much broader sampling of the movement's shaping processes.

My desire has been to put elements of the Baptist experience together in a way that might allow for new possibilities. To do that, new elements have needed to be addressed in unconventional ways. Black Baptists, Native Baptists, and Asian Baptists are among the many that needed to be placed within their non-Anglo historical and cultural contexts. Baptist women needed to be interpreted from contexts different from those of male Baptists – out of which their stories typically have been told. Although many important persons, contributions, church traditions, and identity issues could not be developed, it is hoped that enough essential indicators have been included to encourage the research necessary for development of those primal sources for Baptist identity. Furthermore, because this is an introduction, numerous ideas necessarily are presented in seminal form without full elaboration and often without the extended supporting arguments that would be desirable. Many opportunities exist for correcting, nuancing, and extending the research that could only be presented here in a perfunctory fashion.

For many years, I have struggled with the unsatisfying results of trying to make Baptist identity fit around one center. Repeatedly, that effort resulted in major parts of the global Baptist community being pushed to the margins. Women, non-Anglo Baptists, and numerous other persons could never remain an integral part of the story but continually became relegated to its periphery despite their undeniable and indispensible contributions. The perspectives of emerging postmodern social analysis have offered promising clues for addressing that dilemma.[1] The tools of postmodernist sociopolitical critique have enabled views of social ontology and of relationships between order and structure that unlock new possibilities for interpreting Baptists' history. Utilization of some of those methodologies in this study has accentuated global Baptists' nature as a culturally polycentric movement characterized by elements that are too diverse to permit the movement's identity to be contained under a singular cultural vista. The modernist tendency to look for one center to which all other centers must conform has prevented Baptists from recognizing the vast possibilities available to them for exploring those identities more fully. Placing Anglo cultural traditioning sources in a broader framework allows many independent and differing centers to stand side by side in the Baptist quest for identity, each with its own cultural DNA, traditioning sources, and contexts of experience. This intentionally polycentric approach offers possibilities for new understandings and practices that have the potential to transform Baptists' personal and communal lives. Baptist history has

---

[1] Naturally, these methodologies include critiques derived from the insights of philosophers like Jean Baudrillard, Jean-François Lyotard, Jacques Derrida, and Michel Foucault (who rejected a postmodernist identification). More specifically, however, I found helpful the synthesizing work of John W. Murphy in *Postmodern Social Analysis and Criticism* (New York: Greenwood Press, 1989) and John Murphy and Jung Min Choi in *Postmodernism: Unraveling Racism and Democratic Institutions* (London: Praeger Publishers, 1997). In those works, the authors contrast modernist forms of social analysis with those of postmodernist thinkers and illumine the opportunities they believe postmodernist perspectives offer critical social analysis. Murphy is also very helpful in the attention he gives to postmodern religious attitudes. Although this study offers no pretense of presenting a serious sociological study of Baptists, many perspectives found here are indebted to insights gained from these scholars.

long recognized this movement's theological polycentrism, including the independent identities and practices those diverse centers have generated, along with the exclusivist claims they often have engendered. Exploration of Baptist's polycentrism now needs to be extended to include cultural, social, and gender sources and should be done in a manner that values both difference and the evolution of identity.

This book's intended audience primarily includes college and university students, seminarians, clergy, interested laity, and scholars who want to know more about the history and theology of the Baptist family of denominations and their interactions with the wider cultures in which the movement's adherents have lived. Because many readers likely will have little or no knowledge of Baptist origins, the first chapter seeks to contextualize the movement by examining its traditioning processes, early cultural settings, and primal theological sources. Although much of that information is not new, it is included here as essential background material for those unfamiliar with Baptist studies. This section attempts to help the noninitiate reader understand the location of the Anglo Baptist movement within the larger ecclesial and theological contexts of Western Christianity. It also illumines the cultural and theological roots from which the Anglo Baptist movement was forged while pointing out the early existence of additional cultural and theological sources that have not generally been included in Baptists' recounting of their history. Furthermore, the incorporation of previously excluded cultural and theological traditions adds new dimensions to Baptist identity that are explored in the chapters that follow.

Chapter 2 identifies seminal elements within early Baptist life that contributed to diversity, although the prevalence of Anglo constituents tended to obscure this fact. Here, pathways are traced revealing how Baptist denominations of the seventeenth and eighteenth centuries wove specific theological and cultural elements together in pursuit of their dreams for a life that was temporally and eternally better. Those quests became the shaping forces of major early Baptist traditions.

The nineteenth century was a frontier age for the global Baptist movement. Chapter 3 examines what this meant in the British Empire, Chapter 4 illumines the frontier experiences of Baptists in the United States, and Chapter 5 explores what this age meant for Baptists on the European Continent and in Africa, Asia, and Latin America. Although still largely an Anglo cultural force, missionary and evangelistic success extended the Baptist movement into a variety of new cultures, spawning additional dreamers who began to address matters relevant to their own contexts and bringing fresh sources for the enhancement of Baptist identity. Mostly unaware of what this meant, Anglo Baptists tended to interpret their own traditions as the truly and divinely inspired perceptions of the way life, church, government, gender roles, and all of culture should be. But the period since 1890 has witnessed the emergence of challenges to the prevailing Anglo interpretations. During this age of proliferating traditioning sources, variant Baptist communities appealed to the same Bible, the same basic faith traditions, and the same family name to espouse convictions that have sometimes clashed violently. Chapter 6 signals the start of a shift – slow at first but gaining momentum by the dawn of the twenty-first century. Baptist growth in the West began to slow and in some cases decline, whereas in Africa, Asia, and Latin America dramatic growth was occurring. Chapter 7 traces those trends into Latin America, Europe, and Eurasia, and Chapter 8 outlines the continuation of Baptist fragmentation in the United States and the multitudes of traditioning sources that were evident there by the close of the twentieth century.

A global overview of Baptist beliefs and practices is presented in Chapter 9. That survey indicates how growing diversity and proliferating traditioning sources today are reshaping Baptist identity in important ways. Although such multiformity is not totally new, it is becoming more obvious. Culturally related differences that in the past might have been ignored because geographical distances and Euro-American dominance permitted them to be subsumed under Anglo Baptist metanarratives are not so easily cast aside today. These considerations transition into the closing observations that address the new contexts in which Baptist identity is being shaped at this time.

The intent of this book, therefore, is to point toward potentially new and more inclusive dimensions for interpreting and presenting Baptists' histories and identities. My desire is not to devalue any heritage. Instead, the aim has been to construct a framework that allows each tradition (or center) to be known through its own set of experiences and beliefs without the need to judge it in light of some other tradition (except on occasions when one tradition has violated the freedom of some other tradition, thereby making critique necessary). The Anglo and Anglo-American traditions of Baptist life have contributed much to the foundations of Baptist identity. Those traditions likely will continue to offer a great deal. Yet those voices cannot be the dominant definers of Baptist identity in the future. Other voices also have much to offer. Finding helpful ways to include the "other" Baptists not only could enrich the movement's self-understanding but also could awaken Baptists to new possibilities capable of making this family of denominations far more relevant for today's world.

PART I

Foundations

And let no man be offended at us for that we differ from the ancient brethren of the separation in the Liturgy, Presbytery, and Treasury of the Church: for we hold not our faith at any man's pleasure or in respect of persons, neither do we bind ourselves to walk according to other men's lines further than they walk in the truth: neither let the world think that we approve them in all their practices: let them justify their proceedings or repent of them. We have (we willingly & thankfully acknowledge) received much light of truth from their writings, for which mercy we always bless our God: & for which help we always honor them in the Lord and in the truth. But as Paul withstood Peter to his face & separated from Barnabas that good man that was full of the holy ghost & of faith, for just causes: So must they give us leave to love the truth & honor the lord more than any man or Church upon earth.[1]

John Smyth
Differences of the Churches of the Separation, 1608

A BAPTIST PROFILE

In his "I Have a Dream" speech, delivered prophetically on the steps of the Lincoln Memorial in Washington, D.C., on August 28, 1963, Martin Luther King Jr. proclaimed his vision of a new reality for the world in which he suffered. He envisioned a day when "little black boys and black girls will be able to join hands with little white boys and white girls as sisters and brothers." King was not the first to indulge such a dream, and he was not the only person in the multitude gathered that day to aspire to this new reality. The fact that his words resonated so powerfully with so many people both then and now testifies to the fact that his dream lay latent in the hearts and minds of countless people. But King, on that day, to a degree surpassing everyone before him, succeeded in giving voice to a dream that had been struggling for birth over generations. Indeed, when expanded to global proportions, this dream continues its contest for actualization. King's words both expressed and express the hopes of many individuals for a new reality that would end brutal oppression and its debilitating wounds

---

[1] John Smyth, *Differences of the Churches of the Separation*, 1608. Reprinted in W. T. Whitley, ed., *The Works of John Smyth*, 2 vols. (Cambridge: Cambridge University Press, 1915), 1:269–92. The typeface and spelling in this quotation have been modernized to accommodate a global readership.

and pain. This dream took King to the "mountaintop," from which he could faintly glimpse the Promised Land, although others, not he, would be the earthly benefactors of that dream.[2]

Martin Luther King Jr. globally stands among Baptists' best-known luminaries. And because his character and ideals are so widely known and respected, his dream illustrates a powerful metaphor through which the Baptist story might be communicated to a global audience. For King's dream was not only a product of his social and political experiences; it also was born in the matrix of his African American Baptist heritage and was thereby informed by particular ways of reading and valuing the Bible, by the dreams of his larger faith community, and by his understanding of how God engages in the human condition. Captured in a memorial inscription erected outside the Lorraine Motel in Memphis, Tennessee, where King was martyred, are words expressing the truth that he embodied best: "And they said one to another, Behold, this dreamer cometh. Come now therefore, and let us slay him . . . and we shall see what will become of his dreams." King's legacy as a man of dreams epitomizes the essence of the global Baptist tradition – a people of dreams.

---

[2] Martin Luther King Jr. "I Have a Dream Speech," qtd. in *The Autobiography of Martin Luther King, Jr.*, ed. Clayborne Carson (New York: Time Warner Book Group, 1998), 223–7.

CHAPTER I

The Primal Shaping Processes of the Global Baptist Movement

Dreams for a life that is new and better (however a particular Baptist group might define that) characterize the global experience of Baptists more than any other single set of qualities. Baptist identity has been marked less by a commonly acknowledged body of valued traditions preserved from the past than by the power of dreams to forge the future. Over their history, Baptists, individually and collectively, have been guided by a wide variety of dreams. Among them was the dream of freedom to worship without external coercion; the dream of liberty to study and apply the Bible as conscience, knowledge, and reflection might dictate; the dream of freedom to organize and govern themselves in churches free of ecclesiastical and governmental interference; the dream of liberation from human enslavement; the dream of freedom from cultural discrimination in the formulation of belief and practice; the dream of being trusted as true servants of the common good and not as enemies of the people in socialist regimes; the dream of deliverance from gender bias in religious and communal life; and the list could be continued in extenso.

The foregoing Baptist profile highlighted Martin Luther King Jr. as an exemplar to the global community of Baptist dreaming. He also demonstrates another aspect of the Baptist experience – living a dream is not easy. Power holders tend not to like dreamers, for power holders prefer to keep things as they are. Dreamers, however, like to think revolutionary thoughts. They hope for a new way, being unwilling to accept the hopelessness of things as they currently stand when injustices prevail. Inspired by the Bible, faith traditions, courageous leaders, and the unacceptable situations of the societies in which they have been located, Baptists have been people of many dreams. Sometimes those dreams have clashed with one another. Too often some within the Baptist family have assumed positions as power holders seeking to ossify their own dreams into structures that would enslave or deny the dreams of others, even those of fellow Baptists. During such times, Baptists have entered into conflict with one another as competing dreams have struggled for expression. At their best, Baptists have found the toleration and forms needed to give life to the dreams of all. At their worst, they have tried to crush opposing dreams, usually with less-than-satisfying outcomes. Still, their dreams have provided the force that has propelled the Baptist movement onto a global stage.

Dreams are not born in a vacuum, however. They are products of historical realities, cultural traditions, personal experiences, imagination, hope, faith, and related qualities. The motivating power of Baptist dreaming becomes intelligible only as we comprehend the processes of theological, cultural, and historical traditioning that give form to Baptist convictions. Furthermore, dreams require dreamers. The Baptist story includes individuals and communities whose lives, in significant ways, have embodied the things dreamed. Woven together, these elements form the tapestry of a family of denominations whose most consistent thread is their dreams of achieving life that is abundant, both now and eternally. Baptists believe the blueprints for that life should be drawn from the Bible. Different expressions of Baptist life have emerged as individuals and communities have interpreted the biblical texts, Christian traditions, and human societies in varied ways.

Baptists cannot point to a single individual or group as the fundamental shaping source of their faith tradition. They have never been inspired by just one dreamer. Although numerous histories point to the Anglican priest John Smyth (introduced in the next chapter) as the first Baptist, in reality, he significantly influenced only one strand of the Baptist movement and remained Baptist for only a short period of time. Several of his followers rescued his early Baptist dreams and gave them organizational life through the English General Baptist denominations. Yet various other Baptist denominations have originated without any knowledge of Smyth's teachings and without any contact with or influence from descendants of his movement. Some sources make a case for the Jacob-Lathrop-Jesse church in London (also discussed in the next chapter) during the 1630s as the starting point for the mainstream of the Baptist tradition, thereby laying claims to it and its views as the source of the "true" Baptist tradition. Again, none of the original pastors of that church were Baptist – although the church itself became the source of several Particular Baptist congregations in the mid-seventeenth century.[1] Still other Baptist bodies have emerged without reference to or influence from either of those sources. Something other

---

[1] Henry Jessey later embraced Baptist convictions and was baptized by Hansard Knollys in 1645, at least seven years after the first Particular Baptist church was formed.

than a historical succession is needed to explain the essence of Baptists' traditions.

Neither can Baptists point to a single theological tradition. A large part of the Baptist movement either is a product of or is heavily influenced by the Reformed or Calvinist tradition. Yet from the beginning, many Baptists embraced other theological foundations, including Free Will or Arminian positions; Seventh-Day principles; either strict or ecumenical attitudes toward communion; an African sacred cosmos, an Anglican sacred cosmos, or a sacred cosmos that somehow blended or modified the two; in addition to numerous other sources. Contemporary Baptists also are not the product of a single cultural influence. The cultural shapers of the global Baptist movement are almost as varied as humanity itself. Consequently, when the Baptist movement is examined closely, one finds an amalgam of traditions – many totally independent of the others – that defies serious efforts genuinely to interpret them as one. Herein resides the problem of justly structuring and articulating a global history of the Baptist movement.

BAPTISTS' TRADITIONING PROCESSES

Traditioning is a complex interplay of power and dreams. Power attempts both to arrange and maintain affairs to preserve a desired status quo; the dream hopes to change that arrangement. Frequently during their history, Baptists have experienced bitter battles over which or whose dreams, definitions, and descriptions are (or should be) the authoritative ones. Various Baptist individuals and groups have produced histories designed to highlight and give support to the qualities and characteristics that each has perceived as expressing the true version of who Baptists are, what they think, and how they practice their faith. Such interpreters usually prefer an established tradition over the dynamic visions of those who dream.

The greatest drawback with efforts to interpret the Baptist story as a single or even unified tradition has been the tendency to judge alternative traditions as somehow erroneous or defective. Such approaches are inclined either to leave out or to marginalize significant parts of the story that don't fit the singular tradition's values, priorities, and preferred doctrines and practices. Recognizing that the Baptist story is not just one tradition but a complex of traditions with an ongoing process of traditioning helps to reduce the tendency to overlook, exclude, or evoke prejudice against different traditions within the Baptist movement. This allows each part of the tradition to be examined in its own context, have value in its own right, and be viewed as contributing to the continuing process of Baptist traditioning as it pursues its own set of dreams for a better world, both within history and beyond.

The fact is, the history of Baptist beliefs and practices constitutes an intricate traditioning process that incorporates multiple and sometimes disparate sources. This process includes three major elements: the appropriation of beliefs and practices from varied origins (many outside the boundaries of Baptist faith communities themselves), the transformation of those elements to fit a Baptist ethos, and an ongoing interpretive intentionality aimed at managing the Baptist community's understanding of what does and does not constitute part of its theological and operative heritage and thus become admissible as standards for Baptist belief and praxis.[2] No interpretive intentionality, however, is able to prevail at all points in the complex of traditions that contribute to the movement that has become known by the name *Baptist*. Consequently, the movement itself reflects ongoing tensions among a variety of primal traditions and influences out of which many elements continue to express themselves independently. Those voices continue to speak the matters relevant to their own contexts and apart from the interpretations assorted Baptist authorities would like to impose on them. At the same time, a theological intentionality continually seeks to find articulation and bring coherence to the complexity and variety of those sources, whether they appear as conflicting faith traditions, cultural influences, theological insights, or other concerns. A perennial part of Baptist experience has been the effort by varied Baptist entities to lay authoritative claim to interpretative oversight and, where necessary, to prevail over the initial claims of extant sources.

Traditionally, the more critical studies of the sources of Baptist faith, tradition, and practice have focused on the elements of complexity and variety in the Baptist movement. This has tended to be the work of historians, theologians, and scholars of the tradition. The so-called church interpretation has focused primarily on the theological intentionality produced by particular sources in the traditioning process. This has most often been the task of pastors, denominational leaders, and folk theologians. As a global history, this work attempts to include both of these elements in the traditioning

---

[2] In describing the complexity of process involved in ancient Israel's production of the Torah, Walter Brueggemann furnishes a model very useful for interpreting the Baptist tradition. He speaks of a twofold process of appropriation and transformation as the cornerstones of this traditioning process, one that "does not everywhere prevail in the text that becomes Torah." Similar elements can be helpful for identifying and interpreting the traditioning processes at work in Baptist experience. See Walter Brueggemann, *An Introduction to the Old Testament: The Canon and Christian Imagination* (Louisville, KY: Westminster John Knox Press, 2003), 17.

process, not allowing either one to silence or deprecate the other. Effort is made to take seriously both the need for critical attentiveness to the variety and complexity of the sources contributing to Baptist traditions and the impetus of Baptist praxis to achieve a constancy and coherence that satisfies the needs of a given body of adherents. The former dimensions are treated under the rubrics of theological and cultural traditioning sources. The latter are explored as formative of Baptist traditions.

INCUBATORS OF EARLY BAPTIST DREAMING

What frequently has come to be referred to as the Baptist tradition originated in identifiable theological and cultural contexts. This fact might seem to be self-evident. Yet many members of the global Baptist family have tended to view Baptist identity as something suprahistorical – that is, as something derived unadulterated from the Bible and capable of being verbalized noncontextually through a concise list of qualifications or characteristics. Furthermore, Baptists do not lack a supply of persons willing to oblige such wishes for authoritative definitions. But experiences associated with cultural contextualization and today's questions surrounding social, medical, and scientific advances place increasing pressures on persons caught in the concomitant moral dilemmas and spiritual concerns. "What do Baptists think about the topic?" is a common query. In such cases, the inability to produce a definitive declaration of identity that is suitable for all Baptists becomes more evident, despite the imperious claims of self-appointed authorities who would suggest otherwise. In addition, many of the more thoughtful attempts to sketch a broadly satisfactory identity have made global assumptions based on very culturally specific interpretations of who Baptists are and what they believe and practice. Overall, the Baptist movement seems to be reaching the limits of the capacity for such approaches to supply needed direction for its future.

This chapter is intentional in its proposal to delineate the theological and cultural settings out of which Baptist origins and early identity have been interpreted. It also seeks to narrate some of the theological and cultural backgrounds that constitute part of early Baptists' global heritage but have not been included in the movement's stated identity. If nothing else, these pages should make readers more aware of the challenges Baptists face to broaden the ground of their sources of identity formation.

The following pages introduce readers to the two principal incubators of early Baptist traditioning – theological sources and cultural sources. The Anglo theological and cultural sources are the ones more familiar to the prevalent body of Baptist histories. The Native and African sources addressed in this chapter tend to be found mostly in the ethnic Baptist studies of each marginalized group. Consequently, even though some overlap is unavoidable in the effort to trace independently the theological and cultural sources of early Baptist identity, it seems important for our understanding of Baptist traditioning to keep the two distinct.

Early Baptist's Anglo Theological Traditioning Sources

European Theological Traditioning Sources

The religious seeds from which Anglo Baptists' earliest dreams flowered germinated in the soil of the broader theological mainstream of Western Christianity. Almost all Baptist traditions have been significantly shaped by Trinitarian concepts of God, Chalcedonian Christology, and doctrines of atonement reflective of the broad-based consensus of Western churches. Consequently, Baptists' faith dreams have been beneficiaries of a long history of theological traditioning, although many Baptists seem not to be aware of this.[3] Decades of hostility between Protestants and Catholics influenced numerous Baptists to voice their dreams in terms that denied their indebtedness to early theological sources derived either from or through the Catholic tradition. The core of Baptist doctrines about God, Christ, salvation, and many other topics has evolved out of a theological groundwork laid by classical and medieval Eastern and Western theologians and later refined through the Protestant Reformations. Additional refinements have been made regionally as varied bodies of Baptists throughout the globe have attempted to express their dreams via doctrinal interpretations reflective of their own understanding of Scripture and within the contexts of their own cultural realities.

Among the earliest sources of Baptist dreams were faith traditions that stemmed from theological roots located in the Renaissance and Reformation. At the core of those sources were Baptists' views concerning the authority of the Scriptures. Renaissance humanism introduced a distinctive literary and cultural program that eventually affected biblical studies. This approach is summed up in the term *ad fontes*. Alister McGrath describes the atmosphere of Renaissance Europe as an age of geographical, physiological, and scientific discovery. Humanist literary endeavors led these scholars to the realization that much ancient literature bore a similar spirit of discovery.

---

[3] For examples of this, see Steven R. Harmon, *Towards Baptist Catholicity: Essays on Tradition and the Baptist Vision* (Bletchley, Milton Keyes, U.K.: Paternoster, 2006), 36–7.

Homer, Virgil, Galen, and others give descriptions of such discoveries. A sense of immediate connection between the discoverers of the fifteenth century and those of antiquity emerged. Over time, this gave birth to the conviction that returning to the original literary sources in their original languages offered a unique means for discovering truth. Humanist scholars believed the approach held the potential of mediating authentic experience to posterity.[4] This became the source for a very common dream among Anglo Baptists who longed to establish the Bible as the supreme authority in all matters of faith without any government or church hierarchy overriding the convictions of believing individuals and congregations of such persons.

Late in the fifteenth century, these insights, initially based on secular literary studies, were applied to biblical interpretation as well. The conviction emerged that if the Bible were approached in the proper way and in the original languages then contemporary readers could personally encounter the risen Christ as had the original apostolic witnesses. This offered an alternative to the Catholic Church's emphasis on historical succession. Soon scholars were hard at work producing the textual and philological tools needed to enable this venture. Erasmus, considered by many the premiere ecclesiastical Renaissance humanist scholar, added to this his own belief that the laity was the key to a much-needed reform of the Catholic Church. He was convinced that the laity's ability to read the Bible for themselves was essential for a proper lay spiritual formation.[5] This added incentive to the already centuries-old efforts by persons like John Wycliffe and groups like the Waldensians to make the Bible available to the masses in vernacular languages.[6]

Sola scriptura identified a widespread Protestant way of valuing the Bible that is built on the *ad fontes* tradition. This doctrine refined further the methodology reformers believed the faithful should employ when approaching Scripture. All authority (e.g., popes, bishops, councils, theologians, creeds) was subordinate to the teachings contained in the Bible. This meant that any authority exercised within the church was derived not from the office held, the longevity of the institution's existence, or extrabiblical traditions but from faithfulness to God's Word.

---

[4] Alister McGrath, *Reformation Thought: An Introduction* (Oxford, U.K.: Basil Blackwell, 1988), see especially chapter 3.

[5] Desiderius Erasmus, *Enchiridion Militis Christiani* (1503).

[6] Translations from the Latin Vulgate were made into French, Piedmontese, Catalan (Northeast Spain), German, Italian, and Czech. A growing belief that the Catholic Church had based some of its doctrines on faulty Latin translations sent Renaissance theologians scurrying to produce vernacular translations from more reliable texts in the original biblical languages.

Protestant reformers rejected Catholic assertions that tradition constituted a separate and distinct source of revelation in addition to the Bible.
However, they did acknowledge a doctrinal continuity that was accepted as
an authoritative tradition. This tradition speaks of a "fixed interpretation"
that originates among the early Christian teachers as recognized by the
church and extends to the present.[7] Baptists tended, as had the Anabaptists, not to acknowledge any such authoritative tradition. Every individual
was believed to be competent to interpret the Bible according to the dictates
of conscience and subject to the guidance of the Holy Spirit.[8] Therefore,
Baptists recognized no authoritative revelation outside the Bible itself and
no authoritative tradition of interpretation, although many Baptists have
argued on biblical grounds that the individual's interpretation is account-
able to the gathered community of faith and must be exercised within such
boundaries. However, this conviction emerged in political contexts that
strongly opposed any such notions. Consequently, among Baptists' earliest
dreams were those surrounding liberty of conscience and freedom to read
and apply the Bible's teachings to one's life without civil or ecclesiastical
interference.

When Baptists began to emerge in the early seventeenth century, almost
a century of Catholic and Protestant experiments with humanist-inspired
approaches to biblical interpretation had transpired. Many of those ideas
had become widely disseminated among significant segments of European
populations by the late sixteenth century. Largely unaware of the basis for
their approach, Baptists began to embrace the Bible as their only recognized
source of authority for doctrine and practice. In 1611, the early Baptist
leader Thomas Helwys wrote in his confession of faith, "The scriptures
off the Old and New Testament are . . . to bee vsed withal reverence, as
conteyning the Holie Word off God, which onelie is our direction in al
thinges whatsoever."[9] Explaining the Baptist view of Scripture in contrast
to Quaker emphasis on the inner light, Thomas Lover in 1640 wrote,
"It's the Scriptures of the Prophets and Apostles that we square our faith
and practice by. . . . Let the Scripture therefore be the rule of thy faith and

---

[7] See Alister E. McGrath, *Historical Theology: An Introduction to the History of Christian Thought*
(Oxford, U.K.: Basil Blackwell, 1998), 181–3.
[8] For a discussion of this doctrine, see Molly T. Marshall, "Exercising Liberty of Conscience: Freedom
in Private Interpretation," *Baptists in the Balance* (Valley Forge, PA: Judson Press, 1997), 141–50. Also
see H. Wheeler Robinson, *The Life and Faith of Baptists*, rev. ed. (London: Kingsgate Press, 1946)
for discussion of the weaknesses as well as the strengths associated with this Baptist position.
[9] "A Declaration of Faith of English People Remaining at Amsterdam" (n.p., n.p.: 1611), reprinted in
William L. Lumpkin, *Baptist Confessions of Faith* (Valley Forge, PA: Judson Press, 1959), 122.

practice."[10] Thus, not only did the Renaissance and Reformation traditions furnish the foundation on which Baptist dreams and later traditions would be built (i.e., the Bible), they also supplied the ground on which they would be approached (i.e., personal conviction and insight). In Anglo Baptist experience, these convictions were closely associated with another Reformation tradition – *sola fide*.

Interwoven with Martin Luther's doctrine of justification was his doctrine of faith. For him, faith is profoundly personal, involves trusting in God's promise for salvation, and actively unites the believer to Christ. Exercising such faith leads to the real and true presence of Christ in the believer. In justification, God provides everything. The individual simply receives what God has already made available. Through faith, the individual accepts what God has done, which leads to a personal transformation that enables him or her to comprehend God and God's Word in new ways. In justification, the believer is declared perfect, not made perfect. He or she continues to experience sin (*simul justus et peccator*). The Christian life begins by faith alone, but as a consequence of God's transforming work, the believer gradually grows in righteousness and good works.

Baptists generally embraced this view of faith and justification but with an important difference from most mainline reformers. Baptists tended to conclude that God's transforming work leading to the real and true presence of Christ in the life of the believer included the ability of each individual, at least in some measure, to interpret the Scripture under the guidance of the Holy Spirit. Luther and other magisterial reformers had been frightened by such a notion. They attempted to counter this by emphasizing the church's traditional interpretation wherever the tradition was seen to be consistent with Scripture. Departure from this standard on the part of early English Baptists likely had its roots in certain pre-Baptist conscience-restricting experiences they had suffered while still congregants in the Anglican Church. This was but one of many expressions of Baptist reaction against the established Church of England, which had prohibited much that they dreamed of implementing on the basis of their understanding of biblical teachings. Consequently, English Baptists sought to protect the individual believer's conscience against coercion by any ecclesiastical authority, even those within their own ranks.

Closely aligned with the doctrines of *sola scriptura* and *sola fide* is another conviction that has supported the dreams of many other Baptists – the priesthood of all believers. Luther considered this a result of justification.

[10]   Ibid., 191.

Being declared right with God enhanced believers' status before God, sanctified their vocation, and provided the motivation for a life of Christian service.[11] However, Luther applied this to the church in such a way that the doctrine had to be understood in the context of confessionalism. For Baptists, priesthood of the believer signified "the profound capacity and responsibility each human being has in relation to the Holy One who addresses us one by one, who abides within each Christian, and who gifts us for distinctive contributions to the *missio dei*."[12]

About the time Anglo Baptists were emerging, a major theological rift occurred among adherents of the Reformed tradition, especially in Holland. This became a significant traditioning source for several bodies within the Baptist movement. The genesis of the division grew out of Calvinism's doctrine of divine election, which some Reformed scholars had pushed to its limits. Franciscus Gomarus, for example, taught a very fatalistic version of Calvinism that made God the author of every human action. In response, Jacob Arminius advanced theological opinions that attempted to find room for human volition in matters of faith, especially in soteriology. A year after his death, Arminius's views were published in a document titled *Remonstrance*.[13] This became the origin of a theological position known as Arminianism. In reaction, supporters of a strict Calvinist perspective issued *Countra-Remonstrance*,[14] embracing the doctrines of total depravity, unconditional election, limited atonement, irresistible grace, and perseverance of the saints. Throughout the seventeenth and eighteenth centuries, both of these supplied additional components for the theological shaping processes at work among conflicting dreams within the Anglo Baptist movement. Arminian sources influenced some Baptists to stress the role of human free will in their theologies of decision making. Calvinist sources, in contrast, prompted other Baptists to distrust the notion that humans possess the capacity to choose anything that might be ultimately good. Some Baptists adopted such an extreme version of this viewpoint that they left little room for human volition at all.

A second theological traditioning source among early Anglo Baptists derived from dreams of making the Church of England less Catholic in

---

[11] William R. Estep, *Renaissance and Reformation* (Grand Rapids, MI: William B. Eerdmans, 1986), 159.

[12] Marshall, "Exercising Liberty of Conscience," 142.

[13] Also known as "The Five Arminian Articles," 1610, or the "Articuli Arminiani sive Remonstrantia." See Philip Schaff, ed., *The Creeds of Christendom*, 3 vols. (San Francisco: Harper & Row, 1931; reprint, Grand Rapids, MI: Baker Book House, 1983), 3:545–9.

[14] Also known as "The Canons of the Synod of Dort," 1618–19, or the "Canones Synodi Dordrechtanae." See Schaff, *Creeds*, 3:550–97.

doctrine and practice. After Queen Elizabeth's death in 1603, Puritanism intensified its efforts to reform the Church of England. Despite its repeated attempts, however, the endeavor never succeeded. Puritanism's more enduring impact would be experienced among the Separated churches. Frustrated over their inability to purify the Anglican Church of its Catholic corruptions, many Puritans formed independent churches. There they practiced their interpretation of biblical teachings on matters of church doctrine and polity.

Among the more noted of the early Separatist congregations were the Privy Church of Pastor Richard Fitz; the Pioneer Church of pastors Robert Browne, Henry Barrow, and John Greenwood; the Ancient Church of Pastor Francis Johnson; and the Pilgrim Church of Pastor John Robinson. The earliest identifiable Baptists emerged out of conventicles like these, making Puritanism and Separatism important theological sources of many early Anglo Baptist dreams for an authentic restoration of primitive Christian faith and practice.

Conflicts over Sabbath observance became a third source of conflict among Anglo Baptists, and likewise produced additional diversity among their dreams of what biblical Christianity should look like. In 1595, Nicholas Brownde published a work titled *The Doctrine of the Sabbath*, intending to provide support for a strict Sabbath observance of Sunday. What he did not foresee, however, was the huge controversy it would generate concerning which day of the week was biblically appropriate for Sabbath observance. Although most churches decided the matter in favor of Sunday (first day), several smaller groups opted for a Saturday (seventh day) observance. Among Baptists, this gave rise to the Seventh Day Baptist denomination and their dreams of Christian communities that would value and restore this Old Testament practice.

In the eighteenth century, rationalism sparked major debates over the nature of the person and work of Jesus. Those controversies generated yet another variety of dreams within the early Baptist movement. Several forms of anti-Trinitarian theology arose from those debates. Some anti-Trinitarians taught that Christ existed prior to creation and held that he was more than a mere human being. Nonetheless, he was a created being and therefore less than God. Another group embraced a Socinian Christology that denied both Christ's preexistence and deity, interpreting him as being an enlightened teacher but not divine. These ideas won acceptance among a small portion of the early Baptist movement and became part of the traditioning influences that shaped a few of England's General Baptists.

A fifth major European source of theological influence generative of yet other Baptist dreams came through the Wesleyan revivals. The Pietist movement, associated with Philip Jakob Spener's publication of *Pia disideria* in 1675, influenced the Anglican pastor John Wesley's religious thinking. As a student at Oxford University, Wesley had been attracted to William Law's ideals of a consecrated life and by the disciplines inculcated through the academic club at Oxford. While serving as a missionary to the Georgia Colony between 1735 and 1738, Wesley became deeply impressed by the devotion of the Moravian Brethren, a Pietist group. On return to England, he studied Pietism more seriously and eventually incorporated some of its teaching into his own theology. After a deeply moving spiritual experience on May 24, 1738, Wesley began including his new birth and biblical holiness theologies in his preaching. Although he never intended to leave the Anglican Church, Wesley soon found that his new ideas were not welcome in most Anglican pulpits. Influenced by the example of George Whitefield, Wesley began preaching outdoor meetings – a practice that appealed to England's masses. The resulting spiritual movements became known as the Wesleyan revivals. Wesley's movement notably influenced the religious life of England and America, awakened a spirit of humanitarianism toward the suffering masses among the newly created industrial urban populations, and resulted in a new denomination – Methodist. These developments also helped shape both British and American Baptists in numerous ways and significantly contributed to Baptist growth during the eighteenth century.

Colonial American Theological Traditioning Sources
Prior to 1700, Baptists in America were few and widely scattered. Their largest numbers were located in New England, with small contingents beginning to appear in the regions around Philadelphia as the seventeenth century came to a close. Only in the eighteenth century did Baptists begin to settle permanently in the southern colonies of what was to become the United States.[15] The principal theological systems among which they developed within these environments were those of Puritanism, Anglicanism, and Quakerism.

English Puritans dreamed of transforming England's established church into an institution fashioned along the lines of the one in John Calvin's Geneva. To this end, they set out to transform the character, liturgy, theology, and government of the king's church. They had no notion of

---

[15] Except for a small group in the area of Charleston, South Carolina, perhaps as early as 1684.

separating from it, but they intended to reform the church, freeing it from the political controls of the English monarchy and Parliament and from the ecclesiastical controls of its bishops. When this proved impossible, many made their way to the colonies of Massachusetts, Connecticut, and New Hampshire, where they came closer to achieving their ideals.

The Calvinist-oriented theology of Puritanism emphasized the doctrine of divine sovereignty above all else. Human beings were dust, unworthy worms, incapable of pleasing God or producing true righteousness on their own. Salvation, therefore, was totally dependent on the unmerited grace of God's election. Once given by God, salvation was secured forever. Such selection placed the elected one in covenant with God, a relationship the Puritans believed should govern both personal and community life in all matters. John Winthrop, the Bay Colony's first governor, wrote, "[If we neglect God's covenant] the Lord will surely break out in wrath against us [and] be avenged of such a perjured people and make us know the price of the breach of such a Covenant."[16] Like the postexilic Pharisees, fear of God's wrath led Puritan divines to strongly resist anything that seemed to compromise or threaten the vision.

Even after removing themselves to America, Puritans continued to consider themselves part of the Church of England. Eventually, however, they became too distinctive to persist in this notion and finally assumed the name *Congregationalists*. Doctor John Cotton, a prominent early Puritan pastor in Boston, documented several complaints the faithful in New England had against England's "National Church." The list included use of the Book of Common Prayer, which they viewed as a violation of the Second Commandment; the church's authority should be congregational, not national; and governance should come by covenanted agreement from below, not legislated decisions from above. In these points can be seen the seeds of the emerging Congregational denomination.

Puritan worship theology focused on simplicity. Every effort was made to rid their churches of everything "papist." Clergy were not to dress in vestments that implied a spiritual distance between them and laity. The minister was not a priest and possessed no intermediary position between God and the believer. Two sacraments, baptism and the Lord's Supper, were acknowledged. Baptism initiated one into the faith community and was given to infants. The Lord's Supper was to be simple, with no hint of transubstantiation. Sunday was to be strictly observed, but feast days, such

---

[16] John Winthrop, "A Modell of Christian Charity," *Winthrop Papers*, 1623–30 (Boston: Massachusetts Historical Society, 1931), 292–5.

as Christmas and Easter, were not given special observance. Preaching was the focus of worship, a time when the Word of God was expounded.

Colonial Anglo Baptists, having emerged themselves out of similar theological foundations, held many of those convictions in common with the Puritans. On at least two points, however, they differed greatly, and with serious consequences. First, and of fundamental importance, like Calvin in Geneva, Congregationalism established itself as the official religion of New England. All who failed to conform to this religious establishment could suffer the same penalties that were being inflicted by the National Church in England. Ministers did not govern the colonies, but the alliance between civil and ecclesiastical authorities was such that "mutual understanding of common obligations all carried out under the watchful eye of Providence" left little room for deviation.[17] John Cotton expressed his view on the matter in a pamphlet titled "Liberty of Conscience," in which he allowed diversity of opinion with two qualifications: dissenting views could only differ from those of the established church on peripheral matters, and those entertaining such views must hold them quietly to themselves. Such was the state of religious diversity in colonial New England. Baptists often found themselves at odds with local authorities over these matters.

Closely allied to the issue of an established church was the practice of infant baptism. Because the privileges of citizenship were closely associated with membership in the state's church, infant baptism helped serve the needs of both state and church. For Baptists, who believed that baptism was only for those old enough to experience conversion and request the ritual with understanding, their practice of withholding infants from baptism singled them out for punishment.

In the southern territories of England's American colonies, Anglicanism was established, beginning with the Virginia Colony. In contrast to Puritanism's dream of recreating Geneva's church, Anglicanism longed to recreate the English king's church in the Americas. In Virginia, the Thirty-Nine Articles were identified as the single doctrinal standard to be tolerated, and only those ministers sent by a bishop in England would be allowed to serve the newly created parishes. Stern warning was offered to any who might think otherwise: "if any other person pretending himself a minister shall . . . presume to teach or preach publicly or privately, the Governor & Council are hereby desired and empowered to suspend & silence the person so offending."[18] Oversight of each parish was entrusted to a vestry

---

[17] Edwin S. Gaustad, *A Religious History of America*, rev. ed. (San Francisco: Harper & Row, 1990), 59.
[18] Quoted in Gaustad, *A Religious History of America*, 42.

of twelve capable and trustworthy men residing in that parish. This would ensure support, protection, and exclusive franchise for the king's church. To varying degrees, similar efforts could be found in the Carolinas and Georgia.

Despite the desire to re-create a church like the one they had known in England, physical conditions made such an undertaking impossible. Parishes were too large and sparsely settled for a minister to meet adequately the spiritual needs of the colonists, especially beyond the eastern plantations. Chronic shortages of clergy, together with the low standards of many who did come, often left the parishes in a weakened condition throughout the seventeenth century. Still, official opposition to anything non-Anglican was so strong that Baptists made few inroads among settlers in the American South prior to the early eighteenth century; even then, it would be midcentury before significant growth would occur.

The first major crack in Anglicanism's establishment in the southern colonies appeared in the frontier regions beyond the Piedmont plantations. A different type of settler was being attracted to those regions – persons less cultured and less attracted to the formal liturgies associated with the Church of England. Here, the Presbyterians, Baptists, and later the Methodists confronted the Anglican establishment head-on. Once again, their contest for freedom of conscience against the Anglican establishment became a formative part of Anglo Baptist identity in North America.

In the middle colonies of New York, New Jersey, Delaware, and Pennsylvania, and in the New England colony of Rhode Island, Baptists encountered a variety of Protestant faith traditions, especially those of the Dutch Reformed, Lutherans, Quakers, and Presbyterians. Of these, by far the one that exerted the greatest influence on Baptist traditioning was that of the Quakers. Anglo Baptists experienced major competition with this communion and were influenced both by what they rejected in Quakerism as well as by what they embraced from that source.

The Society of Friends, known more popularly as Quakers, had its origin in the left wing of Puritanism. It pressed Puritanism's rejection of ecclesiastical hierarchy, sacramentalism, and formal liturgy to the extreme, focusing on individualism and direct illumination by God's Spirit. If Puritanism were thought of as focused in Christocentric experimentalism, with little value given to the mystical and moral dimensions of salvation, Quakerism might be thought of as occupying the other end of that polarity. The Quaker tradition minimized "the liturgical and teaching function of an ordained ministry, [abandoned] the idea of objective sacraments, and [inspired] conduct which was attributed to the promptings of an inner voice."[19] Consequently, Quakers had no church government that was recognizable to "real Christians."[20] They had no traditional church buildings, no paid clergy, no social distinctions, and they did not follow generally accepted social conventions.

Anglo Baptists embraced the Puritan inclination away from hierarchy, sacramentalism, and formalized liturgy. However, their soteriology and ecclesiology could accept neither infant baptism nor an established church. Yet Baptists were equally reluctant to go as far as the Quakers in jettisoning many of the external expressions of the church in favor of individual spiritual experience. Baptist losses to the Quaker movement increased Baptist resistance, although a few (e.g., the Keithians) experimented with a combination of Baptist immersion and church life with Quaker spirituality. But those experiments were not lasting.

Colonial Canadian Theological Traditioning Sources

Early Canadian Baptists had a very diverse and complex traditioning history that was complicated by immigration, regionalism, and ethnicity. One important dimension of their story relates to the fact that French Catholicism constituted a presence and influence in Canada that affected almost every aspect of the nation's religious history, even in those areas where Protestants were in the majority. Although Canadian Baptists seem to have drawn very little directly from Canadian Catholicism for their theological traditions, the way they chose to respond to and relate to the significant Catholic presence did influence their identity and traditioning in a variety of ways.[21]

Of much greater significance to Canadian Baptist life during this period, however, were the influences of British Baptist, colonial American (later U.S.) Baptist, and revivalistic traditions. The same religious awakening that spread Wesleyanism throughout England also fueled revivals in the English American colonies – initially in the Middle and New England colonies. Soon, New Light Congregational preachers, as well as others, took the revivals both southward (to the American southern colonies and Caribbean Islands) and northward into Canada. Baptists benefited greatly from the revivals, especially in the fact that many New Light Congregationalists

---

[19] Sidney E. Ahlstrom, *A Religious History of the American People* (New Haven, CT: Yale University Press, 1972), 178.
[20] Cotton Mather's label for faith traditions outside the Anglican, Congregational, and Reformed core of denominations that he considered to have some validity.
[21] See Mark A. Noll, *A History of Christianity in the United States and Canada* (Grand Rapids, MI: William Eerdmans Publishing, 1992), chapter 10.

eventually became Baptists.[22] This new source of Baptist life drew on theological traditions that emphasized personal experience in religion and resisted institutionalism and doctrinal confessions. However, New Light Baptists often found themselves vulnerable to proselytism from more organized denominations. Over time, many Canadian and American New Light Baptists were ushered into Calvinist churches, which emphasized discipline, regular observance of the Lord's Supper, and closed communion. Traditions with their roots in British and American Calvinist and Arminian sources established themselves in Canadian religious soil, especially in the Maritime Provinces, and exerted major influence in Canadian Baptists' traditioning processes.

In Upper and Lower Canada, Baptists faced a tougher environment, and very little penetration into the surrounding culture was possible during the period. Here, the Baptist movement consisted of a complex mixture of English, Scottish, and American theological influences that were often at tension with one another throughout this era and beyond. Most of the early Baptists in these regions were United Empire Loyalists, thus introducing a new tension into Baptist life, the choice between British or American patterns of Baptist structure, doctrine, and practice. This can be detected in struggles over styles of churchmanship, doctrinal beliefs, levels of Calvinism, church practices, open versus closed communion, and structural models.[23] Although Canadian Baptists would develop an identity that is reflective of their unique history and context, these externally derived identities are among the early factors contributing to their faith traditions.

Early Baptists' Native Theological Traditioning Sources

Notions of Amerindian theological traditions as vehicles for expressing Baptistic faith convictions are mostly a product of twentieth-century religious thought.[24] We find little evidence for such modes of understanding in the sixteenth and seventeenth centuries. Yet the seeds of all faith traditions are initially planted in the soil of a particular culture's worldview.

---

[22] William L. Lumpkin, *Baptist Foundations in the South: Tracing through the Separates the Influence of the Great Awakening, 1754–1787* (Nashville, TN: Broadman Press, 1961).

[23] H. Leon McBeth, *The Baptist Heritage: Four Centuries of Baptist Witness* (Nashville, TN: Broadman Press, 1987), 335.

[24] The title *Amerindian* has been employed here to refer to the people of the indigenous nations of the Americas. This term is used in an effort to avoid geographical limitation of these peoples to the United States, as the term *Native American* would, or confusing of them with citizens of India, who also will be treated in this book.

Despite frequent efforts on the part of the evangelizing religious tradition to deny any influence from the religious traditions of the evangelized peoples (a cultural annihilationist approach), elements of those cultures' primal faith traditions live on and express themselves in unpredictable ways. They form part of the corpus that is transformed to fit a Baptist ethos. They also constitute part of the complex of traditions that no interpretive intentionality can absolutely obliterate. Professor Brooks Holifield has observed, "Historians construct traditions as heuristic aids that help identify patterns that may not have always been apparent to actors of the past."[25] This is just as true of European and New England Puritan theologies as of Native theologies. The student of history pursues components of his or her identity by searching through their sources in the past. Therefore, it is significant to Amerindian Baptists and others that, in their study of history, they encounter the worldviews through which they have interpreted the Baptist witness they embrace. Traditioning sources of indigenous peoples merit a place in global Baptist history because theirs are among the pre-Baptist North America theological strands contributing to the story of at least one part of the early Baptist family, even if their primal theological traditions were not constitutive of the majority Baptist traditions during the movement's incipient period.

Charles Eastman, a Santee Sioux who possessed extensive life experiences in both the Anglo American and Native cultures, observed early in the twentieth century, "The religion of the Indian is the last thing about him the man of another race will understand."[26] Perusal of four centuries of Baptist descriptions and interpretations of Native religious practices supports the accuracy of that statement. Attempts to survey this dimension of Amerindian heritage within parameters admissible for an historical introduction suffer incompleteness. The need to include more and to explain more everywhere abounds. Still, effort must be made to ground the Native Baptist experience to its world of origin or the alternative that is likely to emerge will be the denial of indigenous cultural sources for Baptist Amerindians. To do this would validate approaches that make Native and Baptist mutually exclusive categories and deny the possibility of a Baptist identity that could also include Amerindian cultural groundedness. This is a conclusion most Native Baptists justly cannot accept.

---

[25] E. Brooks Holifield, *Theology in America: Christian Thought from the Age of the Puritans to the Civil War* (New Haven, CT: Yale University Press, 2003), 306.

[26] Charles Alexander Eastman (Ohiyesa), *The Soul of the Indian* (Mineola, NY: Dover Publications, 2003), xv.

Native or *Amerindian* encompasses a wide range of people whose identity is frequently expressed through the terms *Native American, Eskimo, Inuit, Native Hawaiian, First Nations peoples*, and the like.[27] These persons are also designated by myriad tribal names, some of which are chosen and others imposed. Furthermore, geopolitical templates imposed by European conquerors have prescribed nontribal designations that further obscure the roots of Native identity. But to be Baptist generally identifies an outlook and experience quite different for the Amerindian than for the Anglo-American. To be Baptist does not place the Anglo at odds with an English, Welsh, or American cultural affiliation in the same way that being Baptist and Native does. To be Amerindian and Baptist often means taking up a life struggle to reconcile two seemingly contradictory allegiances. Thus, although Catholic, Anglican, Calvinist, and other theological traditioning processes play a role in Native Baptist identity, a more significant source for their theological traditioning derives out of interaction with Native cultures themselves (this perspective is explored more fully in subsequent chapters).

Historically, Indians of the Americas tended to understand their world in terms of spiritual forces. Every action and occurrence could have meaning in this cosmos of spiritual influences.[28] Those forces could affect how persons or tribes cooked, ate, danced, told stories, made pottery, painted their bodies, arranged their living quarters, organized the village, wooed a partner, married, spoke, and were buried. "Wisdom [came] by paying attention to the living world, discerning the spiritual dimension within it, and debating its significance with others in a community. . . . Everyday realities [could] carry extraordinary significance. Dreams [could] matter."[29] Such religious understanding meant that each tribe had to interpret its reality within the context of its own physical environment. This made pre-Baptist Amerindian religion very pluralistic long before experiencing any contact with European cultures.[30] In fact, European religion initially did more to undermine Indian religious pluralism than encourage it. Only after the emergence of postcolonial cultures did Western Christianity become

---

[27] See James Treat, "Introduction: Native American Narrative Discourse," in *Native and Christian, Indigenous Voices on Religious Identity in the United States and Canada* (New York: Routledge, 1996), 2.

[28] Joseph Epes Brown, *Teaching Spirits: Understanding Native American Religious Traditions* (Oxford: Oxford University Press, 2001), 5–6.

[29] Joel W. Martin, *The Land Looks after Us: A History of Native American Religion* (Oxford: Oxford University Press, 1999), 5.

[30] Gaustad, *A Religious History of America*, 3.

significantly cognizant of the value religious pluralism might have for the peaceful functioning of multicultural and multireligious societies.

Amerindian religious stories and practices played an important role in helping Native peoples understand and accommodate to their specific environments. "If rains were scarce and crucial to survival, then much religious ritual center[ed] on urging or sacrificing or praying that rains might come. If the success of the hunt or the fertility of the soil were central to tribal life, then religion was called upon to do its part."[31] In addition, Amerindian religion furnished a means for addressing many of the same questions with which European religious traditions struggled:

Where did I (we) come from? Why must I (we) die? What is permitted (or forbidden) to me (us) to do? What separates us from or unites us with, other peoples of other tribes or totems or lineages? What rules the sun, or the seasons, or even the affairs of the heart?[32]

Amerindian religion also served a vital function in helping its practitioners through the vital transitions of life. "Countless ceremonies helped to usher the vulnerable individual from the womb to the world, from childhood to maturity, from a single to a conjugal state, and from life into and beyond death."[33] An Amerindian who accepted the Baptist faith tradition might substitute child dedication, baptism, the Eucharist, and hymns for some of the tribe's traditional ceremonies, and he or she might interpret those through a new faith lens. Somehow, though, those new practices and understandings had to make sense in the indigenous cultural and theological world of spiritual forces. If this could not happen, the individual or tribe became alienated from its world in ways that robbed it of its soul – its vital being.[34]

Baptist missionaries to indigenous tribes often are among those singled out for condemnation for their culturally and theologically insensitive ways of dealing with Amerindians. As one author puts it, "They tried to bring the indigenous peoples under the rule of Anglo-Saxon law. Later Christian missionization would be an agent of cultural assault and violence against the peoples and their way of life."[35] Although it is true that Anglo-American Baptist missionaries (along with other evangelizers) too often "were more

---

[31] Ibid., 4.   [32] Ibid.   [33] Ibid.
[34] David Bebbington describes this notion as being among the "other identities" Baptists possess alongside their "religious qualities" in his foreword to Ian M. Randall, Toivo Pilli, Anthony R. Cross, eds., *Baptist Identities: International Studies from the Seventeenth to the Twentieth Centuries* (Milton Keynes, U.K.: Paternoster, 2006), xiii–viv.
[35] M. Shawn Copeland, "Black, Hispanic/Latino, and Native American Theologies," in *The Modern Theologians*, ed. David Ford (Oxford, U.K.: Blackwell Publishers, 1997), 376. Also see the description

concerned to transform Indians into good Englishmen or women than into good Christians," they were not alone in their cultural imperialism. Those missionaries were part of a much larger cultural assault that included most of colonial North America's political, commercial, colonization, and religious interests. In a few cases, Anglo Baptist missionaries at least partially recognized the devastating effect this was having on Native populations and attempted to buffer Amerindians against the harshest forms of this inhuman pogrom.[36] Having noted this, however, Baptist Amerindians have justly observed that their encounter with Western Christianity did much to deprive them of their indigenous modes of theologizing. Among other problems, the oppressive nature of their evangelization created confusion over which elements of the Christianity they had embraced constituted the essence of Christian faith and which were the accoutrements of Western cultural and theological modalities. Awareness of this distortion has sent some Amerindian theologians on a quest for their roots in an effort to reconnect their indigenous modes of theologizing with the Christian kerygma. At least some Amerindian Baptists are among them.

Early Baptists' African Theological Traditioning Sources

Questions surrounding the nature and degree of influence of African native religious thought and ritual on African American Christian belief and practice are still strongly debated. Most scholars agree that African influence is much stronger and clearer in many dimensions of South American and Caribbean black religious life than is the case in North America.[37] Determining the ways in which African religious sources contributed to black religious traditioning in North America has proved much more challenging. Melville J. Herskovits has argued that slavery did not eradicate important elements of African culture among those held in slavery and that a significant amount of Africanism lives on in African American theology and culture in the United States.[38] E. Franklin Frazier vehemently disagrees with Herskovits and asserts that very little of African thought and culture was able to survive North American slavery. He maintains that slavery's

---

offered by Liliuokalani, *Hawaii's Story* (Honolulu, HI: Mutual Publishing, 1990), which treats the violence suffered by Hawaii's Native populations.

[36] See, for example, Jerry L. Faught's article "Isaac McCoy: Successful Missionary or Successful Humanitarian?" *American Baptist Quarterly* 23, no. 1 (March 2004): 65–77.

[37] This is more easily discernable via the influence of such practices as voodoo in Haiti, Obeah in Jamaica, Santeria in Cuba, and candomblé and *umbanda* in Brazil.

[38] See Melville J. Herskovits, *The Myth of the Negro Past* (Boston: Beacon Press, 1958).

systems and the gradual passing away of the first generations of those born in Africa destroyed any significant vestiges of Africanism. The resultant void was filled by the Christian religion.[39] Numerous treatments of that theme since the 1960s have tended to yield less extreme positions and have generally defended the notion of African religio-cultural influences, but in less straightforward and obvious ways than those suggested by Herskovits.[40]

African religion was very diverse, and slavery drew its captives from many parts of the African continent. The fact that many African nations, tribes, and language groups made up the slave population means that any attempt at summarizing African theologies is tenuous. Still, Albert J. Raboteau makes a good case for the possibility of identifying "similar modes of perception, shared basic principles, and common patterns of ritual" as a starting point for discussion of African sources of religious traditioning among black Baptists in North America.[41]

Raboteau argues that the African religious belief systems among slaves relocated to the Americas were complex. They were integral to the African community's worldview, which was built on a close relationship between the natural and supernatural worlds. Consequently, "the welfare of the community and of each individual within it derived from the close relationship of man to the gods, the ancestors, and the unseen spirits."[42] African religion was practiced to promote harmony among these relationships. The essence of evil was understood in terms of disrupting this harmony. Among the most common religious dimensions of this worldview were belief in a high God; in a plethora of lesser divinities or secondary gods who possessed powers for good or evil; in the spirits of ancestors, whose involvement in the lives of the living was thought to be very important; in the power of magic as a way to influence the spirits; in priests, whose role was vital in proper worship and performance of rituals; and in the necessity of ritual as the means for enacting religious beliefs. Dancing, drumming, and singing were essential aspects of the ritual experience.

Eric Lincoln and Lawrence Mamiya make a strong case for the possibility of detecting the influence of this African traditioning source in American black Christianity through what they identify as "the black

[39] Frazier argues his point in several books, including *The Negro Church in America* (New York: Schocken Books, 1964), *The Negro Family in the United States* (Chicago: University of Chicago Press, 1966), and *The Negro in the United States* (New York: Macmillan, 1957).

[40] Cf. C. Eric Lincoln and Lawrence H. Mamiya, *The Black Church in the African American Experience* (Durham, NC: Duke University Press, 1990).

[41] See Albert J. Raboteau, *Slave Religion: The "Invisible Institution" in the Antebellum South* (Oxford: Oxford University Press, 2004).

[42] Ibid., 16.

sacred cosmos."[43] They argue that "black people created their own unique and distinctive forms of culture and worldviews as parallels rather than replications of the culture in which they were involuntary guests."[44] They find evidence of this influence in forms of music, styles and content of preaching, modes of worship, and especially in the distinctives of black Christian "emphases and valences given to certain particular theological views."[45] Among those distinctives were the core values of freedom, justice, equality, Africanness, and racial parity.

EARLY CULTURAL TRADITIONING SOURCES

In addition to theological traditioning sources, each expression of Baptist life also includes traditioning elements that derive from the culture of which it is part. A major portion of the earliest Baptist traditions grew out of the Anglo and Anglo-American cultures, but as previously noted, that was not exclusively the case. Important contributions also came from African culture via the North Atlantic slave trade, Amerindian cultures, and similar sources. In the nineteenth and twentieth centuries, the variety of cultural sources expanded significantly. However, even though the non-European cultural sources for Baptist life as it existed prior to the nineteenth century generally were limited by colonialists' attitudes of racial and religious exclusiveness, those sources grew in importance over time and, therefore, demand attention as part of the earliest Baptists' traditioning processes. It is possible that, at least in some cases, non-Anglo-American cultures influenced dominant Anglo and Anglo-American Baptist groups in ways not yet fully researched. But at the very least, recognizing the cultural diversity present in the full scope of Baptist life during the movement's early stages is essential to an adequate understanding of subsequent developments. Early Baptists' cultural gene pool was far larger than most Baptist histories have tended to recognize.

Early Baptists' Anglo Cultural Traditioning Sources

European Cultural Traditioning Sources
Some of Baptists' earliest traditions have the residue of British culture deeply embedded in them, especially as they developed during the sixteenth and seventeenth centuries. The complicated and fluctuating nature of relations between the papacy and England's monarchs during this period form

---

[43] Lincoln and Mamiya, *Black Church*, 2–7.   [44] Ibid., 2.   [45] Ibid., 3.

the cultural matrix through which the first known Baptists were shaped. Over the course of the reigns of Henry VIII, Edward VI, Mary Tudor, and Elizabeth I, ecclesiastical policies, together with Continental Reformation influences, left many groups dissatisfied, including Catholics, Calvinists, and adherents of numerous other theological systems. When Elizabeth came to the throne, she had little choice but to allow a modest amount of religious diversity. Her religious settlement in 1559, while reestablishing Protestantism, was carefully balanced to avoid alienating those of Catholic sentiment unnecessarily. This became the source for Anglicanism's famous middle way.

After Elizabeth came to the throne, many who had chosen to go into exile during Mary's reign returned to England. Scores of those persons, along with others who were reform minded but had remained in England during the Marian persecutions, were not happy with the queen's new Anglo-Catholic church. It was not Protestant enough, they felt. They pressed for additional reform, hoping to bring the church into closer conformity with the patterns they gleaned from the Bible. For the most part they were disappointed. Some grew increasingly dissatisfied and called for additional purification of the Church of England. From among those elements, the so-called Puritans emerged. Although they did not officially break with the Anglican Church, they often found ways to incorporate some of the reforms they sought into their religious practices. Others, however, became so dissatisfied with the state of religious practice in the established church that they withdrew altogether and organized independent congregations. These became known as Separatists.

By the time of Elizabeth's death in 1603, Puritan and Separatist dissatisfaction with the Anglican Church had resulted in an explosion of sects, schisms, and separatist movements.[46] Elizabeth had pursued policies aimed to contain and eradicate such dissent, producing actions her counselors viewed simply as law enforcement but which religious dissenters interpreted as persecution. The forerunners of the early Anglo Baptist movement can be found among those in the latter group.

Hopeful at first that James's succession to England's throne – and therewith the installation of a new dynasty – would bring greater toleration of religious diversity, Dissenters soon discovered this would not be the case. Many in England had become concerned about the rapidly growing ranks

[46] For example, see T. L. Underwood, *Primitivism, Radicalism, and the Lamb's War: The Baptist-Quaker Conflict in Seventeenth-Century England* (Oxford: Oxford University Press, 1997), chapter 1.

of religious Nonconformists and wanted to see remedial steps taken. King James agreed. He is reported to have stated that if every citizen were given freedom to hold his or her own views, then "Jack and Tom and Will and Dick shall meet, and at their pleasure censure me and my Council and all our proceedings. Then Will shall stand up and say it must be thus; then Dick shall reply and say, nay, marry, but wee will have it thus."[47] James determined that such a scenario would not occur in England and set about to enforce adherence to the laws supporting England's established church. It was during his reign that the first General Baptist churches were formed, which entailed them finding their way amid a hostile political environment.

As religious persecution grew stronger in England, numerous Separatists went into exile during the reigns of Elizabeth I, James I, and Charles I. Holland became a favored destination for many such exiles, as that nation was relatively close geographically, it allowed a great deal of religious toleration, and the English exiles often found those who welcomed them there. Among one of these groups, under the leadership of John Smyth and Thomas Helwys, the first known Baptist church emerged in 1609. The religious milieu of Holland during this period was dominated by two major traditions – Dutch Anabaptism (which arose in the sixteenth century, rejecting both Catholicism and Protestantism) and the Dutch Reformed Church (which was Calvinistic in its theology). The Smyth-Helwys Separatist congregation that migrated to Amsterdam had close association with at least one group of Anabaptists – the Waterlander Mennonites. Comparisons of their subsequent confessions of faith suggest the probability of at least some degree of influence.[48] After only a few months of existence, in 1611, disagreements within the newly organized Baptist church generated the movement's first division, resulting in the Smyth party's decision to remain in Holland and the Helwys faction's courageous resolve to return to London. These formative cultural experiences and associations significantly influenced General Baptist's views on ecclesiology, government, church-state relations, and Christian discipleship.

In 1525, James was succeeded to the English throne by his son Charles I, who not only continued his father's religious policies but also did so with increased resolve. During his reign, a second Anglo Baptist tradition, one

---

[47] Edward P. Cheyney, ed., *Readings in English History Drawn from the Original Sources* (New York: Ginn and Company, 1922), 431.

[48] For a detailed treatment of this association and influence see James Robert Coggins, *John Smyth's Congregation: English Separatism, Mennonite Influence, and the Elect Nation* (Waterloo, ON: Herald Press, 1991), especially 117–54.

more thoroughly Calvinist in nature, was born. Those Baptists, known as Particular Baptists, differed in several important respects from General Baptists, but both shared the cultural experiences of persecution and threat because of their religious convictions. Consequently, both shared similar attitudes toward freedom of conscience and legal separation of church from government.

By 1640, tensions between Charles I and Parliament had grown so strong that the king decided to disband it. Parliament refused to disband, instead forming an army under the command of Oliver Cromwell. A civil war ensued, resulting in Charles's defeat and subsequent execution. During the years of the Cromwellian Regime (1648–60), Anglo Baptists experienced increased freedom to participate in government, to pursue their dreams of building a better life, and to disseminate their ideas among the general populace. However, the new situation exposed the fact that dissenters were not of one mind and lacked the political experience to govern effectively. Considerable tension arose within their ranks, making meaningful consensus impossible on most issues and ultimately dooming the Saints regime to failure. The Cromwellian interlude did enable Anglo Baptists to become bolder in publishing their views, in openly debating their opponents, and in establishing churches that publicly identified themselves as Baptist. But this freedom did not last, ending abruptly in 1660 with the Royal Restoration. The ensuing enactment of the Clarendon Code penalized all dissenters, including Baptists. The period between 1660 and adoption of the Act of Toleration in 1689 were difficult years for British Baptists. Their experiences of struggle for survival, persecution, and social ostracism seriously influenced development of their self-image, theology, and attitudes both toward government and religious establishment. The impact was so pivotal during the formative stages of Anglo Baptist life that it became an enduring feature of their traditioning processes and, thus, a product of their faith dreams and cultural environments.

Britain underwent major political, sociocultural, and economic change over the course of the eighteenth century. Six aspects of this transformation had particular significance in shaping subsequent Anglo Baptist traditions. First was a major political shift. With the accession of the monarchs William and Mary, toleration was granted to religious dissenters. This change of policy gave new life to British Baptists, who had sunk into considerable despair.[49] However, despite having won toleration, Baptists never felt secure in the privilege and remained hypervigilant on matters even remotely

---

[49] Gilbert Burnet, *The History of My Own Times*, 6 vols. (Oxford: Clarendon Press, 1833), 4:550.

touching on religious freedom. Moreover, gaining official toleration did not bring public welcome, and "nonconformity was rarely without vociferous enemies at any time in the century."[50]

Eighteenth-century England also was awash in anti-Catholic polemic. Such sentiment was not limited to Dissenters; it was shared by the Anglican establishment as well. Louis XIV's revocation of the Edict of Nantes fueled English Protestant fears that the same might happen in their country should the wrong monarch gain office. The influences fanned the embers of an existing anti-Catholic sentiment among Baptists. Strong suspicion of anything Catholic already was part of Anglo Baptists' Puritan-influenced heritage, which fueled a strong we-are-the-opposite-of-Catholic identity. British Baptist pamphlets and sermons from the period became filled with warnings against perceived threats of "popery," which caused Baptists' anti-Catholic dispositions to become even more deeply ingrained.

The rise of rationalism, exemplified in the works of authors like John Toland and John Locke, popularized the role of reason in deciding matters of religion. Gradually, the supernatural elements of Christian faith became an embarrassment to growing segments of British society. Many concluded that exemplary comportment was more important than orthodox theology. This distressed some among Baptists who lamented that "moral conduct [had] begun to displace the quest for personal salvation."[51] Baptist traditioning was affected in two major ways. Some within the General Baptist ranks utilized rationalistic systems of thought in ways that rejected conventional Christology and Trinitarianism and guided them along a path toward Unitarianism. Among Particular Baptists, rationalism was used to maintain "a rigid quasi-rationalistic framework, seriously distorting the doctrine of grace."[52]

The early stages of the Industrial Revolution that would eventually generate massive social changes in England, together with major challenges to British churches, emerged early in the eighteenth century. But the nature of those challenges affected different churches in differing ways. Tens of thousands of job hunters migrated into England's growing textile cities, which were unprepared to receive them. The multitudes of common people, whose lives were radically disrupted by this transfer from agriculture to industrial urban life, became receptive to the voices of dissenting churches. Some Baptist churches in these centers grew large and became influential.

---

[50] Raymond Brown, *The English Baptists of the Eighteenth Century*, vol. 2, *A History of the English Baptists*, ed. B. R. White (London: Baptist Historical Society, 1986), 3.
[51] Ibid.   [52] Ibid., 5.

But throughout most of the century, 80 percent of England's citizens continued to live in rural areas. Most Baptist churches were located there as well. Consequently, the typical Baptist church was characterized by insularity, not urban innovation. Agrarian society often gave these churches stability, dependability, integration, and continuity, but it also produced some less desirable qualities. "Generations of inter-marrying meant that members of such churches were closely related. Lay leadership was often confined to privileged families who had served for many generations.... Corporate life [often degenerated] into self-regarding independence, even doctrinaire superiority."[53]

In contrast, urban areas fostered changes that many Baptists interpreted as evidence of moral decline. "Many believers . . . blamed the theatre; these 'academies of hell' and 'nurseries of all vice'" for the "threatening" moral changes.[54] Others saw evidence of God's wrath against those innovations in nature itself. An outbreak of plague (1665), the great fire of London (1666), a major earthquake (1691), and a series of devastating storms (1703) became signs of God's displeasure with English waywardness. Throughout the following century, "'storm' sermons were preached annually in which congregations were urged to repent, avert the wrath of God, abandon their unworthy behavior, and turn dependently to Christ."[55]

Another product of eighteenth-century British culture was the frequent controversies within and among denominations. These heightened Baptists' defensiveness, forcing them to explain their beliefs and practices more clearly as well as to focus more attention on doctrinal matters. Many people in eighteenth-century England experienced faith as an inseparable part of everyday life. Therefore, whenever a contrary view happened to be put forth, the issue was easily interpreted as a question of personal obedience to God, not a simple matter of hermeneutical difference. Baptists became adept at the publication of confessions of faith, engagement in public debates, and preaching sermons that forcefully asserted the correctness of the Baptist claims against contrary opinions. Such behavior may have been normative for denominations of the period, but it tended to produce heightened claims for one's own position together with concomitant prejudices against contrasting views.

---

[53] Ibid., 11.
[54] William Bisset, "Plain English: A Sermon Preached at St. Mary-le-Bow . . . for Reformation of Manners" (1704), quoted in Brown, *English Baptists of the Eighteenth Century*, 2:6.
[55] For representative examples, see Benjamin Stinton, "A Sermon Preached the 27th November 1713 in Commemoration of the Great and Dreadful Storm in November 1703" (1714), and Andrew Gifford, "A Sermon in Commemoration of the Great Storm Commonly Called the High Wind (1703) . . . with an Account of the Damage Done by It" (1733).

Colonial American Cultural Traditioning Sources

Three great colonial powers furnished cultural foundations of significant consequence in North America – the Spanish, French, and English. Besides this, the Dutch made an important attempt to establish a permanent colonial presence in the region of New York and the Swedish in Delaware. Although early Spanish, French, Dutch, and Swedish colonial efforts in eastern North America did not endure, one could hardly call them unsuccessful by several important measures. Each left behind enduring cultural legacies. Those legacies did not seem especially significant to Anglo-American Baptists in the seventeenth and eighteenth centuries, as few Baptists could be counted among their ranks in North America. Yet, over time, their importance would grow so that, by the twentieth century, substantial Baptist communions would value one or another of those cultures as furnishing an undeniable part of their identity.

Without belaboring the point here, we should note that Spain established the first permanent European colony in what became the United States at St. Augustine, Florida in 1565. Eventually, Spanish culture would dominate in the regions now known as Florida; New Mexico; Arizona; Texas; California; and to a lesser extent, many other areas of the southwestern quadrant of the United States. The chief Spanish institutions in these regions were the presidio and the mission, which became the centers of commerce, religion, and education. Although these borderlands of Spain's American empire were eventually lost to the politics of Manifest Destiny by the United States, Spanish architecture, linguistic influence, and ethnic heritage continued to exert a vigorous cultural influence. The strongly Catholic nature of this culture made it an object of Anglo-American Baptist concern and evangelism, especially over the course of the nineteenth century.

French colonial influence in North America during its early stages cannot meaningfully be divided into the national boundaries of the United States and Canada, a fact that might seem self-evident but often is obscured by subsequent political developments. In the United States, the influence of France's colonial presence became greatly diluted by later migrations whereas, in Canada, French cultural dominance was maintained in major regions, especially the territories of Quebec and Ontario. Consequently, the importance of French culture as a shaping influence worked very differently for Baptists in the United States than was the case in Canada. In that regard, national boundaries became important shapers of Baptist tradition.

In what became the United States, French exploration and colonial influence began primarily with trading ventures and was characterized by only modest interest in establishing French settlements. This presence was strongest in regions around the Great Lakes and along the Mississippi

River. Led by the Jesuits, the French culture established in those areas gave Roman Catholic institutions and faith a centrality unequaled in most other colonies. The names Marquette, Francis Xavier, and Jean de Brébeuf are enduring reminders of that heritage. Yet Sydney Ahlstrom is probably correct in his declaration that the lasting impact of New France on religious life in the United States was "slight." "Little that was French or Roman Catholic endured except . . . a treasure of melodious but soon hopelessly mispronounced place names."[56] Ultimately, only in those regions of the United States where exiled Acadians settled – primarily New Orleans and the Louisiana bayou country – did French culture make a significant ongoing impact. Besides that, although exiled Huguenots created pockets of culturally interesting episodes of French influence, they were soon absorbed into the larger culture of the British colonies.

In the end, perhaps the greatest shaping influences that French culture exerted on the developing American colonies and subsequent United States came in the form of political rivalries with Britain that helped fuel the American Revolutionary War and intensified British and American hatred of popery. In the French-Anglo culture wars, use and abuse of the Amerindian peoples for political purposes became horribly destructive to those tribal populations. Ahlstrom concludes, "Only one misfortune to befall the Indians was greater than his being caught up on the crosscurrents of imperialism; his greatest tragedy was to be overrun and enveloped by the 'Atlantic Migration.'"[57]

Although the early Spanish and French cultures in the United States might seem to be of such little consequence for Baptist history that they do not deserve attention, in both direct and indirect ways the cultures do influence varied dimensions of Baptist traditioning processes in the United States. This theme will be explored more thoroughly in chapters that follow.

For England's colonies in North America, the seventeenth and eighteenth centuries were primarily a period of laying foundations. This was fortuitous for Anglo-American Baptist development, as this was a time of beginnings for them as well. Although initially unwelcome in many colonies, Baptists were emerging within a society experiencing great flux. Their fortunes tended to ebb and flow with those of the new nation in germination. In the end, many Anglo-American Baptist values – such as democratic principles of church governance, separation of church and state, and freedom of conscience – found fertile soil in the emerging American society.

[56] Ahlstrom, *Religious History*, 68.   [57] Ibid.

During much of the seventeenth century, the territories that came to constitute the early United States could culturally be divided into three regions – the New England colonies, the southern colonies, and the middle colonies. Culturally, these colonies owed much to the European communities that had spawned them. In New England, this meant Puritan values built on the conviction that their move to America was bound up with a divine commission. Thus, life and relationships were often approached from a mentality of covenant agreements. Such religious convictions were so important that Puritan leaders generally insisted only property owners and members of the official church could share in the colony's government. This attitude met with debate and opposition from various lay and clerical elements within their colonies – especially noteworthy were the objections of Ann Hutchinson and Roger Williams. Williams believed so strongly in his views regarding relations between civil and ecclesiastical authority that he founded the independent settlement of Providence in 1636 and the colony of Rhode Island in 1644, which included religious liberty for all residents as the centerpiece of their governance.

As the century progressed, population growth and diversity of viewpoints began to erode the covenantal ideals established by New England's Puritan founders, thus opening the way for greater religious differentiation. The economic, moral, and religious changes that accompanied the transition generated varied responses, from religious persecution to the Salem witch hunt of 1692. These changes brought new, though challenging, possibilities for Baptists. As had been the case in England, their struggles against the Congregational establishment did much to shape Anglo-American Baptists' dreams of securing both religious liberty and separation between the church and civil government.

Religious life did not preoccupy early Southern culture in the same way it did in New England. Southern society was largely divided between the more established, eastern tidewater settlements and the newer, less cultured lifestyles of the interior pioneers. The Anglican Church was favored by the eastern planter classes. Baptists and other "dissenting" traditions experienced greater acceptance among the frontier populations.

The middle colonies included widely diverse populations from various cultural and national backgrounds, including communities from Dutch, Finnish, Swedish, German, Welsh, Scottish, and English heritages. The region offered a mix of cultures, denominations, and nationalities unmatched in the other two regions and had no official church. Consequently, the great American religious experiment had its roots there, requiring that each church make its own way. This turned out to be the environment in which the Anglo-American Baptist movement would began to thrive.

The region around Philadelphia became the numerical center for Anglo Baptist life in America through most of the eighteenth century. The climate of religious toleration, pluralism, and competitive opportunity proved favorable for the Baptist cause. Soon churches began to multiply, followed by early stages of denominational formation. In 1707, the first enduring Baptist association was formed (the Philadelphia Baptist Association), which became a center for evangelism, mission work, education, and doctrinal coherence for many Anglo-American Baptists.

By the early eighteenth century, numerous religious leaders began to express concerns that the quality of spiritual life in the colonies was declining.[58] Such worries helped fuel efforts toward religious renewal resulting in a series of revivals that swept through the colonies in the 1720s through the 1750s. Collectively known as the First Great Awakening, revivals did much to establish the character of American religious life – especially that of Anglo-American Baptists – for the following two centuries. Among the characteristics of the new revivalistic tradition were flamboyant and emotional preaching, increased intensity of physical manifestations as part of the conversion experience; heavy focus on personal religious experience; and emphasis on practices like itinerant preaching, devotional reading, and individual "exhorting."[59]

The revivals proved a watershed for Anglo Baptists in America. They likely did more to establish the future course for this wing of the Baptist movement than did any other single event of the eighteenth century. As a consequence, Anglo-American Baptists grew from about 24 churches with approximately 839 members in 1700 to about 979 churches and almost 67,500 members in 1790. Collectively, Baptists in America were transformed from the position of being a barely perceptible group in 1700 to being one of the largest denominations in the nation by 1800. To a significant degree, the First Great Awakening and the cultural transitions associated with the Revolutionary War were the determinative cultural factors of the nineteenth century that would fashion the future of America's Anglo Baptist movement.

The complex body of factors that contributed to America's Revolutionary War is too extensive for detailed treatment here. In general, the story might be summarized as the outgrowth of tensions that developed as a

---

[58] See, for example, "The Necessity of Reformation, with the Expedients Subservient Thereunto, Asserted in Two Questions," in *The Results of Three Synods* (Boston, 1725), 94–117.
[59] Ahlstrom, *Religious History*, 286–7.

result of England's early extension to colonists of the same rights enjoyed by citizens in the mother country, along with limited freedom for self-government, privileges that the monarchy later sought to restrict and even rescind. However, years of colonial government had produced assemblies accustomed to exercising certain liberties in colonial decision making as well as many colonists' being habituated to sharing in local government. Royal efforts to gain more control over the colonies served only to push them further toward independence. This trend was furthered by the spirit of liberty fostered through conditions on the American frontier. The crisis came to a head in 1776 with America's Declaration of Independence, thereby setting in motion processes that resulted in American nationhood and eventually to organization of the U.S. government under its current constitution in 1789.

The processes leading up to this achievement were important ones for Baptists. American independence was a product of philosophical ideals, political opportunity, and social demands for changes that would guarantee greater personal liberties. Anglo-American Baptist dreams of religious freedom grew out of their convictions regarding the nature of the individual's relationship to God. It was to be personal and uncoerced. Therefore, a parish system could not fit either Baptist soteriology or ecclesiology. But achieving such liberty had not only been impossible for Baptists, it often had been an unpopular position among the general populations in which Baptists had resided up to this point. The American Revolution brought together many forces that normally would not have tended to cooperate with each other – John Locke's philosophy with its emphasis on religious toleration, Enlightenment principles which valued personal liberties, the ideals of the First Great Awakening with its focus on personal religious experience, and the biblical views of groups like the Baptists. Thus, in this great American social experiment secular and religious ideals came together in a unique fashion, uniting dreams for political liberty with those of religious liberty. Consequently, Anglo-American Baptists had the fortune of being situated at the right place, with the right theology, at the right time in history to attract masses of adherents into their movement.

Colonial Canadian Cultural Traditioning Sources
Canadian identity, and tangentially Canadian Baptist identity, has been shaped by three major cultural factors: its beginnings as an *"ad hoc* colonial outpost," its cultural location between the United States and Europe,[60]

---

[60]   Mark A. Noll, *A History of Christianity in the United States and Canada* (Grand Rapids, MI: William Eerdmans Publishing), 246.

and its vast and diverse geographical reality.[61] The English presence in Canada prior to the mid-eighteenth century was primarily motivated by commercial interests and a desire to contain the French. The earliest waves of English-speaking immigrants were mostly British Anglicans and Presbyterians and American Congregationalists who came to the region for economic, not religious, incentives. This, together with the scarcity of clergy, contributed to a de facto religious toleration.

As the eighteenth century opened, Baptists had joined the ranks of Canadian immigrants. Expulsion of the French Acadians in 1755 opened the doors for a new wave of immigration, mostly from America and mainly into the French Maritime territories. In addition, the American Revolution helped double Canada's population as Loyalists made the decision to resettle there, especially in Quebec and the Atlantic Coast (or Maritime) Provinces. Freed and escaped African slaves were significant among this group, the majority of who were Baptists. Among the important leaders in this company were the black Baptist preachers David George (1742–92) and Richard Preston (1790–1861).[62]

In 1791, Canada's cultural identity was further complicated with the creation of Upper and Lower Canada. Lower Canada, which constituted modern Quebec and the Maritime Provinces, was religiously diverse, with significant numbers of Anglicans, Methodists, Congregationalists, Mennonites, Lutherans, Moravians, Quakers, and Baptists. By 1812, as a result of the Loyalist migrations, perceptibly American forms of some denominations existed alongside more British-oriented ones.[63] Quebec was French-speaking and strongly Catholic, while Upper Canada (modern Ontario) hosted a wide range of denominations.

As Canada gradually developed toward nationhood, no initial overarching vision or consensus existed regarding what kind of colony this was to become.[64] Therefore, Baptists, like others, lacked a centralized identity. The business of survival was their focus. Resources were lacking, in terms of both leadership and church buildings. Urban communities usually could afford buildings, support a minister, and maintain a program of ministry, but smaller rural settings were isolated and needy. Much like the similar

---

[61] Darren C. Marks, "Canadian Protestantism to the Present Day," in *The Blackwell Companion to Protestantism*, ed. Alister E. McGrath and Darren C. Marks (Oxford, U.K.: Blackwell Publishing, 2004), 189.

[62] Terrence Murphy, "The English-Speaking Colonies to 1854," in *A Concise History of Christianity in Canada*, ed. Terrance Murphy and Roberto Perin (Oxford: Oxford University Press, 1996), 116.

[63] Ibid., 113.   [64] Marks, "Canadian Protestantism," 190.

frontier situation in the United States, this isolation contributed to the success of revivalism in the latter half of the eighteenth century.

In a general sense, the cultural context of eighteenth-century Canada meant three things for Baptists as well as most other church bodies. First, limited resources required a degree of cooperation among denominations. Although this cannot be interpreted as a full-blown ecumenism, it does help explain the surprising degree of sharing across denominational lines, especially with those denominations closest in belief and practice. Second, the character of churches in larger urban centers was different from that of the rural areas. In these centers, churches often had the resources to sustain denominationally independent programs in ways rural churches could not. Finally, the laity constituted the backbone of Canada's ecclesiastical institutions. "Any form of ecclesiastical establishment or centralized control . . . was met with resistance and suspicion."[65] These cultural characteristics furnished the matrix in which early Canadian Baptists came into being.

Early Baptists' Native Cultural Traditioning Sources

Native American culture encompasses such a multitude of tribes and other social units that attempting to offer any meaningful generalizations adequately describing all of them is almost impossible. Often numerous tribes are categorized together because of certain shared practices or traits, when in reality each tribe has its own practices and customs. Thus, to speak of Amerindian culture as a unit can easily assume too much. The popular image of the American Indian as a tribe of people with a chief, braves who ride horses (a sixteenth-century Spanish contribution), and life centered on buffalo hunting is most representative of the Plains Indians, but even among them, it fails to reflect the great variety among the Plains peoples. However, if we keep the factor of an incredible diversity in mind, a few generalizations might be offered to assist us in our efforts to grasp the significance of this complex body of cultures as one of the many sources for early Baptist traditioning.

Although theories shift from time to time, it still seems most likely that Amerindian tribes are descendents of a proto-Mongoloid population in northeastern Asia. Linguistic and archaeological links have not been clearly delineated, but they probably were part of the circumpolar and circumboreal culture extending from Scandinavia to Siberia. Characteristics

---

[65] Ibid., 191.

of those cultures included animal ceremonialism, hunting taboos, belief in spirits, and shamanism.[66] They seem to have shared the common bond of being hunting cultures as they migrated to America but gradually took different paths of development over time. In a very general sense, Amerindian cultures developed according to two main patterns – a hunting pattern and a horticultural pattern. Other major patterns usually reflect a blending of these two.

The Amerindian hunting cultures were characterized by animal ceremonialism, the quest for spiritual power, a male supreme being, an annual ceremony of cosmic revitalization, shamanism, and life after death – either beyond the horizon or in the sky. The horticultural cultural pattern generally included rain and fertility ceremonies, priestly rituals, goddesses as well as gods, ongoing fertility rites, fixed shrines and temples, medicine-society ritualism, and life after death – either in the underworld or beyond the clouds.[67] In general, patterns of religious practices developed that correlated to these major cultural patterns.

When Baptist missionaries and others representatives of Christianity came into contact with Amerindian cultures, two very different systems of traditioning were encountering each other. Anglo-American Baptist religion was representative of a tradition that had been established by a particular founder, Jesus of Nazareth, and had been preserved essentially through literary forms. Amerindian religions, however, did not have a single founder and were transmitted by tribes in oral forms. This meant, among other things, that Indian cultures did not lend themselves to religious creedal or dogmatic expression in the way Christianity did. Among most indigenous groups, "it was common for a person to enter into direct contact with the supernatural powers and receive their directions."[68] Thus, the old traditions, though valued and passed on to the next generation, were capable of being changed through visions, which gave rise to new traditions. Consequently, when Amerindians were urged to become Christian, they were being asked to exchange a rather charismatic, innovative, and spirit-focused faith tradition for one that seemed more rigid, rational, and form focused.

American Indians also held a very different view of creation and its interrelated parts than did Anglo-American Baptists. Sharp lines of distinction between divinity, humans, and animals generally did not exist. A very different concept of existence from that of conventional Christianity

---

[66] Ake Hultkrantz, *Native Religions of North America* (San Francisco: Harper Collins, 1987), 12.
[67] Ibid., 14.   [68] Ibid., 16.

shaped this contrast. Amerindian mythology presented the view that in the beginning "all beings on earth were more or less human." Then, for reasons that varied from tribe to tribe, "many primal beings [turned] into animals and birds."[69] This meant that humans and much of the animal kingdom were "brothers," so animals should be treated with respect. This was the underlying attitude for much Indian ceremony – for example, imitation of animals in dress, actions, and thought projections. Not only were some animals thought to have spirits; usually, the preferred form for a spirit that wished to project itself into the natural world would be that of an animal (animalism). To some extent, similar patterns existed relative to other aspects of nature, especially any feature that seemed unusual.

When a natural phenomenon or cultural object was understood as "saturated with supernaturalness,"[70] it would be set aside as taboo. This meant its sacredness was of such a nature as to render it dangerous if not treated properly. Transgressing taboo could cause sickness, paralysis, or even death. Myths and rituals helped draw the supernatural powers and humans close together, producing a culture in which nature, world, and universe flowed into one another and made existence alive with spiritual activity to a far greater degree than normally would be the case for the Anglo-American Baptist.

In *The Soul of the Indian*, the Native American Charles Eastman (Ohiyesa) argues that primitive Christianity includes much that naturally would have appealed to the religious sensibilities of Native peoples. "Jesus' hard sayings to the rich and about the rich would have been entirely comprehensible. . . . Yet the religion that is preached in our churches and practiced by our congregations, with its element of display and self-aggrandizement, its active proselytism, and its open contempt of all religions but its own, was for a long time extremely repellent."[71] Eastman concedes that Christianity itself should not be rejected just because of the poor models observed through Anglo behavior but argues that "bad national faith" was hard to overlook. When representatives of Anglo government, some of them ministers of the gospel, pledged to the Indian nations "in solemn treaty the national honor, with prayer and mention of their God; and when such treaties . . . were promptly and shamelessly broken, is it strange that the action should arouse . . . contempt?"[72] In the brief book, Eastman meticulously makes the case that much affinity existed between the best in Christian theology and the best in Native theology, with the potential that both could have benefited from the encounter. The

[69] Ibid., 21.   [70] Ibid., 23.   [71] Eastman (Ohiyesa), *The Soul of the Indian*, 5.   [72] Ibid., 6.

cultural exclusiveness that characterized most Anglo Baptists made that connection almost impossible for the early Native inquirer.

Today's Native Baptist, who seeks solid theological foundations on which to establish a vibrant Indian Baptist faith identity, frequently experiences the need to deal both with the strongly ingrained worldviews of Native cultures and the kinds of issues Eastman has clarified. Long frustrated in their efforts to give concrete expression to their faith dreams, those persons who are both Native and Baptist have lived in enduring bifurcation of these two vital aspects of their identity. Their experience, too, is a part of Baptists' cultural DNA and an important part of the traditioning processes that shape Baptists' identity as a global movement.

Early Baptists' African Cultural Traditioning Sources

A worldview might be thought of as a culture's way of defining and interpreting reality. It describes the integrated systems of beliefs, values, feelings, and relationships that constitute the mental maps individuals and groups use for interpreting the meaning of life experiences. Worldviews furnish the fundamental and unquestioned assumptions a culture makes regarding the nature of things. In that sense, a worldview supplies the categories through which a people think and declare what is real and important and what is not.

Early black Baptists drew significantly from both a West African worldview and a Euro-American worldview in ways that make their versions of Baptist traditioning distinct from the Anglo and Anglo-American Baptist traditions. As with the Amerindian cultures, there was no singular West African worldview during the seventeenth and eighteenth centuries. Each subgroup had its own explanations and interpretations of reality. However, enough similarity existed that one might speak of a "shared basic outlook,"[73] thus making possible some general observations regarding the role of West African culture in early African and African American Baptist life.

In a very general sense, over the past two millennia, Africa has been the home of a complex network of cultures whose developments frequently have been altered and shaped by outside civilizations. "White" Africa has tended to dominate the northern and southern regions of the continent, whereas black Africa has developed its strongest cultures along the two outer margins of East Africa and West Africa. Among those cultures, two basic categories might be identified – those that developed written languages

[73] Mechal Sobel, *Trabelin' On: The Slave Journey to an Afro-Baptist Faith* (Princeton, NJ: Princeton University Press, 1979), 5.

and thus preserved traditions that have subsequently become better known to the modern world and those lacking written languages and therefore available to us only through oral traditions, archaeology, and sporadic eyewitness accounts preserved by foreign visitors over the centuries.

Since ancient times, the development of "higher" cultures in black Africa has generally occurred in regions where three elements converged to produce a stable balance: agriculture, livestock maintenance, and contact with the outside world. This has most often occurred along the edges of the Sahara between the desert and the Indian Ocean to the east and the Atlantic Ocean to the west. In both instances (since the Greco-Roman period), black Africa's earliest major outside contact was with Islamic culture. In the seventh and eighth centuries, commercial outposts formed links between Africa and the Muslim Middle East extending from Mogadishu southward to Zanzibar. The main commodities sustaining this trade were slaves, gold, and ivory. Commercial interests of this type led to the rise of several important African kingdoms, including the kingdom of Monomotapa (modern Zimbabwe) to the southeast and the Niger empires in the west. The major Niger empires included those of Ghana (c. 800–1077); Mali (or the Manding Empire or Manden Kurufa, a medieval state of the Mandinka from 1235 to 1645); and the Songhay (early fifteenth century to 1591), with its famed capitals in Gao and Timbuktu. By the eighteenth century, these empires had disappeared – victims of a declining trans-Saharan trade.[74]

A more elusive dimension of African culture developed among the tribal peoples without written languages. In contrast to the empires with their well-ordered societies and governments, the oral cultures of Africa left a less clearly defined heritage. As Ferand Braudel describes the situation, there was "one Africa with kings – whose history is not wholly unknown – and another without them, lost in oblivion."[75] For early Baptist development, the latter Africa is its more significant cultural source, thus making definitive answers to some of the movement's most perplexing questions almost impossible to achieve. The result has been significant disagreement among scholars concerning the connections between African culture and African American Baptists. Fortunately, investigation of the connections has become an important area of research in African American Baptist

---

[74] Fernand Braudel, *A History of Civilization*, trans. Richard Mayne (New York: Penguin, 1993), 126–30.
[75] Ibid., 126.

scholarship in recent decades and has yielded important insight into this aspect of Baptists' roots.[76]

Mechal Sobel carefully defends the argument that "Africans brought their world views into North America where, in an early phase of slavery, the core understandings, or Sacred Cosmos, at the heart of these world views coalesced into one neo-African consciousness."[77] This supports the conclusion that African culture is one important aspect of the early Baptist traditioning process, but one that has tended to be overlooked and marginalized. Sobel demonstrates that the majority of African slaves brought to North America came from one of four language groups, that "had originally come from one source, the 'Niger-Congo and Kurdoganian' language group."[78] Through a detailed study of language, similarities of outlook, and tribal mythology, she builds the case that for the North American slave a distinct West African worldview confronted the Anglo worldview to produce a unique tradition that is reflected in African American Baptist experience.

Sobel identifies six elements or categories of being in this worldview, which she labels the "West African sacred cosmos." The most important of these elements was the human being. "Every Spirit and thing exists in its relationship to him and is actually defined as it relates to man."[79] However, the other elements were neither created by nor ultimately controlled by humankind. Spirit is the key to power, and the guiding motivation in this worldview is to connect with this force and properly to order individual and group being so that spirit works in your favor, not to your detriment. Hence, God (the first creator), the spirits of the recent dead and of great predecessors, humanity, animals and plants (also possessing spirits), phenomena and objects, and force all work together in the West African worldview according to patterns and relationships that must be discovered, comprehended, and honored. The motivating element in this complex web of relationships is found in "a dialectic of creation: opposites are created within each whole, and the activity generated by the working out of these given contradictions leads to development."[80]

The overall effect of this complex of worldviews seems somewhat Hegelian, with the guiding *Geist* being the human "spirit" (or spirits, or perhaps aspects of the one spirit), which "must develop and fulfill itself in order to live with the Supreme Spirit."[81] As will be seen later, this aspect

---

[76] See, for example, Sobel, *Trabelin' On;* Walter F. Pitts Jr., *Old Ship of Zion: The Afro-Baptist Ritual in the African Diaspora* (Oxford: Oxford University Press, 1993); Lincoln and Mamiya, *Black Church*; and Melva Wilson Costen, *In Spirit and in Truth: The Music of African American Worship* (Louisville, KY: Westminster John Knox Press, 1993).

[77] Sobel, *Trabelin' On*, xvii.   [78] Ibid., 5.   [79] Ibid., 10.   [80] Ibid.   [81] Ibid.

of West African culture will contribute a key component to a significant part of the early Baptist traditioning process – the black Baptist dimension. Without this cultural component, the early African American Baptist experience loses sight of an essential part of its identity. From West Africa came the notion that every person (in relation with the tribal community) must be "responsible for making himself and taking his proper place in the ongoing continuum."[82] Every person is responsible for the "little man" who "existed before his body came into the world and who will continue to exist after his body dies."[83] This way of interpreting reality was among the important shaping factors in the early African American Baptist traditioning processes.

CONCLUSION

Baptist identity is the product of extensive and complex traditioning processes that are multicultural, varied theologically, and subject to the specific experiences of particular groups of Baptists. A defining characteristic of Baptists is their dreams for life that enables persons to grow into their God-given potential, both temporally and eternally. But, as we have seen, those dreams are born in theological and cultural contexts that vary widely. Such environments not only shape the forms through which Baptist dreams find expression but also fashion the pathways by which those dreams seek their realization. Martin Luther King Jr., as a person of global notoriety, epitomized this Baptist quality. His dreams for the correction of an unjust and oppressive social system in the United States were at the same time shaped by the cultural contexts and theological insights of his day and also exerted a powerful influence that helped change both culture and theological perception. In this, he illustrates processes that also characterized Baptist development during the movement's first centuries – a period when persons of Anglo cultural heritage predominated. But King's persona also demonstrates at least one reason the parameters of Baptists' conceptualization of their cultural and theological roots must be expanded to include the cultural heritages of the varieties of persons who made up the movement's early constituency.

Traditionally, presentations of Baptist history have tended to take unisource, linear approaches that focus the story around Anglo, Anglo-American, and male-dominated traditioning sources. In this schema, non-Anglo Baptists and women have tended to be addressed on the peripheries

---

[82] Ibid., 21.   [83] Ibid.

of that tradition and treated as partakers of the blessing, but as stepchildren, not as full-blooded heirs. Because of this long-standing practice, a fuller treatment of Baptists' theological and cultural foundations requires both acquaintance with what is Anglo and patriarchal in those foundations and acknowledgement of a much more extensive cultural and theological base on which those who call themselves Baptist are grounded. These have been the objectives of this chapter. In the early stages, Baptists' theological and cultural base included Anglo, Anglo-American, Anglo-Canadian, Native, African, and African American cultures and theologies. Recognizing this complex traditioning process (originating early in Baptist history) is essential for an exploration of the full possibilities of what being Baptist could and should mean. Placing the Anglo Baptist cultural-traditioning sources in a broader cultural framework opens possibilities for exploring Baptist identity in fuller and richer ways.

PART II

Age of Emerging Baptist Denominational Traditions

Global Baptist Development Phase 1, 1600–1792

> Trusting that we have through the power of Divine Grace, been enabled to yield ourselves up to God: So we do now covenant with each other, looking up to the great Head of the church for assistance in fulfilling our most solemn engagements. That we will by the grace of God; walk with each other in humility and brotherly love. Watching with Christian candor and care over each other for good, warning, rebuking, admonishing each other in love according to the gospel: and will ever strive to stir up each others [sic] minds to love and good works. That we will try to maintain the character of a Christian family, participating in each others [sic] joys and with tenderness and sympathy bearing each others burdens and sorrows. That we will respect our aged brothers and sisters and as far as we have opportunity, we will comfort them in their declining age.
>
> Chief Charles Journeycake, Pastor
> Portions of the "Covenant," *Original Minutes of the Delaware Baptist Church*, 1871

A BAPTIST PROFILE

In September 1769, about two years before his death, Shubal Stearns, a charismatic Separate Baptist preacher and founder of the rapidly growing center of Baptist work in Sandy Creek, North Carolina, had a troublesome dream. When climbing a hill near his home, he saw clouds on the horizon that appeared as though a heap of snow. Approaching the cloud, "he perceived the heap to stand suspended in the air 15 to 20 feet above the ground. Presently it fell to the ground and divided itself into three parts; the greatest part moved northward; a less towards the south; and the third, which was less than either but much brighter, remained on the spot where the whole fell."[1] As the clouds slowly vanished, Stearns instinctively sensed that this was a message to him about the future. He had given himself

---

[1] Morgan Edwards, *Materials towards a History of the Baptists* (1770–92), reprint prepared for publication by Eve B. Weeks and Mary B. Warren in 2 vols. (Danielsville, GA: Heritage Papers, 1984), 2: 94.

tirelessly to building the ministry that was now thriving at a strategic wilderness crossroads in central North Carolina. Was this a divine message that all was to be lost?

Shubal deliberated over what the phantom, the division, and the movement of the clouds meant. Finally, the message seemed clear: "The bright heap is our religious interest; which will divide and spread north and south, but chiefly northward; while a small part remains at Sandy-creek."[2] Morgan Edwards recorded this dream in his *Materials towards a History of the Baptists*, and whether historical or apocryphal, the narrative outlines the extension of Separate Baptists into the American South as religious awakenings breathed new life and new traditions into the Baptist movement. This narrative illustrates the transforming impetus that revivalistic activity in both Britain and America had on Baptist developments during the period.

[2] Ibid.

CHAPTER 2

Seeds for Diversity amid an Early Anglo Prevalence

The preceding chapter mapped the complex and variegated theological and cultural backgrounds out of which the numerous traditions that collectively constituted the early Baptist movement developed. In the process, the requisite components were assembled from which to identify and evaluate the distinctive features characteristic of the Baptist movement during the first phase of its evolution. This foundation enhances our possibilities for exploring the ways Baptist denominations have woven specific theological and cultural elements together in pursuit of the dreams that have motivated them. This chapter identifies some of the dreams that guided the development of major early Baptist traditions and explores the shaping influences originating from their cultural and theological environments.

ANGLO, ANGLO-AMERICAN, AND ANGLO-CANADIAN BAPTIST TRADITIONS

Attempts to define accurately Baptists under a single denominational rubric tend to generate confusion and frustration because this aggregation of churches lacks the centralizing authority often associated with an officially recognized denominational bishop, episcopacy, creed, or unifying structure. For that reason, the ensuing pages illustrate how, within its first two centuries of existence, the Baptist movement came to incorporate several independently generated traditions that had no connections to prior Baptist bodies. Other independently spawned Baptist traditions came later in time. Therefore, the movement cannot be conceived as originating out of a single core from which subsequent schisms produced division (although schismatic separations certainly did occur). This means that efforts to characterize Baptist churches predominantly according to the characteristics they tended to share in the early phases of their history can easily brand them with an Anglo identity that obscures the contributions derived independently from other cultural sources, which make the varied traditions within the Baptist movement distinctive. So, how might the world of Baptist churches best be understood? To answer that question, the major Baptist traditions that emerged during the first phase of Baptist development must be introduced and their distinguishing characteristics isolated. Subsequently, their meaning as parts of the larger Baptist movement can be explored.

General Baptist Traditions of the Seventeenth and Eighteenth Centuries

The term *general* as applied to the General family of Baptist denominations carries certain theological implications, mostly related to doctrines of Christ's atonement. Early General Baptists were united with most of Western Christianity in their core assumption that all humankind existed under a sentence of divine judgment due to sin. General Baptist theology was especially characterized by the view that Christ died as a vicarious sacrifice on behalf of all humanity, even though the benefits of that act would be experienced only by those who chose to trust Christ for salvation from God's condemnation (the dominant theological image here is Anselmian). In other words, the benefits of God's covenant were thought to be available to all, but participation was possible only for those who bound themselves to it through faith in Christ. Their view on this specific theological issue was the same as that held by adherents of the Arminian tradition (which originated about the same time), which led many to equate General Baptists with Arminian beliefs. Although some General Baptists were very close to Arminianism on a wide range of issues, and some were fully Arminian, the two traditions did not necessarily agree on all points.

Another doctrine that tended to distinguish early General Baptists – and a major reason they were labeled "Arminian" – was their conviction that each person had the freedom to believe or not believe in Christ. This meant that no one had been predestined to either salvation or damnation but had the ability to decide the matter personally under the influence of biblical persuasion and the witness of God's Spirit. In addition, because one could choose salvation, most General Baptists also believed that individuals could freely renounce their faith and depart from the ranks of the saved.

English General Baptists
The English General Baptist tradition is chronologically the earliest to emerge in the Baptist movement, originating among English Separatist exiles in Amsterdam in 1609. They were one outcome of developments within English Separatism in its quest to restore the truly biblical church.

Theologically, this tradition arose out of the same Calvinistically influenced heritage that produced Puritanism, and therefore, in its pre-Baptist stages, it emphasized the notion of a covenant relationship with God and other like-minded believers.

Culturally a product of late- and post-Elizabethan England, the earliest General Baptists began as part of a Separatist congregation in Gainsborough on the Trent under the leadership of John Smyth, a Cambridge graduate. A number of local persons, having concluded that the Church of England was simply a "revised edition of the Church of Rome," chose to reconstitute the Church according to biblical standards.[1] Among them were John Robinson, William Brewster, and William Bradford, each noted for the role he played in establishing the Plymouth Colony in America. Bradford later recorded the substance of this covenant:

Touched with heavenly zeal for his truth, they shook off this yoke of antichristian bondage and as the Lord's free people joined themselves, by a covenant to the Lord, into a Church estate in the fellowship of the Gospel to walk in all his ways made known, or to be made known, according to their best endeavors whatsoever it should cost them.[2]

The Gainsborough Separatist congregation grew rapidly, which raised concerns that its illegal religious activities might be detected by authorities. Consequently, the group decided to divide into two congregations, one to continue at Gainsborough and the other to meet at Scrooby Manor. Within two years, those precautionary measures proved inadequate, so both bodies decided to migrate to Holland. Once there, Smyth's congregation settled in Amsterdam, and Robinson's moved to Leiden. Afterward, the two congregations developed along different ecclesiological paths.

In Amsterdam, Smyth and his congregation had significant interaction with two other groups – the Waterlander Mennonites and the Ancient Church (also an English Separatist congregation in exile, led by Francis Johnson who, like Smyth, began his Separatist pilgrimage as a result of influences he experienced while at Cambridge). Johnson possessed an inquiring nature and was prone to raise challenging questions, a practice that kept matters stirred up among Smyth and his followers. One of Johnson's queries proved to be pivotal for the Smyth group: "Who are the rightful members of a church?" Smyth's efforts to answer that question produced the first theory and practice of Anglo Baptist doctrine.

---

[1] Walter H. Burgess, *John Smith the Se-Baptist, Thomas Helwys and the First Baptist Church in England with Fresh Light upon the Pilgrim Fathers' Church* (London: James Clarke & Co., 1911), 83.

[2] William Bradford, as cited by Burgess, *John Smith the Se-Baptist*, 84.

Somewhat like Martin Luther King Jr., John Smyth was guided by a dream – that the authentic New Testament church somehow could be restored. Bishop Joseph Hall of Exeter recognized that idealistic quality in Smyth, referring to him as "a Schollar of no small reeding, and well seene and experienced in Arts," who, being led about by his dreams, was "exceedingly malleable."[3] Observing that he had moved from Anglicanism to Puritanism to Separatism to Baptist convictions and finally to Anabaptism in less than a decade, Richard Barnard wrote that Smyth was "a wavering Reed, a mutable Proteus, a variable Chameleon" whose "course is as changeable as the Moone."[4] In reality, Smyth was far more stable than his critics perceived him to be, the discrepancy being explained by the standard with which his malleability might be gauged. When measured against the goals that guided his ecclesiastical pilgrimage, Smyth appears to be quite persistent.

Smyth's response to Johnson's plaguing question came in two short statements: infants should not be baptized, and "Antichristians converted" (a reference to followers of the Anglican establishment) should be admitted into the true church through baptism. In essence, he had concluded that the baptism practiced by the Church of England was not valid and that the true church should consist only of those "properly" baptized. In that, he was declaring a new basis for constituting the "true church." This church was not to be established on the basis of historical succession or of a divine covenant but on the basis of an uncoerced and regenerate membership. While Johnson continued to debate the issue, in 1609, Smyth took action. He persuaded his followers to dissolve their covenanted church, then baptized himself upon his profession of faith in Christ and subsequently baptized the others.

For Smyth, this was the culmination of a process that likely began sometime between 1586 and 1600 while he was a student at Cambridge University. Debates among those holding historical succession views of the church and those adhering to Reformed covenant ideas had awakened in him a quest for a church that would be biblically "correct" in its precepts and practices. The quest took him from Anglicanism through Puritanism and Separatism, and then to Baptist views. The same quest for the true church subsequently led him to seek admission with the Dutch Anabaptists. After he had formed his Baptist church, an observer asked Smyth why, on

[3] Joseph Hall, *A Description of the Church of Christ, . . . against Certaine Anabaptisticall and Erroneous Opinions* (London, 1610), 108.
[4] Richard Bernard, *Plaine Evidences: The Church of England Is Apostolicall, the Separation Schismaticall* (London, 1610), 18, 21–2.

arriving at his particular convictions regarding church membership, he had not simply joined an Anabaptist church. After investigating Anabaptist tenets, Smyth concluded that such a church as he had envisioned already existed. He then decided to dissolve his newly formed church and seek membership with the Mennonites, descendants of the sixteenth-century Anabaptist movement. For Smyth, the ecclesiastical pilgrimage had been completed.

The same was not true for several other members of his Baptist con-gregation, however. Debate arose among them concerning whether or not baptism and church ministry should be by succession (i.e., only from someone who already possessed it). Smyth and a majority of his followers concluded that succession was necessary and proceeded to renounce their earlier actions and unite with the Dutch Mennonites. But others, led by Thomas Helwys, concluded that their earlier actions had been correct and that baptismal succession was not biblically necessary. This group refused to give up the church Smyth had led them to form and proceeded to exclude Smyth and about twenty other members.

Having achieved their initial dream – to determine the nature of the true church – Helwys and his followers now pursued a more difficult one: to convince their fellow English that the true New Testament church was finally recovered. In 1611, Helwys's group returned to England and relocated its congregation in the Spitalfields section of London. There they took up the formidable challenge of convincing fellow citizens and English authorities that the Bible revealed not an established church, or a parish church, or a church of the bishops but a church of authentic believers. This so-called believers' church held revolutionary implications not only for the Church of England but also for the very fabric of English society. Dreams for a separation between church and state and for religious freedom soon derived from this concept of ecclesiology. Pursuit of those goals would steer these Baptists down a long and bloody road.

As the seventeenth century progressed, Thomas Grantham emerged as the recognized spokesperson for English General Baptist beliefs and practices, clarifying and advocating their views. He was their first signif-icant theologian and exerted major influence in shaping their theological positions. In 1678, he completed the first General Baptist theology, titled *Christianismus Primitivus*. This work not only explained General Baptist thought but also preserved descriptions of early General Baptist worship, presented their views on numerous controversial topics, and expended sig-nificant effort explaining Baptist convictions regarding religious liberty. Among other important subjects, he illumined English General Baptists'

threefold ministry of elders, deacons, and messengers. The office of messenger as employed by General Baptists was unique in many respects, but
reflective of General Baptists' tendency to view local churches as constituent
parts of one larger church. The office helped maintain cohesiveness among
early General Baptists' widely dispersed congregations. Local churches were
united into associations, and in 1660, English General Baptists were united
into a national assembly.

From 1611 until 1689, General Baptists were held together by their common struggle for religious liberty. But after Parliament approved the Edict
of Toleration allowing a measure of the religious freedom that they sought,
English General Baptists found themselves unprepared to take advantage
of their changed legal status. Members were largely located in rural areas,
many congregations were still meeting in members' homes with no permanent buildings of their own, doctrine was inflexible, and ministerial education largely was unappreciated. In addition, after the mid-seventeenth
century, the practice of laying on hands following baptism (a rite based on
Hebrews 6:1–2) had become increasingly divisive, which resulted in losses.
Furthermore, they were not equipped to handle the new theological challenges that surfaced during the course of the eighteenth century. English
General Baptists were most devastated by the anti-Trinitarian teachings
of Matthew Caffyn early in the century and William Vidler during its
latter decades. Schisms, failed attempts at resolution, and theological drift
resulted in major decline. By the mid-nineteenth century, most English
General Baptist churches had ceased to exist, many having either drifted
into Unitarian meetings or joined other Baptist bodies.

New Connection of General Baptists

In 1763, a Methodist lay preacher named Dan Taylor decided to unite with
General Baptists. After his baptism, he organized a Baptist church populated mostly by former Wesleyan converts and led them to affiliate with
the Lincoln Association of General Baptists. A product of the Wesleyan
revivals, Taylor was boldly Arminian in his theology and zealously evangelical. He soon found himself in tension with General Baptists because of
their lack of vision, loss of spiritual zeal, and doctrinal decay. Their laxness
over the doctrine of the Trinity was especially appalling to Taylor, and
he grew weary of their so-called impertinent quibbles. Finally, on June 6,
1770, he and about twenty other ministers met in Whitechapel, London
and organized the Assembly of Free Grace General Baptists, soon afterward
designated the New Connection of General Baptists.

New Connection General Baptists clearly reflect the theological and cultural conditions of England during the period when they were in formation. In contrast to the inflexible adherence to outworn customs and doctrinal laxity of the older General Baptists, Taylor affirmed the complete divinity of Christ, Wesleyan-style evangelism and Arminianism, and such "modern" practices as the active participation of women in ministry and church leadership and in congregational hymn singing. New Connection Baptists also embodied a moderate form of Wesley's holiness ethic. As the nineteenth century dawned, New Connection General Baptists were thriving, whereas the old General Baptists continued on a downward spiral.

North American General Baptists
Many of the earliest Baptist churches established in North America were either General Baptist or had persons of strong General Baptist sentiment among their membership.[5] In 1827, the General Baptist historian Richard Knight identified fifteen churches in Rhode Island, eight in Massachusetts, three in Connecticut, six in New York, one in Pennsylvania, one in Vermont, and numerous others in the South as having been General Baptist at the time of their organization.[6] During that period, North American General Baptists were strongest in New England, South Carolina, and North Carolina. The efforts of William Sojourner, Paul Palmer, and Joseph Parker produced an especially vibrant General Baptist tradition in the central regions of North Carolina. However, aggressive proselytizing by Regular Baptists between 1765 and 1794 succeeded in winning over most of those churches.

Two issues slowly eroded the strength of General Baptist churches – Calvinism and the ordinance of laying on of hands. The Philadelphia Baptist Association, organized in 1707, was Calvinistic in its theological orientation and effective in efforts to proselytize General Baptist congregations. Fearful that associations might gain too much power, General Baptists remained reluctant to exploit associational connectionalism at the very time when Regular (Calvinistic) Baptists were organizing aggressive programs to win over their churches. The battle against Regular Baptist persuasion was hard fought by New England Generals, but a combination of factors such as congregational reactions against a rigid application of the

[5] Some sources prefer to identify them as moderate Calvinists who later became Arminian. Disagreement persists over how numerous such churches should be characterized theologically.
[6] Richard Knight, *History of the General or Six Principle Baptists, in Europe and America* (Providence, RI: Smith and Parmenter, Printers, 1827), 319.

laying on of hands, the onslaught of a militant Calvinism, and a lack of strong leadership had produced major declines in the numbers of General Baptists in North America by the end of the eighteenth century.[7]

General Six-Principle Baptists

Around 1644, many General Baptists in England became convinced that the Bible required a third ordinance in addition to baptism and the Lord's Supper – the laying on of hands for new converts. Churches that practiced the rite were known as Six-Principle Baptists. Although often used synonymously with General Baptists, many English Particular Baptist and North American Regular Baptist churches adopted the rite as well. The Calvinistic Philadelphia Confession of Faith in 1742 included the practice.

In England, William Jeffrey, Thomas Grantham, and John Griffith were the strongest advocates for the doctrine. In North America, General Six-Principle Baptists traced their roots to Roger Williams. In *The Bloody Tenet of Persecution*, Williams argued forcefully for the practice, even stating that no true profession of Christ could exclude the doctrine.[8] Following his lead, by the late seventeenth century, many of the most prominent Baptist churches in North America were Six Principle. In 1670, the Baptist churches at Providence, Newport, and North Kingstown in Rhode Island formed the Yearly Meeting, probably the oldest associational meeting in America. Gradually, other Six-Principle Baptist churches organized Yearly Meetings, bringing them together into one large Meeting on June 21, 1729. Insistence that only those under hands could commune with them gradually disillusioned many congregations and motivated them to join with the Regular Baptists or New England Free Will Baptists. Subsequently, Six-Principle Baptists experienced persistent decline and today have almost died out.

Distinctive Contributions to the Baptist Traditioning Process

The General Baptist family of churches was born in the cultural matrix of post-Elizabethan England, out of forces seeking to recover and re-create the essence of the New Testament church. The one unifying factor among those entities was the conviction that the Church of England was not all it should be and therefore its reform was absolutely essential. The General Baptist

---

[7] See the critique presented by Ollie Latch, *History of the General Baptists* (Popular Bluff, MO: General Baptist Press, 1954), 111–14.

[8] Roger Williams, *The Bloudy Tenent of Persecution for the Cause of Conscience Discussed in a Conference between Peace and Truth* (London, 1644), reprint by Edward B. Underhill, ed. (London: J. Haddon, 1848), 40.

distinctive in this process was the conclusion that believers' baptism was the biblically established foundation for the true church. The concomitant assertion that a regenerate membership constituted the fundamental nature of the church carried with it major implications for the relationship among church and society, religious liberty, church government, and the focal activities of church life.

General Baptist efforts to live out that dream placed their members in conflict with established authorities in England and colonial America. From those struggles, doctrines of separation of church and state, freedom of conscience, and uncoerced church membership emerged. Those beliefs, in addition to General Baptists' emphasis on the freedom of the individual to determine one's own eternal destiny, led to strong convictions regarding the individual conscience. The high value placed on personal freedom before God made them more open to doctrinal and theological experimentation but also gave them less doctrinal unity. This diffused adherents' spiritual development in a variety of directions. Old General Baptists became inflexibly bound by customs derived from their earlier struggles, the laying on of hands being an example. Holding fast to such symbols helped some members preserve the essence of their core values but failed to allow for an expansion of vision that could accommodate the experiences and ideals of new generations. Theological experimentation guided many General Baptists into other movements, such as Unitarianism. Schism erupted in some instances, especially when new sources of spiritual vitality from other religious movements were drawn into General Baptist traditions. The New Connection illustrates that response. Also, other groups with stronger organizational and doctrinal foci at times made inroads into General Baptist life, draining away resources and personnel.

The General Baptist traditioning process was guided by a dream that wove elements of seventeenth-century Anglo and Anglo-American culture together with theological convictions concerning human free will, a general atonement, and beliefs about the nature of the church to produce a distinctive expression of what it means to be Baptist.

Particular and Regular Baptist Traditions of the Seventeenth and Eighteenth Centuries

The terms *particular* and *regular* identify a family of Baptist denominations – Calvinistic in orientation – that embraced a "particular" or "limited" view of Christ's atonement. Like General Baptists, they agreed that all humanity was condemned because of sin. A major theological distinction was their belief that Christ died only for the elect – those whom God had chosen for salvation. Thus, predestination was an important component of Particular Baptist doctrine. God only redeems "particular" persons.

Particular Baptists had an independent origin from that of General Baptists. While it is natural to speak of General and Particular Baptists as contrasting and often competing groups, Particulars did not begin as a division of General Baptists. From the start, Particular Baptists held to a thoroughgoing Calvinism that gave little credence to an individual's ability to choose salvation. Only God's prevenient grace could enable a person to respond to the divine offer of salvation; thus no free will was possible in the matter. Once elected, however, an individual could never turn away from that salvation. God's work of redemption having been initiated must by all means be completed successfully.

English Particular Baptists
English Particular Baptists originated in the same cultural environment as that of English General Baptists – early seventeenth-century British Puritan-Separatism. An influential figure in the denomination's origin was a Separatist by the name of Henry Jacob, who never became a Baptist himself. Jacob, an Oxford graduate, supported further reform of the Anglican Church, but never rejected it as a true church. After a period as pastor of a Separatist congregation near Leyden, he returned to England desiring the freedom to form a different type of church while at the same time not totally denying validity to the Church of England. In 1616 he formed a Separatist church in the Southwark section of London known historically as the "Jacob-Lathrop-Jessey" (JLJ) church. While not Baptist, the church became the mother of the first Particular Baptist church on record. In 1622 Jacob immigrated to Virginia, where he died in 1624.

Under the pastorates of John Lathrop (1624–1634) and Henry Jessey (1637–1663) disagreements arose within the congregation over questions of baptism. Initially the debate seems to have focused around whether or not baptisms performed by a "corrupt" Church of England were valid. Apparently the congregation was divided over the legitimacy of the Anglican Church by this time. In 1633 Samuel Eaton formed a strictly Separatist church that included only persons who renounced the Church of England. A number of these persons were rebaptized. Some scholars regard this as the first Particular Baptist church. Others have concluded, however, that the basis for constituting the church is not clear enough to declare it Baptist at this time. They support the year 1638 as the point of origin of Particular

Baptists, when six members who specifically embraced believer's baptism left the JLJ church to form their own congregation.

As the issues surrounding these congregational divisions suggest, the biblical basis upon which the "true" church should be established was of supreme importance to early Particular Baptists. Even after deciding that this church's membership should consist only of the regenerate elect who had received believers' baptism, debates continued. Between 1638 and 1641, the method of baptism became a matter of serious discussion. Soon a small group within Jessey's church determined that immersion was the only biblically acceptable form of baptism, and knowing of no one who could legitimately baptize them according to that method, a deacon in the congregation named Richard Blunt, who could speak the Dutch language, was sent to Holland to seek help from the Rijnsburgers (or Collegiants), a small Mennonite group at Rijnsburg, Holland. How they knew the Rijnsburgers practiced immersion is uncertain, but from them Blunt either received baptism by immersion or received instruction concerning this form of baptism from John Batte(n), an elder among the group. Blunt then returned to England to baptize others via this method.[9] The group then separated from Jessey's church and organized themselves into a Baptist congregation. Within a few years virtually all Baptists, General and Particular, had adopted believers' baptism by immersion as the only legitimate form of Christian baptism.

In 1644 Particular Baptist churches in the London area issued a joint confession of faith setting forth the essence of their belief and practice. A motivating factor may have been a desire to distinguish their movement from that of the Anabaptists who, after the Munster debacle in 1534–35, were considered by many to be little more than terrorists. Another reason may have been related to the success of Oliver Cromwell's regime, which gave them the freedom to publish such documents. Among the noted signers of this confession were John Spilsbury, William Kiffin, Samuel Richardson, and Thomas Patience. During the years 1644 to 1660, Particular Baptists grew rapidly. Many joined Cromwell's New Model Army, establishing Baptist churches wherever the army went, even in Scotland, Wales, and Ireland. By the end of the seventeenth century, Particular Baptists were the leading Baptist group in England with success in urban as well as rural areas.

---

[9] The so-called Kiffin Manuscript is the source of this information. Analysis of the account is furnished by Champlin Burrage in *The Early English Dissenters in the Light of Recent Research (1550–1641)*, 2 vols. (New York: Russell & Russell, 1967 [first published 1912]), 1:326–7.

During the eighteenth century, English Particular Baptists became strongly influenced by a strict form of Calvinism that, in some instances, took the doctrines of predestination and divine election to fatalistic extremes. John Gill, John Brine, and John Skepp are among the noted definers of this deterministic outlook. Gill's influence was so great that his rigid Calvinistic perspective was referred to as "Gillism." This theology impacted Particular Baptists in numerous ways, especially their diminished motivation for evangelism. Still, they were successful in developing denominational structures. A few of their congregations managed to accrue substantial resources, pastors formed venues for meeting to seek advice and address political concerns, and educational endeavors were initiated. In the West Country, Baptists formed the Bristol Baptist Education Society to support the Bristol Academy, a leading institution of ministerial education for British Baptists. These endeavors became the vehicles by which Particular Baptists succeeded in establishing institutions based on voluntary methods of engaging and supporting religious undertakings.

Several Baptist women were crucial in these endeavors. Dorothy Hazzard of the Bristol Baptist Church was noted for her leadership, evangelism, and outspoken conviction, which helped that church to develop as an important agent of Baptist work. Katherine Peck supplied much of the driving force that kept the Baptist church at Abingdon alive during the years of the Clarendon Code. In 1684 she was taken to London and put on trial for her religious activities. Ann Dutton gained notoriety as an author, producing thirty-eight tracts and books expressing her Baptist views. Her autobiography *A Brief Account of the Gracious Dealings of God with a Poor, Sinful, Unworthy Creature* included a defense of women's right to write and publish. In addition, women served as deacons, deaconesses, preachers, and sometimes as pastors.[10] Their involvement, leadership, support, and vision were integral parts of Baptist institutional development during this period of structural formation.

By the end of the eighteenth century, this tradition of employing voluntary methods for supporting religious work gave rise to one of Baptists' most far-reaching enterprises – overseas missions. A strict Calvinist theological environment would seem to have been an unlikely place from which such initiative would have arisen. Yet, William Carey, a Particular Baptist pastor at Moulton, became convinced that God intended the Christian message to be shared with all people. His vision and effort helped launch the Baptist Missionary Society in 1792. He was appointed a missionary to

[10] See H. Leon McBeth, *Women in Baptist Life* (Nashville, TN: Broadman Press, 1979), 37.

India by that society in 1793, and spent the remainder of his life teaching, preaching, translating, and laying the foundations for a strong Baptist communion there. Today Baptists in India constitute the second largest aggregate of Baptist communities in the world.

The theological foundations laid by Andrew Fuller, a Particular Baptist pastor at Soham and Kettering and later secretary/treasurer of the Baptist Missionary Society, were important for Particular Baptist development in the latter part of the eighteenth and into the nineteenth centuries. Fuller was the major advocate for a renewal movement called "evangelical Calvinism." In *The Gospel Worthy of All Acceptation* (1786) he articulated an understanding of Calvinist doctrine that upheld the church's responsibility to proclaim and invite persons to accept God's free grace. His views countered the influence of "Gillism," and were effectual in opening Particular Baptist minds to the possibility of the work undertaken by the Baptist Missionary Society. "Fullerism" gave Particular Baptists the theological vision that guided them throughout much of the nineteenth century.

Regular Baptists of North America

In colonial America, Calvinistically oriented Baptists were referred to as Regular Baptists. Essentially they held to the same views and practices as English Particular Baptists and are sometimes designated Particular-Regular Baptists. Most early Baptists churches in America contained a mixture of Calvinistically inclined and Arminian-inclined Baptists, confounding efforts to label them according to these categories. Eventually, however, Regular Baptists became the largest of the early Baptist bodies and created the most extensive organizational structures.

During the First Great Awakening, Regular and Separate Baptists stood in contrast to each other in several significant ways. Regular Baptists tended to support an educated and paid ministry, preferred worship that was orderly and not overly emotional, and discouraged women from involvement in public ministry. Initially strongest in the Philadelphia area, Regular Baptists formed the influential Philadelphia Baptists Association in 1707. This body supported itinerant preachers who helped establish Regular Baptist churches throughout the southern colonies and into the Ohio Valley. Other well-known and influential early Regular Baptist bodies include the Charleston Association (organized in 1751), the Warren Association (organized in 1767), and the Kehuckee Association (organized in 1769). In 1742, Particular Baptists adopted a confession of faith in the Philadelphia region, which influenced Baptists throughout the colonies. They also founded America's first Baptist college, Rhode Island College (now Brown University), in 1764.

In the late eighteenth century, Regular Baptists (especially in the Philadelphia and Warren Associations) waged campaigns intended to influence General Baptists toward becoming Regular Baptists. The efforts were largely successful among General Baptist pastors, but less effective among the laity. In addition, Regulars experienced significant growth through an influx of Separate Baptist churches into their denomination. The common struggle among Baptists for religious liberty, reactions to Free Will Baptists' growing influence, and Regular Baptists' moderation of their Calvinist views induced most Separate Baptist churches to migrate toward affiliation with the Regular Baptist associations. By the nineteenth century, most Separate and Regular Baptists had merged into one body on the basis of the Philadelphia Confession of Faith.

Five Principle Calvinistic Baptists

Early Baptist churches in colonial America included a mixture of members, some of whom inclined toward General Baptist principles and others toward Particular Baptist principles. As tensions mounted within and among congregations over these issues, coalitions of churches gradually emerged. One such coalition was that of the Five Principle Calvinistic Baptists.

This body of Baptists formed mostly in Rhode Island, Massachusetts, and Connecticut during the decades between 1640 and 1740. The name was derived from their adherence to the five doctrines associated with the Westminster Confession of Faith's definition of Calvinism – total depravity, unmerited election, limited atonement, irresistible grace, and perseverance of the saints. Prior to 1740, two of these congregations were seventh day and ten were first day churches. In general, Five Principle Baptists adhered to the doctrines that characterized the Particular Baptist churches of England and Wales.

Distinctive Contributions to the Baptist Traditioning Process

The Particular Baptist family of churches shared much of the same cultural heritage as General Baptists. Like the Generals, they dreamed of somehow re-creating the church of the New Testament, which they believed had become distorted over the course of the Catholic Middle Ages. In Britain, they were shaped by the turmoil of post-Elizabethan religious strife, the experiments of the "Saints' Regime," and the persecutions following the Royal Restoration. In the American colonies they were formed through

the frontier experience, the disadvantages of religious dissent, and the struggles for religious liberty. In contrast to General Baptists they drew more
heavily upon Calvinist ideals for their soteriological and ecclesiological
definitions, thereby interpreting the nature of the "true" church somewhat
differently. Perhaps it was the Calvinist theological tradition that influenced
them to give greater emphasis to "correct" doctrine (reflected in the stress
given to predestination and divine election) than to the unfettered personal
decision and experience so valued by the General Baptist tradition (accented
in their focus on free will). Consequently, Particular-Regular Baptists
tended to highlight the need for some amount of doctrinal unity among
adherents through the significance they placed on confessions of faith.

Like Calvin, Particular-Regular Baptists embraced a somewhat more
reflective form of Baptist spirituality than their Separate Baptist cousins.
Their doctrinal orientation made them more distrustful of the emotional-
ism and evangelistic appeals associated with the Wesleyan revivals and the
First Great Awakening. Consequently, the Particular-Regular Baptist traditioning process was guided by a dream that also wove together elements
of the Anglo and Anglo-American culture but bound them together via
theological convictions that were influenced by Calvinism. Their emphasis on God's sovereignty, divine predestination and election, and doctrine
distinguished their understanding of the Christian life. Yet their insistence
on believers' baptism, the uncoerced nature of religious life, congregational
decision making, and voluntary methods for ecclesiastical work gave them
much in common with other families of Baptists from this period.

Seventh Day Baptist Traditions of the Seventeenth and Eighteenth Centuries

The Seventh Day or Sabbatarian Baptist tradition originated amid the
cultural and theological chaos of mid-seventeenth-century England. In
that environment of fast-paced and often apocalyptically charged religious
innovation, Nonconformists spawned a wide variety of movements based
on literalistic interpretations of the Bible. As the name suggests, Seventh
Day Baptists became enamored of the Hebrew Bible's emphasis on the
seventh day as God's required day of rest and worship. This stood in
contrast to the practice of most Baptists, who worshiped on the first day
of the week – the day Christ was resurrected. After a failed revolt under
Thomas Venner aimed at helping usher in Christ's millennial kingdom,
many adherents of the Fifth Monarchy Movement joined the Seventh Day
Baptist movement and thereby extended its significance.

English Seventh Day Baptists

The first identifiable Seventh Day Baptist church was the Mill Yard Church, established around 1653 under the leadership of Peter Chamberlen. Its association with radical millennialism was viewed with suspicion by English authorities, and its second pastor, John James, was executed in 1661. Still, other churches, from both the General and Particular Baptist traditions, joined the movement. Among their earliest leaders were James Ockford, William Saller, and Thomas Tillam. The movement flourished in England for only a few decades, however. By 1730, it had almost ceased to exist.

North American Seventh Day Baptists

The Seventh Day Baptist movement in the United States began as a schism within Regular Baptist churches over questions associated with the biblically correct day of the week for worship. The issue first appeared within the membership of the Baptist Church in Newport, Rhode Island, through the influence of Stephen Mumford. A member of the Bell Lane Seventh Day Baptist Church in London, Mumford migrated to Rhode Island in 1665. He joined the first-day Baptist church because Newport had no Seventh Day Baptist church at that time. At first, adherents of the two views coexisted, but under the ministry of Obediah Holmes, tensions gradually mounted. Finally, in 1671, the division produced a schism, and the first Seventh Day Baptist Church in America was organized with William Hiscox as its first pastor. From there, other Seventh Day Baptist centers developed in Hopkinton, Rhode Island; in Philadelphia (especially through the work of Abel Noble); in New Jersey (under the influence of Edmund Dunham); and from those three centers, it extended northward into Connecticut and western New York and southward into Virginia, the Carolinas, and Georgia.

Distinctive Contributions to the Baptist Traditioning Process

Seventh Day Baptists' primary distinctive was their belief that the Bible required Saturday as the day of worship. In most other respects, they were like other Calvinistic Baptists of seventeenth-century British origin. In the American British colonies, the Sabbath question surfaced within many Baptist congregations and was quite divisive. First-day Baptists accused Seventh Day Baptists of returning to the Old Testament Law and of preferring Moses to Christ. Seventh Day adherents argued that the Ten Commandments remained unaltered by New Testament developments, including the requirement for Sabbath (seventh-day) observance. In the nineteenth and twentieth centuries, Seventh Day Baptist structural development closely paralleled that of other Baptist denominations in America.

Separate Baptist Traditions of the Seventeenth
and Eighteenth Centuries

The eighteenth century proved decisive for the Baptist movement in the American British colonies. In 1700, Baptists there had only twenty-four churches with a total of 839 members. They had little denominational structure beyond that of the local church and no institution for the training of ministers. By 1790, however, Baptists had 979 churches with approximately 67,490 members in a new nation whose population totaled 3,929,000. Much of that growth came as a result of the First Great Awakening and a developing social climate of independence that was favorably disposed to the democratic ideals already embraced by Baptists.

Although it is popular to think of the pre-independent U.S. as an intensely pious and religious nation, this was hardly the case. Naturally, some persons were serious practitioners of their faith. But a reading of key documents from the era indicates that many religious leaders detected spiritual lethargy among the colonists. Some point to the Halfway Covenant of the Congregational churches as one indicator of that spiritual inertia. Theodore Frelinghuysen was another person who described such decline. Having moved to the Raritan Valley of New Jersey from Amsterdam, Holland, in 1720, he encountered stiff resistance to his pietistic style of preaching and practice. Some members of his church did not like his effort to change their head religion for a heart religion. Affairs in the parish eventually reached a crisis point, and Frelinghuysen was on the verge of being dismissed from his charge when revival broke out among his churches in 1726. This was the first documented evidence of the First Great Awakening in the colonies.

Among other noted preachers of revival were Gilbert Tennent, Jonathan Edwards, and George Whitfield. Their preaching and writing helped spread revivalistic religion throughout the thirteen colonies and establish the distinctive character of American Christianity. Among the results of the First Great Awakening were a strong emphasis on religious experience, emotional fervor (which led certain persons to react strongly against the new form of piety), divisions within denominations between those who supported the revivals and those who opposed them, an aggressive and itinerant evangelism that challenged the familiar boundaries of the old parish system, and unprecedented growth among Baptists.

Much of the numerical expansion was related to the emergence of a new Baptist tradition known as Separate Baptists, which originated within the Congregational Church. Many New Light Congregationalists (members of Congregational churches who accepted the First Great Awakening's revivalistic theology and practices) were forced to leave the older and stricter Congregational churches and establish new congregations of their own – often referred to as Separate Congregationalists. During the mid-1740s, many of those congregations experienced internal struggles over the issue of baptism. Some decided that the Bible taught believers' baptism, whereas others continued to embrace infant baptism (practiced by the Congregational Church). This division resulted in many New Light Congregationalists becoming Baptists, but they became the creators of a new Baptist tradition in the process.

Among the New England Separate Baptists who exerted a significant influence on Baptist life in America were Shubal Stearns, Daniel Marshall, and Martha Marshall. In 1755, the three, together with members of their families, established the Sandy Creek Baptist Church in Sandy Creek, North Carolina. This became a significant center from which Separate Baptists spread throughout the colonies of Virginia, North Carolina, South Carolina, and Georgia. Eventually, from those centers, they extended westward into Tennessee and the newly settled areas of the Ohio Valley.

The First Great Awakening also brought about a great increase in itinerant preaching, which increased tensions between Baptists and colonial authorities. For example, Virginia law required dissenting preachers to be licensed. However, Separate Baptists rejected that law, insisting that no government had the right to say who could or could not preach. They believed that the right belonged only to God and the local church. Even when dissenting preachers attempted to obtain the required license, they were often refused. Furthermore, licenses were usually granted to only one dissenting meetinghouse per county – insufficient for the Baptist demand.

James Ireland and John Leland illustrate the challenge Baptists faced in Virginia. Ireland was imprisoned in Culpeper County in 1769 for persistently preaching without a license. He gained notoriety for the heroic witness he bore from his "palace" (jail cell) in the center of town where large crowds gathered to hear him preach. John Leland (1754–1841) served in Virginia long enough to gain a reputation for having influenced James Madison to agree to propose the adoption of the First Amendment to the U.S. Constitution.[11] Leland is noted for his major treatise on religious liberty titled *The Rights of Conscience Inalienable* (1791).

---

[11] The authenticity of this claim has been debated among those historians who have seriously explored the matter.

Distinctive Contributions to the Baptist Traditioning Process

Separate Baptists made several significant contributions to Baptist life and development during the eighteenth century. First, they appeared at a critical moment in American religious history. Social, political, and economic conditions made people aware of their religious needs. The situation called for messengers who could speak to those needs in ways the common person might understand. Separates emerged with the right message at the right time and with the ability to communicate in terms accessible to frontier settlers. That enabled Separate Baptists to gain a role as agents in helping establish the character of American evangelical Christianity. The revivalism they helped popularize marked the beginning of an aggressive Christianity on the American frontier. They also provided a significant part of the religious leadership on that frontier. This world was untamed and immigrants often entered a culture that lived on the verge of degenerating into lawlessness. Among those who helped settle the rapidly growing frontier were Separate Baptists, who urged obedience to both God's law and the laws of the nation.[12]

Separate Baptists also contributed to the success of America's struggle for religious liberty. Their love for democracy and freedom of conscience put them in the forefront of the Revolutionary movement. Those values also motivated them to take serious interest in the spiritual life of African Americans, as they were among the first Anglo-American Baptists to preach among the slave populations. In all their activities, Separates employed methodologies that appealed to the masses. This included the utilization of an indigenous ministry among both frontier and black Baptist populations, widespread use of lay preachers, and employment of an individualized and emotional style of worship. Such qualities appealed to many individuals among the frontier and African American peoples.

At the same time, Separate Baptists had certain weaknesses that worked to the detriment of the movement, and eventually Regular Baptists capitalized on that. They had a one-sided emphasis on mass evangelism and excessive emotional appeal. Sometimes that led to manipulation of listeners. More often, however, it awakened emotionally starved and often-struggling peoples of the frontier regions and slave populations to sources of spiritual support. Unfortunately, Separate Baptists often failed to follow through with the necessary spiritual disciplines, which would have contributed to a maturing and well-balanced faith. That failure was accentuated by certain

---

[12] For a good analysis of this Baptist tradition, see William L. Lumpkin, *Baptist Foundations in the South* (Nashville, TN: Broadman Press, 1961).

weaknesses in their understanding of ministry. The value of ministerial education was lost among Separate Baptists. This was an understandable reaction against the established church, which to them seemed to emphasize education to the exclusion of personal piety, but their "correction" to the problem created long-term problems of its own. Although their lack of education often gave the Separate preachers an advantage in the early days of the movement, over time it weakened the doctrinal moorings of church members. This made Separates susceptible to other religious movements that tended to siphon off their members.

Separate Baptists generally did not pay their ministers. At first this was attractive. It helped restore an air of dedication and piety that many felt was lacking among the frontier Anglican clergy. In the long run, however, their churches suffered from the practice.

Ultimately, doctrinal indefiniteness, lack of attention to organizational structure, and untrained leadership proved detrimental to Separate Baptist development. Two or three doctrines were preached over and over while others went neglected. Their practices did help them avoid the Regular Baptist "error" against which they reacted – that of making confessions into creeds. Yet Separate Baptists faced too much theological and systemic looseness. That left them defenseless against the appeals of other frontier religious movements.

The unique features of the seventeenth- and eighteenth-century American frontier formed the cultural context for the Separate Baptist dream. Their dream was more closely associated with re-creating "authentic" Christian experience than with recapturing the true church. The frontier focus on individualism was highly valued, which led Separates to emphasize the Bible and distrust education, confessions of faith, or any church organization that might threaten the freedom of the individual soul. Again, believers' baptism, the supreme authority of the Bible (as they understood it), religious freedom, congregational government, and voluntary methods of support were among the qualities that connected this Baptist tradition to other Anglo Baptist traditions of the period.

Free Will Baptist Traditions of the Seventeenth and Eighteenth Centuries

The Free Will family of Baptists emerged from cultural roots in New England that date to the 1770s and derive from the work of several ministers in the New Hampshire colony. These believers were heavily influenced by the revivalistic religion gained from the First Great Awakening, which also contributed to their acceptance of certain Baptistic values. However, Free

Will Baptist interpretation of the Bible led them to embrace Arminian sote-riological perspectives in contrast to the strict Calvinism that was prevalent among other Baptists in their geographic area. The result was the creation of yet another distinctive Baptist tradition.

A New Hampshire tailor and farmer named Benjamin Randall is cred-ited as the founder of the Free Will Baptist tradition. Although religious in his early years, he had refrained from identifying with any particular church, and as a young man, he had completely rejected the revivalism associated with the First Great Awakening. He was especially critical of George Whitefield's preaching. When the famed evangelist suddenly died in 1770, Randall began to reflect on his own life and finally decided to join a local Congregational church. This action did not end his spiritual struggle. In 1776, he concluded that he was inclined more toward Baptist convictions and joined a Baptist church. He recognized soon afterward that the stern Calvinism of those New England Baptists was not compatible with his own understanding of the Bible. His public expression of doubts regarding the issues resulted in his being disciplined by his Baptist church for holding un-Calvinistic views. Finally, on June 30, 1780, he and seven other like-minded persons organized the first Free Will Baptist church in New Durham, New Hampshire.[13]

Theologically, Free Will Baptists are similar to General Baptists, but their origins have no historical connection to that body. A General Baptist group in Chowan, North Carolina, under the leadership of Paul Palmer held comparable views but exerted no influence on the Randall group. Both traditions emphasize the doctrines of a general atonement, human freedom to choose salvation (meaning there is no divine predestination of those who are to be saved or lost), and open communion.

Benjamin Randall actively itinerated in Vermont, New Hampshire, and Maine, quickly extending the movement into those regions. His successor, John Buzzell, became the person most responsible for shaping Free Will Baptists' denominational structure. The body's Monthly and Quarterly meetings constituted organizational schemes that were roughly equivalent to the Regular Baptist associations.

Distinctive Contributions to the Baptist Traditioning Process
Religious and cultural conditions specific to the American New England colonies formed the context in which the Free Will Baptist dream devel-oped. Supportive of revivalism, their dream grew out of a desire to unite

---

[13] See William F. Davidson, *The Free Will Baptists in History* (Nashville, TN: Randall House Publica-tions, 2001), 126–32.

Baptistic ecclesiology with Armenian soteriology. Believers' baptism, their views on biblical authority, religious freedom, congregational government, and voluntary methods of support were practices they held in common with other Anglo Baptist traditions. However, the cultural and theological threads they wove together, along with the dreams that guided them, were combined in ways that gave them a unique expression of what it meant to be Baptist.

Canadian Baptist Traditions of the Seventeenth and Eighteenth Centuries

When France and England signed the Treaty of Utrecht in 1713, the status of thousands of French settlers in British Canada became uncertain. They now lived in English territory, but what that ultimately would mean for them remained undecided for a generation. Finally, in 1755, Nova Scotia's British governor, Charles Lawrence, demanded that French inhabitants (called Acadians) should swear full allegiance to England's monarch or depart the colony. Many refused to make that commitment and were expelled, leaving cultivated farmland vacant and in need of new proprietors.

Numerous British colonists residing further south (in what is today the United States) were attracted to the prospects of settling those lands but were reluctant to undertake such a migration because of the colony's Anglican establishment. Desperate to attract additional British settlers who would help secure the region's future, in 1759, Lawrence issued a proclamation known as the Charter of Nova Scotia, which granted dissenting Protestants liberty of conscience, freedom to erect their own church buildings, the right to choose their own ministers, and exemption from paying taxes to support the established Anglican Church. The provisions were more liberal than the ones governing most colonists in New England, so thousands of so-called Planters decided to make their way to the regions that today constitute the provinces of New Brunswick, Nova Scotia, and Prince Edward Island. Religiously, the Planters were overwhelmingly Congregationalists (both Old Light and New Light) and Baptists. The wave of immigrants was motivated by economic opportunity, not political issues, and therefore they became known as Planters not Loyalists.

A Baptist preacher named Ebenezer Moulton was among those settlers. Born in Connecticut and converted during one of the revivals associated with the First Great Awakening, he became pastor of Brimfield Baptist Church of Massachusetts Colony in 1741. Financial reversals that resulted in debt problems forced him to flee to Nova Scotia in 1760. He settled initially in the area of Yarmouth, where he served as a government agent commissioned to assign new lands to immigrants. Moulton seized every opportunity to preach and was especially active in the Annapolis Valley. His itinerant work led to the organization of a Baptist church in Horton (today known as Wolfville) in 1765, which has become Canada's longest-surviving Baptist congregation.

A slightly older church (the first Baptist church to exist in Canadian territory) was organized initially at Swansey, Massachusetts, in 1763 with Nathan Mason as pastor and was transplanted to Sackville (then known as SacVille) in Nova Scotia (today in New Brunswick Province) soon afterward. The church was disbanded in 1771 when most of its members returned to Massachusetts. Prior to the First Great Awakening, most Baptist churches in the American colonies were either Calvinist (Regular Baptists) or Arminian (Six-Principle or General Baptist). After the Awakening, churches with a more moderate Calvinist perspective emerged (Separate Baptists). The first Sackville Baptist Church was Six-Principle in its theological tradition. The Horton Baptist Church was Separate Baptist. In 1766, a second Baptist church, of Separate Baptist conviction, was organized in Sackville. Indicative of the uncertainties of the period, all three churches had ceased to function by the mid-1770s, although the Horton church was revived in 1778 and has survived to the present.

Another temporary but significant Baptist work was begun among the black population in the Halifax region by the former slave David George. After the American Revolution, a sizable number of blacks migrated to Nova Scotia seeking freedom from slavery. John Burton, pastor of the Baptist church in Halifax, initially encouraged the group, but George's leadership was required before a settled church could be established. George faced harsh opposition at first but finally succeeded in organizing a black Baptist church at Shelbourne. In 1793, the group was offered the opportunity to relocate to Sierra Leone, Africa. Interpreting that as a chance for a new life free of persecution, the entire congregation set sail in 1793, taking most of Nova Scotia's remaining Baptists with them.[14]

Among the early Planters, New Light Congregationalists and Separate Baptists frequently did not segregate themselves into denominationally distinct churches until late in the eighteenth century. Consequently, numerous instances are found of pastors of Baptist inclination having led churches that contained persons of Baptist conviction among their members, but

---

[14] See John Rippon, ed., *The Baptist Annual Register, for 1790, 1791, 1792, and Part of 1793* (London: n.p., 1793): 573–83.

the churches did not designate themselves as Baptist. On the reverse side, Henry Alline, a New Light Christian from Newport, Rhode Island, never became Baptist but exerted considerable influence on the future of Baptist work in Nova Scotia. That fluidity of denominational identity was a distinctive feature of many early congregations and constitutes a characteristic important in later ecclesiastical developments.

Prior to America's Revolutionary War, Nova Scotia was simply one of fourteen British colonies strung out along the Atlantic Coast of North America. No one at the time imagined that the colony was destined for a national identity different from that of the other thirteen. But the Revolution forced each colony to make a decisive choice, and Nova Scotia alone (which then included New Brunswick and Prince Edward Island) chose to remain loyal to the king. Persons residing within the rebelling colonies to the south who chose fidelity to the crown were forced to leave. Known as United Empire Loyalists, the political refugees immigrated in such great numbers that they soon became the new majority in many regions of Nova Scotia. The fact that most were Anglican challenged the prevailing order and threatened the religious freedoms Planters had gained earlier. For decades the matter was contested in varied ways. Ultimately, religious freedoms were regained and dissenters mollified, but only after considerable effort. Many Old Light Congregationalists suffered the reverse experience of the Loyalists. Having decided in favor of the Revolution, they were forced to emigrate back to the rebelling colonies. Their removal paved the way for an era of Baptist growth in Nova Scotia.

After an unpromising start, the late 1790s foreshadowed better days for Maritime Baptists. Beginning with the work of Theodore S. Harding at Horton, and extending through the ministries of John Burton at Halifax, Thomas H. Chipman at Annapolis Royal, John Payzant and Edward Manning at Cornwallis, Harris Harding at Yarmouth, Joseph Dimock at Chester, Joseph Crandall in a newly established church at Sackville, and Enoch Towner in the Digby region, Baptist congregations were established. This time they achieved stability and were successful in attracting increasing numbers of committed adherents.

Distinctive Contributions to the Baptist Traditioning Process

Early Canadian Baptist traditions were forged out of a unique blend of New England Separate Baptist roots, New Light Congregational influences, Loyalist Anglican opponents, and political commitments that ran counter to those of Baptists in the other American colonies. Never having sanctioned slavery, British Canada became a refuge for an independent black Baptist population, which subsequently was lost to recolonization efforts in Africa. The churches that survived those volatile beginnings were mostly Anglo in culture and therefore shared many features of the Anglo congregations south of the border. However, diverging conclusions about relations with the British Empire and a particular set of contextual influences generated yet another tradition within the Baptist movement.

NATIVE AMERICAN BAPTIST TRADITIONS

Native American acceptance of Baptist religious identity was negligible prior to the nineteenth century. By 1790, probably there were only 159 Baptist Indians in North America. The reasons for such low receptivity are many and complex, but clearly Anglo Baptist perceptions of Indian culture and religion did not help their appeal to indigenous populations. Roger Williams is noted for his work among Indians in the Massachusetts and Rhode Island colonies. Among other things, he recognized Amerindian rights of ownership to the lands European settlers were occupying, rejected the English monarch's right simply to usurp North American lands as though Native populations had no legitimate land claims, studied the Pequot and Narragansett languages, and published *A Key into the Language of America* as an aid to Europeans in their interaction with those indigenous tribes. He seems to have had good relations with most New England Indian tribes and even was sheltered by an Indian tribe when exiled by Massachusetts authorities in the winter of 1636.

In spite of Williams' good relations with the Narragansetts, he found them resistant to his Euro-Christian theology. John Callender, Baptists' first American religious historian, observed in 1738 that Williams became discouraged in his efforts to "instruct" the Indians. The difficulties of communication and his feeling that he lacked clear divine commissioning for the work led him to conclude that "there is no more reason to expect religion should, by human means, thrive among such people, than among the lazy and abandoned poor in London."[15] Callender, after noting the

---

[15] John Callender, Romeo Elton, and Rhode Island Historical Society, *An Historical Discourse, on the Civil and Religious Affairs of the Colony of Rhode Island by John Callender, M.A. with a Memoir of the Author; Geographical Notices of Some of His Distinguished Contemporaries; and Annotations and Original Documents, Illustrative of the History of Rhode Island and Providence Plantations, from the First Settlement to the End of the First Century by Romeo Elton* (Philadelphia: Knowles, Vose & Company, 1838), 139.

miserable state of most local Native peoples, offers his interpretation for the reason. He ascribes it to "their insuperable aversion to the English industry, . . . alteration from the Indian method of living, their laziness, and their universal love of strong drink."[16] He attributed God's judgment as the cause for this, "The Lord is King forever, and the Heathen, are perished out of the land! [In their place] God hath planted this [the English] people."[17] Given such interpretations of Amerindian culture, it is not surprising that Indians were not attracted to the Baptist faith. The great wonder is that a few actually did find something attractive in Anglo Baptist witness.

Early Native acceptance of Baptist beliefs was not an indigenous development but a result of Anglo mission efforts. But, after hearing the missionaries' message, numerous Amerindians saw a potential compatibility between Amerindian culture and Christian faith in its primal forms. The problem resided in the fact that Indians found the Anglo race generally a poor model for the religion they taught. An excellent example of this is found in the autobiography of Hawaii's last reigning queen, Liliuokalani. She writes that "the habits and prejudices of New England Puritanism were not well adapted to the genius of a tropical people, nor capable of being thoroughly engrafted upon them. But Christianity in substance they have accepted."[18] As did many Amerindians, she and her people endured deceptions and betrayals from Anglo Christians but continued to find meaning in the faith, although in terms that were their own.

Peter Folger, a teacher, surveyor, missionary, and interpreter, moved to Martha's Vineyard about 1642 and to Nantucket about 1657. While he was employed as an instructor by Thomas Mayhew Jr., Folger became a Baptist. A number of Indians who had converted to Christianity under Mayhew's influence also became Baptists and joined Folger in becoming part of a Baptist church in Newport, Rhode Island. From that foundation, three Native Baptist churches developed: Gayhead, Nantucket, and Chappaquiddick.

After the efforts of Williams and Folger, Baptist interest in mission outreach among Native Americans seems to have waned until the mideighteenth century. In 1750, in part as a result of interests growing out of the First Great Awakening, a Native congregation called Indian Baptist Church was organized in Charleston, Rhode Island. Samuel Niles was the most noted among the church's pastors, and under his leadership, the

---

[16] Ibid., 141.   [17] Ibid., 146.
[18] Liliuokalani, *Hawaii's Story By Hawaii's Queen* (Boston: Lothrop, Lee and Shepherd, 1898), 367.

church's first "meeting house" was constructed.[19] In October 1772, David Jones was sent out by the Philadelphia Baptist Association to work among the Shawnee and Delaware tribes. However, he became discouraged over the lack of response and soon abandoned the project.

Distinctive Contributions to the Baptist Traditioning Process

As might be expected, Anglo Baptists demonstrated no perception that there might be a distinction between the Christian faith and their European culture. This blindness quickly became evident in their associations with Amerindians. Theologically, Native peoples may have possessed greater insight into the essence of the Christian message they were presented than did their Anglo instructors, and Indians might have experienced stronger attraction to it had they been permitted to embrace it within their own cultural terms. However, power rested with those whose understanding of Christianity was limited to but one cultural possibility. Thus, serious tension was created between Native identity and Christian identity making the two exclusive of each other. Becoming both Baptist and Native often meant a lifetime of identity struggle and exclusion from both the Anglo and Native cultures.

From the beginning, Baptist Amerindians have lived out the challenge to interpret the essence of Christian faith in cultural settings other than European. This has never been easy. Many Native Baptists express the feeling that they "face a fundamental dilemma in attempting to resolve their hybrid identities in an organic unity."[20] Being both Native and Christian is problematic in many dimensions. Yet numerous Native Baptists have demonstrated the courage to take up this challenge. As people who have taken seriously both a Baptist cultural and religious heritage and a Native cultural and religious heritage, Amerindian Baptists model for the larger Baptist world an ability to value "their own spiritual perceptions and experiences" and a commitment to work through this problem in ways that "facilitate personal and communal survival."[21] From the early phase of Baptist life, Amerindian Baptist experience has honed insight and skills

---

[19] Frederic Denison, *Westerly and Its Witness for Two Hundred and Fifty Years* (Providence: RI: J. A. & R. A. Reid, 1878), 81.

[20] James Treat, "Introduction: Native American Narrative Discourse," in *Native and Christian, Indigenous Voices on Religious Identity in the United States and Canada* (New York: Routledge, 1996), 9.

[21] Ibid., 2.

needed by the entire Baptist community, although few from other Baptist traditions have recognized or welcomed them.

AFRICAN AMERICAN BAPTIST TRADITIONS

Mechal Sobel has identified three distinct phases in the religious development of early African American Baptists: the quasi-African phase, the African-Christian phase, and the black Baptist sacred cosmos phase.[22] She argues that each phase can be identified through linguistic characteristics integral to that phase. In the first phase, spiritual life and thought functioned primarily in the African mother language and culture and reflected primarily that worldview. In the African-Christian phase, both cultures coexisted but did not coalesce. Major contradictions existed in life, thought, and theology. In the third phase, a coherent worldview emerged, but one that still was tied to the African sacred cosmos. Black Baptist traditioning during that period reflects those phases.

During the initial period of African American history in North America, the quasi-African phase of religious development predominated. This was a period when slavery overwhelmingly dominated the African American experience. Anglo-American Baptists of America's colonial era showed little interest in addressing the spiritual needs of blacks. A few isolated instances of concern for the spiritual nurture of African Americans can be found in Virginia, Rhode Island, and Massachusetts, but even there the evidence is scarce. Separate Baptists may have been the first to take an active interest in the spiritual life of African Americans, and it is possible that they helped organize a black Baptist church on the plantation of William Byrd III in Virginia as early as 1758.

In 1772, Robert Steven and eighteen other blacks were members of First Baptist Church of Providence, Rhode Island. In the same year, First Baptist Church of Boston was receiving black members. In most cases, however, membership privileges were limited for black Baptists, and almost no sensitivity to the value of African culture was evidenced. Generally, blacks were expected to conform to Anglo-American cultural preferences. In reality, Anglo-American Baptists too often were willing to set aside the fundamental Baptist principles they espoused for themselves to accommodate the institution of slavery.[23]

---

[22] Mechal Sobel, *Trabelin' On: The Slave Journey to an Afro-Baptist Faith* (Princeton, NJ: Princeton University Press, 1979), xxiii–xxiv.

[23] Leroy Fitts shares several illustrations of this fact in *A History of Black Baptists* (Nashville, TN: Broadman Press, 1985), 24–6.

As the African sacred cosmos and the Anglican sacred cosmos converged in the black experience, many black Baptists came to prefer a separate black Baptist worship. This allowed them greater freedom to incorporate African cultural traditions and worldviews into practices of worship and preaching that had derived from Anglo-American Baptist sources. The developments are indicative of Sobel's African-Christian phase. Achieving this was not easy, however. Plantation owners usually were very reluctant to permit such religious independence among the slaves, especially under the preaching of a black Baptist pastor, although a few exceptions can be found. Uncle Harry Cowan in North Carolina was given privilege papers, which allowed him to preach anywhere on the four plantations of his owner, Thomas L. Cowan. Likely the names of other preachers with similar privileges have been lost to history.

Usually, slaves were not allowed to own their own churches, have their own pastors, or meet without the owner's permission. Some slaves managed at times to sneak away to forests, barns, canebrakes, or similar locations to pray and have preaching. Laws that limited such preaching by black Baptists gradually came to be ignored by masters who held compatible views of faith. Over time, a few independent black churches emerged. Reverend George Liele was the pioneer black missionary and preacher in America, and his work led to the establishment of independent black churches. Two noted black preachers who developed under his influence were David George and Andrew Bryan.

The First Great Awakening became an important stimulus for religious work among slaves. Preachers of revivalistic religion helped to reduce the gap between the Anglo-American and African American religious cultures. Revival preaching emphasized personal experience with God. This experience was equally available to those of African and Anglo heritage. Theologically at least, social position, wealth, race, and the like were irrelevant to God's promise of forgiveness.

Out of this culture of revivalism, churches organized by and for black Americans began to appear. This development reflected the African sacred cosmos phase. The first continuing black Baptist church was the Silver Bluff Church in Aiken County, South Carolina. Around 1773 or 1774, David George established the congregation, which was pastored by other black leaders until 1791, when Jesse Peter led the congregation to locate in nearby Augusta, Georgia. There it was incorporated as the Springfield Baptist Church.

During the Revolutionary War, David George and much of the Silver Bluff congregation moved to Savannah, Georgia, when that city was under

British occupation. After British evacuation from the city three years later, George fled to Nova Scotia, Canada, and helped establish a tradition of black Baptist churches in that province. In 1793, he emigrated to Africa, where he helped colonize the nation of Sierra Leone and also the first Baptist church in West Africa.

One of George's coworkers in both South Carolina and Georgia was George Liele (c. 1750–1820). Converted under the ministry of an Anglo-American Baptist preacher, Liele soon afterward began exhorting fellow slaves. Shortly before the British occupation of Savannah, Liele's owner granted him his freedom. Liele remained in Savannah during the British occupation, but when English armies left, he fled to Jamaica, fearing that he might be forced back into slavery if he remained. In Kingston, he established a church that had grown to 350 members by 1791. This made Liele the first foreign missionary among Baptists in North America.

Before leaving Savannah, Liele baptized Hannah and Andrew Bryan. When other black leaders left the city with the British, Bryan quickly emerged as leader of the African American community. In 1788, Bryan was ordained and installed as the founding minister of the Ethiopian Church of Jesus Christ (known today as the First African Baptist Church of Savannah). Bryan and members of his church suffered continuing harassment and repeated imprisonments because of their status as independent blacks – a matter of great concern in the antebellum South. Those conflicts persisted until after the Civil War.

Distinctive Contributions to the Baptist Traditioning Process

The African American Baptist tradition was distinctive among the Baptist traditions that emerged during this period. Weaving elements of African culture and theology together with elements of Anglo-British and Anglo-American culture and theology – and doing so from the experience of slavery – black Baptist theological emphases, styles of worship, and ways of structuring their faith communities stand apart from Anglo Baptist traditions in significant ways. The guiding dream was one of freedom that drew heavily on themes from the Old Testament, especially those of deliverance from bondage, oppression, and abuse. Although believers' baptism, views of biblical authority, voluntary methods of support, and the faith community's involvement in governing the church might be identified as qualities that this tradition held in common with other Baptist traditions, the African American Baptist generally had unique ways of understanding and applying those features, ways that were reflective of an African cultural foundation. These distinctions will be explored in subsequent chapters.

WOMEN IN EARLY BAPTIST TRADITIONS

In Baptist history, women have faced challenges that have presented them with gender-specific identity issues. Those challenges have included questions surrounding their exercise of leadership, voice in decision making, Bible teaching and interpretation, authority, and ministerial offices. As in other matters, Baptist traditions were not uniform in their views regarding women's freedom to participate at all levels of church life. In addition, the nature of women's identity as Baptists has varied significantly across cultures. Yet it is certain that the Baptist movement could not have survived without the dedicated and sacrificial contributions of its women leaders and adherents. This fact requires a representative sampling of Baptist women's contributions to the movement's traditioning processes.

Anglo Women and English Baptist Traditioning

One does not need to search far to confirm the fact that seventeenth- and eighteenth-century British social structures were shaped by patriarchal systems. With notable exceptions, women were not generally permitted to exercise leadership or assert power in the oversight of public institutions. In general, this was true also for women in Baptist life. However, as Dissenters, Baptists did not enjoy the usual privileges experienced by those fully accepted into British public life. Perhaps this dissenting status explains why at least a few Baptist women were able to exercise voices of leadership in ways atypical of the culture in general. Beyond this, even when women were denied public voices in leadership, they still often played significant roles in founding and sustaining Baptist and other Separatist churches. Patricia Crawford has documented cases where women exercised decisive and pivotal roles in church life, but she found that often their contributions have been overlooked "by historians' concentration on the role of ministers in the 'foundation' of a particular church."[24]

British culture at the time tended to hold rather rigid views of class and gender roles. Capable and astute individuals occasionally found means to transcend the social norms, but usually widespread public condemnation was the price to be paid for doing so. Few persons possessed the fortitude or political skills needed to overcome such barriers. Consequently, most people chose to live within their culturally assigned roles. British culture tended to shape male gender identity in terms of a man's profession (or public persona) and female gender identity in terms of her family

---

[24] Patricia Crawford, *Women and Religion in England, 1500–1720* (London: Routledge, 1993), 141.

responsibilities (or private persona). Baptist men and women both faced formidable identity and legal challenges when they stepped outside the normal boundaries of established religious conventions. Those men who went even further and transgressed culturally accepted professional roles by assuming ministerial duties within a dissenting congregation augmented those challenges exponentially. A tract from the period expressed typical popular sentiments against such innovators: "Is it a miracle or wonder to see saucie boyes, bold botching taylors, and other most audacious, illiterate mechanicks to run out of their shops into a pulpit? To see bold, impudent, huswives to take upon them to prate an hour or more."[25] For women, the price required for attempting to follow God's call into unconventional Christian vocation was daunting, as doing so required them to step outside practically every major culturally recognized gendering tradition. Despite the fact that actions of this sort might have offered ways for Dissenters to express disdain toward the established church, the religious identity struggles in the face of such rejection were not easy to bear.[26]

For reasons that are not completely clear (possibly related to social conditions leading to the English Civil War), women preachers first begin to appear on record around 1641. Robert Baillie traces the phenomenon to Baptist churches in Holland, stating, "The continental Baptists allowed women's preaching, and every one of their members the power of public preaching."[27] He then adds, "Many more of their women do venture to preach among the Baptists than among the Brownists, in England."[28] This practice elicited swift reactions from Baptists' public detractors. *Lucifer's Lackey, or the Devil's New Creation* poked fun at women preachers through what became an often-cited rhyme: "When women preach and cobblers pray, the fiends of Hell make holiday."[29] Similar attitudes were expressed in other publications, such as "Idolater's Ruin and England's Triumph, or the Meditations of a Maimed Soldier" (1644) and "Tub Preachers Overturned, or Independency to be Abandoned and Abhorred" (1647).

The Presbyterian minister Thomas Edwards offered analogous appraisals, portraying Baptists as spiritual gangrene. Women's preaching was among the Baptist practices he found most objectionable. He mentions examples of women preachers in Lincolnshire (where "a woman preacher who preaches [it's certain] and 'tis reported also she baptizeth, but that is

---

[25] *The Schismatics Sifted; or, The Picture of the Independents* (London: n.p., 1646), 34.
[26] See Crawford, *Women and Religion in England, 1500–1720.*
[27] Robert Baillie, *Anabaptism, the True Fountaine of Independency, Brownism, Antinomy* (printed by M. F. for Samuel Gellibrand, at the Brazen Serpent in Paul's Churchyard, 1647), 30.
[28] Ibid.   [29] *Lucifer's Lackey; or, The Devil's New Creation* (London: n.p., 1641), 244.

not so certain"), Isle of Ely (a land of "eerors and sectaries), Hartfordshire (where some women preachers "take upon them to expound the scriptures in houses, and preach upon texts"), and London (where "there are women who for some time together have preached weekly . . . unto whose preaching many have resorted"). He gives major attention to the preaching of a Mrs. Attaway, whom he describes as "the mistress of all the she-preachers in Coleman Street."[30] Robert Baillie adds that many of the "feminine preachers in Kent, Norfolk, and the rest of the shires [had] their breeding in the same school."[31] He seems to connect the source of these preachers with the principle General Baptist Church in London. These and similar sources make clear the fact that Baptist women did preach in England during the seventeenth century. It also seems clear that public opinion made it difficult for them to continue in those roles, even though some did manage to persist.

Early British Baptists recognized two biblical offices of ministry in the church – the ministry of the word, exercised by the elder or pastor, and the ministry of daily necessity, entrusted to the deacons. Numerous English Baptist churches list women among their deacons. A few of the churches designated women deacons as deaconesses, although the earliest Baptist confessions of faith did not make this distinction. The Baptist church in Bristol equated the office of deaconess with that of "widows" (1 Timothy 5:9) and therefore identified it as a scriptural office. A service of ordination for deaconesses in 1679 identified among their roles the duty "to speak a word to their souls, as occasion requires, for support or consolation, to build them up in a spiritual lively faith in Jesus Christ."[32]

Throughout the seventeenth and eighteenth centuries, Baptist women were active in some fashion at every level of church life, including leadership and ministry. Among the British Baptist women most recognized for their leading roles were Dorothy Hazzard of the Baptist church at Bristol, Katherine Peck of Abingdon, and Ann Dutton of the Cripplegate Church in London. Women tended to experience greater freedom to exercise leadership roles within the General Baptist tradition, especially among the New Connection of General Baptists, and much less opportunity among Particular Baptists. As the period drew to a close, however, women's voices in decision making were being diminished within practically every Baptist

---

30 Thomas Edwards, *Gangraena: Or a Catalogue and Discovery of Many of the Errours, Heresies* (London: Ralph Smith, 1646).
31 Baillie, *Anabaptism, the True Fountaine of Independency, Brownism, Antinomy*, 30.
32 A. C. Underwood, *A History of the English Baptists* (London: Baptist Union of Great Britain and Ireland, 1970), 397.

tradition. The following period witnessed a complete reversal of the historic leadership roles British Baptist women exercised during the movement's formative period.

Anglo Women and American Baptist Traditioning Processes

In the seventeenth century, Anglo Baptist women in the American colonies seem to have enjoyed precious little status as church leaders and decision makers. However, a couple of sources indicate at least a few exceptions to this general conclusion. Governor John Winthrop records the influence of Catherine Scott – sister of Anne Hutchinson – on Roger Williams of Rhode Island by convincing him to accept believers' baptism and to aid in organizing the First Baptist church in America. In *Wonder-working Providence of Zion's Saviour in New England*, Edward Johnson writes, "And here these sectaries [i.e. Baptists] had many pretty knacks to delude withal, and especially to please the female sex, they told of rare revelations of things to come . . . says one of them, I will bring you a woman that preaches better gospel than any of your black coats, that have been in the university."[33] Beyond this we know very little about the activities of most Baptist women in American church life. The fact that some churches did not even list the names of women, children, or slaves in their membership indicates much about their lack of status as leaders. Yet we can surmise that Baptist women exerted a great deal of informal if not official influence.

During the eighteenth century, the question of women's roles in Baptist churches gained much greater attention. In the years around 1746, the Philadelphia Baptist Association debated whether women should be allowed to vote in church assemblies. Only men delegates were allowed to decide the matter, and they concluded that "there must be times and ways when women . . . may discharge their conscience and duty towards God and men. . . . A woman may, at least, make a brother a mouth to ask leave to speak, if not ask it herself; and a time of hearing is to be allowed."[34] However, women were to refrain from "all degrees of teaching, ruling, governing, and leading in the church of God."

---

[33] Edward F. Johnson, *Wonder-working Providence of Zion's Saviour in New England* (1654), quoted in Backus, *History of the Baptists of New England*, 2 vols., 2nd ed. (Newton, MA: The Backus Historical Society, 1871), I: 64.

[34] A. D. Gillette, ed., *Minutes of the Philadelphia Baptist Association, 1707–1807* (Philadelphia: American Baptist Publication Society, 1851), 53.

The early Baptist pastor and historian Morgan Edwards furnishes a significant source for information about women's leadership roles in American Baptist churches, especially those of the Regular Baptist traditions. In *Customs of Primitive Churches* (1768), Edwards reveals that many Baptist churches in the colonies had both deaconesses and eldresses, although his account indicates very little difference in the responsibilities associated with each office. The deaconess, he writes, "is of divine original and perpetual continuance in the church. It is the same in general with the office of deacon."[35] The ministry of the eldress "consists in praying, and teaching in their separate assemblies[,] . . . consulting with sisters about matters of the church which concern them, and representing their sense thereof to the elders; attending at the unction of sick sisters, and at the baptism of women, that all may be done orderly."[36] Although Edwards defends the biblical nature of the offices (eldresses based on 1 Timothy 5:9, deaconesses on Romans 16:1, and widows on 1 Timothy 5:9), he does not consider women to be full partners with men in decision making. He argues that "the scripture forbids women to speak, ask questions, teach, dispute, rule, or vote in church. Yet they may make their minds known by means of a brother, and ought to have a just regard paid thereto."[37] The fact that women did vote during most Baptist church assemblies in the colonies was a source of concern for Edwards, who felt the practice was an innovation. The heart of his rejection of women's full partnership in the church seems to have rested on issues of control. Women, he writes, "who are always the most numerous (in Baptist churches); have in their power any time to decide everything against the men."[38] Likely, Edwards spoke the minds (and perhaps the fears) of many if not most Regular Baptist men, the tradition to which he adhered.

Among Separate Baptist churches, women shared much more fully in leadership and decision-making roles. During a trip through the Southern colonies, Morgan Edwards observed that, in North Carolina, the Sandy Creek, Shallow-Fords, and Haw-River Baptist churches included eldresses and deaconesses among their ordained leaders.[39] In addition, Separate

---

[35] Morgan Edwards, *The Customs of Primitive Churches; or, A Set of Propositions Relative to the Name, Materials, Constitution, Power, Officers . . . of a Church* (Philadelphia: Printed by Andrew Steuart, 1768), 42.

[36] Ibid., 41.   [37] Ibid., 102.   [38] Ibid.

[39] Morgan Edwards, *Materials towards a History of the Baptists* (1770/1792), reprint prepared for publication by Eve B. Weeks and Mary B. Warren in 2 vols. (Danielsville, GA: Heritage Papers, 1984), 2: 91–6.

Baptists accepted women preachers. Three of their most famous women preachers were Martha Stearns Marshall, Margaret Meuse Clay, and Hannah Lee.[40] In some regions of Virginia, women Separate Baptist preachers were the first Baptist ministers in the area.[41]

During the Revolutionary War and early national eras, Baptist struggles to secure religious liberty and the separation of church and state generated pressures for the two groups to unite. One major hindrance to that lay in the very different attitudes the two traditions held toward women's roles in the church. Separate Baptists accepted women as preachers and deaconesses and allowed them to speak freely in deciding matters of church business. Regular Baptists withheld those privileges. Eventually, the need for unity overpowered Separate Baptists' preservation of those freedoms. Gradually, Separate Baptists conformed to Regular Baptist concepts of doctrine and church governance. In the process, Anglo Baptist women lost most of the public voice they had once enjoyed in the church life of some Baptist traditions.

Native Women and Baptist Traditioning Processes

As previously observed, social life and interaction were vastly different for Native populations than for Anglo-Americans. Consequently, the temptation must be resisted simply to discuss Amerindian Baptist women according to the same paternalistic categories as Anglo women. European Christian definitions of gendered behavior had deep roots in the Hebrew and Christian Bibles, as filtered through Greek and Roman cultural interpretations, a world that was foreign to the Amerindian heritage. Any perceived similarities of pattern, therefore, must be approached through Native cultural systems and not those of Europe.

Amerindian theologies tended to guide adherents toward accommodating to their specific environments rather than dominating them. This usually translated into metaphors of balance and complementation rather than hierarchy. A persistent Native assessment of European behavior during this period has focused on greed: "we suspect that the greed that motivated the displacement of all indigenous peoples from their lands of spiritual rootedness is the same greed that threatens the destruction of the earth

---

[40] See William L. Lumpkin, *Baptist Foundations in the South* (Nashville, TN: Broadman Press, 1961) and William L. Lumpkin, "The Role of Women in 18th Century Virginia Baptist Life," *Baptist History and Heritage* (July 1973): 158-67.

[41] William L. Lumpkin, "The Role of Women," 163.

and the continued oppression of so many peoples."[42] In contrast, Native perceptions of creation as sacred inform every aspect of the community's activity and are especially attentive to the ways all live together. This means that, prior to European conquest, the roles of Amerindian women in relation to men must be interpreted in complementary rather than hierarchic terms, although that does not necessarily signify perfect relationships.

Among the roles Amerindian societies tended to assign to women were those of preserving tribal wisdom and of being the mothers of future generations. Such roles often meant that lineage and residence were traced through female lines, something Anglo culture would call matriarchal, although Native concepts of balance would not interpret this in the same way. In many tribes, homes were owned by the women. Growing out of that social system, tribal decision making "was predicated on a domestic basis, that is, on the smallest social unit of the female-controlled home."[43] The tribal council, rather than embodying a top down power structure, actually functioned as a deliberative voice reflective of the collective voices of the community.

The "balanced" nature of male and female also was expressed in Native religions through bigendered concepts of the divine. Male-female reciprocity was expressed through ideas like earth and sky, day and night, and grandmother and grandfather. Women's roles in the creation process as "life givers" are reflected through Native recognition of "female spiritual power in the larger creational process."[44]

When Native culture was disrupted (and in many instances destroyed) by European conquests, those ways of perceiving and relating were derailed. Yet many of the underlying Native values persisted, although often in distorted and confused cultural forms. From the Anglo cultural perspective, those qualities frequently were categorized as laziness, lack of self-discipline, lack of personal motivation, and paganism. The few Native women who found their way into the Baptist movement during this phase of development often were pressured to understand their femaleness in foreign, more hierarchical terms. Any concept of gender reciprocity in Anglo culture was interpreted quite differently from that inculcated in Native cultures. Still, the primal traditions Native women brought with them into their new

---

[42] George Tinker, "Spirituality, Native American Personhood, Sovereignty, and Solidarity," in *Native and Christian: Indigenous Voices on Religious Identity in the United States and Canada* (New York: Routledge, 1996), 128–9.

[43] Clara Sue Kidwell, Homer Noley, and George E. Tinker, *A Native American Theology* (Maryknoll, NY: Orbis Books, 2001), 17.

[44] Ibid.

religious lives could not be obliterated, thus making these women "strong reminders of a different way of being" even as they embraced Anglo versions of Baptist life.[45]

Although individual voices of Amerindian Baptist women are very hard to find during this period, their presence and silent influence cannot be ignored. As one scholar has explained, "Indian men know the truth of the old Indian aphorism that our nations will never die until the hearts of our women lie on the ground."[46] Therein resides an invaluable resource on which the future of Baptist traditioning could benefit.

African American Women and Baptist Traditioning Processes

Under slavery, the African cultural roots of early black Baptist women were seriously disrupted. Lincoln and Mamiya argue that vestiges of that heritage can still be found in black Baptist life but usually in altered forms.[47] Understanding that heritage requires a return to African religious traditions.

John Mbiti's research has helped identify the prominent roles women exercised in African traditional religion. Among the significant sacral offices he distinguishes as commonly having been exercised by women were priest-ess, queen, midwife, diviner, and herbalist. Each role accomplished essential functions in the religious world of the African tribal community.[48] Geoffrey Parrinder's investigation concluded that in the traditional religions women could fill religious functions "as prominent as men. . . . The psychic abilities of women have received recognition and scope to a much greater degree in African religion than they have in Islam or Christianity where women are still barred from the priesthood."[49] As slaves in the Americas, African women often continued to exercise those religious roles among African populations, especially through the "ministries" of herbal healing, mid-wifery, fortune telling, and storytelling. Because literacy was prohibited for most slaves, the oral transmission of values and traditions received great attention in black culture.

Black women began losing their priestly roles as increasing numbers of African Americans adopted Christianity. Few if any women preacher

[45] Ibid.   [46] Ibid.

[47] C. Eric Lincoln and Lawrence H. Mamiya, *The Black Church in the African American Experience* (Durham, NC: Duke University Press, 1990), 277.

[48] See chapter 11 of John Mbiti, *African Religions and Philosophy* (New York: Praeger Publishers, 1969).

[49] Geoffrey Parrinder, *African Traditional Religion* (New York: Harper & Row, 1976), 101.

models were exhibited by those who initially proclaimed Christianity to slave populations; consequently, no precedent was offered for their inclusion in ministerial offices. Following emancipation, the male freedmen and former slaves who assumed leadership of black Baptist congregations perpetuated the same paternalistic structures and hierarchy they had received from Anglo congregations. Because, in that context, the role of the black preacher offered one of the very few opportunities for recognized status in American society, and "the inclusion of women seemed very much like a gratuitous defeat for everybody," black women were refused admission into the ranks of Baptist leadership and decision makers.[50]

However, the persistence of the African primal culture could not be eradicated and black women preachers continued to surface in spite of efforts to keep them quiet. Their cultural traditions in religious leadership, their influence as preservers of black oral traditions, the internal strength they had developed under a social system that deprived them of permanent family relationships, and the Protestant belief that God could call anyone God chose to preach and minister continued to motivate black women to exercise preaching vocations. Some black women apparently were among those who preached clandestinely in plantation settings. But after emancipation, most women were forced to follow subliminal paths to exercise their calling. Those paths included ministries like exhorters, teachers, missionaries, evangelists, writers, and preacher's wives.[51] Although the importance of those offices in black Baptist life should not be underestimated, they clearly limited the decision-making and leadership voices of women in the church's ministries to a secondary status.

The sense of call experienced by some black women was too strong to be repressed, however. A few of the women whose exercise of religious vocation during this period is known to us include Phyllis Wheatly, Elizabeth, Jarena Lee, Rebecca Jackson, and Amanda Smith. None of these was a Baptist woman, and much work remains of historians to uncover the Baptist dimensions of this topic. Phyllis Wheatly exercised her preaching voice through poetry. A former slave known only as Elizabeth gained renowned as a preacher in Virginia, even though she was harassed by authorities.[52] The careers of Jarena Lee, Rebecca Cox Jackson, and Amanda Berry Smith demonstrate the challenges black women preachers faced, even from leaders in the black community itself. Still, they offer irrefutable evidence that

---

[50] Lincoln and Mamiya, *The Black Church*, 278.   [51] Ibid., 279.

[52] Elizabeth, *Elizabeth, a Colored Minister of the Gospel Born in Slavery* (Philadelphia: Tract Association of Friends, 1889).

Figure 1. First Baptist Church in America, organized in Providence, RI, in 1638, under the leadership of Roger Williams (courtesy of American Baptist Historical Society, Valley Forge, Pennsylvania).

Figure 2. Sandy Creek Baptist, organized in Sandy Creek, NC, in 1755 under the leadership of Shubal Stearns and Daniel and Martha Marshall (photo courtesy of L. McKay Whatley, Asheboro, NC).

female preachers continued to emerge in the black community even while the institution of slavery flourished.

Distinctive Contributions to the Baptist Traditioning Process

The experiences of women varied greatly across Baptist traditions, although in general, women discovered that the freedom to exercise their gifts was restricted by gender roles. Patriarchal patterns dominated in Anglo culture, often prohibiting women from such vocations as preaching, leading worship, or even exercising full voice in congregational decision making. Different patterns can be found in General and Separatist Baptist life and in the primal traditions of the Native and African cultures. However, as Anglo cultural assumptions and Particular-Regular Baptist traditions came to dominate in Baptist life, women's voices in leadership and decision making tended to be diminished or silenced altogether.

However, a rich heritage of gender inclusive religious leadership roles can be found in the broad range of cultures from which the Baptist movement draws. Those primal traditioning sources have persistently refused to be silenced. They have resurfaced periodically in varieties of ways to confound, inspire, and advance the dreams of numerous Baptist traditions. The same sources hold much potential for enriching Baptist life in new and unimagined ways in the future.

SUMMARY OF THE BAPTIST TRADITIONING PROCESS DURING
THE DEVELOPMENTAL PERIOD

Historians have struggled with whether to think of Baptists as a movement, a tradition, or a denomination. This chapter has utilized all three categories in its attempt to describe this family of churches. As a movement, Baptist men and women of different cultural backgrounds have tended to value a sometimes vaguely defined set of ideas that compels them to mobilize for actions that are intended to influence the social order.[53] This chapter has frequently referred to several of these ideals – Baptists' definition of the church as a body of believers whose salvation by and commitment to Christ is expressed in believers' baptism and the fact that out of this have derived convictions concerning freedom of conscience, the nature of the church's relationship to government, the nature of group decision making, voluntary principles of association, and related themes. As we shall observe later, those convictions are not always interpreted or applied the same way from culture to culture, but they tend to be present in some fashion.

As denominations, specific groups of Baptists defined and organized themselves to achieve particular goals. This chapter has often referred to such goals as dreams because they often have been unrealized hopes around which adherents rally and toward which they organized their efforts. Some of these dreams have been focused toward a better life in this world; others have been aimed toward preparing adherents for life after death.

As specific traditions, Baptists have been inclined to unite their particular cultural experiences and interpretations with certain theological assumptions in ways that have tended to create identifiable families of Baptist denominations – General, Particular, Free Will, Native, African American, and numerous other groups. The characteristic procedures and reasoning each group employs to accomplish this have been identified as traditioning processes. In the historical annals of each Baptist denomination, church interpretations are found that select theological, cultural, and historical sources for the purpose of illumining and encouraging allegiance to that group's dream. Often Baptist denominational families have developed subdivisions based on different interpretations of how the dream should be achieved or what elements should constitute the resources for the pursuit.

Collectively, by the end of their formational period, Baptist churches constituted a movement made up of many denominations, each

---

[53] See the discussion of this issue by William H. Brackney, "Introduction," *Historical Dictionary of the Baptists* (Toronto: Scarecrow Press, 1999), xxv–xxvii.

distinguished by cultural and theological particularities. Each Baptist denomination was characterized by identifiable traditioning processes that were complex, intentional, and often difficult to decipher in relation to fellow Baptist denominations. Although certain tendencies might be identified as common characteristics, how these were defined and employed varied, even within a specific Baptist tradition. Traditioning processes evolved with the aim of managing the organization's understanding of what did and did not constitute part of its theological and operative heritage. Each denomination tended to define itself in contrast to its significant competitors.

During the Baptist movement's formative period, Baptist bodies drew most heavily on three cultural sources – the Anglo, Anglo-American, and African cultures. The Amerindian culture constituted an important presence, but its major applications in Baptist life occurred during the next phase of Baptist development and will be developed more fully there. Theologically, Baptists depended heavily on the mainstream traditions of Western Christianity, although reactions to specific ecclesiastical and soteriological practices tended to obscure this fact and caused Baptists to identify themselves in stark contrast to those denominations that historically identified with the broader Christian heritage. Baptist faith communities built on this theological foundation, utilizing varying elements derived from Calvinist, Arminian, Pietistic, revivalistic, African, Amerindian, and other theologies to fashion their distinctive perspectives. The way those theological and cultural threads were woven together produced varied Baptist denominations and traditions that collectively formed the tapestry of a vibrant and growing faith movement.

By the end of the eighteenth century, seven significant Baptist traditions could be identified: General Baptists, Particular-Regular Baptists, Separate Baptists, Free Will Baptists, Seventh Day Baptists, Amerindian Baptists, and black Baptists. Free Will Baptists were relatively new and still small and undeveloped. Seventh Day Baptists were more established but few in numbers. General Baptists were also few in numbers and representative of a more Arminian theology. Particular and Regular Baptists were more numerous than Generals and were more Calvinistic in their theology. Their worship styles were characterized by less enthusiastic expression than was the case among the Separates. Separate Baptists had become the fastest-growing group of Baptists by the mid-eighteenth century because they strongly appealed to America's newly arriving frontier immigrants. Over time, Separates tended to merge with Regular Baptists to form a mainstream American Baptist body that included a mixture of qualities that had been drawn from the two groups. The preferences of individual congregations and regional populations influenced the selection and combination of those properties and produced incredible variety among Baptist churches in America.[54] Amerindian Baptists faced an entirely different set of identity issues, which were not generally recognized by the Anglo Baptist cultures and consequently limited the movement's appeal among Native peoples. Black Baptists had begun to develop distinctive theological perspectives and worship styles but had little opportunity to constitute independent churches or develop denominational structures during the period. Nevertheless, each Baptist tradition, through its particular struggles, embraced dreams that refused to die. Some of those dreams and their dreamers embraced faith expressions that often did not find their way into denominational history books. Those traditions therefore must be recovered and given their rightful place along side the better established ones.

[54] See Walter B. Shurden, "The Southern Baptist Synthesis: Is It Cracking?" *Baptist History and Heritage* (April 1981): 2–11.

PART III

The Frontier Age

Global Baptist Development Phase 2, 1792–1890

Our Lord Jesus Christ, a little before his departure, commissioned his apostles to "Go, and teach all nations"; or, as another evangelist expresses it, "Go into all the world, and preach the gospel to every creature." This commission was as extensive as possible, and laid them under obligation to disperse themselves into every country of the habitable globe, and preach to all the inhabitants, without exception or limitation. They accordingly went forth in obedience to the command, and the power of God evidently wrought with them.

But the work has not been taken up, or prosecuted of late years . . . with the zeal and perseverance with which the primitive Christians went about it. It seems as if many thought the commission was sufficiently put in execution by what the apostles and others have done; that we have enough to do to attend to the salvation of our own countrymen; and that, if God intends the salvation of the heathen, he will some way or other bring them to the gospel, or the gospel to them. It is thus that multitudes sit at ease, and give themselves no concern about the far greater part of their fellow sinners, who to this day are lost in ignorance and idolatry . . . .

We must not be contented however with praying, without exerting ourselves in the use of means for the obtaining of those things we pray for . . . .

Suppose a company of serious Christians, ministers and private persons, were to form themselves into a society, and make a number of rules respecting the regulation of the plan, and the persons who were employed as missionaries, the means of defraying the expense, etc.

William Carey
*An Enquiry into the Obligations of Christians to
Use Means for the Conversion of the Heathens, 1792*

A BAPTIST PROFILE

Several editions of the Latvian newspaper *Baltic Messenger* (*Baltijas Wehstnesis*) in 1889 carried stories about Brazil. They described the nation's fertile lands, agreeable climate, rich vegetation, abundant wildlife, bountiful crops, liberal government, and grand opportunities for settlement. From those articles, another Baptist dream was born. Like many other

Baptist dreams of this era, it involved migration to a new location where a prosperous and happy life might be established. That dream included land ownership, fruitful agriculture, religious freedom, and personal liberties. It also included the vision of organizing a local Baptist faith community, one that could thrive in peace with ample liberty to pursue its version of biblical teaching. On March 20, 1892, one group of Latvian Baptist dreamers founded the New River Latvian Baptist Church (Igreja Batista Leta de Rio Novo) with seventy-five members. This marked the beginning of a wave of Latvian Baptist immigration to Brazil – one of the early significant constituents of Brazilian Baptist life.[1] This episode in the Latvian Baptist story is representative of similar Baptist experiences in scattered regions of the world during the frontier phase.

[1] See Osvaldo Ronis, *Uma epopéia de fé: A história dos Batistas Letas no Brasil* (Rio de Janeiro: Junta de Educação Religiosa e Publicações da Convenção Batista Brasileira, 1974).

CHAPTER 3

Baptists' Frontier Age in the British Empire

Baptists' frontier phase was characterized by geographical expansion, challenges from new intellectual venues, quests for organizational and theological definitions, and experimentation on a variety of fronts. Baptist emigrants from England established churches in South Africa, New Zealand, Australia, and beyond. Baptist emigrants from the United States spread their faith communities to new regions of the American West (some of which were Mexican territories at the time), to Brazil, and Africa. German Baptists pioneered work in many parts of Eastern Europe, Scandinavia, the United States, and elsewhere, especially among German-speaking populations. Swedish Baptists established a growing presence in America's Midwest, eventually constituting one of that nation's significant Baptist traditions. These migrations illustrate but one dimension of the myriad experiences that constitute Baptists' frontier age.

In addition, this was an era when Baptists were awakening to global mission engagement. This core feature of Baptist identity grew from creation of the Baptist Missionary Society (BMS) in Kettering, England, in 1792. By the end of the following century, BMS missionaries were actively deployed in India, the West Indies, Cameroons, the Congo, Sri Lanka (Ceylon), and China. Baptists in the United States formed the General Missionary Convention in 1814, which became the American Baptist Missionary Union (ABMU) after 1845. By the end of the century, it supported work in Burma (Myanmar), Northeast India, and Africa. Southern Baptists created their Foreign Mission Board (FMB) in 1845, which by the century's end directed mission stations in China, Africa, Italy, Mexico, Brazil, and Japan. Black Baptists in America organized the African Baptist Missionary Society in 1815. By the century's end that society had established a significant mission enterprise in Africa, focused especially on Liberia. Baptists in Jamaica organized the Jamaican Baptist Missionary Society in 1842, which at the close of this period supported work in Africa and Central America. Collectively,

Figure 3. Bloomsbury Chapel, London, as it appeared in about 1848, noted for its social activism (courtesy Bloomsbury Chapel).

this was an era of frontiers that shaped the entire Baptist movement in profound ways.

Through these means, the cultural gene pool from which the movement would draw continued to expand, although few Baptists of the period

Figure 4. Johann Gerhard Oncken (1800–84), a German Baptist pastor and evangelist who pioneered Baptist work in many parts of the European Continent, 1834–84 (see Chapter 5) (courtesy of American Baptist Historical Society, Valley Forge, Pennsylvania).

perceived the potential of this development for future change. To the Anglo and Anglo-American Baptist mainstream, Western-oriented Baptist traditions seemed to be conquering (converting) lost and benighted peoples, enlightening and civilizing them and cultivating them into what they believed were the truly biblical patterns and practices of church. Cultural myopia and naïveté blinded them to the fact that such interactions could never be one-way exchanges. Consequently, the theological seeds Baptists planted on their geographical and cultural frontiers during the nineteenth century took root and began to produce wonderfully diverse cultural and theological traditioning sources for the late twentieth century and beyond.

BAPTIST FRONTIERS IN THE BRITISH ISLES

English Baptists

During Baptists' frontier phase, England's governmental and social institutions underwent gradual but dramatic changes. In the century prior, the

Whig and Tory aristocracies had developed a new form of government administration that centered on the cabinet and prime minister. As the nineteenth century progressed, government was challenged to adapt this system to the new social realities created by the Industrial Revolution. This adaptation involved the inclusion first of the middle class and then of the working class as partners in England's evolving political machinery. Leadership was keenly aware that failure to achieve the transition could result in social upheavals similar to those associated with the French Revolution. Thus, by increments, advancements toward democracy extended political rights to all classes with concomitant impact on developments among England's Baptist churches.

This political transition was accomplished without catastrophic social conflicts largely because the Victorian age was one of peace, freedom from external threat, and prosperity. Those conditions provided citizens with a sense of stability out of which peaceful change might take place. In addition, England's government developed a national education system to supplement the existing piecemeal efforts offered by private and ecclesiastical educational entities, thereby equipping more citizens for participation in social and political decision making.

Ongoing antagonisms between the established church and dissenting churches supplied the underlying principles that motivated and defined this political evolution. Such antagonism furnished the fundamental ethos that connected Victorian Liberals and Conservatives with the Whigs and Tories of Charles II's era. As long as certain monopolies were retained for the Anglican Church, this tension continued to be reflected in political affairs. The nineteenth-century working-class movement was integrally connected to dissent and lay mostly beyond the influence of the ecclesiastical establishment. The movement's interests were most often advanced by the Liberal Party, which sought to further causes like the political enfranchisement of the working classes; to improve economic and social conditions to the masses; and to promote trade unions, cooperative societies, and emancipation of slaves. Such interests stimulated churches, universities, and newly formed organizations to involve themselves in improving every dimension of life. Trade unions, benevolent societies, committees, and multitudes of similar organizations were created for a host of philanthropic causes, including education, health care, working conditions, voting rights, and humane treatment. They also fostered a new conception of the role of women in society. As Dissenters, English Baptists were involved in and shaped by this cultural atmosphere.

In addition, Enlightenment philosophies and modern methods of scientific inquiry confronted England's churches, whether established or dissenting, in new ways during this period. Critical methods of historical and literary investigation subjected both the institution of the church and the Bible to scrutiny, which seemed to undercut long-held traditions and theological assumptions. Prosperity afforded more leisure and new forms of entertainment. Churches were forced to reconsider their sometimes-strict teachings about such pastimes as reading novels, frequenting the theater, and enjoying popular magazines.

These are among the developments that prompt the designation of this period as being a frontier age for English Baptists. Their frontiers involved identity struggles, new organizational structures, and new ways of engaging themselves in society for which there were no internal traditions on which to draw. In this post-industrial-startup period both the established church and dissenting churches were obliged to accommodate themselves to new social realities and to the permanent existence of alternative church bodies. The established church gradually accepted the fact that religious dissent would not disappear. Baptist churches, in contrast, were challenged to relax some of their exclusivist attitudes. Most Baptists slowly accepted their status as that of being one among numerous legitimate expressions of Christian faith.[1] A few Baptist denominations, however, persisted in their rigorously sectarian positions.

A major new frontier and source of life for English Baptists appeared in the last decade of the eighteenth century. In 1792, the Particular Baptist Missionary Society for Propagating the Gospel among the Heathen (better known as the Baptist Missionary Society) was organized through the vision and prodding of ministers like William Carey and Andrew Fuller. In addition to expanding Baptists' view of the world, the new venture also helped awaken them to the needs of people and churches at home. In 1797, the Baptist Society for the Encouragement and Support of Itinerant Preaching was formed to commission national missionaries and itinerant preachers, to help train lay preachers, and to cooperate with the colleges to connect student preachers with opportunities for service. These activities helped inaugurate a period of growth. Between 1789 and 1835, the number of Particular Baptist churches grew from about four hundred to more than one thousand.

As the century progressed, English Baptists developed an increasingly national perspective for their work and organizations. During the previous

---

[1] J. H. Y. Briggs, *The English Baptists of the Nineteenth Century*, vol. 3, *A History of English Baptists*, ed. B. R. White (Didcot, England: Baptist Historical Society, 1994), 9–10.

period, their outlook had often been very narrow and local in scope. In 1813, the first step in a process of creating a general Baptist union was begun. During the first decade of the nineteenth century, the London Baptist pastors Joseph Ivimey and John Rippon promoted the need for greater cooperative effort among Baptist churches. Ivimey issued a call for interested churches to send representatives to a meeting in the summer of 1812 to plan a union of Baptist churches. About sixty churches responded. The following year, the Baptist Union was founded. It took time for Baptists to grasp the value of this organization, and reorganizations were necessary in 1832 and 1863. But finally, in 1891, the process reached full implementation when English General Baptists and Particular Baptists united into one body under the auspices of the Baptist Union of Great Britain and Ireland.

Several Baptist leaders pressed for a shift in theological emphasis and for modifications to some church practices. Andrew Fuller in Kettering urged Baptists toward a more moderate Calvinism. Robert Hall advocated a more accepting attitude through practicing open communion. Dan Taylor led New Connection General Baptists to organize fully as a denomination, including educational institutions, publications, church relations, and mission societies. Not all Baptists were happy with the changes. Alternate publications were created to reflect specific lines of doctrine. New schools were established as well. In addition to Bristol College, other colleges were founded at Horton in Yorkshire and at Stepney in London. The famed Metropolitan Chapel pastor, Charles Spurgeon, organized a preachers' college in 1856 specifically to train ministerial leaders. And Manchester Baptist College was opened in 1860 as a reaction against open communion Baptist views.

These changes generated a significant schism by Strict and Particular Baptists. This body held high-Calvinist beliefs and practices, and therefore stood in opposition to the views advocated by Hall and Fuller. Believing that Baptist doctrine was being compromised, they began forming their own associations in the 1820s. Among the early leaders were George Wright, William Gadsby, William Tiptaft, Charles Banks, and Joseph Philpot. Early organization included the Suffolk and Norfolk Strict Association (1829), the Strict Communion Society (1841), and the London Strict Baptist Association (1852). Naturally, they did not join with the Baptist Union. As the century progressed, Strict Baptists experienced further division over doctrinal matters, mostly related to differences associated with Christological interpretations.

The Victorian age also brought changes to the political landscape in which English Baptists flourished. Until 1828, they had lived as second-class citizens, unable to participate in local government; disqualified from royal appointments; required to pay taxes for maintenance of the state church, though they had no part in it; and excluded from state universities. Over the course of the nineteenth century, those limitations were gradually removed. The history of Regent's Park College, Oxford, illustrates the impact of this transition on Baptist education. Some saw those changes as a mixed blessing. New careers were opened to Baptists, draining some of the talent needed to guide the movement through challenging days. The new situation meant that Baptist colleges entered into competition with Oxford or Cambridge for Baptist students. New developments in scientific inquiry generated worldviews that seemed to undermine religious beliefs and values.

These advances fomented yet another schism in English Baptist life. English Baptists' best-known and often most controversial pastor in the nineteenth century was Charles Spurgeon. Toward the end of the century, he expressed concern that British Baptists were degenerating doctrinally by embracing elements of new scientific theories. His views sparked the downgrade controversy, creating division, suspicion, sometimes-groundless accusations, and bitter strife. Finally, Spurgeon withdrew from the Baptist Union. A Spurgeonic Baptist tradition grew up among churches that identified with Spurgeon in his concerns and ministries. This was a serious blow to the Baptist Union. Although the organization continued to thrive, the division was a drain on Baptist energies at a time when all resources were needed to confront the new challenges that were soon to emerge.

One other transformative development in British Baptist life during the frontier phase came in the area of social causes. In the nineteenth century, Baptists developed what was sometimes referred to as the Nonconformist conscience. British Baptists had long voiced their convictions about issues of personal morality, such as strict Sunday observance, temperance, gambling, and sexual promiscuity. Nineteenth-century social and cultural changes created additional tensions concerning the acceptability of new forms of entertainment such as frequenting the theater, reading novels and magazines, and participating in similar practices that offended an underlying Puritan spirit. But, beyond this, British Baptists began exercising their voices in behalf of social affairs, such as parliamentary reform, voting rights, slavery, education, poverty, employment, and housing. William Knibb and

John Clifford were among English Baptists' most noted spokespeople for such causes.

The events and challenges of the nineteenth century captured English Baptists in processes that reshaped their identity in significant ways. Moving from the status of social and political outsiders to full participants, from lower class to mainstream, and from theological exclusivists to broader views of their place in England's religious landscape involved noteworthy shifts. One indicator of this can be seen in the changing status of English Baptists' educational institutions. Modifications to British laws allowed Baptist colleges to retain their independence while developing formal relationships with universities like Oxford, Cambridge, and the University of London. This permitted some Baptist leaders to prepare themselves far better for the challenges of a new day. It also allowed others to exercise roles in British social and political decision making of which previous generations of Baptists had only been able to dream.

But English Baptists were not alone among British Baptists in their evolution amid political, social, and intellectual transformations. Parallel experiences accompanied the Baptist congregations that were reintroduced into Scotland, Wales, and Ireland during this period. Each nation was unique in its development, and Baptists were shaped in distinctive ways as a result. In contrast to the English, however, these Baptists struggled as peoples whose cultures were gradually losing ground to the irresistible power of England. This reality together with their nationalistic particularities forged bodies of Baptists with marked though intertwined identities.

Scottish Baptists

The 1707 Act of Union essentially bound England and Scotland into one government. Following the Jacobite Rebellion's failed attempt to undo the union, British authorities took serious steps to abolish the Scottish clan system. Several severe acts were passed with the intention of totally disrupting traditional Highland culture and making further rebellion impossible. As a consequence many Highlanders relocated to Scotland's lowland cities, eventually constituting a major part of the labor force for the region's emerging industrial revolution. Some Scots were banished to other parts of the British Empire, particularly Nova Scotia, eastern Quebec, and Upper Canada (modern Ontario).

At the same time, an agricultural revolution transformed the system of subsistence farming traditional to the Lowlands into a more stable and productive agricultural strategy. This also brought disruptions to the population and forced massive migrations by Lowlanders. These and associated changes increasingly wedded Scotland's well-being to that of the United Kingdom as a whole. As the nation began to prosper, the concerns that had produced the Jacobite Rebellion diminished and the laws aimed against the Highland culture were repealed. The concomitant social, economic, and political disruptions created openings among some Scottish citizens for the kinds of theological concerns that were voiced by Baptists.

Glasgow and Edinburgh experienced tremendous growth toward the end of the eighteenth century, creating a new environment for intellectual and literary productivity. Adam Smith, David Hume, and James Boswell emerged as leading thinkers in the Scottish Enlightenment, whereas Robert Burns and Sir Walter Scott captured the literary limelight for their portrayals of what many came to view as the authentic Scottish culture. As the nineteenth century unfolded, Glasgow became a major shipbuilding center and one of the world's largest cities.

While these cultural, economic, and political developments were occurring, Baptist ministry in Scotland began to reemerge following a century of dormancy subsequent to their introduction by soldiers in Cromwell's army. The earliest churches at Leith (1652), Cupar (1652), and Perth (1653) had consisted mostly of members of English ethnicity. In the mid-eighteenth century, the first truly indigenous churches were organized. The earliest of these was established at Keiss in 1750 by William Sinclair (known as the Preaching Knight). Over the course of the late eighteenth and the nineteenth centuries, two independent traditions emerged in Scottish Baptist life. The first derived from the influence of Robert Carmichael and Archibald McLean. Influenced by the Glassite movement, these pastors strongly emphasized rational assent and adherence to New Testament church order. Composed of Independents, Old Scots, dissenters from the Church of Scotland, and Bereans, this tradition adopted a Scottish order characterized by weekly communion and multiple leaders rather than a single pastor. The second tradition grew out of the evangelism of Robert and James Haldane and employed the English order of having a single pastor as leader. Gradually, the English order became the dominant one among all of Scotland's Baptist churches.

In 1859 and for several years afterward, revivals breathed fresh spiritual life into these churches. This influence helped moderate their strong Calvinist theology and inspired the introduction of hymn singing, instrumental music, and choirs. Also, following two unsuccessful attempts in 1835 and 1843, the Baptist Union of Scotland finally was organized in 1869. Baptist

Theological College of Scotland was founded in 1893 in Glasgow as a center for training Scottish Baptist ministers.

Welsh Baptists

In the early decades of the nineteenth century, portions of Wales, especially in the South, became heavily industrialized. This development pushed Wales from a predominantly rural society in 1800 to a generally urban one by the twentieth century. The social impact of industrialization and major social change produced serious conflicts between Welsh workers and English factory owners. Those tensions were inflamed seriously in 1847, when three English commissioners produced a report that characterized the Welsh as lazy, immoral, and ignorant and blamed those qualities on the Welsh language and customs. Prevailing socioeconomic conditions along with culturally arrogant attitudes on the part of some British administrators fed a popular attraction to socialist ideals and religious nonconformity. As a consequence, campaigns arose to disestablish the Church of England, which was accomplished in the early twentieth century. Out of those general conditions, by the early twentieth century, Wales had developed the greatest concentration of Baptist churches in Europe.[2]

The possibility exists that some Baptist work in Wales could date to as early as the 1630s. Without doubt, Baptists did preach and organize churches there during Cromwell's government a few years later. General Baptist preachers Hugh Evans and Jeremy Ives were among the earliest Baptist witnesses to this region, but stronger foundations were established a bit later by John Miles and Thomas Proud. These two evangelists founded a Particular Baptist church at Ilston near Swansea in 1649. Other congregations were organized soon afterward at Hay, Llantrisant, Carmarthen, and two years later at Abergavenny. Despite Baptists' strong position favoring the separation of church and state, Miles accepted support from Cromwell's government to advance this mission. Following the Royal Restoration in 1660, however, persecution of Baptists in Wales became so great that Miles and his congregation relocated to the Massachusetts Colony in America.

In the nineteenth century, Christmas Evans emerged as Welsh Baptists' most noted leader. He possessed exceptional preaching abilities that attracted large crowds. He was especially revered for his popular open-air preaching campaigns that were conducted throughout the country and

---

[2] Albert W. Wardin, ed., *Baptists around the World: A Comprehensive Handbook* (Nashville, TN: Broadman & Holman, 1995), 191.

attracted multitudes into the Baptist movement. His work not only helped revive the Baptist movement in Wales but also restored interest in the Welsh language as well.

As the century progressed, Welsh Baptists slowly consolidated their work in spite of their strong reservations against the dangers of centralization. The Baptist Union of Wales was organized in 1866 and included two assemblies, each with its own leadership – one for English-speaking and the other for Welsh-speaking churches. In addition, two Baptist colleges have survived – South Wales Baptist College organized in 1807 at Abergavenny, Monmouthshire, now located at Cardiff, and the North Wales Baptist College organized in 1862 and now at Bangor.

Irish Baptists

In 1801, the Act of Union terminated Ireland's independence and created the United Kingdom of Great Britain and Ireland. Under that arrangement, Irish members of Parliament served in Westminster, and Ireland was administered by a lord lieutenant appointed by the British monarch and a chief secretary appointed by the British prime minister. From 1801 until Irish independence in 1922, these appointees were all Protestant.

In the 1830s, the Irish political spokesperson Daniel O'Connell launched a series of unsuccessful but peaceful campaigns to have the Act of Union repealed. Unrelated grievances on various occasions did lead to violence, however, and frequently those causes became enmeshed with nationalist sentiments. Among those were the conflicts between landlords (most of whom were Protestant) and the rural populations (most of whom were Catholic) and the so-called Tithe War over the requirement that Catholics pay taxes that helped support the Protestant Church of Ireland. In addition, economic ups and downs exacerbated the social and political situation. The worst of these downturns, the Great Irish Famine of 1845–49, resulted in about 1 million deaths and the emigration of another million persons. Cultural and economic factors contributed to this social disaster in that only small plots of land were available for a growing population to eke out a living. This contributed to an almost complete dependence on potatoes as a source of survival, as potatoes were the single crop capable of feeding a family on such small acreage. In addition, the lack of an adequate infrastructure for transporting crops and land enclosure for cattle grazing seriously exacerbated the situation. When the potato blight hit in 1845, inadequate responses on the part of the British government turned the problem into a catastrophe. The outcome was the virtual elimination of

Ireland's farmworkers and the first great wave of Irish immigration to the United States, creating a diaspora that helped encourage and finance a growing Irish independence movement. Such disruptions created space in which a small but determined Irish Baptist presence was able to emerge.

Growing resistance to the landlords and to British administration spawned the creation of organizations like the Irish National Land League and the Irish Republican Brotherhood and the use of boycotts to force the matter. The British government initially responded with arrests and imposition of martial law, but it eventually passed a series of acts that effectively created a large class of small property owners and greatly diminished the power of the landed class.

During the latter part of the century, Ireland became divided between supporters of home rule and supporters of a strong union. Isaac Butt, William Shaw, and Charles Stewart Parnell transformed home rule into a major political force. In contrast to O'Connell's earlier attempt to return to Irish independence, the home rule movement sought to gain the right of Ireland to govern itself as a region within the United Kingdom. Unionists formed a small but very significant minority of persons strongly opposed to home rule. Centered in Ulster, Unionists feared that a Dublin-based, Catholic-dominated Parliament would be detrimental, especially because most of Ireland was agricultural and Ulster was Ireland's primary center of industry with needs for different economic policies than those desired by agriculturalists. This complex economic, social, and political context shaped a distinctive Irish Baptist identity.

The earliest roots of Baptist life in Ireland may be roughly contemporaneous with those of Particular Baptists in England. However, the movement did not appear in force until the arrival of Baptists in Cromwell's armies in 1649. Between 1652 and 1653, congregations were established in Dublin, Waterford, Clonmel, Kilkenny, Cork, Limerick, Galway, Wexford, Kerry, and Carrick Fergus. At that point, the strength of the Baptist movement existed in southern Ireland. However, that strength was deceptive, as it mostly consisted of an English, not Irish, membership. With the Royal Restoration in 1660, Baptist life in Ireland declined precipitously.

Baptist vigor was renewed in the nineteenth century, mostly from two sources. The first was creation of the Baptist Irish Society in 1813 under the influence of Joseph Ivimey. The society supported an auxiliary organization through the Baptist congregation at Dublin called the Baptist Society for Propagating the Gospel in Ireland. These twin organizations were formed consequent to an appeal made from a band of young Baptist men at Dublin seeking help in evangelizing their homeland. Despite their indigenous origins, at that point, Irish Baptists still depended heavily on Anglo Baptists for their survival. Culturally, they were bucking a strongly Catholic social order in their attempts to spread the Baptist message. Later, the society was renamed the Irish Baptist Home Mission, and its operations were placed under direction of the Irish Baptist Association.

A second important source of Baptist life in the nineteenth century derived from the work of Alexander Carson. Heavily influenced by the Haldane movement in Scotland and employing that movement's methods to introduce Baptist work into Ireland, Carson organized a Baptist congregation at Tobermore in 1814. This became a center for his effective evangelistic work that continued to thrive for the next three decades.

Emigration during Ireland's economic crises exerted a steady drain on Irish Baptist membership. The Dublin revival in 1859 furnished a much-welcomed source for renewal. By 1862, Irish Baptists had gained sufficient strength to form their own association and ongoing success enabled them to form the Baptist Union of Ireland in 1895. That final step of independence was hastened in part by the downgrade controversy. Motivated by the fact that the more conservative Irish Baptists tended to find merit in Spurgeon's criticisms, they followed him in withdrawing from the Baptist Union of Great Britain.

In summary, early Baptists in Scotland, Ireland, and Wales experienced many similarities in their early challenges and developments. Most suffered a major disconnect between their initial Anglo Baptist origins in the mid-seventeenth century and the more indigenous developments of the nineteenth. In the first half of the century, Baptist churches in those countries often affiliated with the Baptist Union in England but later developed independent unions that allowed them to address more effectively the distinctive challenges presented by their particular contexts.

Baptist Women in the British Isles

As with other groups in Baptist life, the situation of women in nineteenth-century Britain was complex. Generalizations must be approached with caution, recognizing that variations of social class, urban or rural settings, economic resources, and individual circumstances often made local experiences different from the broad overviews offered here. That having been stated, some attempt is necessary toward identifying the conditions within which British Baptist women's theological and ecclesiastical identity was formed. Efforts to incorporate women into Baptist history studies have often focused exclusively on their accomplishments, which harbors value as a step toward rectifying a long neglected area of historical research. But such attempts to recognize the roles of women in Baptist history often have obscured the disadvantages and disappointments many Baptist women experienced because of social conditions that detracted from and often limited their achievements. The impression is often generated that women were permitted a level of leadership in Baptist life that was hardly the case. Recovery of Baptist women's history requires treatment of these conditions as well as recognition of their substantial contributions to the life of the church.

In general, Victorian women had little real control over their lives. Most had no true option but to marry, and when they did, everything they either already possessed or ever would possess became the property of their husbands. Consequently, the masses of women lived lives that had much in common with those of slaves. They had to obey their husbands, right or wrong, good or bad, because their spouses controlled all their assets. Women were given less opportunity for education than men, were not allowed to attend the universities, and for the most part could attain only low-paying jobs. Consequently, their possibilities for achieving any significant amount of personal independence were very limited. Naturally, the specifics of what this status meant for an individual woman depended significantly on her social status and the character of her husband, if she were married. At the top of the social order were those very few women, such as Queen Victoria, who held significant and genuinely powerful positions of authority in government and beyond. Also very high in the social hierarchy were women whose families or husbands were independently wealthy. Although still dependent on the fortune and goodwill of their husbands, these women might exercise a good deal of personal power in administering large household staffs, planning and organizing social and other events, and exerting personal influence within the circles of significant decision makers. Next were the wives of professionals whose positions furnished significant status and income. The risk of losing such status was frightening in nineteenth-century British society because of what it would mean for the well-being of the woman involved. Most Baptist women were members of the working class. The women of that rank worked at jobs ranging from the trades and shopkeepers at the high end to washerwomen and street venders on the lower end. At the very bottom of the social ladder was an underclass. This category included women reduced to begging for survival (which often included harassment and imprisonment by constables), as well as women whose lives were consumed with vices (such as alcoholism).

By the mid-twentieth century, it was common to think of Anglo women from the frontier period as having been mostly homemakers who were supported by their husbands. This was often true of women married to wealthy or professional men. However, this was certainly not the case for most women: working-class wives had to work for wages. It has been estimated that, at midcentury, about 43 percent of British women older than twenty had no spouse. Of those, roughly 70 percent were single and 30 percent were widowed. Ten percent of these women lived on personal or family wealth, and 90 percent worked for wages to survive. About 30 percent of the workforce was female.[3]

The social ideal of marriage could make life very miserable for women at a time when there were not enough marriageable men in England. This situation prompted many unmarried women to emigrate to one of England's colonies where men outnumbered women. In any case, if a woman happened to enter into a bad or even abusive marriage, there was little she could do about her situation. Divorce was rare, and like a slave, if she tried to flee her husband and was apprehended, she would be returned. These practices were upheld by most churches, sanctioned by laws, inculcated by British customs, and generally approved by society. Many women themselves sanctioned this status quo. Rebellion against the existing state of affairs was quickly squelched.

It is interesting that while women were robbed of almost any means of self-determination, womanhood was placed on a pedestal.[4] But the realities of life for most women were quite different from this ideal. Working-class women usually began some sort of employment at around ten years of age and would continue their occupations until they were married. After that, whether a woman worked for wages or not depended on her husband. If she worked, whatever she made legally belonged to him. Among working-class women, most held jobs in domestic services; the others worked either in factories or as agricultural laborers. The emergence of employment as seamstresses in the mid-nineteenth century offered a new and welcome employment opportunity for many women of this class.

In spite of the British society's pressure to conform to this state of affairs, as the century progressed, a few women did begin questioning their situation. Dale Spender in *Feminist Theorists* presents an overview of

---

[3] Wanda Fraiken Neff, *Victorian Working Women: An Historical and Literary Study of Women in British Industries and Professions, 1832–1850* (New York: Routledge, 1966), 12–14. Also see Joan Perkin, *Victorian Women* (London: John Murray Publishers, 1993).

[4] See, for example, the analysis offered by R. J. Cruikshank, *Roaring Century* (London: Hamish Hamilton, 1946).

critiques, complaints, and arguments offered by women through published works in the nineteenth century.[5] Also, as the century wore on and other social causes were taken up, women's concerns began to be voiced as well. Working-class men demanded their right to vote and hold office. Liberty, personal freedom, and legal reform increasingly characterized the newly emerging social order. Abolition of slavery was being advocated. So a few women, like Barbara Leigh Smith, saw opportunities to advance the cause of women's emancipation as well.[6]

As might be imagined, the notion of a new, more independent status for women did not find easy acceptance among the working-class Baptists. And yet the part that women should have played in Baptist churches could not be ignored. In 1809, *Baptist Magazine* addressed the issue of whether women should be allowed to vote in church meetings. The following year questions were raised concerning the practice of women giving testimony before the church prior to acceptance into membership. In general, British Baptists allowed women to offer public testimony, but not vote on important issues of church life.

But many Baptist women did find public venues from which to make their voices heard. Hymn writing became one avenue. Marianne Hearn, Mary Leslie, Sarah Medley, Maria Saffery, Elizabeth Trestrail, and Caroline Dent became hymn writers of note. Other women found opportunities for service through education. Henrietta Neale, schoolmistress of Luton school, and Martha Trinder, proprietor of Northampton school, were both prolific writers and skilled administrators. Baptist women also made major contributions to charities. These included the Young Women's Christian Association, Christian Endeavor, orphanages, and similar ministries. In no other sphere did Baptist women attain so much, however, as in the area of foreign mission engagement and support.

Several Baptist women joined their husbands and took up ministries in distant mission locations. Hannah Marshman actively engaged in the work of the Serampore mission in India. Marianne Lewis prepared for mission service in Ceylon but transferred to Calcutta, where she dedicated herself to the work of educating Indian women. Elizabeth Sale and her husband began work in Barisal, India, where she engaged in medical work and youth development programs. When they moved to Jessore in 1854, she began working in a Hindu zenana (the secluded living quarters of Indian

---

[5] Dale Spender, ed., *Feminist Theorists: Three Centuries of Key Women Thinkers* (New York: Pantheon Books, 1983).

[6] See, for example, Pam Hirsch, *Barbara Leigh Smith Bodichon, 1827–1891: Feminist, Artist and Rebel* (London: Chatto & Windus, 1998).

women). Previously, most missionary women had limited their work to Christian Indian women. Elizabeth continued her work in the zenanas even after moving to Calcutta. Marianne Lewis popularized Sale's work in a book titled *A Plea for Zenanas* published in 1866, which marks the initiation of the Baptist Zenana Mission (BZM). When Elizabeth died in 1898, the mission employed sixty-seven women missionaries, of whom fifty-eight were single. By then, the mission's work had extended to China, Ceylon, Congo, and Italy. The BZM offered single women opportunities for service that were difficult to obtain through most missionary-sending agencies at the time.[7]

The missionary enterprise also gave Baptist women opportunities to develop and exercise administrative talents. These included organizational leadership, fund-raising, and mission education. While acknowledging the value of women's efforts in these activities "in bringing both lower and upper-middle class women out of their homes and . . . [making] a small contribution to that expansion of their occupational opportunities," Olive Anderson noted that "such developments did not explicitly challenge either the social convention that respectable women played no public part in mixed society, or Christian teaching that women should be silent in the church."[8] Yet, as Thomas Moscrop observed, British Baptist women did advance Christian ministries beyond their very limited opportunities to challenge existing social conventions. He recognized that "India's future is bound up with the regeneration of her women . . . not until woman everywhere has the status and opportunity which Christ would give her and which are her right in Him, will His purposes be accomplished. Without her perfecting and endeavor, His Kingdom cannot fully appear."[9] The fact slowly began to dawn that British Baptists were prepared to allow women to minister overseas in ways they were not prepared to accept at home. Recognition of this inconsistency helped force changes in the thinking of at least some Baptists in the British Isles during the following period.

As the century drew to a close, women's appearances as speakers at gatherings like the Baptist Union Assembly, together with reconsideration of what the Bible actually teaches about women in the life of the church, signaled the beginning of reform: "Some Baptists accordingly welcomed the evangelistic potential of women employed in the church's mission, whilst

---

[7] Briggs, *English Baptists of the Nineteenth Century*, 279–83.
[8] Olive Anderson, "Women Preachers in Mid-Victorian Britain: Some Reflections on Feminism, Popular Religion and Social Change," *Historical Journal* 12, no. 3 (1969): 469.
[9] Thomas Moscrop, quoted in, *Jubilee, 1867–1917: Fifty Years['] Work amongst Women in the Far East* (London: The Carey Press, 1917), 5–6.

others were unable to persuade themselves that the Pauline prohibitions did not still apply."[10] As the century closed, British Baptist women's frontiers for achieving full inclusion remained unsettled.

BAPTIST FRONTIERS IN BRITAIN'S OVERSEAS EMPIRE

During the reign of Queen Victoria, Britain's primary external interest was trade. The nation's industrial machine required colonies and raw materials to prosper, and the victories at Trafalgar and Waterloo helped promote imperial expansion. Overpopulation and unemployment, generated in part by economic and social transitions prompted by growing industrialization, drove hundreds of thousands of English, Scottish, and Irish agricultural workers to seek a new start in Britain's colonies. Baptists were among them, and their migrations were the primary sources for Baptist expansion into those extended regions during this period. To the extent that Anglo Baptists attempted to influence compatriots toward Baptist views, the work was indigenous. Many early churches in those parts of the empire were founded by Baptist laypersons and remained for long periods without pastors. Consequently, efforts to reach beyond the Anglo community into the indigenous populations of those colonies were slow to develop. Much of that type of ministry was initiated through missionaries and often was not indigenous in nature. Given such conditions, the fact that Baptists in those regions tended to be more conservative than the ones in England is not surprising.

Some portions of Britain's nineteenth-century empire (e.g., India) are treated in other chapters of Part III of this work. This section focuses on Baptist developments in Canada, Australia, New Zealand, and South Africa.

Canadian Baptists

The Evolving Context
The War of 1812 had strategic significance for Canada as the nineteenth century continued to unfold. Among the likely causes for the conflict, related to growing antagonisms over the fourteenth colony, which did not join the United States in revolution against England, was the Maritime Provinces of modern Canada. Another reason was questions over how to achieve the westward expansion that many U.S. Americans believed was

---

[10] Briggs, *English Baptists of the Nineteenth Century*, 288.

critical to their nation's future. Some were convinced that the only way to accomplish expansion would be through conquest of both Canada and of the Native populations to the west and north. While England was occupied with Napoléon, Americans took advantage of Britain's distraction to invade Ontario, causing the British once again to employ Native peoples in their cause. Ultimately, Native tribes became the greatest losers in the war. Some American-born Baptist pastors in Canada took the side of the invaders, a position that set them against the general Canadian preference on the matter. But more detrimental for Baptist work was the fact that, for at least five years, American Baptist missionaries were unable to be sent into Canada, and after they did return, their numbers never returned to prewar levels. For the American Baptist missionaries who did venture back, postwar anti-American sentiments (especially among Canadian Loyalists) made effective ministry treacherous. The primary effect the war had for Canada was to divert American migrations away from what had been their early-nineteenth-century pattern – to travel first into Upper Canada and then westward into the regions of Michigan and Ohio. America's westward settlers now stayed south of the Canadian border. Those populations gradually assumed increasing amounts of American Baptist missionary attention, leaving Canadian Baptists to fend for themselves.

Internally, Canada itself struggled over its future relationship with England. Although rejecting annexation by the United States, some Canadians wanted independence from England. This desire created several rebellions in 1837–38. One series of rebellions broke out under the leadership of William Mackenzie and resulted in skirmishes around Toronto, London, and Hamilton. In Lower Canada, French and English revolutionaries also led rebellions against British authorities. Robert Nelson was among the most notorious of the rebels. But the nascent independence movement was defeated rather quickly, and Canada's identity as a Crown colony was secured.

Following these incidents, John Lambton, First Earl of Durham, was sent to Canada to investigate the situation. Among the recommendations he sent back in his report was the suggestion that Upper and Lower Canada be united into one colony, the object of which would be a forced assimilation of the French-speaking population into Anglo culture. This recommendation was made fact with the 1840 Act of Union, which created the United Province of Canada from the former independent colonies. However, this arrangement never was popular with most citizens of both regions and would consequently endure only until 1867. The priorities, organization, and working relationships among Baptists in the regions reflect these shift-ing political attitudes and arrangements.

After Britain and the United States agreed to the forty-ninth parallel north as the border between the Canadian and American territories, the Pacific colonies of British Colombia and Vancouver Island were formed. In 1866, they were united into one province. Once again, political develop-ments had an important impact on factors that would affect the nature of Baptist enterprising in the region, including migration patterns, commerce, settlement policies, and public institutions.

In 1864, processes were set in motion toward uniting the British colonies in North America into a federation. Three reasons prompted this move-ment: nationalist sentiments that wanted to unite the territories into one country, fear that U.S. expansion westward would ignite a desire to annex Canada's western territories, and the urge to undo the union of Upper and Lower Canada. On July 1, 1867, Parliament granted the desired feder-ation, which united the Province of Canada, New Brunswick, and Nova Scotia into the independently governed Dominion of Canada. Construc-tion of the Canadian Pacific Railway, together with the establishment of the North-West Mounted Police, helped extend the federation's authority into the western territories. Manitoba joined the dominion as a territory in 1870, and British Columbia in 1871. In 1905, Saskatchewan and Alberta became provinces of Canada.

These political developments, together with their concomitant cultural, economic, and social transformations, shaped the world in which Canadian Baptists developed during the nineteenth century. Not only did Canadian Baptists reflect the political and geographical identities of their specific regions; they also embodied the great diversity of those regions. While Maritime Baptists were becoming more integrated and conscious of fit-ting into the larger Canadian culture, other Canadian Baptists remained more isolated. Baptists also mirrored the nation's varied national, ethnic, and linguistic culture. Finally, they echoed the different theological and ecclesiological patterns of Baptist life inherited from British and American Baptist sources.

The dreams of Canadian Baptists for a better life had to survive amid significant hardship, as the ensuing depiction will reflect. The external chal-lenges of cultural, political, and ethnic developments were compounded by the internal struggles that surrounded differences over doctrine, prac-tice, and organization. Consequently, the disparate sources of Baptist life together with geographical separation and theological fragmentation made the survival of any Baptist dream formidable. Because of the distinctive ways Canadian Baptists developed during the nineteenth century, it seems helpful to treat their development according to the nation's three major geographical regions: Baptists of the Atlantic Coast provinces, Baptists of Upper and Lower Canada, and Baptists of the western provinces.

Baptists of the Atlantic Coast Provinces
In 1798, churches of the Alline tradition (see Chapter 2) formed the Baptist and Congregational Association. This historic alliance symbolized the source of much tension and division in Maritime Baptist life for the subsequent several decades. When the New Light evangelist Henry Alline led in the organization of churches throughout Nova Scotia, he made minimal doctrinal requirements, thereby allowing Baptists and Congregationalists to coexist in the same congregations. As the nineteenth century unfolded, however, issues arose that divided the churches. Particularly troublesome were questions surrounding Calvinist doctrines, baptism, and communion. In 1800, the name *Congregational* was dropped from the association, making it an exclusively Baptist body. Among other casualties was the exclusion of a beloved and dedicated pastor, John Payzant (see Chapter 2), who was expelled for not having been immersed. The Nova Scotia and New Brunswick Baptist Association afterward entered into a relationship with the Danbury Association in New England, bringing additional matters of church order to the surface. As a result, in 1809, the association passed a resolution "to withdraw fellowship from all churches [that admitted] unbaptized persons to what is called occasional communion, and to consider themselves a Regular closed-communion Baptist Association."[11] This decision cost the association a third of its members. In 1821, the association was divided into two. Noteworthy among the significant early achievements of the Nova Scotia Association was its formation of an academy at Horton (now Wolfville) to train Christian leaders. That institution eventually evolved into Acadia University. Guided by parallel concerns, New Brunswick Baptists organized the New Brunswick Baptist Seminary in 1836 at Fredericton for the same purpose.

In the early decades of the nineteenth century, the Scottish laymen John Scott and Alexander Crawford organized several Baptist churches on Prince Edward Island. But progress there was very slow. By 1844, Baptists in the Atlantic Coast provinces recognized that their work in education and missions would be strengthened by a united effort. Consequently they

---

[11] "Association Minutes," June 26, 1809, Acadia University Archives, cited in Renfree, *Heritage and Horizon*, 60.

combined to form the Baptist Convention of Nova Scotia, New Brunswick, and Prince Edward Island, which was renamed the Baptist Convention of the Maritime Provinces in 1879.

Baptist life in the Atlantic Coast provinces became more complex in the early 1800s, when Free Will Baptists from New England began itinerating in the area. In 1821, Asa McGray organized the first Free Baptist Church in Nova Scotia. The movement spread rapidly and, in 1834, they established a union of Free Baptist churches. Two years later, they formed common cause with the Christian Baptists and formed the Free Christian Baptist movement, which by 1867 had evolved into the Free Baptist General Conference. This body of Baptists was characterized by its emphasis on general atonement, free will, and personal freedom to choose or reject salvation.

After the War of 1812, more freed and escaped slaves made their way into the region, and many joined Baptist churches. Prior to 1840, most had attended white congregations. Few Canadian Baptist churches were segregated, but special sections for black members became more common as the century advanced. Most congregations seem to have preferred that blacks worship elsewhere, but not necessarily because of racism. The newly arriving blacks inclined toward animated preaching and singing. To the Calvinistically inclined Anglo-Canadian Baptists, this seemed doctrinally unsound. So, as the numbers of black Baptists increased, white Baptists took steps to help black Baptists form separate congregations. Often black Baptists preferred this arrangement as well, but only in part because of cultural differences. In the nineteenth century, the most common path to leadership among blacks was through the church. Having their own churches aided their possibilities for exercising governance roles in the black community.[12]

In Canada, the church, along with a temperance society and school, was one of the institutions found in virtually every black community. These helped instill piety, Puritan ethics, and the basics of education but did little to improve blacks' social standing in the face of discrimination. If an abolition society or land association arose within the congregation, the same leadership was responsible for its management, and "such leadership was not progressive." This "interlocking directorate produced a single Negro whom whites treated as the sole spokesman for the entire

---

[12]   Robin W. Winks, *The Blacks in Canada: A History*, 2nd ed. (Montreal: McGill-Queen's University Press, 1997), 338–9.

black community," directing their aid and communications through that person.[13] A few leaders of renown who were generated through this system included Stephen Blucke, Joseph Leonard, Josiah Henson, Mifflin Gibbs, and William Hubbard. The arrangement tended to produce and perpetuate conservatism on the part of Canadian black Baptist churches, because the spokesperson generally did not wish to lose white support.

The one issue on which black churches were activist was the condemnation of slavery. In 1842, Richard Preston, a former slave from Virginia who been ordained in London and had become a black Baptist leader in Nova Scotia, led his congregation to form the Anglo-African Mutual Improvement and Aid Association. In 1846, he helped organize the Negro Abolition Society. But his decision in 1853 to form the African Baptist Association took black Baptists "outside the mainstream of general Baptist development in the province just as the sect was beginning to experience an intellectual flowering not seen among members of the faith in other Maritime colonies."[14] Consequently, white and black Baptists developed along separate lines over the course of the nineteenth century, leaving the black churches of the Atlantic Coast provinces to suffer neglect by the larger Baptist community.

Baptists in Upper and Lower Canada

Baptist ministries in the colonies of Ontario and Quebec included a complex mixture of English, Scottish, and American Baptist sources that generated constant tension throughout the nineteenth century. By 1810, Regular Baptists had established eight congregations, largely through the efforts of American Baptist missionaries. This work was interrupted and then slowed by the War of 1812. United Empire Loyalists were the source of much of the work along the upper St. Lawrence River, the eastern villages of Quebec, the Niagara Peninsula, and along Lakes Ontario and Erie. After the war, American Baptist influence diminished. However, political, economic, and social conditions in Scotland fueled Scottish immigration into the area. A few of those immigrants were Baptists who had been influenced by the Haldane movement. In contrast to the Calvinistic orientation of the churches established by American Baptists, with their emphasis on proper order and polity, the Scottish Baptists practiced open communion and selected leaders from within their membership. Conflicts soon arose between the closed-communion and open-communion Baptists that,

---

[13] Ibid., 340.   [14] Ibid.

together with differences over associational relations, created bitter debates and inhibited cooperative efforts until the last decade of the nineteenth century.

In addition, early in the century, British Baptists sponsored missionary enterprises in the region of Montreal, initially through the Baptist Colonial Missionary Society and later through the Baptist Missionary Society. The first Baptist association in this region, organized in 1802 at Thurlow, was a product of this effort.

By the mid-nineteenth century, Baptist work in Upper and Lower Canada radiated primarily from four centers: Montreal, Woodstock, Brantford, and Toronto. Attempts to bring unity to this work were unsuccessful, with doctrinal differences, ethnic tensions, and geographical isolation creating formidable barriers. Each center established its own work and organized its own schools to train leaders for its particular version of Baptist life. Canada Baptist College was organized in 1838 at Montreal, the Canadian Literary Institute was begun in Woodstock in 1860, Toronto Baptist College (after 1888 McMaster University) was founded in 1881, and Brantford launched the Baptist Training Institute in the twentieth century.

Black-initiated Baptist churches established in Upper Canada in the 1820s and 1830s were originally multiracial, among them being the church in Toronto, which was multiracial until 1829; the church at Colchester until after 1830; and the Niagara church until 1831. However, few remained that way after 1840. The reasons are complex, but generally the trend toward racially segregated congregations related to cultural differences and black distrust of whites. This growing separation, agitated by antislavery concerns, led to the formation of the Amherstburg Association in 1841. Declaring that they were unable to "enjoy the privileges we wish as Christians with the White Churches in Canada," they formed an international association of black churches from Niagara westward to London, Ontario, and southward to Detroit. The association united with the Baptist Convention of Ontario and Quebec in 1927.

In addition, a small French-speaking work was begun in 1835 by Louis Roussy and Henriette Feller. Roussy was employed by the Commission of the Churches of Switzerland Associated for Evangelization, sponsored by the Haldanes. They first ministered in Montreal, then at Grande Ligne, where the noteworthy Grande Ligne Mission was organized. Feller and Roussy called themselves Baptiste Liberaux (Free Baptists) and emphasized local church autonomy. Their open position regarding baptism by immersion resulted in tensions with the more exclusivist Baptists. In 1847, Roussy accepted immersion and influenced the mission to unite with the larger Canadian Baptist fold in 1849.

Baptists in the Western Provinces

Baptist work in the western provinces of Manitoba, Saskatchewan, Alberta, and British Columbia originated largely out of the missionary endeavors of Baptists in Upper and Lower Canada and from immigration. American Baptists assisted with the challenging work undertaken by the Home Mission Board of the Ontario-Quebec Convention and the Women's Home and Foreign Mission Society of Manitoba and the North West Territories in efforts to minister among the rapidly growing ethnic communities, especially the Russians, Ukrainians, Galicians, Germans, and Swedes.

In 1873, the Ontario Convention sent Alexander McDonald to gather and organize Baptist churches in the area of Winnipeg. A church was organized there in 1875, and shortly afterward, others were established in Calgary (1888), Medicine Hat (1890), Edmonton (1892), and Stratcona (1895). The Ontario Baptist sponsors of this work stressed that the mission effort was not only to evangelize but also properly to indoctrinate the converts in Calvinistic Baptist church order. Alexander Clyde was an early leader in Baptist work at Victoria. A multiracial Baptist church was founded there in 1876, some of its black members having migrated from California as early as 1858. Robert Lennie helped establish the first Baptist church in Vancouver in 1887. The British Columbia Baptist Church Extension Society founded in 1896 helped establish numerous other churches in the region. By 1900, four separate conventions had been formed among Baptists in the western provinces. They united to create the Baptist Union of Western Canada in 1909, bringing greater coordination and more resources to Baptists' labors in the territory.

Comprehending Canadian Baptists' Nineteenth-Century
Traditioning Processes

The Canadian Baptist historian Jarold Zeman attempted to capture the essence of the Canadian Baptist experience in his work titled *Baptists in Canada: Search for Identity amidst Diversity*. The struggle for common identity was critical for Canadian Baptists in the nineteenth century because their numbers were small enough to keep the need for unity always before them, but their differences were too great to permit easy cooperation. Thus, an elusive dream to achieve the results that united resources might afford amid the reality of irreconcilable differences tended to characterize Canadian Baptists during this period. The preceding accounts have reflected the often frustratingly disjointed nature of nineteenth-century Canadian Baptist life, especially for those who perceived the potential that could be available through consolidated efforts.

When evaluated carefully, however, the divisions Canadian Baptists experienced were predominantly those endemic to the Anglo Baptist experience in many locations. Although a few French, Scottish, black, and immigrant ethnic Baptists existed on the periphery of Canadian Baptist work – and some of those populations were the object of Canadian Baptist mission efforts – the heart of Baptists' tensions were to be found in the same core issues that had divided Anglo Baptists wherever they predominated: limited (Calvinist) or general (Arminian) atonement, open or closed communion, and whether to place greater emphasis on local church autonomy or on interdependence (cooperation) and toleration of differences. In some contexts, Anglo Baptist communities were large enough that they could ignore the opposition and organize their own work independent of their theological adversaries. The Canadian setting did not allow Baptists easily to do this. In significant ways, their struggles were portents of the larger Baptist experience in a globalized world.

Australia Baptists

On January 26, 1788, Arthur Phillip and 1,305 European colonists began a settlement at Sydney Cove, thereby establishing a British presence and an effective claim to the eastern portion of the continent of Australia. The French also held an interest in the continent and gave some indications that they might have plans for colonization as well. This prompted the English to send a naval vessel in 1829 to claim Western Australia. Soon afterward, James Stirling arrived with another group of colonists to initiate the colony's second settlement at Perth. A large portion of Australia's first settlers were convicts (736 of the 1,305 original settlers at Sydney, for example). About a third of the early convicts were Irish, many having been implicated in political upheavals occurring at the time against the landlords and the British rule of Ireland. Those early convicts effectively substituted for the slaves who had served as the colonial workforce of Britain's earlier colonies. Convicts who proved to be useful could eventually earn their freedom and even become settlers themselves. The ones who rebelled could be sent to one of the penal colonies, where life was incredibly harsh.

This combination of qualities that made Australian origins unique served also as the matrix that helped distinguish Baptist identity there. Although many of the germinal theological and ecclesiological foundations of these

Baptists are familiar from the broader Anglo Baptist movement; specific emphases and concerns of Australian Baptists are products of this distinctive context. Roots of their identity go deep into the nation's past, extending back to the days when Australia bore the reputation of being the dumping grounds for England's social outcasts and a land of high crime, drunkenness, and religious indifference. The earliest Baptists were among those who migrated as pioneer settlers from Great Britain and shared in this infamy. Richard Boots, a convict, was among those. He arrived in 1788 and identified his religious affiliation as Baptist.

In 1831, John McKaeg conducted the first Baptist worship service on record – in the Rose and Crown Hotel in Sydney. Of Particular Baptist background, he had grown up in Scotland, served as a missionary in Ireland, and pastored a church in England before immigrating to Australia. He performed the first known Baptist baptism in 1832 at Woolloomooloo Bay. He had a reputation for gambling, heavy drinking, and dishonest dealings. A failed tobacco business caused his imprisonment for debt. Although clearly not the desired model for Baptist witness, McKaeg's life nonetheless was quite indicative of the struggles common to the masses among whom he served. Despite his shortcomings, he seems to have been sustained by a dream for a better life for both himself and those to whom he sought to minister.

Significant explorations by Australian teams like those of Robert Burke and William Wills, as well as Hamilton Hume and Charles Sturt, helped open the continent's interior to eventual settlement over the course of the nineteenth century. The subsequent influx of settlers offered opportunities for Baptists to extend their work. As frontier settlements grew into established communities, the increased stability helped awaken desires to develop a more cultured Australian society. The explorer William Charles was among those who led movements, on the one hand, to end convict transportation and, on the other hand, to establish representative government. Such efforts helped terminate the importation of convicts by 1840 in eastern Australia, although it continued until 1868 in the West. Of equal importance to the elevation and future of this developing society was the introduction of the wool industry, which became a staple of Australia's early economy. Concomitantly, it was also a source of financial stability for Baptists and their institutions.

The prospects of establishing a new life on almost free Crown land proved a powerful incentive for immigration. After the late 1820s, authorized settlement was limited to specific regions, but a defiant group of squatters chose to ignore those restrictions. By managing to settle lands beyond those limits without reprisals from British officials, a powerful class of landowners was created. In this newly emerging society, the Church of England held the dominant position among religious institutions. The large numbers of Irish convicts meant that Catholicism came to be well represented as well. English religious dissenting groups also were present, albeit in lesser numbers, including Baptists and Methodists.

The advantages that Australia's growing economic and cultural stability held for Baptists during the period can be detected in several areas of development. One indicator is Baptists' growing awareness of opportunities for witness that were going unfulfilled. In the early 1830s, the Baptist Missionary Society sent John Saunders to work in Australia in response to Baptist appeals for assistance. His efforts gave birth to the country's first surviving Baptist church in 1836, the Bathurst Street Church in Sydney, New South Wales. The success of his work and the repeated pleas by Australian Baptists for help motivated the Baptist Missionary Society to contemplate sending additional missionaries to promote the work there. However, the nation's growing Baptist presence induced the BMS to forgo work in Australia and focus on the unevangelized populations in several other lands, concluding that the Baptists in Australia could carry on the work themselves. The society did on several occasions send evangelists to help start churches, but Australian Baptists saw many opportunities pass them by because of limited resources and too few workers.

Somewhat analogous to Baptist beginnings in North America, the work in Australia began among independent colonies that were under British administration. Consequently, Baptist work had different points of origin in the various territories. For example, in 1835, Henry Dowling, a strict Calvinist, organized the earliest Baptist church to be constituted in Australia at Hobart, Tasmania (then known as Van Diemen's Land). However, the church survived for only eight years. Baptist work in Tasmania was continued through the support of William and Mary Gibson and graduates of Spurgeon's College. Thomas Spurgeon, son of the noted London preacher, took great interest in the colony as a result of a visit and promoted the Baptist effort there through Spurgeon College students. By 1885, Spurgeon graduates filled the pulpits of every Baptist church in Tasmania and New South Wales, the best known among them being F. W. Boreham.

Around 1839, a congregation reflective of the Scottish Baptist tradition was organized in Melbourne, Victoria, through evangelistic efforts of Peter Virtue and James Wilson. John Ham organized the Collins Street Baptist Church in 1843. That church, like the ones at Sydney and Hobart, was built on lands donated by the British government. This practice became a source of tension among Australian Baptists, as acceptance of government aid was considered by many to violate the Baptist principle of separation of church and state. W. P. Scott established the Albert Street Baptist Church in 1850 as a closed communion church.

The Baptist movement in South Australia failed to show great promise, however, until the ministry of Silas Mead in the 1860s. Mead was an advocate of open membership and the center of his work was the Flinders Street Baptist Church, which he organized in North Adelaide. This church became the source of numerous new churches that were established throughout the region.

Individual Baptists resided in Queensland at least as early as 1839, but they initially worshipped as part of the United Evangelical Church, not as a Baptist congregation. In 1855, the first independent Baptist work was initiated when a church was established at Moreton Bay. B. G. Wilson was leader of that work until 1878, serving as pastor of the City Tabernacle Church. German Baptist settlers established several of the colony's rural Baptist churches a short time later.

In 1895, J. H. Cole formed a Baptist church at Perth in Western Australia, inaugurating Baptist's first presence there. William Kennedy became a significant Baptist pioneer, founding numerous rural Baptist churches in the territory.

As European immigration and settlement gained momentum, the Aboriginal population of Australia suffered greatly from encroachment on their lands. Diseases decimated their ranks. Construction and farming often destroyed resources needed for their survival, resulting in starvation. By the early twentieth century, about 90 percent of the Aboriginal population had disappeared. For decades the notion reigned that British colonization of Australia has been peaceful, an example of settler and indigenous populations' success at coexisting. More recent studies by Australian historian Henry Reynolds (among others) have challenged that claim. His research has produced evidence demonstrating that a great deal of fear existed among settlers over Aboriginal attacks. Moreover, he also documents numerous instances of Aboriginal resistance. In a few cases, entire settlements were destroyed. In reaction, settlers often took steps to eradicate the threat, including massacring Aboriginal populations. A few of the major massacres included the ones at Pinjarra, Myall Creek, and Tasmania.[15]

---

[15] See Henry Reynolds, *The Other Side of the Frontier: Aboriginal Resistance to the European* (Sydney: University of New South Wales Press, 2007).

Early Australian Baptists were not totally silent about the plight suffered by Aboriginal peoples, although like Anglo Baptists in many other parts of the world at the time, their voices against the abuses inflicted on indigenous populations were far too limited. The BMS missionary John Saunders was among the few Anglos who gained a reputation for speaking out against the mistreatment of Aborigines – which, along with convict transportation and alcoholism, was a major social issue of his day. In the 1840s, Baptist mission effort was initiated in the territory of South Australia among Aboriginal peoples, and in 1848, an Aboriginal Baptist church was organized in Adelaide.

The discovery of gold in 1851 opened a new chapter in Australia's history. The subsequent gold rush was fueled in part by a global economic downturn that occurred around midcentury. The influx of get-rich-quick settlers helped transform the continent politically, economically, and demographically, thereby challenging Australian Baptists with a changing and often-unfamiliar context in which to work. In addition to British and Irish settlers, significant numbers of persons of North American and Chinese heritage migrated as well. As the number of new settlers grew, demands for representative government and other qualities associated with democracies became stronger. Despite resistance from the "squatters," in 1855, New South Wales, Victoria, South Australia, and Tasmania were granted representative governments. In important ways, the patterns of Australian Baptist organizational development reflected this change of status.

Australia's gold rush contributed to an economic boom that lasted through the 1880s. Melbourne in particular benefited from this situation, growing to become the second-largest city in the British Empire for a brief period. With development also came demands for workers' rights and benefits. In response, some employers attempted to circumvent the trade and labor unions by importing Chinese workers. Feeling threatened economically, a reaction set in among Australian working classes against the new immigrants and resulted in adoption of the so-called white Australia policy. Similar to the Chinese Exclusion Act of the United States that was introduced about the same period, this policy placed restrictions on non-white immigration to Australia that continued in force until 1973. This environment fueled attitudes of ethnic exclusiveness, and Baptists were not immune to its impact. A decade-long economic depression, which began in 1891, brought massive unemployment, political pressures, and racism – especially against Chinese, Japanese, and Indian immigrants.

In the late 1880s, strong sentiments for nationalism started to surface. Influenced by other federations (such as Canada and Switzerland), by improvements to transportation and communication, and by the need for greater efficiency, agitation arose favoring an Australian federation. After surviving a series of starts and stops, the federation finally became a reality on January 1, 1901, when the Commonwealth of Australia was created, uniting Australia's separate colonies under one federal government.

Australia's Baptist work during this period was patterned mostly after that in Britain, and consequently, it reflected many of the theological issues prevalent among British Baptists at the time. British Baptist ways of organizing also became the principal models that shaped the Australian Baptist institutions that subsequently developed. Around the mid-nineteenth century, Baptist unions very much like the ones in Britain began to be organized. Because the discovery of gold had stimulated growth in population, economy, and Baptist activity in the territory of Victoria, it was there that, in 1862, the first of Australia's Baptist unions emerged, partly through the influence of F. J. Wilkins. South Australia followed with the nation's second Baptist union in 1863. State unions were organized in New South Wales in 1868, Queensland in 1877, Tasmania in 1884, and Western Australia in 1896. Australian Baptists' first national organization was created in 1926, the Baptist Union of Australia. The union originated as a cooperative venture among the Australian state associations. Somewhat reflective of Australia's political development, each union originated independently and has remained independent. Rather like a federation, the national union serves mostly as an advisory council that helps coordinate the work of the independent regional unions. In addition to Baptist Union work, in 1872, the Particular Baptist Association of Australia was organized in New South Wales.

Australian Baptists have held a commitment to mission work since the early days of their history, organizing an auxiliary to the Baptist Missionary Society of London in 1863, which has evolved into today's Australian Baptist Missionary Society. That society initiated work in Bangladesh (then known as East Bengal) soon after its formation in 1863. Between 1876 and 1880, it supported a mission to Japan.

Comprehending Australian Baptists' Nineteenth-Century Traditioning Processes

Early theological traditioning sources prevalent among Baptists in Australia were predominantly derived from British Anglo Baptists. Consequently, they tended to repeat a familiar litany of theological differences related to questions over limited versus general atonement, degree of Calvinist doctrinal adherence, and open versus closed communion. Any cultural diversity among Australian Baptists during the period was very limited. The extension of Baptist work throughout the Australian continent was painfully slow to occur in most areas for the entire nineteenth century. Several cultural factors were generally cited by Baptist leaders of the period to explain the dearth of growth: a widespread secularist attitude that took little interest in religion; the many and serious divisions among Baptists themselves; the lack of human and financial resources to take advantage of opportunities that did exist; and Baptists' tendency to draw primarily from the lower classes, which limited possibilities for resources and influence. This combination of theological and cultural traditioning factors had the effect of shaping Australian Baptists into a hearty movement that has been rugged and resilient in the face of difficulties. With little outside assistance, they found ways to make effective use of limited resources and to succeed amid formidable hardships. Despite the unfavorable odds, their small numbers, and their lower-class beginnings, these Baptists were able to pioneer new frontiers with fortitude and effect during the nineteenth century and in the process prepare the way for more encouraging results that would come in the century that followed.

New Zealand Baptists

James Cook's expeditions to New Zealand achieved at least two major things: they made New Zealand known to Europeans, who began to see the islands as desirable places for settlement, and they introduced European diseases, crops, and animals, which significantly changed the Maori culture and the islands' environments. In the 1790s, European and American whale and seal hunters began to establish permanent settlements on the islands, followed in the early nineteenth century by increasing trade. Those influences brought considerable change to tribal life. During the first half of the century, Maori culture remained dominant. Their incredible ability to adapt made them more successful than most indigenous peoples at utilizing new technologies for their own purposes. The so-called Musket Wars is an example. Tribes that managed to obtain European muskets used them to conquer tribes without them, until finally all the island's tribes possessed guns, thereby creating a new basis for tribal balance of power.

In the 1830s, many of the Maori tribes converted to Christianity. At the same time, European settlement increased, with Baptists being among the immigrants. Misunderstandings and different concepts of land ownership led to tension and conflicts. Missionaries, who had come to the islands in growing numbers since the turn of the century, appealed to British authorities for intervention on behalf of the Maori. The British had already established prior claims to administration of the islands under Captain Phillip when the New South Wales colony was established in 1788. However, colonial administrators had taken no interest in New Zealand at that time. In 1832, the British government appointed James Busby official resident. With little support, Busby tried unsuccessfully to leverage the Maori chiefs into a position from which he might exert effective administrative control over the European population.

The New Zealand Company announced its intention of purchasing large tracts of land on which to establish colonies in 1839. This news prompted the British to take action. In 1840, the Treaty of Waitangi was signed by Maori leaders, acknowledging British sovereignty over New Zealand. However, translation issues caused differences between what the Maori thought they were granting and what the British insisted they were receiving through the treaty.

The following year New Zealand became a colony in its own right, no longer under the administration of New South Wales. Subsequently, considerable immigration began to occur from Scotland, Wales, Ireland, the United States, India, and Eastern Europe. In the 1870s and 1880s, several thousand Chinese migrated to the South Island, mostly to work in the gold mines. As with other Western governments, the hostility of white settlers resulted in the adoption of laws that excluded Chinese immigration.

As Pakeha (European and American) populations grew, the Maori became more concerned. Pressures from the white populace steadily increased, and whites were demanding that the Maori sell them more land. But land was the basis of Maori identity. It was considered a tribal resource, not owned by individuals, and something not to be given up easily. Tensions mounted to the point that, in the 1860s and 1870s, troops invaded Maori lands and took them by force. The decades of war, disease, and land confiscations generated serious social problems for the tribal peoples, including inadequate housing, unemployment, decay of family systems, and alcohol abuse. Consequently, the Maori race declined from around eighty-six thousand people in 1769 to about forty-two thousand in 1896.

Discovery of gold at Gabriel's Gully in 1861 touched off a gold rush that stimulated increased immigration and further transformation of the islands. As get-rich-quick dreams gave way to more sober realities, settlers turned to other industries for livelihood. New Zealand's colonial economy began to take shape after a pattern that led the white population to concentrate mostly on the South Island. The situation would become reversed during the twentieth century, however, as the North Island outpaced the South Island in white population growth. During the 1890s, the invention of refrigeration caused the economy to shift from wool exports to frozen meat and dairy products. It was during that decade that New Zealand became the first country in the world to give women the right to vote.[16] Under the leadership of Richard Seddon, prime minister and leader of the Liberal Party, legislation was implemented that made New Zealand a pioneer in social welfare through programs such as old-age pensions, minimum wage requirements, and children's health services.

Baptists were among the early Europeans who settled in New Zealand, but organized work did not begin for several decades. Initially, Baptist settlers were few in number and worshipped with other denominations. When their numbers became sufficiently large, groups of laypersons began to form meetings, where sermons were read accompanied by other acts of worship. Eventually many of those meetings developed into churches.

Baptists' first church was established in the city of Nelson on South Island in 1851 by Decimus Dolamore, an English Baptist. Within a few years, other Baptist centers sprang up in the cities of Auckland, Wellington, Christchurch, and Dunedin. Leaders in those centers felt the work would be strengthened should an association be organized to help coordinate and encourage the ministries. Unfortunately, early efforts to create such a union among the churches were unsuccessful. Finally, in 1873, the Canterbury Baptist Association was formed. As earlier leaders had hoped, the union advanced the Baptist movement in New Zealand. Among other things, the association established circuits of itinerant preachers who provided stable ministerial leadership to the churches and opened new centers of Baptist witness. Within a few years, the association had established thirty such circuits led mostly by laypersons.

The outstanding success of the Canterbury Association inspired the formation of the Baptist Union of New Zealand in 1882. Led by Charles Dallaston, the union encompassed Baptists of both islands and gradually brought a connecting focus to their widely scattered work. Among other things, the union organized mission efforts at home and abroad, established institutions for ministerial education, and laid the foundations for Sunday-school work. In the 1880s, ministries were established among the Maori people and among new settlements along the western coast. The New Zealand Baptist Missionary Society was created in 1885 and the following

---

[16]   Keith Sinclair and Raewyn Dalziel, *A History of New Zealand; additional material by Raewyn Dalziel* (Auckland: Penguin Books, 2000).

year sent Rosalie MacGeorge to India as its first missionary. Finally, Baptists' dream of having their own educational institution was realized when the Baptist College of New Zealand was established at Auckland in 1924. Now able to address the need for trained leadership, New Zealand Baptists could bring an added dimension of theological and organizational unity to their work.

Comprehending New Zealand Baptists' Nineteenth-Century Traditioning Processes

Certain unique features of the Baptist context in New Zealand generated special tensions within Baptist life there. Much of their diversity grew from the sources so common among Anglo Baptists – open or closed communion, cooperation or local church independence, and degree of Calvinism. Other differences grew out of the ecumenism practiced by early New Zealand Baptists. Some Baptists embraced doctrinal features from those sources that created tensions with other Baptists. The lack of harmony contributed to the so-called dismal decade between 1882 and 1892, when collectively Baptist churches lost about as many members as they gained. By the end of the century, Baptists in New Zealand numbered about 2 percent of the total population.

South African Baptists

In the mid-seventeenth century, Dutch authorities decided to establish a permanent settlement on the southern tip of Africa around what came to be known as Cape Town. Initially, the settlement was intended to serve only as a supply stop for ships that sailed the spice route to the East. Over time, a few Dutch colonists were allowed to set up farms as a means for supplying the station. The venture proved successful, and the number of farmers grew and expanded into the territory of the Khoikhoi tribes. These Dutch Reformed burghers were eventually joined by French Huguenots fleeing persecution in their homeland. In addition to the free burghers, Dutch settlers frequently wedded slaves imported from Madagascar and Indonesia, thus providing the source for what later became known as the Cape coloreds. Eventually conflicts broke out with the Khoikhoi, who were easily conquered. They, too, were absorbed into the colored population.

As the Dutch burghers continued to expand, many adopted a semi-nomadic lifestyle reminiscent of that which had been characteristic of the Khoikhoi they had displaced. The settlers formed the basis for the Trekboers, later simply called Boers. The harsh conditions in which they lived shaped them into rugged individualists who knew the land and lived lives rigidly based on their understanding of the Bible.

As Dutch maritime power began to decline, the British moved in to fill the void. In 1806, they conquered the Cape and established British sovereignty over the region. At that point, Cape Town was a colony of about 20,000 whites, 15,000 Khoisans, 25,000 slaves, and 1,000 freed blacks, together with the Trekboers scattered throughout the hinterland. The colony was rigidly differentiated along racial lines, with power clearly in the hands of the white colonists.[17]

British administrators began to encourage Anglo settlers into the region in the 1820s. In the initial wave, 4,500 British citizens moved to South Africa, among them several Baptist families, some of whom came from Joseph Ivimey's church in London. By 1823, those British immigrants had established trading communities at Grahamstown and Port Elizabeth. The Baptist community soon selected the layperson William Miller to give oversight to their spiritual lives and development. Miller had no training for this role but evidenced an extraordinary dedication to the task. Within three years, he had led the small Baptist fellowship to construct the first Baptist chapel in Grahamstown. But, as in many other colonies, the Baptist immigrants were not all of one theological mind. Soon, the familiar Anglo Baptist divisions over Calvinist versus Arminian theological interpretations began to surface, creating conflict and division.

William Davis, sent by the Baptist Missionary Society in England, was the first ordained minister to serve in South Africa. Arriving in 1832, he helped organize, encourage, and unite the fragmented Grahamstown church. Following his departure, two other missionary pastors were sent out by the BMS, but the society's resources at the time were focused in the Congo, so South Africa's Baptists had to find a way to thrive without significant outside help. Still, they managed to extend Baptist work into the farming district of Kariega, about sixteen miles east of Grahamstown. The work periodically was interrupted by conflicts between settlers and nomadic black tribes.

As the decade unfolded, two distinct white communities emerged: the urbanized English-speaking community that dominated politics, trade, and business, and the largely rural and uneducated Boers. Britain's abolition of slavery in 1833 widened the gap between the two even farther. In the 1850s, this mix became even more diversified by the immigration of German

---

[17] See Leonard Monteath Thompson, *A History of South Africa*, 3rd ed. (New Haven, CT: Yale University Press, 2001).

settlers. The initial wave was made up of German soldiers who had been allotted land by the British government for fighting in the Crimean War. They were followed in 1858 and 1859 by other waves of German farmers seeking land. Among them were a few Baptists who managed to organize several small and scattered Baptist congregations between 1858 and 1861. The lay leaders Carsten and Dorothea Langhein organized one of the strongest churches at Frankfort. By 1861, when Carsten was ordained as the church's pastor, the congregation numbered three hundred members.

In the early nineteenth century, the Nguni tribes of KwaZulu-Natal began to centralize, creating a fortifiable fighting and expanding force. At the same time, the Boers, increasingly dissatisfied with British rule, decided to migrate further into the interior to seek greater independence. In 1835, groups of Boers reached a region northeast of the Orange River that seemed like a promised land of extensive and deserted pasture lands. In reality, they had found a land deserted as a result of Zulu campaigns of expansion, not abandonment. The subsequent conflicts between the Boer settlers and Zulus over this land reached a decisive point in the Battle of Blood River in December 1838, when several thousand Zulu warriors were killed with only a few Boer losses. The Boers saw this as divine approval for their cause and established the Republic of Natal. The British moved in to annex the area in 1843. Trapped between the British on one side and Native African peoples on the other, most Boers decided to move even further north.[18]

As the British pushed further into the Natal region, they discovered that the Zulus constituted a formidable fighting force. Despite suffering humiliating defeats, the British eventually succeeded in extending their control over Zululand (modern KwaZulu-Natal Province). However, they were less successful in attracting African labor for their sugar plantations in the newly acquired lands. A solution was found through turning to another of their colonies: the British secured indentured labor from India. Among those immigrants were members of the Telugu tribes, who were Baptists. In the early twentieth century, India's Telugu Home Missionary Society sent the missionary John Rangiah to serve as pastor to this thriving Baptist community. An Indian association was eventually formed that became part of the Baptist Union of South Africa. By the end of the nineteenth century, Indian settlers outnumbered whites in Natal.

As their needs for pastoral leadership grew stronger, German immigrants appealed to Johann G. Oncken to send help. The German Baptist assembly

---

[18] For a perceptive treatment of this complex series of developments, see Thompson, *A History of South Africa*.

at Hamburg sent Carl H. Gutsche (1845–1926), a student of Oncken, in 1867. Over the following twenty-five years, he established twenty-five churches, each with its own building. Through his efforts, greater unity was achieved, and in 1870, an association (*Bund*) of German Baptist churches was created. English Baptist work was augmented about the same time by the efforts of American Baptist missionary Moses H. Bixby (1827–1901), who, on a stopover while en route to Burma, organized the first Baptist congregation at Cape Town in 1860.

The Boers eventually established several republics (e.g., Transvaal, the Orange Free State). Although they lacked industry and provided only minimal agricultural potential, the republics offered hope to the Boers for independent states. The discovery of diamonds in the region of Kimberley in 1869 changed that. Once again, Britain stepped in and annexed the area. The discovery, however, sparked a flood of both European and African immigration into the region.

The German Baptist Carl Gutsche baptized J. D. Odendaal, a Dutch farmer, in 1867. For several years, Odendaal served as a lay preacher among the German and Dutch Baptists and in 1875 was ordained into the Baptist ministry. Largely through his efforts, in 1886, the Afrikaanse Baptiste Kerk, the first Dutch-speaking Baptist church, was organized in the Orange Free State at Sugarloaf (later renamed Cornelia).

Boer resentment against the British exploded into the Anglo-Boer War in 1880. A crushing defeat suffered by the British at the Battle of Majuba Hill in 1881 returned Boer control to the Transvaal region, which took the name Zuid-Afrikaansche Republiek (or South African Republic). The British, however, moved ahead with plans to unite their South African colonies into a federation. This process was hastened by the discovery of gold in the Witwatersrand in 1886. With another explosion of population, the Boers found themselves threatened once again by a massive influx of foreign laborers. Tensions between the Boers and Cape colonies erupted into war once again in 1900, this time ending in a British victory recognized by a superficial peace agreed to in the Treaty of Vereeniging signed by the Boers in 1902. These developments brought together all the necessary elements for creating the Union of South Africa in 1909.

The Baptist Union of South Africa was formed in 1877, uniting many of the culturally diverse Baptist groupings. In 1878, the American Baptist Missionary Union began work in Natal. In 1892, the South African Baptist Missionary Society instituted evangelistic and church development initiatives among South Africa's black populations. The ministries eventually included Transkei, Natal, Transvaal, and the Orange Free State, as well as other locations.

Although most deeply rooted among populations of British and German heritage, the Baptist movement in South Africa was also beginning to spread among both colored (mixed-race) and Native African populations by the end of the nineteenth century. As early as 1876, the German Baptist Carl Pape initiated a Baptist ministry among the Xhosa tribes. The first Baptist work among the colored population was begun in 1888. Most colored Baptist churches developed out of white churches, with the strongest being located in Western Province. After its formation in 1892, the South African Baptist Missionary Society became the focal agent for Baptist work among the black populations. Black Baptists in the United States also initiated work among these groups – by the end of the century, the Foreign Mission Board of the National Baptist Convention, USA, had begun work there, followed later by the Lott Carey Baptist Foreign Mission Convention. In the twentieth century, the work of these two organizations merged, and their converts became known as National Baptists. They, in turn, later united with South Africa's Bantu Baptist Church.

Comprehending South African Baptists' Nineteenth-Century Traditioning Processes
The cultural, political, social, and ethnic makeup of South Africa presented a complex and tension-filled environment for Baptist ministry. Against all odds, by the end of the nineteenth century, Baptists, with very limited outside assistance, had established work among the British, German, Afrikaner, Asiatic Indian, and black populations. Their fragile and struggling union was held together by three goals: their evangelistic enterprise, their commitment to biblical teaching, and their missionary vision. Growth was slow. South African Baptists lacked the needed financial resources, suffered a shortage of pastors, and were scattered over vast distances. But their fortitude and creativity in meeting those challenges became the source of the very qualities that would shape South African Baptists' character, witness, and identity during the century that followed.

Baptist Women in the British Empire during the Frontier Phase

In general, Anglo Baptist women in the colonies of the British Empire faced the same identity challenges as women in Britain itself. Largely, the same ideals of womanhood dominated, along with the same gender restrictions.

Often, however, life was harder in the colonies and the possibility of achieving the Victorian or the true-woman ideals was never a possibility for most women. Once again, social class and location often made a huge difference.

In Baptist life, Anglo women sometimes experienced greater freedom to participate in group decision making when a Baptist congregation was still in the meeting stage and lacking the formal structures of a fully organized church. However, in normal church life, women were not full participants in matters of church governance. Even in New Zealand, where women gained the right to vote in 1893, in Baptist life, that right was not granted until 1908. Women engaged in educational work for the church; organized women's prayer meetings; taught Sunday-school lessons; and as the century unfolded, became increasingly involved in organizing, promoting, and leading women's missionary societies. It was quite unusual, however, for a woman to preach. But the irony of this prohibition was already becoming clear to some as the century closed. In a 1910 editorial carried by the *New Zealand Baptist*, G. T. Beilby wrote, "How delightfully illogical we are. We allow a woman to grace the throne of this mighty Empire [Queen Victoria], and forbid her a seat in our legislative halls. We make her pastor in all but name of our most difficult charges in India [female missionaries], and shudder at the bare suggestion of the Rev. Mrs. Smith."[19] Most colonial Baptists were not convinced that the status of women in Baptist life should change, however.

Non-Anglo Baptist women in regions encompassed by the British Empire often faced a rapidly changing world that threatened traditional gender identity in significant ways. However, most missionaries at the time were from Anglo or Anglo-American cultures, where the ideals of woman-hood were quite foreign to the traditions these women would have known. What it meant to be Aboriginal, female, and Baptist or Maori, female, and Baptist involved theological transitions that still need to be researched. It is clear, however, that being Baptist did not mean the same thing to every person, everywhere, and all the time.

General Identifying Characteristics of British Empire Baptists
The core of the Baptist movement in the lands ruled as part of the British Empire was culturally Anglo. In most instances, Baptist communities were formed by settlers from Britain who wanted to maintain their faith traditions wherever they migrated. Over time, as the communities took on

---

[19] Cited by Bill J. Leonard, *Baptist Ways: A History* (Valley Forge, PA: Judson Press, 2003), 302.

more regional identities (e.g., Australian, South African), their Anglo Baptist identity naturally transitioned into meaningful local versions of Baptistness.

Along with imperial expansion also went Anglo Baptist mission efforts. This work often focused on the non-Anglo, indigenous populations. Those efforts usually included more than Christianization; they also sought to enlighten and civilize. In most instances, the endeavors ignored the complexities associated with introducing Baptist theology into a totally different culture. Consequently, in many parts of the British Empire, what it meant to be Baptist developed with different undertones among the varied populations that happened to dwell in a given geographical location. Usually, the organizational structures for the Baptist work that emerged were those of the Anglo Baptist traditions. For some parts of the Baptist community, there seemed to be a commonality in all of this diversity. For others, failure to address adequately the basic theological tensions that surfaced as part of the encounter between Christianity and a new culture left less-than-satisfying results. During the ensuing phase of Baptist life, many presumed commonalities would emerge as sources of debate, contention, and further division.

CHAPTER 4

Baptists' Frontier Age in the United States

The War of 1812 was determinative for the shape the United States would take over the course of the nineteenth century. To that point, many leaders had believed the key to fulfillment of America's Manifest Destiny lay with the conquest of British holdings to the north. Two things changed this. One was the Louisiana Purchase of 1803, which opened up vast new territories to the west. The other was America's inability to conquer Britain's Canadian colonies and thereby unite colonial North America under a U.S. government. In the end, expansion went westward, not northward.

As the century unfolded, the United States began to emerge as a growing force in the community of nations. The vast wealth of raw materials and lands attracted immigration, fueled development, and stimulated a growing transatlantic trade. Industrialization gradually sprang up, especially in the northeastern region of the country. Railroads were being built to transport America's products to markets and its people to ever more distant places. It was a period of prosperity and optimism, at least for much of the Anglo and European part of America's population. Two major groups were not integrated into the newly emerging political, economic, and social structures – those of Native and those of African heritage. These exclusions festered like open sores, igniting wars and social justice concerns that stretched throughout the century and beyond.

During the early decades of the nineteenth century, a delicate balance was achieved between two rival cultures and economies in America – those of the North and those of the South. While the nation expanded westward, the institution of slavery increasingly emerged as the test over where a new state's loyalties would lie. Consequently, the moral question of slavery could no longer be ignored, and the Civil War broke out to decide the matter. These developments precipitated a division that would have lasting consequences on Baptist life in America.

The decade after the close of the Civil War has long been known as the Reconstruction Era. During that period, the Thirteenth, Fourteenth, and

Fifteenth Amendments to the U.S. Constitution were passed, outlawing slavery; guaranteeing citizenship to all born within U.S. territory; and granting the vote to all men, regardless of race. In response, the Ku Klux Klan – a white supremacist group – arose, using violence as a tactic for resisting black inclusion in political decision making in the South. The election of Rutherford B. Hayes ended Reconstruction and marked the South's reentry to the national political scene.

The Gilded Age is a label often used to designate the years 1876 to 1890. Dramatic expansion of industry brought unparalleled wealth to the U.S. economy, and especially to a few industrial barons. It also was characterized by unethical business practices, monopolies in commerce, and scandalous political dealings. Such behavior motivated legislation like the Interstate Commerce Act and the Sherman Antitrust Act in efforts to curb some of the abuses. It also led to the rise of the labor movement, amid frequent acts of violence. The American Baptist John D. Rockefeller built Standard Oil into one of the nation's largest corporations and utilized a portion of his wealth to benefit Baptist and other philanthropic causes. Another Baptist, Walter Rauschenbusch, however, strongly criticized the emerging industrial society for the way it abused the working classes. He developed the social gospel theology to expose and confront such corporate evil. Thus, Baptist leaders often found themselves trapped and confused amid the counter forces at work on multiple fronts in the rapidly changing world of late-nineteenth-century America.

Throughout the period, growing waves of immigration provided labor for industry and sped up settlement of the West. But immigration and industrialization also aggravated social injustice and created pockets of ethnic poverty. Moral decay stimulated efforts at reform. Labor laws, education reform, temperance movements, and the like sought to improve American society. Consequently, the decade between 1890 and 1918 is known as the Progressive Era – characterized by reform movements intended to protect society against the decay caused by industrial corruption and abuse. The century ended with the Spanish-American War and the 1898 Treaty of Paris, which recognized Cuba as an independent nation and made Puerto Rico, Guam, and the Philippines territories of the United States.

ANGLO-AMERICAN BAPTISTS ON THE U.S. FRONTIER

Anglo Baptists in America reflect the impact of the nation's major developmental events in their own stories. They began this period full of enthusiasm and optimism, having gained a more positive public image as a result of the stands they took favoring the Revolutionary cause, religious liberty, and the separation between church and civil government. They had grown from obscurity at the start of the eighteenth century into one of the largest families of denominations in America by the opening of the nineteenth century. The Second Great Awakening added to the number of Baptist churches, significantly increased their members, and expanded the geographical extent of their work. Between 1814 and 1832, they attained a significant degree of national unity and developed institutions to facilitate their foreign mission, home mission, and educational ministries.

But like the nation itself, in the nineteenth century, Baptists suffered repeated controversies, conflicts, and divisions that destroyed their earlier efforts at unity. Among the lesser controversies were those derived from the challenges of Unitarianism, experienced mostly by Baptists in New England; Mormonism, encountered mainly by Baptists on the American frontier; and membership in secret lodges (such as the Masons), which troubled scattered groups of Baptists throughout the East Coast states. But several other controversies produced major divisions within Baptist ranks, including the antimission movement, the Restoration movement of Alexander Campbell, the Landmark movement, and the antislavery movement. Each of the latter controversies resulted in serious schism and losses for the mainstream of the Baptist movement in America and significantly rewrote the future of Baptist life.

Early Organizational Frontiers

A milestone was achieved in American Baptist life with the inauguration of the General Missionary Convention of the Baptist Denomination in the United States for Foreign Missions, better known as the Triennial Convention. This body was established on May 18, 1814, to send "the glad tidings of Salvation to the Heathen, and to nations destitute of pure Gospel-light."[1] Ann and Adoniram Judson and Luther Rice became the catalysts for the founding of this institution when they decided to become Baptists while en route to their mission assignments in India as Congregational missionaries. Rice returned home to help raise support with the intention of returning to foreign mission service. His labor as an agent for Baptist mission support kept him from ever returning to India. Ann and Adoniram moved on to Burma (modern Myanmar), where they established American Baptists' first overseas mission work.

[1] *Minutes of the General Missionary Convention*, May 21, 1814, Archives, American Baptist Historical Society, Mercer University, Atlanta, Georgia.

While engaged in missionary promotion, Luther Rice developed a vision for what eventually became American Baptists' first nationwide organization. Almost from the beginning, Baptists differed over how to organize the work. Should they utilize a society approach that would promote multi-church ministries while maximizing local church independence, or should they use an associational plan that would give greater emphasis to a centralized administration? The U.S. Baptist historian H. Leon McBeth believes that regional differences played a major role in deciding the organizational preferences made by Baptists in the North and those in the South. He suggests that Baptists in the North were fiercely defensive of local church autonomy, held suspicions that any form of centralized organization could jeopardize that autonomy, and lived in a social climate that favored individualism. Baptists in the South, however, possessed a General Baptist strand in their heritage that favored a strong denominational identity, had been strongly influenced by the more centralized Philadelphia Association, lived in a social environment influenced by the plantation system that emphasized community, and had strong leaders who attracted large and widespread followings.[2] These two tendencies confronted each other for the first time in the organizational structures of the Triennial Convention. During its first twelve years, the convention tended toward an associational approach for its work, gradually encompassing foreign mission, home mission, educational, and publishing ministries at a centralized location in Washington, D.C. However, at the 1826 Triennial Convention, meeting leadership abruptly decided to change its approach. Two powerful Baptist personalities clashed over the matter: Luther Rice, who favored the associational approach, and Francis Wayland, who preferred the society method. Wayland's position emerged victorious. The Triennial Convention divested itself of home mission, educational, and publication ministries and concentrated exclusively on its foreign mission task. This difference revealed a fault line in the mainstream of early-nineteenth-century American Baptist life and may have been the beginning of the division between Baptists of the North and those of the South. It might also offer an import insight into the reason the two communities of Baptists were never able to reunite after the Civil War, even though most other divided denominations succeeded in doing so.

New Theological Frontiers

The Baptist historian Walter B. Shurden in *Not a Silent People* approaches the question of Baptist identity from the perspective of the controversies

---

[2] Leon H. McBeth, *The Baptist Heritage: Four Centuries of Baptist Witness* (Nashville, TN: B&H Publishing Group, 1987), 349–50.

that have significantly marked their histories. He suggests that Baptist identity has been notably shaped by the theological battles Baptists have fought, usually with multiple streams of identity flowing out of each conflict.[3] Although Shurden's applications deal specifically with Southern Baptist history, the principle he advances is applicable to the larger experience of Baptists in America during the nineteenth century. Over that period, four major controversies proved especially formative in shaping the American Baptist landscape.

The Antimission Controversy
One factor that contributed to Baptists' rapid growth on America's western frontier in the mid-nineteenth century was the farmer-preacher. These preachers were not theologically trained but gained their status as ministers through congregations that recognized their having the gift of preaching. Their immediate availability, close identity with the people, and ability to survive the hardships of life on the frontier offered certain advantages for Baptist churches. At the same time, the world of these preachers was very different from that of Baptists in the more settled East. Creating institutions to extend the ministry of a local church into foreign lands seemed to carry the threat of emerging denominational machinery, something frontier preachers tended to associate with a pope. Strong reactions erupted producing the so-called antimission movement, which began about 1819 – only five years after creation of the Triennial Convention.

Although the antimission movement had many leaders, three stand out as having particular importance – John Taylor, Joshua Lawrence, and Daniel Parker. John Taylor, though not formally educated, did possess great natural eloquence in his preaching. This made him a very convincing personality on the frontier (at that time extending from the Appalachian Mountains to barely west of the Mississippi River). In 1819, he wrote *Thoughts on Missions*, in which he charged that the principal motives of Rice and other agents of the Triennial Convention were to enrich themselves. Questions over how the money collected would be used, fears that a hierarchical structure was developing in the convention, and suspicions that Rice and other agents were only in it for the money continued to feed the movement. Joshua Lawrence became a noted antimission leader in the western regions of North Carolina and Georgia and the northern portion of Alabama. He so turned the Kehuckee Association of North

---

[3] Walter B. Shurden, *Not a Silent People: Controversies That Have Shaped Southern Baptists* (Macon, GA: Smyth & Helwys Publishing, 1995).

Carolina against mission organizations that the term *Kehuckeeism* became synonymous with antimissions. Some of his followers declared that mission society agents like Luther Rice "are ready to rob the poor, drain the coffers of the rich, and are the most dangerous robbers and murders, and ever ready to cut throats. . . . They have been, are now, and ever will be a curse to the church of God and the nations of the earth."

Daniel Parker first opposed the Triennial Convention's mission work in 1815, saying that its efforts reflected Arminianism and were contrary to the gospel. He condemned mission societies, theological seminaries, benevolent organizations, and Bible societies. In 1820, he published a thirty-eight-page pamphlet strongly attacking denominational newspapers, as well as religious tracts and books. In 1826, he published two pamphlets based on Genesis 3:15, the first titled "Views of the Two Seeds" and the second "The Second Dose of the Two Seeds." In those works, he presented his two-seed-in-the-Spirit predestinarian views. The churches organized in association with his movement became known as the Two Seeds in the Spirit Predestinarian Baptists.

The antimission movement spread rapidly among Baptists in the frontier regions that were undergoing settlement during the 1820s through 1840s. The Primitive Baptist family of churches is among the heirs of this tradition. Since the mid-nineteenth century, they have variously been called Ancient Baptists, Old School Baptists, Primitive Baptists, Predestinarian Baptists, Original Baptists, Antimissionary Baptists, and sometimes derisively Hardshell Baptists.

The Restoration Movement Controversy

The Restoration movement was an outgrowth of the work of a father and son ministry team – Thomas and Alexander Campbell. In 1807, Thomas immigrated to America from Ireland for health reasons. Having experienced difficulties with the narrowness of the Presbyterian church in which he had ministered in Pennsylvania, he withdrew and organized the Christian Association of Washington, Pennsylvania. He soon adopted a principal that became the watchword for his movement: "Where the Scripture speaks we speak, where the Scripture is silent we are silent."[4]

In 1809, Alexander joined his father in the United States. As a student in Scotland, he had been greatly influenced by the views of John Glas and Robert Sandeman, by John Locke's theory of knowledge, and by

---

[4] Robert Richardson, *Memoirs of Alexander Campbell* (Indianapolis, IN: Religious Book Service, 1897), 1:231.

Francis Bacon's inductive method of reasoning. In October 1810, Alexander and Thomas sought acceptance into the Presbyterian synod of Pittsburgh. When they were refused, they formed the Bush Run Church and ordained Alexander a pastor. A few months afterward, Campbell began conversations with Baptists concerning possible affiliation with them. But from the beginning, this relationship had problems. Alexander and his congregation held strong convictions against any doctrinal creed (including confessions of faith) outside the Bible itself and against any ecclesiastical authority beyond the local church. In 1813, after having refused to affiliate with the Philadelphia Baptist Association, Campbell's congregation was accepted into the Redstone Baptist Association of Pennsylvania.

Over the following decade, however, questions developed among many Baptists concerning several of Campbell's theological views. Most troublesome were his interpretations of the nature of saving faith, the meaning of baptism, the frequency of celebrating the Lord's Supper, rejection of organizations beyond the local church, and ordination. Those differences became more apparent between 1823 and 1830, when he served as editor of a paper titled the *Christian Baptist*, where his ideas came to be more widely disseminated. During this period, numerous Baptists embraced Campbell's position, and as he gradually moved away from his Baptist affiliation, they followed. In 1829, Campbell severed his Baptist connections to launch his own Reformer movement. In 1832, the Christian churches associated with Barton W. Stone's movement and the Disciples churches associated with Alexander Campbell united into one fellowship. By 1840, Campbell was in open conflict with Baptists, and the two movements began to divide. In the aftermath of this division, numerous Baptist churches in the frontier regions of the American Midwest experienced major loss of membership. In some areas, half of their members aligned themselves with Campbell's movement. This bitter experience forced Baptists to give more careful attention to some of their beliefs and practices. One particularly influential attempt to establish Baptist identity more clearly came through the Baptist Landmark movement.

The Baptist Landmark Controversy

During the nineteenth century, many denominations in America confronted questions of religious authority – on what basis could their church claim to be the true church? In part, this was a product of disestablishment and was aggravated in the United States through the arrival of large numbers of immigrants with a wide variety of religious positions. Consequently, an attitude of competition and hostility developed among denominations, especially on the American frontier. The Baptist Landmark movement was born in this environment and was strongly characterized by the search for a Baptist identity capable of answering those concerns.

In 1834, James R. Graves left the Congregational Church to become a Baptist, and from the start encountered conflicting notions of Baptist belief and practice. Among the influences that shaped his concept of Baptist identity were the controversies between Baptists and pedo-Baptists over infant baptism, the New Hampshire Confession of Faith of 1833, and the views of Francis Wayland, a strong defender of the absolute autonomy of the local church. Conflicts surrounding the Restoration movement also made a powerful impact on Graves. The legacy of bitter struggle between Baptists and those who left the Baptist church to follow Alexander Campbell convinced Graves of the importance of being absolutely faithful to one's group.[5]

Baptist Landmarkism took its name from two verses in the Old Testament – Proverbs 22:28, "Do not remove the ancient landmark that your ancestors set up," and Job 24:2, "The wicked remove landmarks." Both texts refer to the ancient property markers that set the boundaries of ancestral lands. To move a landmark was the worst sort of crime in that world. J. R. Graves became convinced that the landmarks of Baptist faith also had been moved as persons had diminished their commitment to ancient Baptist beliefs, and he determined to reset them. He was assisted in this effort by two other committed Landmark leaders, J. M. Pendleton and A. C. Dayton.

The seeds of the Landmark movement seem to have been planted around 1832, when Graves became concerned about questions related to baptism. The issue was raised for him when he observed a pedo-baptism minister employ several different modes of baptism during a single worship service. Graves seriously studied the practice and concluded that only Baptist immersion constituted valid baptism. The topic surfaced in earnest after Graves became editor of the *Tennessee Baptist* in 1846. He first became involved in an open conflict with John L. Walker, editor of the *Western Baptist Review*, and Richard B. Burleson of Alabama. The conflict surrounded the validity of a baptism performed by a pastor who had not been immersed. Graves supported a position that was the same in essence as baptismal succession. Burleson argued strongly that the faith of the person baptized was of greater importance than the qualifications of the person performing the baptism. Graves strongly disagreed and insisted on the necessity of baptismal successionism. In substance this was the ancient

[5] James E. Tull, *Shapers of Baptist Thought* (Valley Forge, PA: Judson Press, 1972), 129–51.

Donatist controversy reborn. The newspaper debates led to a meeting of Graves's supporters at Cotton Grove, Tennessee, on June 24, 1851, when the Cotton Grove Resolutions were developed. These declarations present the earliest organized expressions of Landmark views and offer the first clues that a denominational division was in the making.

Conflicts between Graves and R. B. C. Howell, pastor of the church Graves attended in Nashville, elevated the debate among Baptists throughout the American South. However, messengers at the 1859 meeting of the Southern Baptist Convention voted a series of resolutions that systematically dealt Landmarkism a crushing defeat within the convention. From that point, adherents of Landmark Baptist theology gradually withdrew to form their own churches and associations and create an independent Landmark Baptist tradition.

Several characteristics distinguished Landmarkism. One was its belief that the Baptist Church was the only true church. Because only the Baptist Church was an authentically biblical church, all other so-called churches were merely human societies. This meant that only ordinances performed by this true church were valid. All other rites were simply rituals performed by leaders of religious societies. The Lord's Supper could correctly be administered only to members of the local congregation (closed communion). Pastors of other denominations could not be true pastors because their churches were not true churches. Therefore, such pastors should never be allowed to preach or speak from Baptist pulpits. Landmarkism also placed great emphasis on Baptist secessionism. Generally, Landmark leaders supported the view that Baptists began with John the Baptist and could be traced in an unbroken chain from New Testament times to the present. Landmarkism also held that the local church was the only true expression of biblical church activity, meaning that any ecclesial organization outside of the church usurps its authority and should thus not be allowed to exist. Hence, Graves was against mission societies, boards, or any other extrachurch organizations. This did not mean he opposed mission activity, but such work was to be directly under the authority of a local church.

The Antislavery Controversy

The most divisive controversy American Baptists suffered in the nineteenth century was the antislavery controversy. This produced a division that set the tone for much of subsequent Anglo-American Baptist work. As the nineteenth century progressed, a serious problem emerged between the northern and southern regions of United States, known as sectionalism or regionalism. The source of this territorialism was essentially economic and political. The southern regions of United States had an agricultural economy. The northern states had a more industrial economy. Each region sought federal laws and policies that would favor the economic interests of that region. Unfortunately, the needs of one region would prove to be antithetical to the needs of the other region.

In 1832, the American Baptist Home Mission Society was organized, with one of its major goals being the evangelization of the West. This objective became increasingly fraught with political pitfalls, however, because of divisions over the institution of slavery. In an effort to maintain a balance of power between the North and South, each time a territory became a new state, a battle erupted in the U.S. Congress and within the affected territories over whether the new state would be slave or free. In reality, slavery had been a moral issue since the early days of American colonization. But in the mid-nineteenth century, it also became the touchstone for political struggles between North and South. With so much political tension between the two regions, it was inevitable that Baptists would at some point reflect that division as well.

In an effort to avoid division, the Triennial Convention decided to remain neutral on the subject of slavery. However, in 1833, the English Parliament adopted a law to end slavery in all British-controlled territories by the year 1838. Baptists in England had been very involved in the struggle to pass this law and felt an obligation to urge Baptists in America to join them in the abolition crusade. In December 1833, a group of English Baptist pastors sent a correspondence to Baptist leaders of the Triennial Convention describing the victory of their emancipation movement. In the letter, they urged Baptists in America to take up the campaign to abolish slavery in their nation as well. For the sake of unity, leaders of the Triennial Convention attempted to avoid addressing the issue, fearing it would alienate their Southern constituents and cause a schism among American Baptist churches. However, a few Baptist leaders in America held such strong feelings against slavery they could not accept nor abide by the convention's neutrality. In May 1835, a group of ministers met in Boston and formulated a letter of response to the English pastors' correspondence. In April 1840, the American Baptist Anti-Slavery Convention was formed. On May 4, 1843, a group of Baptist abolitionists refused to continue participating in the American Baptist Foreign Mission Society. They formed the American and Foreign Mission Society, also known as the American Baptist Free Mission Society, which refused to appoint slaveholders as missionaries.

The American Baptist Home Mission Society, like the foreign mission society, also tried to follow a policy of neutrality. However, it appeared to Baptists in the South that the society was actually not appointing missionaries who were slaveholders. In August 1844, the Executive Committee of the Georgia Baptist Convention recommended James E. Reeve to the Home Mission Society for missionary appointment. The committee specifically mentioned the fact that Reeve was a slaveholder. The executive committee of the Home Mission Society refused to consider the application on the grounds that it was a test case and not a serious application. In November 1844, the Baptist General Convention of Alabama sent a resolution to the Triennial Convention asking for a statement to the effect that slaveholders had equal rights with nonslaveholders in being appointed as missionaries. In December 1844, the Executive Committee responded that if anyone, being a slaveholder, presented himself for missionary appointment and insisted on keeping his slaves, then he could not be appointed as a missionary. In response, 327 delegates from several states in the South met in Augusta, Georgia, on May 8, 1845, to consider a possible course of action. After discussion, they determined to form a new Baptist convention separate from that of the North. This decision gave birth to the Southern Baptist Convention.

The formation of the Southern Baptist Convention did not seem particularly noteworthy to most Baptists in 1845. Many interpreted the action simply as the creation of one more foreign mission society. Adoniram Judson even wrote a letter congratulating the convention's leaders for founding an additional mission-support organization. However, the separation of the Southern Baptist Convention from American Baptists would prove a permanent schism and the beginning of an entirely new Baptist denomination.

Northern Baptist Frontiers

During the second half of the nineteenth century, Baptists in the American North faced the challenge of ministering in a rapidly changing context that included massive European immigration, growing religious and ethnic diversity, the rise of an industrial and urbanized society, a rapidly growing population in the West, and assistance to the educational efforts of African American Baptists in the South. Consequently, they often developed different approaches to ministry than those employed by Baptists in the South. They struggled with different emphases in theology, as was reflected in the social gospel movement. Baptists in the South were confronted with the demands of ministry amid postwar devastation. Political turmoil, an economy in shambles, sharecropping, and poor health care were but a few of the pressing needs they faced. By the dawn of the twentieth century, regionalism, bitterness over the Civil War, and differing theological emphases had caused a wide gulf to develop between Baptists in the American North and those in the South.

Work among northern Baptists was coordinated under the ministries of four societies by the end of the nineteenth century: the American Baptist Missionary Union, the American Baptist Home Mission Society, the American Baptist Publication Society, and the American Baptist Education Society.

Following the schism of 1845, the Triennial Convention changed its name to the American Baptist Missionary Union. The schism between Baptists in the North and those in the South had little effect on the union, as receipts actually grew between 1845 and 1851 and surpassed $500,000 (equivalent to about $128 million in 2008 dollars) by 1900. By that time, the union employed more than 474 missionaries. American Baptists had ninety-four mission stations in seven regions of the world: Burma, Assam, South India, China, Japan, Africa, and the Philippines. American Baptist mission work experienced particular success among the Karens of Burma, the Assam tribes of Northeast India, the Telugus in India, and among tribal groups in the Belgian Congo. In the latter half of the nineteenth century, Baptist women became concerned about their involvement in mission. Reluctance on the part of the union's leadership to appoint single women as missionaries resulted in the creation of three women's foreign missionary societies: the Woman's Baptist Foreign Mission Society (Boston, 1871), the Woman's Baptist Missionary Society of the West (Chicago, 1871), and the Woman's Baptist Foreign Mission Society of the Pacific Coast (San Francisco, 1874).

The American Baptist Publication Society developed out of the former American Baptist Tract Society. The society's purpose was "to promote evangelical religion by means of the Bible, printing press, colportage, and the Sunday school."[6] Among the major accomplishments of the American Baptist Publication Society in the latter half of the nineteenth century was formation of new Sunday schools, adoption of a uniform lesson plan, employment of colporteur missionaries to promote and sell its literature,

---

[6] *The Work of the American Baptist Publication Society Defined* (Philadelphia: American Baptist Publication Society, 1879), preface.

Bible distribution, chapel car work (specially equipped Pullman cars outfitted as chapels transported by train to new communities to serve as centers for starting new Baptist churches), colportage wagons, and gospel cruises. In the latter half of the nineteenth century, tensions developed between the American Baptist Publication Society and the American Baptist Home Mission Society concerning the overlapping dimensions of their work. In 1899, the former agreed to concentrate more in the areas of literature and Sunday schools, leaving church development work to the Home Mission Society. During the final years of the nineteenth century, serious conflicts arose between leaders of the American Baptist Publication Society and the Southern Baptist Sunday School Board, resulting in the society's loss of the Southern market.

The American Baptist Home Mission Society faced difficulties in gaining support from Baptist churches during the first half of the nineteenth century. However, European immigration, the spiritual needs of Southern black freedman, explosive population growth in the West, and the capable leadership of Henry L. Morehouse elicited greater favor for the society's work. By 1900, after sixty-eight years of work, the Home Mission Society recorded 24,242 home missionaries, more than 2 million sermons preached, 163,361 baptized converts, and 5,387 church starts. Other work directed by the society included constructing new churches, assisting freed slaves in establishing a new life, organizing and supporting black Baptist colleges, and ministering to immigrant groups.

The American Baptist Education Society was formed in 1888 to help coordinate the highly local and scattered Baptist educational endeavors. In the year of its creation, Baptists in the North had twenty-five academies, nineteen colleges, and five seminaries. In 1890, the society was instrumental in founding the University of Chicago.

Southern Baptist Frontiers

During the nineteenth century, Southern Baptists had three organizations to carry out their denomination-wide ministries: the Foreign Mission Board, the Home Mission Board, and the Sunday School Board. The Foreign Mission Board was Southern Baptists' strongest institution, and in the early years, it functionally was the convention. At the close of the nineteenth century, the Foreign Mission Board had missionaries serving in China, Africa, Italy, Mexico, Brazil, and Japan.

The Home Mission Board (HMB) faced major challenges from the moment of its creation. In 1874, following several name changes and shifting work assignments, the Home Mission Board assumed the name by which it would be known through much of the twentieth century. A crisis of leadership was among the greatest challenges the HMB faced in the nineteenth century, which was finally resolved when Isaac T. Tichenor became corresponding secretary in 1882. He is credited with bringing new energy, vision, creativity, and a highly developed sense of denominational unity to the organization. Other problems the HMB was forced to confront included the local focus of most Southern Baptist churches, lack of funds, opposition from the antimission movement, and the disruptions of the Civil War.

In the 1880s, Henry L. Morehouse of the Northern Home Mission Society and I. T. Tichenor of the Southern Home Mission Board collided over mission work in the South. Morehouse cherished the national scope of the Home Mission Society's work and saw no reason for withdrawing from the South. Tichenor held and transmitted to others a strong sense of loyalty to the Southern Baptist Convention. Conflict broke out between the two organizations in 1892 when E. T. Winkler, president of the Home Mission Board, wrote an article challenging the right of the Home Mission Society to work in the South. After considerable disagreement, a series of accords was worked out between the two organizations establishing the bases for relationship. Popularly known as the Comity Agreements, the two agencies agreed on three points: the Southern Home Mission Board would create advisory committees to work with the Northern Home Mission Society in governing black colleges, the two organizations would cooperate in mission work among African Americans and in sponsoring ministers' and deacons' institutes, and there would be territorial limits – the Northern society would not continue its work in the South. In the end, the agreement recognized the territorial limits that the Home Mission Board had long sought.

After four unsuccessful attempts, in 1891, Southern Baptists established a permanent publication organization. Long-standing tensions between the American Baptist Publication Society and the Southern Baptist Sunday School Board erupted in 1896. By 1897, the Sunday School Board of the Southern Baptist Convention had succeeded in gaining the support of most Southern Baptists. Its publications became an important source for establishing a strong denominational loyalty among the Southern Baptist constituency.

As did Baptists in the North, Baptists in the South established colleges and other educational institutions during the nineteenth century. Although many of the Baptists in the region had long-held traditions against the corrupting nature of education, especially for the ministry, the growing number of educated pastors who made a positive impression as spiritual leaders helped Baptists begin to overcome their fear.

Frontiers for Other U.S. Baptist Bodies

In addition to the two large Anglo-American Baptist denominations, many other Baptist bodies also flourished during the nineteenth century. These included several families of Baptists designated by particularities of theology, practice, ethnicity, or nationality. The following are a few representative groups.

General Baptists

Unconnected to the seventeenth-century General Baptist movement, numerous General Baptist churches appeared in the American Midwest in the nineteenth century. They are the fruit of a movement begun in 1823 by Benoni Stinson at Evansville, Illinois. In 1824, four Baptist churches united around their affirmation of Christ's general atonement and organized the Liberty Association of General Baptists. The movement continued to spread, and in 1870, a national union called the General Association of General Baptists was formed. The Home Mission Board was organized in 1871, Oakland City College in 1891, and the Foreign Mission Board in 1903.

Free Will Baptists

Two major groupings of Free Will (or Free) Baptists existed in North America during the frontier phase of Baptist development – a Northern grouping derived from Benjamin Randal's pioneer ministries in the eighteenth century and a Southern grouping derived largely from North Carolina General Baptists. All are characterized by the emphasis they placed on free grace, free choice, and free communion. Randal's Free Will Baptists continued to unite in cooperative association in the nineteenth century, creating the General Conference in 1827 and other single ministry voluntary associations, such as the Free Will Baptist Foreign Mission Society (1832), the Free Will Baptist Home Mission Society (1834), and the Free Will Baptist Education Society (1840). Free Will Baptists in the North united with the Free Communion Baptists (mostly located in upstate New York) in 1841 to form the Free Baptist denomination. Across the border, Canadian Free Will Baptists organized the Free Christian Baptist Conference in 1836.

These two Free Will Baptist bodies continued in fellowship with the New Connection of General Baptists through much of the century. The basic Arminian-oriented convictions of each provided the theological glue that held them together.

The Southern or Original Free Will Baptists were challenged by major theological struggles during the nineteenth century and lost many of their churches to Alexander Campbell's Restoration movement. Perhaps for those reasons, they took a more conservative turn and embraced a stricter code of conduct. By the close of the century, they were characterized as "Arminian and conservative in theology, severe in lifestyle, revivalistic, mission-minded . . . , somewhat anti-intellectual, fearful of alliances with other movements, and predominantly rural."[7]

Seventh Day Baptists

Four values informed Seventh Day Baptist development during the nineteenth century: missions, education, ecumenics, and civic duty. Similar in nature to the concerns discussed earlier in connection with Baptists in the North, Seventh Day Baptists strongly valued local church autonomy. Consequently, they also chose independent societies as their approach for implementing missions, publication, and educational ministries. The General Conference of Seventh Day Baptist Churches was formed in 1802 to serve as the central coordinating agency of independent local churches. Several missionary societies assisted pastors in itinerant preaching tours intended to win converts and start churches. The Seventh Day Baptist Missionary Society was organized in 1843 and sent its first missionaries to China in 1847. They maintained medical and educational ministries there until the mid-twentieth century. The importance placed on an enlightened conscience led them to form the Education Society and establish colleges at Alfred, New York; Milton, Wisconsin; and Salem, West Virginia; and a seminary at Alfred.

Distinctives of Frontier-Era Anglo-American Baptist Identity

Anglo-American Baptists shared significantly in the ideals and experiences of the dominant culture of the United States during the nineteenth century.

---

[7] William F. Davidson, "Free Will Baptists," in *Baptists around the World* (Nashville, TN: Broadman & Holman Publishers, 1995), 425.

That reality helped generate the energy, opportunity, and means for accomplishing their far-reaching visions of ministry and growth. Their values of spiritual freedom, personal religious experience, separation of church and civil government, and free church decision making fit well with those of the culture in general at the time. For many Europeans, becoming Baptist did not require a negation of one's cultural identity. Being Baptist and white American often fit easily together. Such was not always the case with South European immigrant groups of Roman Catholic heritage, nor was it the case for Native or African Americans.

In general, Anglo-American Baptists were successful in organizing, developing, and extending their work, especially among other Anglo portions of the population. Of the challenges they faced, the greatest seem to have been internal ones – disagreements and schisms that arose from within their own ranks. Four core sources might be identified as the cause for most of those divisions: theological differences, methodological preferences, cultural identity, and matters of polity. Of the three major groupings of Baptists entering the nineteenth century – Calvinistically oriented (Regular or Separate) Baptists, Arminian oriented (Free Will and General) Baptists, and Seventh Day Baptists – the group that grew and expanded with greatest success (Calvinistically oriented Baptists) was also the group that divided the most. During the course of the frontier phase of Baptist history, Calvinistically oriented Anglo-American Baptists generated three major new families of Baptists: Primitive Baptists, Landmark Baptists, and Southern Baptists. In its own way, each of those denominations reflected the concerns, values, and identity issues of a particular segment of the American religious and cultural landscape. The intersection of Baptist views with other segments of that vista must now be addressed.

BAPTIST FRONTIERS IN NATIVE AMERICAN LIFE AND CULTURE

Notions of the frontier era hold a very different connotation for the Anglo-American than for the Native American. The Anglo tends to view the period as one of conquest, progress, settlement, and taming. The Native tends to experience it as a period of humiliation, destruction, confusion, and loss. Unfortunately, Baptist history has not generally acknowledged this two-sided aspect of the same set of events with resulting differences in theological outlook. Evolving nationhood accelerated the degree of interaction between the Anglo and Native cultures, and power was clearly in the hands of the former. Consequently, the policies that would determine the outcome of this interaction rested mostly in the hands of the agents of Anglo-American culture. In general, one of three options was considered: extermination, removal, or assimilation.

Some Anglo Americans favored extermination, and instances can be found when this policy was employed. However, in general, that approach could not withstand public opposition, even in the nineteenth century.

As a national policy, removal was preferred. Policy makers believed the differences between the Anglo and Native cultures were too great for assimilation to work, and after all, an unlimited supply of "empty" land was available out west. The two cultures could simply be segregated into two separate worlds. This would not be the last instance of a national policy developed on the basis of faulty information. First, the designated lands were not empty. Tribal resettlements usually meant other tribes inhabiting the empty lands had to be displaced, thus generating ongoing intertribal tensions. Second, a transplanted tribe's culture and theology had been developed in relation to a specific geographical context. Removal to a different region usually meant the old customs became ineffective for dealing with the new situation. Also, the policies did not account for the magnitude of Anglo immigration that quickly pushed beyond the intended cultural boundaries. In addition, broken treaties, dishonest administrators, and unenforced laws repeatedly deprived Native populations of needed and promised cultural space.[8]

Some Anglo-American Baptists, especially missionaries, defended the reservation system at first, believing it to be the only protection Indians had against the European onslaught. As the century progressed, however, many missionaries concluded that the removal policy was not working and that assimilation was necessary. This meant Native peoples would need to adopt Anglo culture – the Indian would have to become "white" to become acceptable. Even the most sympathetic missionaries believed themselves to be doing the right thing by "civilizing" Indians through a process of compulsive assimilation into Anglo Christian culture. This strategy was translated into a national plan under President Grant's peace policy of 1869, which gave several Protestant denominations major control over Indian reservations for purposes of "civilization." Baptists were among the major participants in the program and consequently became recipients of the significant criticism and condemnation offered by later generations who more clearly recognized the cultural arrogance involved in the assimilation projects. The plan did not succeed for a variety of reasons, a major one

---

[8] Susan Hill Lindley, *You Have Stepped Out of Your Place: A History of Women and Religion in America* (Louisville, KY: Westminster John Knox Press, 1996), 160.

being denominational rivalries. In 1887, Grant's policy was replaced with
the Dawes Act, which gave each Indian an allotment of land. The ultimate
result, however, was a major additional loss of Indian lands.

Over the course of the nineteenth century, individuals from several
Anglo Baptist traditions committed themselves to missionary work among
Amerindian peoples. Isaac McCoy is representative of this effort. In 1817, he
was appointed by the Triennial Convention to establish a Baptist mission
among the Indians near Fort Wayne, Indiana. There he was assisted by
Johnston Lykins in ministries among the Wea, Miami, and Kickapoo
tribes. Convinced the work would be more successful if it were isolated
from the influence of white settlers, he relocated among the Potawatomi
and opened the Carey School in 1823. In 1826, a second mission station
was opened near Grand Rapids, Michigan. This work was uprooted when
those tribes were forced to resettle further west.

McCoy and Lykins moved to the region of Kansas City on the Missouri-
Kansas border in July 1829. Lykins promptly established the Shawnee
Mission and began his teaching and publishing ministries among the
Indian tribes in that territory. In 1830, McCoy became an agent of the
U.S. government responsible for "general Indian improvement." Twelve
years later, he helped create the American Indian Mission Association in
Louisville, Kentucky, an organization dedicated to evangelizing and minis-
tering among Native peoples. He became the first agent of the association,
serving from 1842 to 1846.[9]

Other representative missionaries illustrate the geographical expanse
and tribal variety of Baptist work during the nineteenth century. Elkanah Holmes worked among the Mohegans in upstate New York during
the late 1790s, establishing a Baptist church in Brothertown. Lee Com-
pere ministered among the Creeks in Georgia between 1819 and 1829.
Humphrey Posey began several schools near Andrews, North Carolina, and
Evan Jones became superintendent of the Valley Towns Mission, which
Posey had started. When the North Carolina Cherokees were forced to
relocate to Indian Territory, Jones accompanied them. Almon C. Bacone
initiated widely recognized educational programs among the Cherokees
near Muskogee, Oklahoma, especially Indian University (later renamed
Bacone College). Munday Durant, a free black, became one of the first
Baptists to serve among the Seminoles in Indian Territory. Later, Joseph

---

[9] See Isaac McCoy, *History of Baptist Indian Missions* (New York: H. and S. Raynor, 1840), reprint
(Springfield, MO: Particular Baptist Press, 2003).

Samuel Murrow, an Anglo, organized Ash Creek Baptist Church, one of the earliest Seminole Baptist churches.[10] Samuel Gorman served as a missionary to the Laguna and Navajo in New Mexico between 1852 and 1866. In many instances, the missionary's work focused around establishing an Indian school and launching an accompanying Baptist church.

In the mid-nineteenth century, "civilization" for Anglo Baptists usually meant Protestant Christianity, for which the Bible was central. Reading the Bible required literacy, which made schools important. Schools implied social, economic, and political systems that could maintain them and thus civilization. The preferred kinds of schools were boarding schools, where young Indians could be removed from the "harmful influences of tribe and parents" and have their values and character shaped while learning how to read, write, do math, and make a living.[11] In the process, children were forced into Anglo cultural roles, regardless of the prior cultural understanding held by their tribe. In addition to the Christian faith, boys learned to be farmers and girls to be good homemakers.

As Anglo Baptist missionaries experienced success in their work, Native Baptist leaders soon emerged from within the tribes to carry the work forward. This was not always easy, however. James Factor – thought to be the first Seminole to become Baptist – was deprived of his position on the Seminole council because he had been bewitched by the Baptist missionary. His conversion was perceived by tribal leaders as a threat to the loyalty of its members. Only after disruption of traditional tribal leadership and customs could Christianity begin to make inroads among the Seminoles. The conversion of the Seminole principal chief John Jumper became the real key to Baptist success.

Jumper embraced Christianity as a result of Presbyterian mission work in 1857. However, three years later, he decided to become Baptist for reasons that related to divisions among denominational bodies caused by the Civil War and to Baptists' heavier utilization of Native preachers. This proved to be a milestone in the development of Baptist work among the Seminoles. A charismatic personality and effectiveness as a preacher led to his ordination in 1865. Morris Grimes described Jumper as "zealous for Christ, and . . . the chief prop of the Baptist church among the Seminoles."[12] Around 1860,

---

[10] See Jack M. Schultz, *The Seminole Baptist Churches of Oklahoma: Maintaining a Traditional Community, The Civilization of the American Indian* (Norman: University of Oklahoma Press, 1999).
[11] Lindley, *Women and Religion*, 157.
[12] Morris W. Grimes, "Annual Report of the Board of Indian Commissioners, of Indian Affairs to the Secretary of the Department of the Interior," 1869, 39.

Jumper spearheaded the organization of Spring Church, a congregation that continues in the Baptist tradition to this day.

Numerous other Native Baptist leaders played decisive roles in the expansion of this work over the course of this period. Unfortunately, only a few representative leaders can be mentioned here. David Fowler, an Indian Baptist, became a deacon and leader over the work initiated by Elkanah Holmes in New York. John Davis was probably the first Creek Indian to be ordained as a Baptist pastor. Encouraged in his ministry by missionary David Lewis, Davis established an especially fruitful pastorate at Ebenezer Baptist Church near Muskogee, Oklahoma. The Baptist Cherokee chief Jesse Bushyhead assisted the ministry of Evan Jones, a work that resulted in several hundred conversions. Peter Folsom, an Oklahoma Choctaw, started ministering among the Choctaws of Mississippi in 1878. He organized Mount Zion Baptist Church (the first Choctaw Baptist church) later that same year. Two years later, Hopewell Baptist Church was organized, followed by Macedonia Baptist Church in 1891.

Distinctives of Frontier-Era Native American Baptist Identity

By the end of the nineteenth century, Native Baptists and Anglo American missionaries had organized dozens of churches and several associations among tribes that were still suffering the turmoil of relocation and the loss of a long-established way of life. These conditions furnished the harsh context in which Native Baptist traditions took root. Baptist understandings of God and God's activity in the world had appealed to some Indians, and indigenous pastors and missionaries quickly emerged. Some Amerindians may well have imagined life would be less complicated after embracing this new faith. Most found that not to be the case. For many, conversion proved the beginning of the identity conflicts already described. Anglo-American Baptist missionaries were prepared to introduce the rudiments of Baptist beliefs, and they were skilled in supplying the trappings of Anglo civilization, but most could do nothing to help Native peoples inculturate anglicized versions of Baptist thought and practice into their own cultural worlds. That task would remain the ongoing challenge for future generations of Native American Baptists.

FRONTIERS OF AFRICAN AMERICAN BAPTIST LIFE AND CULTURE

The nineteenth-century frontiers most daunting for African American Baptists were not primarily geographical in nature but social, political, and attitudinal. The first great frontier they faced was slavery, which abolition, emancipation, and a civil war helped eliminate. But the end of slavery revealed a far more sinister frontier – racism. Distinctive challenges meant that, during that period, black Baptist traditions were shaped by different theological foci than were Anglo-American Baptist traditions. Issues of local church autonomy, liberty of conscience, and the separation of church and state were far less important to black congregations than were matters of human dignity, oppression, and survival. Even in regions where slavery did not exist, racial discrimination often persisted. Under those conditions, black Baptist churches developed unique characteristics.

The First Great Awakening in the eighteenth century was the occasion that stimulated large numbers of free African Americans to embrace Baptist traditions. However, with a few exceptions, the slave population remained largely untouched at that time. Not until the first half of the nineteenth century did substantial numbers of slaves become Baptist. Intentional efforts, sometimes referred to as plantation missions, were the main source for this growth. Following the Second Great Awakening, plantation owners increasingly were harassed by church leaders, pressuring them to fulfill their Christian obligation to convert the heathen. The oftentimes-reluctant slave owners gave in to the arguments and allowed the evangelization of their slaves. However, even the evangelists themselves tended to resist social reforms. Anglo Baptist church leaders were keener to preach "slaves obey your masters" (Ephesians 6:5) and to emphasize the freedom to be gained in heaven after death rather than the message that in Christ "there is . . . neither slave nor free . . . for you are all one" (Galatians 3:28).

Despite efforts to edit the version of Christianity that was offered the slaves and to keep them from reading the Bible for themselves, blacks found in Christianity something very different from what was presented to them. As had happened among the Hebrews in Egypt and among the early Christians in Rome, this Abrahamic faith tradition encouraged hope, dignity, and willingness to take risks. A so-called invisible institution emerged – a secret religion of the slave populations that was distinctive in its practices and theology. Many blacks found Baptist traditions readily adaptable to the autonomous and informal communities of faith they formed. In those gatherings, Exodus, not Galatians, became the favored text.

After emancipation, African American Baptists continued to suffer under the nearly universal assumption by whites that they were culturally, educationally, and religiously inferior. In spite of that, increasing numbers of African Americans adopted the Christian faith. Through their churches, black Baptists received the Bible's countercultural message challenging assumptions of their inferiority. Against overwhelming odds, they began to establish churches and related institutions capable of addressing the needs of their community that were either denied or left unattended by Anglo-American Baptist churches. Black Baptists' success in these ventures provides the entire Baptist family a lesson – that there is an elemental core within Christianity itself, which was not created or controlled by Anglo-American Baptists or any other human beings and that is as accessible to blacks as to whites.[13] Above all else, they appropriated the Baptist theological traditions' emphasis on a personal experience of God's grace. Sharing that experience was more important than ecclesiastical or social structures and served as an uncomfortable reminder to Baptist racists that in God they were one. Perhaps it was their emphasis on this shared experience that made Separate Baptists surprisingly egalitarian in their early years.

With the increasing appeal of revivalistic religion in the early nineteenth century, itinerant preaching by Baptists expanded. Consequently, larger numbers of black Baptist preachers emerged, augmenting the practice of blacks preaching their own understanding of the Christian message to black hearers. With this, the number of African American Baptist churches grew dramatically between 1800 and 1860, although during that period the overwhelming majority of African American Baptist church members were at least formally attached to white Baptist congregations and denominations, even though informally much of their devotional life may have centered on worship shared with fellow slaves in small groups. In a few cases, black Baptist preachers were ministers of largely white congregations.

Seven general qualities might be identified as characteristic of these early independent African American churches. They stressed local congregational autonomy, allowing African Americans a possibility to exercise decision making and self-determination largely denied them in every other area of life; they were generally slow in creating national organizations but by the end of the nineteenth century had come to the place of organizing national bodies; they tended to be active especially in national mission work (for example, in 1845, African American Baptists formed the African Baptist Missionary Society for that purpose); they generally cooperated with the Underground Railroad prior to and during the Civil War; they supported foreign mission effort (such as the work of Lott Carey); they

---

[13] This basic argument is applied more broadly to black Protestantism in America by Will B. Gravely, "The Rise of African American Churches in America (1786–1822)," *Journal of Religious Thought* 41 (1984): 58–73.

faced particular restrictions in the South, which often made their independent work difficult; and they developed a distinctly African American style of spirituality expressed through music, preaching, and worship.

Gradually, slaves succeeded in merging their African heritage with evangelical doctrine and practice. They did this with a different style of empowerment than Anglo Americans. Walter F. Pitts in *Old Ship of Zion: The Afro-Baptist Ritual in the African Diaspora* writes that the structures of African ritual allowed for "a smooth amalgamation of evangelical practice." The African structure of ritual chant produced a "passive-receptive frame of mind, followed by rhythmic drumming and dancing to induce spirit possession."[14] This paralleled the evangelical revivalist progression from "the preparation period with prayer and quiet hymn singing, followed by dramatic, rhythmic preaching... intended to bring the 'sinner' to a religious experience."[15] Donald Matthews suggests that this had the opposite effect on blacks than on whites. Whites spoke of "breaking down" or "yielding" under pressure. Blacks were "lifted up," being thereby enabled to celebrate themselves as persons because of their direct and awesome contact with divinity.[16]

As the century progressed, African American Baptists gradually brought increased organization and cooperation to their work. Some African American associations and organizations were created prior to the Civil War. Among them were the Providence Association in Ohio, established in 1836; the Colored Baptist Association, Friends to Humanity, established in 1839 in Illinois; and the Union Association of Ohio, founded in 1840. At least six black Baptist associations had been formed prior to the Civil War – two in Ohio, two in Illinois, one in Indiana, and one in Canada.

Missionary work was another cause that united early black Baptists and also one that contributed to their organizational growth. In 1815, the African Baptist Missionary Society was formed, only one year after the Triennial Convention. William Crane served as the society's first president. Two other noted leaders included Collin Teague and Lott Carey. In 1840, the American Baptist Missionary Convention was organized in New York. This was the first known attempt of black Baptists to form a general body.

---

[14] See Walter F. Pitts, *Old Ship of Zion: The Afro-Baptist Ritual in the African Diaspora* (New York: Oxford University Press, 1993), especially chapters 2 and 3. The summarizing statement quoted here is from Thomas A. Tweed, ed., *Retelling U.S. Religious History* (Berkeley: University of California Press, 1997), 69–70.

[15] Pitts, *Old Ship of Zion*, chapters 2 and 3, summarizing quote from Tweed, *Retelling*, 70.

[16] See Donald G. Mathews, *Religion in the Old South* (Chicago: University of Chicago Press, 1977), 215.

The convention undertook mission work in Haiti and planned to begin work in Africa. In 1864, the Western and Southern Missionary Baptist Convention was organized in Richmond, Virginia. Also, the American Baptist Missionary Convention and the Western and Southern Missionary Baptist Convention merged in 1866 to form the Consolidated American Baptist Convention. This was the first effort by black Baptists to form an organization that might genuinely have consolidated their work nationally. Post–Civil War conditions hindered its work, however, and the convention ended in 1877.

The termination of slavery did not end the oppression many black Baptists experienced in American society. The need to find ways out of that oppression led many Baptists to support educational institutions. Although fellowship, sense of belonging, and mutual encouragement were important reasons African Americans formed associations, support of educational institutions seems to have been the strongest motivation. During Reconstruction, African American Baptists left previously white churches and denominations in great numbers, forming new churches and organizations. Those churches soon united to form associations and conventions that were seriously committed to establishing schools. Between 1865 and 1879, at least eleven black colleges were organized, including Shaw University, Virginia Union University, and Morehouse College.

From those foundations, ever-widening circles of union were sought and developed. Several regional, denominational, and even national African American Baptist bodies were created in the latter half of the nineteenth century. These trends culminated in the creation of the National Baptist Convention in 1895.

Generally speaking, black Baptists in America grew in independence, self-government, self-determination, and self-confidence over the course of the nineteenth century in spite of overwhelming odds to the contrary. By the end of the century, black Baptists were aggressively engaging in evangelism and the development of ecclesiastical organizations, and they had begun their long struggle toward gaining full recognition of their equality in U.S. law and society.

FRONTIERS OF HISPANIC (LATINO) AMERICAN BAPTIST LIFE AND CULTURE

Hispanic American designates a heritage that is culturally more diverse than generally has been recognized by the larger society. In a broad sense, the term refers to persons from cultural backgrounds as diverse as those of

Spain, Portugal, Mexico, Central and South America, Puerto Rico, and Cuba. Some of the core commonalities of the Iberian heritage shared by this varied family of cultures have contributed to a distinctive identity in Baptist life.

Hispanic American identity – as distinct from general Latin American identity – has roots that stretch back to the extension of Anglo-American hegemony into what became the southwestern region of the United States. That conquest was favored by virtually all American Protestant bodies in the nineteenth century and was accompanied by belief that Anglo-Americans had a special place in God's plan for the world. Many also held the view that Hispanic Americans had inherited "the cruelty, bigotry, and superstition that... marked the character of the Spaniards from the earliest times."[17] Consequently, the race was doomed to "ignorance, degradation, and misery."[18] Abiel Abbot Livermore expressed the sentiments of many when he wrote that this "mongrel race [had cheapened] the American birthright" by being granted citizenship through the 1848 Treaty of Guadalupe Hildago.[19] But, because the act was a fait accompli, Protestants had the mission of extending republican forms of government to the Southwest and purifying the "Mexicans who were 'indolent' and lacked 'consistency' as a people." Along with correct religion missionaries must extend "civilization,.... the arts, and... good government among [the Mexicans]."[20] This would gradually impart energy and industry to the "indolent" people.

Those developments brought a new population with a distinctive and enduring identity into American Baptist life – a people whose identity had changed even though they had never moved from their original homes. In the thinking of the new Anglo-American immigrants, the Hispanic population of the American Southwest was foreign, and spoke a foreign language, even though the Spanish-speaking people were not the latest immigrants to that land. Some Baptists believed their task included helping these "new Americans" (*neomexicanos*) become good citizens and correcting their many errors of thought and practice. This required evangelization and education. Because Hispanic Americans were judged as being morally

---

[17] W. W. H. Davis, *El Gringo or New Mexico and Her People* (Santa Fe, NM: Rydal Press, 1938), 85.
[18] William Jay, *A Review of the Causes and Consequences of the Mexican War* (Boston: Benjamin B. Mussey and Company, 1849), 270.
[19] Abiel Abbot Livermore, *The War with Mexico Revisited* (Boston: American Peace Society, 1850), 177.
[20] William W. Phillips, "An Address Delivered at Peerkskill, New York, October 21, 1846, before the Synod of New York" (New York: Board of Foreign Missions of the Presbyterian Church, 1846).

degenerate, mentally weak, and lazy, they had to be shown a new way. Because Baptists often attributed the negative analysis of the Hispanic character to Catholicism, converting them to the true faith was necessary. But the challenges of the American West at the time were too great. There were not enough resources to reach the rapidly growing numbers of "white" settlers. Hispanics would have to wait.

As with many other groups, Anglo-American Baptist missionaries were the early agents for disseminating Baptist beliefs among the Hispanic American populations. Prior to the Civil War, New Mexico and Texas were the primary centers for Baptist efforts. By 1861, however, the mission endeavors had ended because of three impediments: lack of response from Mexican American populations, inadequate resources, and the disruptions caused by the Civil War.

Hiram Read established Baptists' first work in New Mexico. In 1849, he organized an Anglo congregation in Santa Fe and decided to learn Spanish to work among the Hispanic American population. He even took the title of bishop to better accommodate their religious background. In the 1850s, the American (Northern) Baptist Home Mission Society sent Lewis Smith, John Shaw, and Samuel Gorman to minister in New Mexico. Their initial plans had been to work among the Anglo-American populations, but finding few Anglos, they extended their efforts among the so-called new Americans and Native peoples. A center was established in Albuquerque for which a missionary circuit was extended to Isleta, Pajarito, Peralta, Tomé, Los Jarales, and Manzano. Another center was established at Socorro, with work extending from there. Soon Hispanic preachers were identified who joined the effort, including José María Cháves, Santos Telles, Antonio José García, Blas Cháves, and Romaldo Cháves. Between 1849 and 1860, at least 112 baptisms were recorded. Yet, for all their efforts, no permanent Baptist ministry was achieved. Baptist missionary activity in the area ended with the Civil War, and many of their converts joined the Methodists. Baptist work was not resumed among the Hispanic populations in New Mexico until the twentieth century.

Lasting work among Hispanic Americans in Texas (*tejanos*) began after the Civil War, mostly under the auspices of the Baptist General Convention of Texas (BGCT). Earlier agents such as Thomas J. Pilgrim, James Huckins, and William Tryon had attempted ministry among the Hispanic as well as Anglo-American populations, but no Spanish-speaking church had been formed. At that stage, Hispanic converts became members of Anglo churches. Angela María de Jesus Navarro, a charter member of First Baptist Church of San Antonio, is one example of the practice. However, during the last two decades of the nineteenth century, numerous independent Hispanic churches (often called Mexican) were organized. In 1881, John and Thomas Westrup, Southern Baptist missionaries to Mexico, crossed the border and preached in Laredo, Texas. The baptism of their first convert is commemorated as the beginning of permanent Hispanic Baptist work in Texas. A Hispanic Baptist church may have been established by William Flournoy in Laredo as early as 1883, but it did not survive into the twentieth century. Most sources point to a Primera Iglesia Bautista Mexicana in San Antonio, organized by the missionary William D. Powell in 1887 as the first permanent Hispanic Baptist church in Texas. Shortly afterward, independent Hispanic churches appeared in San Marcos (1889), El Paso (1893), Beeville (1899), and Austin (1899). By the end of the century, at least thirteen such churches existed. Statistical reports from the Blanco Baptist Association between 1879 and 1900 identify several Hispanic pastors, including Manuel Treviño, A. P. Treviño, Pio Quinto Ybaben, and R. E. del Valle.

Among the factors that attracted Hispanic Americans to Baptist churches during the frontier phase were dissatisfaction with the Catholic Church and educational opportunities offered their children. Among Hispanic *penetentes*, spiritual vitality and freedom to choose their own church leaders were crucial issues. But there were also hindrances. Anglo-American attitudes of cultural and religious superiority, anti-Catholic attitudes that blinded missionaries to the true nature of Hispanic relations with the Catholic Church, stronger interest in evangelizing Anglo-Americans than Hispanic Americans, and the desire to Americanize Hispanics were among the major barriers.

Yet, despite the challenges, a Hispanic Baptist identity did emerge. This identity included the self-perception of being a new generation of Protestant reformers who could govern their own churches and develop their own leaders. The Bible, usually interpreted quite literally, became a central symbol for the converts. Their convictions cost them dearly. Their decision to leave Catholicism separated them from other Hispanic Americans and made them a minority within a minority. Many were attracted to Anglo-American culture who, after receiving an education, chose to leave Spanish-speaking congregations for English-speaking ones. But for most Hispanic Americans, becoming Baptist did not protect them from the social, political, and economic pressures their new American status thrust on them.

Throughout the nineteenth century and beyond, Hispanics of the Southwest were treated as foreigners. This attitude was reflected in church life itself. In most instances, Anglo Baptist missionaries held the key leadership positions, controlled publication of Baptist materials, made decisions about the work, and decided who would be trained and who would receive a salary. Hispanic Baptists had little voice in most of the decisions that affected them. In at least a few instances, this caused conflict and sometime divisions. A division between Manuel Treviño and C. D. Daniel is illustrative of this. Treviño already had started several congregations in the area around San Antonio when Daniel, an Anglo-American Baptist missionary, was assigned to oversee the work in 1891. Conflicts arose between the two. Treviño was strongly supported by Hispanic pastors but accused of doctrinal error by Daniel. Daniel went on to become a celebrated leader in Texas Baptist Spanish-speaking work. Treviño resigned and disappeared from Baptist history. This was an often-repeated phenomenon in early Hispanic American Baptist struggles for identity.

FRONTIERS OF ASIAN AMERICAN BAPTIST EXPERIENCE

Asian American Baptists came primarily from three ethnic groups during the nineteenth century – Chinese, Japanese, and Korean immigrants. Social barriers made life difficult for each of these groups and created the conditions out of which early Asian American Baptist identity was forged.

Although initially a very small presence, the Asian American community had occupied a place in American life since the late sixteenth century, when the first known Asians arrived. Those first Asian Americans were Filipino sailors who migrated during the Spanish colonial era. In 1763, the Filipino settlement of Saint Malo was established in Louisiana and continued as such until its destruction by a hurricane in 1915. Large-scale immigration by Asians began in the mid-nineteenth century and was most significant along the West Coast. Political and economic conditions in China constituted the greatest contributing factors to the migration. Several natural disasters and disruptions from civil war and uprisings in the twilight years of the Qing dynasty produced great suffering, driving multitudes of Chinese to seek relief through migrations to Southeast Asia, Europe, and America.[21]

In 1850, only about five hundred Chinese resided in California. As opportunities for employment were generated by the shipping industry, the 1849 gold strike, agriculture, and construction of the Central Pacific Railroad, the Chinese population grew dramatically. By 1852, about 2,200 Chinese had arrived. In 1870, near the beginning of a period of major

---

[21] Jonathan Y. Tan, *Introducing Asian American Theologies* (Maryknoll, NY: Orbis Books, 2008), 20–1.

and decades-long anti-Chinese sentiments in America, about 10 percent of the California's population was Chinese. This dramatic growth fueled interest among both Northern and Southern Baptists to minister to those populations, which paralleled a growing Baptist missionary presence in China itself. J. Lewis Shuck, who previously had served as a Southern Baptist missionary to China (along with his wife, Henrietta, who died there), was the first Anglo-American Baptist missionary sent to work among the Chinese in California. His ministry resulted in the organization of First Chinese Baptist Church in Sacramento in 1860. The American Civil War disrupted funding and forced Shuck to abandon the work.

Numerous nominal Anglo-American Baptist missionaries took up ministries among Chinese Americans only to discover that language, racial prejudice, and cultural differences generated greater barriers to the work than their commitment to overcome them could sustain. The 1860s and 1870s witnessed the rise of white nativism and anti-Chinese prejudice. Many European immigrants were able to "blend in," but physical differences made this impossible for most Asians. Furthermore, many Americans stereotyped all Chinese as "idolatrous, superstitious, filthy, crafty, cruel, dishonest, and intellectually inferior, and as practitioners of intractable vices such as idol worshiping, female footbinding, and female infanticide."[22] Such attitudes were perpetuated in newspapers, books, sermons, and "eyewitness" accounts from the era.

By the 1870s, the economic growth that had prompted much Chinese immigration to California had given way to the Long Depression (1873–1896). A protectionist attitude set in among European Americans that moved beyond prejudice to outright exclusion. The Chinese Exclusion Act of 1882 was extended in 1892 and made permanent in 1902, and it was repealed only in 1943. The American Baptist Home Mission Society declared such discrimination "contrary to the fundamental principles of our free government and opposed to the spirit of Christian religion," but the Chinese issue continued to be as divisive among Baptists as it was for the larger American society. The Baptist preacher O. C. Wheeler is illustrative of those who sided with anti-Chinese advocates, declaring that, "unless the immigration of the Chinese shall be virtually suppressed, they will . . . permeate every portion of our whole country, undermine and control every profitable industry, subvert and destroy all free institutions, replace our sanctuaries with the temples of idolatry, and transform our land

---

[22] Ibid., 22.

into the generator and hot-bed of every foul and unclean thing."[23] Asian American Baptists had to find their own way during the remainder of the nineteenth century, receiving only sporadic and limited assistance from Anglo-American Baptist sources. Dong Gong provides one example of the Asian American Baptist vision, commitment, and achievement during those trying decades. As Baptists' first Chinese convert in San Francisco, he became a prolific agent of Baptist work and influence among Chinese Americans.

John Francis, Roswell Graves, and Fung Seung Nam are noted among those who ministered to the Chinese populations in San Francisco around 1870. Fung Seung Nam experienced particular success, preaching to crowds of between 700 and 1,500 persons on many Sundays. Unfortunately, an illness took his life in 1871, cutting short a very promising work. In 1880, the former China missionary J. B. Hartwell helped organize the First Chinese Baptist Church of San Francisco. That church became an important center for extending Baptist work among Asian American populations throughout California and beyond. Besides this, limited ministries were established among the Chinese by Baptist churches in several U.S. cities by the end of the nineteenth century.

Japanese immigration to America during this phase of Baptist life occurred in three waves – the late 1860s to the mid-1870s, the mid-1870s to the mid-1890s, and the mid-1890s to about 1907. The first wave consisted mostly of diplomats and businessmen. The second came as a result of the Meiji restoration with its emphasis on acquiring Western scientific and technological skills. During this wave, many Japanese students arrived for the purpose of studying in American universities. During the third wave, Japanese immigrants came seeking economic opportunities. Many farmers and young men migrated to Hawaii and California in pursuit of employment.

Baptist work among Japanese immigrants began in the 1890s and centered most heavily in the Seattle area. Fukumatsu Okazaki was important to that work. Born in Japan in 1866, he migrated to San Francisco in 1887; worked for Captain Joshua Holler in Nevada and Walla Walla, Washington, for two years; and then started his own business in Denver, Colorado. While there, he became Baptist and began preaching among Japanese American people in the West. In 1899, he became the first pastor of First Japanese Baptist Church in Seattle.

[23] Rev. O. C. Wheeler, "An Address Delivered in Metropolitan Temple, San Francisco, Dec. 21, 1879, and in the State Capitol at Sacramento, January 16, 1880" (Oakland, CA: Time Publishing, 1880).

Political turmoil in Korea generated the first small wave of Korean immigrants to America in 1883. The earliest major migration occurred in 1903–5, when large numbers of impoverished Korean farmers sought work in the sugarcane industries of Hawaii. The Japanese annexation of Korea in 1910 brought additional refugees from Korea, many being students and intellectuals seeking asylum from Japanese oppression. Baptist work among Korean Americans will emerge only in the next phase of Baptist development.

Distinctives of Frontier-Era Asian American Baptist Identity

Being Baptist as an Asian American in the nineteenth century often meant traversing a great theological frontier from the religious traditions of Asian heritage to embracing the faith of a people among whom one might, on the one hand, find acceptance as a Baptist who is Asian American or, on the other hand, might experience rejection and persecution for no other reason than one's ethnic background. In either case, segregation (accepting a distinct and inferior status) or assimilation (becoming "white," something impossible for most Asian Americans) were offered as the only alternatives. Naturally, this created theological questions for the Asian American Baptist that were quite distinct from the ones most important to the Anglo-American Baptist mainstream. To be Asian in America meant being perpetually foreign and, consequently, bearing the stigma of never being "truly" American, and in many cases not truly Baptist either. Therefore, issues of how to be Christian, American, and of Asian heritage were matters for greater concern to Asian American Baptists than such Anglocentric doctrines as form of church government, Calvinist theology, or the separation of church and state. As the Native American and African American, the Asian American experience presented yet another frontier in what it meant to be Baptist in the nineteenth century – a demarcation that was quite different from that of the Anglo-American Baptist and one that was equally unrecognized by the interpreters of Baptist identity at the time.

OTHER AMERICAN BAPTISTS OF ETHNIC IDENTITY

The Institution of the American Baptist Home Mission Society in 1832 immediately opened Anglo Baptist awareness to the fact of a growing non-Anglo European immigration. As the waves of immigration would ebb and flow, the focus of the society's ethnic work also would shift. In the

1830s, special attention was given to evangelizing the Welsh, German, and Scandinavian immigrants. In the 1840s, more-specific emphasis was placed on the Swedish and Norwegian immigrant populations. In the 1850s, the Danish were added to the list. Finally, in the 1880s, the Finnish and South European immigrants became a special focus. In general, North European immigrants tended to be more responsive to Baptist efforts than those from South European countries. Also, immigrants out of a Pietist or revivalistic tradition tended to be more receptive than those from a Catholic or strongly confessional one.

German Immigrant Baptists

In the nineteenth century, German immigration to America outstripped that of any other non-Anglo group. For German American Baptists, the migration of Konrad A. Fleischmann, who came to the United States in 1839, was especially important. While serving briefly as pastor of a Baptist church in Newark, New Jersey, he was commissioned by the American Baptist Home Mission Society and moved to Reading, Pennsylvania, to work among the German immigrants. There, in 1843, he organized the first German Baptist church in the United States. Fleischmann's dedication and success in this work led many to consider him, along with August Rauschenbusch, one of the founding fathers of German Baptist work in America. In 1851, he led in organizing the German Baptist Conference, from which the North American Baptist Conference was eventually derived. That same year, Rochester Theological Seminary in New York partnered with the conference to provide German-language students training for ministry.

The harsh social and economic conditions suffered by German immigrants in America led the German American Baptist Walter Rauschenbusch to challenge the prevailing attitudes concerning the sources of poverty and evil. The social gospel movement, of which he was a major prophet, addressed the social dimensions of evil, pointing out that individual conversion and holy living cannot address the systemic evils that are written into society's social structures. He argued that the ethics of God's kingdom demands that Christians confront social injustice as well as the need for individual conversion.

In 1893, the Southern Baptists Marie Buhlmaier and Annie Armstrong began a small-scale ministry among German immigrants who arrived in Baltimore. However, Baptists' interest in ministry to German expatriates declined after World War I, when German immigration was halted. From that point, German Baptist denominations became almost the exclusive supporters of this work.

Scandinavian Immigrant Baptists

In the 1840s, Danish and Norwegian immigrants began concentrating especially in the American Midwest. The Norwegian Hans Valder, from a Lutheran background, became Baptist and organized a Norwegian Baptist church in Illinois in 1848 under the auspices of the American Baptist Home Mission Society. Similar churches came to be organized in Wisconsin and Minnesota. Danes tended not to gather into ethnic communities and thus were more readily absorbed into existing Anglo-American Baptist churches, but a few Danish Baptist churches were organized. By 1882, thirty Danish-Norwegian Baptist churches existed in the upper Midwest.

Swedish Baptists came to form a major Baptist group in America over the course of the nineteenth century. Gustavus W. Schroeder embraced Baptists' views in 1845 while in the United States. He returned to Sweden the following year and led Frederick O. Nilsson to Baptist views. Nilsson decided to leave Sweden because of the persecution he suffered because of his Baptist convictions, but before departing, he had contact with Gustaf Palmquist in Stockholm. Palmquist went to the United States in 1852, was baptized and ordained, and soon afterward organized the first Swedish Baptist church in America at Rock Island, Illinois. Nilsson joined him there. His leadership of Baptist work in the Midwest led some to designate him the apostle to Swedish Baptists in America. Anders Wiberg became another noted contributor to Swedish Baptist work in America.

Over the course of the century, Swedish Baptists organized a seminary in 1871 and a general conference in 1879, and they sent out numerous missionaries. Working under the auspices of the American Baptist Foreign Mission Society, Johanna Anderson became their first missionary, appointed for service to Burma in 1888.

Italian Immigrant Baptists

Thousands of Italian immigrants came to America, especially in the latter decades of the nineteenth century. Ariel B. Bellondi was sent by the American Baptist Home Mission Society to initiate work in Buffalo, New York. This was only the beginning of a ministry that resulted in dozens of Italian Baptist churches, especially in the northeastern region of the United States.

French Immigrant Baptists

In the 1830s, the Grande Ligne Mission of Canada led numerous Swiss immigrants to embrace Baptist convictions. In the 1840s, the American Baptist Home Mission Society helped sponsor work among Canadian French Baptists. In 1853, the society appointed its first missionary to minister among French Immigrants in America. The number of French Baptist churches increased to the point that, in 1895, the French-Speaking Baptist Conference of New England was organized.

Distinctives of Ethnic American Baptist Identity During Baptists' Frontier Era

To a degree greater than most other groups, European immigrants who became Baptist had greater success in working out what it meant for them to be both Baptist and persons of non-Anglo origin. At the same time, the fact that they were an ethnic minority created issues of its own. Ethnic Baptist groups organized themselves into churches and denominations according to their distinctive linguistic and cultural lines – German, Italian, Swedish, *cum multis aliis*. However, the children or grandchildren of the original immigrants grew up in a different world from that of their ethnically identified parents, frequently generating tensions between the generations. Over time American-born members of an ethnic Baptist community tended to shift from the language and cultural identity of their parents and grandparents into English-language churches, even if connected to the Baptist denomination of their parents' ethnic identity. North Topeka Baptist Church illustrates this transition. Founded by Swedish Baptists in 1881, the church "changed its name to The West Side Baptist church and decided in 1925 to hold its Sunday Services in English, a Swedish meeting being held on Friday evenings. A number of members of American nationality . . . [subsequently] united with the church."[24] Over time, the church lost any real sense of its Swedish identity altogether, being reminded of this heritage only on occasions when its history would be remembered.

Sometimes these denominations, while making adjustments to the changing situations of their constituents, continued a separate existence – the Baptist General Conference (Swedish Baptist origins) and the North American Baptist Conference (German Baptist origins) are examples. In other cases, Baptist denominations of ethnic origin over time would unite

---

[24] P. Lovene, *History of the Swedish Baptist Churches of Kansas and Missouri: 1869–1927* (n.p.: n.p.), 53–4.

with a larger Baptist body (usually of Anglo-American origin) if that ethnic group's immigration numbers did not persist in replenishing the immigrant culture's traditions – the Norwegian Baptist Conference of America exemplifies that development.

BAPTIST WOMEN IN AMERICA DURING THE FRONTIER ERA

Anglo Baptist Women

Baptist women also confronted and negotiated significant frontiers during the nineteenth century. In Anglo-American life, the nineteenth century was a transitional period during which the ideals for womanhood shifted significantly. Susan Lindley identifies this as the culminating stage of a three-phase ideological evolution from the colonial ideal of the female as good wife, through the post-Revolutionary model as republican mother, to the nineteenth-century paradigm as true woman. The true woman was pious, pure, submissive, and domestic. This notion of woman as naturally moral and pious reflected a complete reversal from the earlier dominating images of women as daughters of Eve who were weaker than men in faith and moral character. While the true-woman ideal was not a possibility or even an acceptable standard for all women, it did significantly shape popular American notions of what women should be. That conceptualization influenced significant segments of Baptist thinking, alternately producing expectations of the roles a virtuous woman should fulfill and a sense of guilt, self-recrimination, and condemnation whenever a woman either chose or was forced to live outside those boundaries.

Numerous sources contributed to this cult of true womanhood. The social and cultural shifts from a basically agrarian to a more urban and industrial society were one of them. That transformation removed men's workplace from the home to an office or factory, creating spheres of domain in the process. Thus, the public sphere became the domain of men, and the domestic sphere became the domain assigned to women. This shift was much more drastic for women than might appear to have been the case. In agrarian settings, the home had served as a center of productivity essential to the family's survival – food preservation, wool spinning, cloth weaving, and the like. In the urban setting, those functions were greatly diminished. Goods were bought, not produced by the family. Thus, a married woman found herself more economically dependent on her husband as the breadwinner and more limited to roles that focused on serving the needs of others. The new ideal generated strongly gendered role expectations of both men and women, but for women, the new expectations were more restrictive.

Shifts in perceptions of the basic nature of the child also affected concepts of motherhood. Calvinist theology had tended to view children as fallen and sinful. In the nineteenth century, new theories emerged that portrayed them as basically innocent and impressionable. Therefore, early influence and training by the mother came to be accentuated. In addition, the pace of change in the public sphere led many people to envision the home as a refuge – a place of stability where family members might escape the chaos of the larger world.

Donald Mathews portrays an ideal of evangelical womanhood in the American South that, though unique in its origin, is consistent with the image of the true woman and has relevance to understanding the "dreams" of Anglo-American Baptist women in such contexts. Interpreting the shift of evangelicals from "being dissenters to shapers of southern culture," Mathews identifies "usefulness" as a major component of the ideal of evangelical womanhood in contrast to the "ornamental" role of earlier aristocratic ideals for women: "Evangelicals began to shape a model of behavior and ideals which was peculiarly the possession of women and was based on their unique contribution to the ideal community."[25] Blends of the true-woman and evangelical-woman ideals contributed to the nineteenth-century Anglo Baptist ideal of womanhood as pure, pious, domestic, submissive, and useful.

The pace of change, the degree of industrialization, and the economic realities of a given community and family varied greatly. Consequently, the sources and impact of the cult of true womanhood differed significantly depending on the context. The ideal itself was probably most closely approximated in white, Protestant, northeastern society, but its influence was felt on a much broader scale. Black, Native, immigrant, and western frontier Baptist women often had to live by a different set of ideals. Yet "the contrast between a homogeneous image and a complex, diverse reality helps to explain the apparent paradox of women in America at this time. Nineteenth-century America saw both a pervasive image of true womanhood within a cult of domesticity and the flowering of women's activities and a women's rights movement."[26] The faith experience of Anglo-American Baptist women during the period might be described as pioneers on a frontier between a socially fabricated true woman and the hard realities of actual life demands, perceptions of God's will, and a need for authentic personhood.

---

[25] Donald G. Mathews, *Religion in the Old South* (Chicago: University of Chicago Press, 1977), 111.
[26] Lindley, *Women and Religion*, 57.

The Second Great Awakening (1795–1830) was significant in the development of Baptist women's religious identity. Among other things, this series of revivals helped establish American religious life on the basis of voluntary institutions. Social and economic changes were disrupting the traditional patterns of identity formation for many women. Nancy Cott is among the scholars who locate in the revivals a means by which women could shape their identities within the new social context.[27] The church offered women an acceptable sphere outside the home for self-expression, peer support, and meaningful involvement. A few women found opportunities to preach. Even fewer attained ordination. But more basically, revivals gave large numbers of women opportunities to pray openly, give testimonies, sing in public, and exhort. The exhorter assisted those persons who continued to struggle while under conviction after a preacher's message, helping them work through to conversion. This was a speaking role that often became almost a preaching role for some women. Exhorters have continued to have a function in some Appalachian Primitive Baptist traditions.

In Baptist life, such developments opened the way for women to organize, assist in, and lead ministries that became integral to the church's work over the course of the nineteenth century. Among those ministries were Sunday school work, charitable organizations, foreign and home mission societies, and reform movements. Especially in frontier settings, women often played critical roles for establishing and sustaining churches. Lucinda Williams's considerable role in founding the First Baptist Church of Dallas, Texas, is illustrative of such work.[28] In addition, women contributed behind-the-scenes support for local churches, the power of which should not be underestimated. The ability of women to raise financial support was crucial to the survival of many churches. And although women often supported causes set forth by male leadership, they also frequently had their own ideas concerning the things that needed to be funded. DeAne Lagerquist has observed that "women . . . used their money as a means of making their voices heard. What the women would pay for could be done; what the women wanted they could pay for."[29]

Baptist women helped organize and promote many reforms during the nineteenth century, especially women's education, temperance, and

[27] Nancy F. Cott, "Young Women in the Second Great Awakening in New England," *Feminist Studies*, no. 3 (Fall 1975): 19–29.

[28] See H. Leon McBeth, *Women in Baptist Life* (Nashville, TN: Broadman Press, 1979), 101–2.

[29] L. DeAne Lagerquist, *From Our Mothers' Arms: A History of Women in the American Lutheran Church* (Minneapolis: Augsburg, 1987), 41.

abolition of slavery. Perhaps no other single ministry undertaken by Baptist women during the frontier phase was more transformative than their involvement in the foreign mission and home mission movements. Through these efforts women organized locally, regionally, and nationally. In the process, many learned to lead meetings, keep records, raise funds, network, and promote mission work. They also developed missionary education programs, designed and produced literature, and taught mission education courses. By the end of the nineteenth century, the vast majority of Baptist groups in America had some form of women's missionary society. Although they usually welcomed the money women raised, male leaders often expressed reservations, concerned that women were assuming too much independence via their mission-support activities. Although such objections at times produced frustrations, ultimately, they were unable to deter the mission causes for which Baptist women gave themselves.

Another dimension of the mission labors of Baptist woman came through their vocations as missionaries. Prior to the Civil War, such service was generally possible only for missionary wives. Married, and therefore ostensibly under the protection of their husbands, such women could step outside the normal boundaries of the Anglo woman and still fulfill the virtues of true womanhood. This allowed many Baptists to honor the strong, assertive, and at times independent actions of Ann Hasseltine Judson, American Baptists' first female foreign missionary. As a missionary wife, she helped Baptists in nineteenth-century America learn to value the significant work women could contribute to the ministry of cross-cultural mission.

Single women, in contrast, found they could not easily be accepted in the same way. As the incidence of single women presenting themselves for missionary service grew, resistance against the idea of such appointments mounted as well. Many persons could not imagine the possibility that a single woman might survive the hardships of life and work in "uncivilized" cultures without a husband's protection and direction. When mission-sending organizations persisted in their refusal to yield on this matter, Baptist women looked for other solutions. Finally, in 1861, women from several denominations united to form the Women's Union Missionary Society of America for Heathen Lands. Its purpose was to send single women as missionaries, because women in other cultures needed medical treatment their social standards would not allow them to receive from a male missionary. Ten years later, a group of Baptist women formed the Woman's Baptist Mission Society for similar purposes. Soon afterward, other Baptist women organized comparable societies. A union of three of those societies in 1913 produced the Woman's American Baptist Foreign Mission Society. The raison d'être was American Baptist women's desire for greater involvement in Christian work and their sense of urgency to address the distinctive needs of women around the world. In 1877, the Woman's Baptist Home Mission Society was formed in Chicago and soon afterward commissioned Joanna P. Moore to promote freedmen's education in the South. Among Southern Baptists, the inspiring ministry of single missionary Charlotte "Lottie" Diggs Moon in China helped galvanize women's support for creation of the Woman's Missionary Union in 1888. Never willing to accept the limitations Anglo-American Baptist society attempted to place on her as a single woman, Lottie Moon expanded the frontiers of ministry possibilities for Baptist women both in America and in China. By the end of the century, home and foreign missionary service, support, and education had become hallmarks of Anglo-American Baptist women's ministries.

Faith convictions, personal needs for creative expression, and unmet pleas for help were preeminent factors that motivated Baptist women to take up missionary and reform causes. They soon discovered, however, that addressing one challenge necessarily meant having to face a second one: defending "their right as women to step out of their place to act and organize in a public way."[30] The tensions between true womanhood and life demands forced many women into undesired frontiers – having to choose between the authority of "man" and that of God. For at least some Baptist women, the superior claim of the latter supplied the fortitude to go against the former.

Native Baptist Women

In a study of Native American women, Susan Lindley contrasts the view of womanhood that was characteristic of Anglo Protestant women with a different tradition that was more typical of Native American women. Almost all Anglo Protestant women, including Baptists, embraced some version of the cult of true womanhood, and all believed that same image should guide Native American women as well. Lindley demonstrates that this expectation failed to acknowledge two important realities: that the two-sphere system of Anglo-American society was very different from the realities of most tribal communities and that Native American women already shared three of the four "cardinal virtues" associated with the

---

[30] Lindley, *Women and Religion*, 90.

true-woman ideal. Although not Christian, Native American women were certainly religious within their own context, and thus they were pious in the terms defined by their own customs. They also could not be thought of as promiscuous. Although Indian sexual practices differed from Anglo-American patterns, in their own world, these women were pure. Furthermore, most Amerindian women were absorbed in child rearing, food gathering, and "homemaking" duties. Therefore, they possessed domesticity. Consequently, a strong basis for commonality between Anglo and Native American women already existed. The one cardinal virtue they did not share was submissiveness: "In many tribes, women had an important political voice and significant economic and personal power and independence as a result of their domestic roles of literally creating homes and producing food."[31] Unfortunately, the basis for commonality was not perceived, which often left Native Baptist women on their own in their search for authentic identity during an era of devastating loss for their traditions.

Disruption of Native American ways of life through geographical relocation followed by assimilationist programs had a serious impact on the livelihood and identity of Native American women. Although some traditional duties continued, others were displaced or uprooted altogether. This loss of the traditional woman's role in tribal life may have been one important factor in some Indian women's decisions to embrace the Baptist faith. This was one of the ways a few women sought to recover the sense of social, economic, and tribal power they had lost. Although the reasons Native women embraced Baptist beliefs are many and complex, the choice to do so was never easy. For most, the struggles between traditional identity and accommodation to Anglo Baptist understandings continued to be a challenge throughout their lives.

In the new Baptist world, an often-uneasy transition was made, limiting the Native woman's sphere in ways not so different from the experiences of many nineteenth-century Anglo-American Baptist women. However, for the Native Baptist woman, the transition occurred amid massive cultural devastation that robbed her and her people of practically all traditional sources of dignity and worth. In the new setting, the Native Baptist woman lost much of her political voice, economic and personal power, and independence. However, in rare cases, remnants of the traditional voice managed to survive in the new Baptist forms. Among some of the Seminole Baptist churches in Oklahoma, for example, one leadership position did emerge in which Native American women were able to continue

[31] Ibid., 162.

at least some elements of their earlier role in tribal life. It was called *hoktake enhomathoyv* (front woman). A similar concept is conveyed in the term *hoktake seme'yupvyv*, which describes "a leader pulling a rope from which the followers are led."[32] Known as women's leaders, they functioned almost as female deacons. Their duties included modeling spiritual disciplines (like prayer and fasting), supervising the spiritual training of younger women, preparing the camps, providing and serving food, and similar activities. The oldest and most experienced of the women leaders was usually honored as the senior woman, although the function was not recognized as a formal position. The senior woman possessed authority to chastise publically the pastor, a function rarely exercised and then only under dire conditions. Use of this authority usually disrupted normal tribal relations within the church and required delicately balanced processes for restoring order. This position, along with those of pastor, minister, and deacon, reflected a close connection to traditional Native leadership positions found in the Seminole bands (*etvlwvlke*).

The frontier many Native American Baptist women traveled during this era involved finding an identity that authentically connected a lost cultural role with a new life situation. Where in Baptist understandings of womanhood and faith could the Native woman find truly useful resources to guide her search for meaning? How might her gifts be exercised both in the church and in the tribal community? This was the heart of what Baptist freedom meant for many Native women. Baptist theology's success or failure to address these types of questions determined that faith's relevance for her long-term pilgrimage.

Black Baptist Women

The American institution of slavery produced a complicated and destructive mix of gender and racial roles. This formed the unavoidable context out of which black Baptist women's identity took shape. For Anglo Baptist women, the true-woman ideal conveyed a Marian-type image of purity, piety, domesticity, and submissiveness. In radical contrast, the experiences of slavery cast the black woman in the image of Eve. She was often perceived as carnal, promiscuous, and morally tainted. Only by becoming "white" could the black woman ever hope to achieve social and moral respectability in that world. In many ways, the limited educational opportunities available to black young women during Reconstruction and afterward

---

[32] Schultz, *Seminole Baptist Churches*, 98.

Figure 5. First Chinese Baptist Church, San Francisco, organized in 1880, representative of the many ethnically identified Baptist churches around the globe (permission by Rev. Don Ng, pastor).

attempted to achieve that goal. At the very least, this negative stereotype made many black women very conscientious of white perceptions regarding black character and awakened a strong desire to counter that stigma.

Slavery fostered a confusion of gender and moral ideals for African American Baptists because the true man was supposed to protect and provide for his family, something the slave could not do. Even the free black often faced social and economic barriers that frustrated his abilities to fulfill this ideal. Anglo-American Baptist cultural realities were very different from those of the black Baptist, yet blacks were generally judged and often found deficient by those same standards. Linda Perkins argues that the twentieth-century tradition of male prerogatives and rigid hierarchy in black church traditions have their roots in nineteenth-century systems that taught the black male an ideal of Christian manhood that those same systems made impossible for him to fulfill.[33] Naturally, this shaped major elements of the context within which black Baptist women struggled for identity.

---

[33] Linda M. Perkins, "The Impact of the 'Cult of the True Womanhood' on the Education of Black Women," in *Black Women in United States History* (Brooklyn, NY: Carlson Publishing, 1990), 3:1065–76.

The church played an analogous role for black Baptist women's development in the nineteenth century to the one it offered for white Baptist women. There they gained essential leadership skills, received mutual support, and found important educational opportunities. This was not a context in which women were likely to find support for ordination into ministry, but their involvement and aid was essential to the church's work. Black women raised money that kept churches alive during critical times, as the women's sewing society of Beale Street Baptist in Memphis demonstrates so well.[34] They also offered educational opportunities to black children, which often was neglected in the larger, white-dominated society. Classes in cooking, music, management skills, sewing, and similar arts were offered.

African American women also created their own organizations to promote and support mission work. By the early twentieth century, they had developed numerous societies and auxiliaries to carry out these efforts. A few of the noted women's missionary organizations include the Women's Auxiliary of the Baptist Educational and Missionary Convention of North Carolina, the Women's Auxiliary of the Lott Carey Baptist Foreign Mission Convention, the Women's General Baptist Missionary Society of Mississippi, and the Women's Home and Foreign Mission Society of North Carolina. A special focus of many black Baptist women's missionary societies was on ministries among African women and children. Much of their financial support sustained black women missionaries. Like their Anglo counterparts, black missionaries tended to promote their own cultural and gender patterns, assuming that Christian "civilization" (Western) would benefit African society. Both black Baptist churches and white mission societies supported black missionaries to Africa during this period. In many cases, the initial mission efforts were closely associated with programs intended to return freed blacks to the continent of Africa.[35]

Laboring under an image of racial inferiority imposed by the dominant culture, black Baptist women often supported black women's clubs as a means for fighting the negative stereotypes and for promoting personal improvements in their lives. Sometimes such programs became enmeshed in promoting Anglo middle-class ideals among black women whose lives

[34] Kathlene C. Berkeley, "Colored Ladies Also Contributed: Black Women's Activities from Benevolence to Social Welfare, 1866–1896," in *Black Women in United States History* (Brooklyn, NY: Carlson Publishing, 1990), 1:63.
[35] See Sandy D. Martin, *Black Baptists and African Missions: The Origins of a Movement, 1880–1915* (Macon, GA: Mercer University Press, 1989).

could not fit that mold. Rarely could the true-woman standards of domesticity fit the economic realities of the black woman. Black Baptist churches were more than religious institutions; they were centers of African American social, economic, political, and educational life as well. And, although black Baptist women seldom demanded equal voice in leadership and decision making, they did "challenge gendered character stereotypes and develop their own female sphere for significant action."[36]

[36] Lindley, *Women and Religion*, 195.

CHAPTER 5

Baptists' Frontier Age in Europe, Africa, Asia, and Latin America

The face of global cultures, economics, and politics shifted enormously over the course of the nineteenth century, affecting the continents of Europe, Africa, Asia, and South America in profound ways. In many instances, the changes benefited Baptists, who discovered new freedoms to witness, resettle, and establish their churches in territories formerly prohibited. In Europe, the Holy Roman Empire ceased to exist, and the Spanish and Portuguese empires – the continent's previous superpowers – weakened and began to disintegrate. Those developments not only created new possibilities for Baptists on the European continent but also often opened new venues in those nations' former colonies. The Napoleonic Wars brought further changes to Europe's political landscape. Gradually, Britain emerged as the world's leading nation, extending its empire until it finally dominated one-fourth of the world's population and about one-third of its land area by the century's end. As noted in previous chapters, this made new spaces available for Baptists among the ever more varied populations that were now under Britain's sovereignty.

Technological advances enabled European powers to dominate much of the rest of the planet. Developments in mathematics, physics, chemistry, and other sciences laid foundations for the transformation of civilizations and cultures. Medical advances, while modest compared to those of the twentieth century, initiated a rapid growth of population among Western peoples. Railroads transformed land transportation and radically altered the ways people lived and worked. They also accelerated urbanization, augmenting the number and locations of cities with populations that surpassed a million inhabitants.

As Western industrialization grew, the demand for raw materials and markets became greater. This stimulated additional Western colonial ventures, introducing Western cultures into ever-expanding areas of the world and in the process transforming local cultures. Almost all of Western Christianity became involved in global missionary ventures. In proportion to their size, Baptists were especially zealous in those efforts. By 1852, Baptists globally numbered almost 1.2 million, with 96 percent located in the United Kingdom, the United States, and Canada. In 1904, their numbers had grown by 500 percent to 6.2 million. The proportion of Baptists from those same regions in comparison to Baptists globally remained about the same, but their numbers on the continents of Europe, Africa, Latin America, and elsewhere were growing significantly. In Continental Europe, Baptists grew by almost 3,000 percent during the last half of the nineteenth century, from 4,200 in 1852 to 124,000 in 1904. During the same period Baptists in Africa grew by 850 percent (from 1,200 to 10,200), in Asia by 1,300 percent (from 12,300 to 161,000), and in the Caribbean by 21 percent (from 35,000 to 42,300). The total numbers of Baptists in the newly entered regions were small by today's standards but indicate that their movement was clearly beginning to take root.

Social changes also exerted important influences on Baptist development. With slavery increasingly rejected as a means for securing needed labor forces in colonial ventures, the drive to replace human power with machine power was strengthened. Britain outlawed slavery in 1833, the Thirteenth Amendment abolished slavery in the United States in 1865 after a bloody Civil War, Brazil ended slavery in 1888 through an act of the emperor, and Russian Tsar Alexander II decreed an end to serfdom in 1861. This slowed the drain of human resources from Africa and brought new dimensions to Baptist life in North and South America through liberation of black Baptist slaves. It also transformed Russian society, opening new possibilities for Baptist development there. Unfortunately, the decimation of Native peoples around the globe continued unabated as lands were confiscated and settled by ever-growing numbers of Western immigrants and other expanding populations.

These political, economic, and technological shifts stimulated major migrations of peoples. Increasing numbers of Europeans moved to colonial lands or to former colonies seeking job opportunities and a better life. New settlements were formed and previous inhabitants were displaced or marginalized. Among those settlers were transplanted Baptists who established churches in the places where they relocated and who also made appeals to churches back home to send missionaries who might aid in the challenges of reaching the un-Christianized peoples around them.

FRONTIERS OF BAPTIST GROWTH IN CONTINENTAL EUROPE

To speak of nineteenth-century Europe as though it were a single culture is as problematic as speaking of a single African or Asian culture. Although there are benefits to reflecting on the European experience in a unified fashion, doing so obscures a complex combination of worldviews, contexts, ethnicities, and histories. Consequently, the broad generalizations we treat here are as filled with controversy, exception, and contradiction as those encountered while dealing with cultures from every other part of the globe.

Norman Davies refers to the nineteenth century as Europe's "triumphant power century."[1] He means by this that during the period Europeans were fascinated with and accommodating to unaccustomed forces. There were new physical (scientific) forces, demographic forces, social forces, commercial and industrial forces, military forces, cultural forces, and political forces. Different from the attitudes of the twentieth century, in the nineteenth century, "power was the object of wonder and hope," not the object of suspicion.[2] The rapid shifts on these frontiers were different from the even more fast-paced changes of the twenty-first century in that a culture of change did not exist. For the most part, Europeans did not comprehend the magnitude of the power they had come to possess.

In the newly emerging situation, there were winners and losers. Among the victims were peasants; home cottage industries; the urban poor; colonial populations; the Turkish, Russian, and Austro-Hungarian empires; and the Irish, Sicilian, and Polish peoples. Failures of adaptation forced millions to migrate – with world-transforming consequences.

Politically, nineteenth-century Europe originated in the aftermath of the French Revolution and ended with the Russian Revolution of 1917. In many ways, the political, cultural, and social tone for the period was set by European reactions to Napoléon's attempted return to power in 1815. After Waterloo, the congress system was determined to restore the rights of monarchy and prevent change to the greatest degree possible. Efforts were made to maintain monarchies, prevent the rise of new republics, and guarantee existing governments and borders in perpetuity. This system established the conservative nature of the Continental order against which any would-be reformers had to contend and delineated the recognized powers that would resist all upstarts and newcomers. Baptists were often categorized among the latter groups.

In a general sense, nineteenth-century Europe would undergo three major stages of development. The first extended from 1815 to 1848, a period in which reactionary forces sought to resist change – until an outburst of revolutionary forces in 1848. The second (1848–71) was one of controlled reform, when constitutions were allowed, the last serfs liberated, and other unavoidable concessions reluctantly agreed. The third stage (1871–1914) was

---

[1] Norman Davies, *Europe: A History* (Oxford: Oxford University Press, 1996), 760. [2] Ibid.

a period of heated rivalry, intensified by diplomatic realignments, military developments, and colonial competition.[3]

Although new philosophies and theories emerged to challenge traditional religious assumptions, in Continental Europe's conservative environment, religious change was not appreciated. Insecurities generated by a changing world caused many to hold on to ancient models of faith and order. Romanticism reflected this need for divine assurance. Consequently, European Baptists began to emerge during a period when any force calling for social, religious, or political change had to reckon with this general cultural climate. Five determinative leaders in these efforts included Johann Gerhard Oncken, Julius Köbner, Gottfried Wilhelm Lehmann, Frederick O. Nilsson, and Vasili G. Pavlov.

Central European Baptist Frontiers

Central Europe includes the territories of Austria, the Czech Republic, Germany, the Netherlands, Poland, Slovakia, and German-speaking Switzerland. For Baptists, Germany became the center from which much of its Continental European work would spread during the nineteenth century. Two other significant centers included Sweden and Russia. Baptists experienced their greatest growth in Central Europe in part because social disruptions promoted large migrations of people. German-speaking peoples became dispersed throughout many European countries, and among those populations, European Baptists experienced their greatest successes during the nineteenth century.

When Johann Gerhard Oncken (1800–84) was a teen, he accompanied his father into political exile. During that period, he was apprenticed to a Scottish merchant in Edinburgh, where he encountered evangelical Christianity, was converted, and began his work of literature distribution and personal witness. After returning to Germany in 1823, he disseminated literature for two Bible societies. At the same time, he began to question the practice of infant baptism. Following a period of careful reflection on the issue, he embraced believer's baptism and subsequently was baptized in 1834 by an American Baptist college professor named Barnas Sears, who was on sabbatical leave in Germany. The next day Oncken organized a Baptist church at Hamburg and served as its pastor for the remainder of his life. That congregation constitutes the oldest surviving Baptist church in Europe.

---

[3] Ibid., 760–1.

Oncken and his church soon came under persecution from German authorities. However, following the great Hamburg fire in 1842, the opposition moderated somewhat after he and his church members gave of themselves sacrificially to assist those devastated by the conflagration. Their sacrifices won the respect of citizens and authorities alike and gained a reprieve from harassment. In 1848, changes in the German constitution allowed greater freedom for religious diversity.

Oncken's ministry was especially characterized by two things: his missionary vision and his belief in the power of the printed word. He carried his message to the Balkans, Russia, the Austro-Hungarian Empire, and Scandinavia. In addition, he distributed Bibles and offered personal witness. These methods also were employed by many of his followers with equal success. Two of his associates, Julius Köbner and Gottfried Lehmann, assisted in missionary travels, church development, and education. Köbner is remembered particularly for his hymns and Lehmann for his church work in Berlin.

Oncken felt that union (*Bund*) and training were essential elements for the success of the Baptist movement in Europe. He promoted a sense of cooperation among his churches, which motivated adoption of a confessional statement in 1847 and creation of the Union of Associated Churches of Baptized Christians in Germany and Denmark in 1849. This organization was modeled after the American Baptist Triennial Convention. The *Bund* eventually included churches in Switzerland, Austria-Hungary, Czech Republic, Slovakia, and Poland. Unfortunately, Oncken succeeded best at reaching German-speaking populations that had been shaped under Lutheran or Reformed traditions. He had very little appeal outside those parameters and therefore failed to penetrate the indigenous populations.

An important ingredient of the German Baptist movement's success was a second wave of Pietism that emerged in the early decades of the nineteenth century. This movement was characterized by an emphasis on personal religious experience, the importance of Bible study, dedication to prayer and piety, and a personal experience of conversion. Those qualities were highly valued by Baptists and provided an easy transition for persons who embraced Pietism to accept Baptist identity.

North European Baptist Frontiers

The North European region includes the Scandinavian and Baltic countries. Although Baptists spread quickly into those regions in the nineteenth century, most adherents were of German heritage. Except for Lithuania and parts of Latvia, these were officially Lutheran countries. Yet, in spite of opposition and persecution, Baptists had successfully established churches in most of these nations by the century's end. In this respect, they were pioneers of the free-church movement within those nations, a fact that eventually became a hallmark of Baptist identity throughout much of Europe.

Sweden emerged as the centerpiece of Baptist success in the region and is illustrative of the Baptist story in the rest of Scandinavia. The major reason for Baptists' accomplishments there is associated with a Pietist awakening influenced by earlier revival movements in England and America. Lutheran church authorities held serious reservations concerning the home Bible studies employed by this *läsare* (readers) movement and attempted to stop them. As a consequence, many practitioners of Pietist devotion broke with the Lutheran church and embraced Baptist views.

Swedish Baptists date their origin from 1848, when Danish Baptist preacher A. P. Föster baptized converts at Vallersvik and then later that same day helped organize Sweden's first Baptist church. A Bible colporteur named Frederick Nilsson was present for the occasion. He had embraced Baptist views about a year earlier through the influence of G. W. Schroeder and had been baptized by J. G. Oncken at Hamburg in 1847. Nilsson traveled to Hamburg and was ordained by Oncken shortly after the church's organization. He returned to Sweden with the intention of pastoring the newly organized church but was arrested and convicted of violating Sweden's state-church laws. In 1851, authorities banished him from the country. Nilsson subsequently settled in the United States and began ministering among Swedish immigrants there. He was pardoned by King Charles XV in 1860 and returned to pastor his Swedish church. But by 1868, he had resumed his previous work in America. This pattern of shuffling back and forth between Continental parishes and immigrant communities in the United States was rather common among Swedish and German Baptist leaders.

Anders Wiberg became pastor of the Baptist church in Stockholm in 1855. Through much of the remainder of the century he stood out as the foremost Baptist leader in Sweden. He led Swedish Baptists to hold general conferences, which helped bring unity to the work. After a period in the United States between 1863 and 1866, he returned to Sweden with support from the American Baptist Missionary Union. In 1866, a seminary was organized to help train church leaders. In 1889, the Swedish Baptist Union was formed. Legislation passed in 1873 granted more religious freedoms to Sweden's dissenters, although certain disabilities remained until the mid-twentieth century. Under these changing conditions, Swedish Baptists grew rapidly over the second half of the century.

Efforts to establish Baptist work in Norway date from 1842 when Enoch Richard Haftorsen Svee returned to his homeland with the intention of launching a Baptist ministry. Svee's untimely death disrupted his dream. Fifteen years later, the Danish sailor Frederick Ludvig Rymker took up Svee's vision and brought it to fruition. In 1860, the First Baptist Church of Porsgrund and Solum was organized. In the following years, Baptist work spread to most parts of Norway through the efforts of leaders like Gottfried Hübert and Ola B. Hansson. By 1877, enough churches had been established to require coordination of their work, leading to organization of the Norwegian Baptist Union.

In Denmark, the first Baptists emerged out of the established Lutheran church as a result of Pietist awakenings in the 1830s. Julius Köbner helped initiate Baptist work during a visit in 1839, followed by Oncken's baptism of converts and the organization of the first Baptist church in Copenhagen later the same year. Between 1849 and 1888, Danish Baptists were part of the German Baptist Union. After that, their closer connections to Baptists in the United States – as a result of the large number of Danish Baptist immigrants – led them to adopt a Western orientation. This produced a strongly international perspective among Danish Baptists that has endured over the decades.

The Baptist movement was born in Latvia amid that country's struggles for independence. The Jaunlatvieši (Young Latvians) movement began laying the foundations for nationhood in the mid-nineteenth century by appealing to compatriots of Slavic identity for support against the prevailing German-dominated social order. Forces for Russification first appeared following the Polish-led January Uprising in 1863 and by the 1880s had gradually spread to the rest of what would become Latvia. In the course of these developments, the New Current (a leftist political movement) displaced the Young Latvians in the 1890s. The 1905 revolution reflected the nationalist fervor of populations in the Baltic region. The first quarter of the twentieth century was a period of political chaos and struggle for the region.

The Memel Baptist Church, a German church in German-held East Prussia (today Klaipeda, Lithuania), introduced Baptist work into Latvia when members from that church who had settled in Libau (Liepaja) formed a Baptist congregation. Another Baptist center was established at Windau (Ventspils) through the influence of Adam Gertners. During the 1860s, all Baptists in Latvia were considered members of the Memel church, but after

1876, the Latvian congregations were constituted as independent churches. John A. Frey and William Fetler were among Latvian Baptists' noted leaders in the latter decades of the nineteenth century.

Finland still was part of the Russian Empire when Swedish Baptists established the first Baptist church in the Åland Islands in 1856. The first Finnish-speaking church was organized in 1870. Erik Jansson, a Swedish-speaking Finn, stands out as the foremost leader among the pioneers of Finnish Baptist work. During the nineteenth century, the impetus for most of this work came primarily via Swedish Baptist assistance, with a limited amount of aid being supplied by the American Baptist Missionary Union.

South European Baptist Frontiers

South Europe tended to be very unresponsive to Baptist work. Consisting of the Latin countries of Belgium, France, Italy, Portugal, Spain, and French-speaking Switzerland, the traditionally Catholic-dominated lands tended to show little interest in the evangelical-type Christianity that characterized nineteenth-century Baptists. In the twentieth century, disaffected Catholics have tended to move toward secularism rather than an alternate form of Christianity. However, Baptist mission effort was strong throughout the nineteenth and twentieth centuries despite the disappointing results.

With the exception of some French-speaking work, most Baptist ministry in southern Europe has depended on foreign mission support. Consequently, Baptists have often been looked on as outsiders "with a heretical creed whose cultural values often proved to be a barrier to the message . . . proclaimed."[4] Even in those places where work has been successfully established, it has advanced best among foreign populations that have relocated to the regions, and even then has tended to grow very slowly.

Baptist Frontiers in the Russian Empire

When Baptists first appeared in the Russian Empire, the kingdom basically included all the territories known today as the Commonwealth of Independent States (CIS), the Baltic States, Finland, and Poland. By the twenty-first century, more than a half million Baptists resided in this great landmass. Because of the strong influence of Orthodoxy in the region, Baptist worship, church life, and moral perspectives included features that reflected

[4] Albert W. Wardin, ed. *Baptists around the World: A Comprehensive Handbook* (Nashville, TN: Broadman & Holman, 1995), 271.

this context. Also, their roots in rural areas and their mostly working-class constituency, together with long periods of government suppression, served to perpetuate a traditional morality and theology that Baptists in many parts of the world considered unduly restrictive.[5]

Three independent sources of Baptist life arose in the Russian Empire during the mid-nineteenth century. The first was a non-Slavonic source, mostly German in nature, that established a Baptist presence in numerous enclaves of German, Swedish, Latvian, and Estonian populations. The second developed from Stundist and Molokan groups in the Ukraine and the Republic of Georgia. The third emerged among members of the Russian aristocracy in St. Petersburg.

The earliest known Baptist work in Russia dates to 1855, when a German Baptist tailor associated with the Memel church in Eastern Prussia (modern Lithuania) named C. Plonus moved to St. Petersburg and formed a small group for worship and Bible study.[6] A few years later Gottfried Alf established Baptist work in Poland and also in Volhynia (western Ukraine). In 1864 Baptist churches were organized among German populations at Horzcik and Soroczin in the Ukraine. Over the subsequent decades Baptists grew among the German ethnic communities in southern Ukraine, the Volga, the Caucasus, western Siberia, and in the Tashkent area. The key to their success was the German Stundist movement – a Pietist-type movement in which members met for one hour of devotions. The pattern of development unfolded as follows: The Memel church extended Baptist work into Latvia, especially among German peoples. German-heritage Baptists in St. Petersburg and Latvia expanded the work into Estonia. From there, Estonian Baptists helped found additional congregations in St. Petersburg. In 1887, the German Baptist churches of Russia separated from the Baptist Union of Germany to form the Union of Baptist Churches of Russia. Toleration was extended to German Baptists within the Russian Empire in 1879 but did not include Baptists of Russian or Ukrainian descent.

Bible society colporteurs and German Stundists became the source for Baptist growth among the Ukrainians, although conversion from Orthodoxy was illegal. Ivan Ryaboshapka and Mikhail Ratushnyi became noted Ukrainian Baptist leaders during the period. The first Baptist church to

---

[5] For a careful study of the dissenting religious context of Russia during the period, see Sergei I. Zhuk, *Russia's Lost Reformation: Peasants, Millennialism, and Radical Sects in Southern Russia and the Ukraine, 1830–1917* (Baltimore: Johns Hopkins University Press, 2004).

[6] Abraham Friesen, *In Defense of Privilege: Russian Mennonites and the State before and during World War I* (Winnipeg, Canada: Kindred Productions, 2006), 108–9.

be organized in the Ukraine was founded at Horstschick in May of 1864. It consisted totally of German colonists who had emigrated from Poland and who came to be closely associated with the work of Gottfried F. Alf (1831–98), a pastor at Adamowo, Poland who itinerated widely in western Russia and eastern Europe. A second Baptist church was established about the same time at Sorotschim. Eventually 15 other such churches came to be founded in an area that extended from Zhitomir to Rozyszcze, together with about 75 preaching points, prayer chapels, and house churches.[7] In 1886, a Baptist church also was organized in the capital city of Kiev.

Martin Kalweit, a German Lithuanian, moved to Tiflis (Tbilisi) in the Republic of Georgia in 1862 and became the catalyst for a thriving Baptist work there. His earliest converts were mostly German ethnic Baptists and Russian Molokans. The Molokans (literally "milk drinkers") were similar to Quakers in their teachings and centered in Tbilisi. Gradually, as the German population left the area, the church became totally Russian. In 1880, a Baptist church was formally organized in Tbilisi. From that center, Baptist work extended to other regions of the Caucasus, up the Volga Valley, and into Molokan communities in Azerbaijan and the Don River region. Vasiliĭ G. Pavlov, V. V. Ivanov-Klyshnikov, Deĭ I. Mazaev, Gavriel Mazaev, Ivan S. Prokhanov, and Johann Kargel were among the noted leaders of the emerging work. By 1884, the Baptist movements in the Ukraine and in the Caucasus had united to the point that a Russian Baptist Union was created.

Through the influence of Lord Radstock, Vasiliĭ A. Pashkov, and Modest M. Korff, a spiritual movement was introduced into the Orthodox Church known as Pashkovism. The movement spread among aristocrats and to some elements of the lower classes in and around St. Petersburg in the 1870s and 1880s. Authorities were unsuccessful in attempts at suppression because of support among the city's aristocracy. Johann Kargel and Ivan Prokhanov – both Baptists – embraced the movement and helped it find acceptance within the Russian Baptist movement in 1903.

As this brief sketch demonstrates, the nineteenth-century Russian Baptist tradition included a wide variety of doctrinal sources, including the Oncken German Baptists, the Stundist movement, the Molokan heritage, and Plymouthism through Pashkovite influence. Many of these elements were quite distinct from the predominant Anglo and Anglo-American interpretations of Baptist identity and often were quite intolerant of those holding moral or doctrinal views different from their own. This generated

[7] See Donald N. Miller, *A History of German Baptists in Volhynia, Russia, 1863–1943* (published by the author, 2000).

a variety of tensions among Baptists in that region, a factor that will be explored more fully in the next phase of the Baptist movement in Russia.

Baptist Frontiers in Southeast Europe

Southeast Europe (which included the modern countries of Albania, Bosnia, Bulgaria, Croatia, Greece, Hungary, Macedonia, Romania, Serbia, Slovenia, and Yugoslavia) teamed with ethnic diversity. With the exceptions of Romania and Hungary, Baptists have faced great challenges and very slow growth. As with much of the rest of Europe in the nineteenth century, the sources for Baptist origins included German Baptist settlers, along with colporteurs sent out by Bible societies. Baptist mission organizations showed little interest in the region during this time frame.

Baptist doctrine was first introduced to Bulgaria by a colporteur of German background. Several Bulgarians in Kazanlik converted but lacked a Baptist leader to establish an ongoing work. In 1880, Johann Kargel moved from St. Petersburg to Ruse, baptized candidates in Kazanlik, and then organized a church at Ruse in 1884. Churches were organized at Lom in 1896 and at Sofia in 1899. The work included ministries among Bulgarian, German, Russian, Hungarian, and Romany populations. Throughout the period, Bulgarian Baptists felt neglected by other Baptist communions because their frequent appeals for help got disappointing results.

Hungary gradually emerged as an important center from which the Baptist movement spread into the rest of Southeast Europe during the nineteenth century. Craftsmen from the region who went to Hamburg, Germany, to work after the Great Fire in 1842, were converted and baptized through the ministry of J. G. Oncken and returned to Hungary as Baptists. In 1846, Oncken commissioned John Rottmayer, Karl Scharschmidt, and Johann Woyka to return to Hungary with the mission of inaugurating Baptist work. Intense opposition kept the movement from taking root, however. In 1873, Heinrich Meyer served as a colporteur in Budapest, and in spite of significant opposition, he succeeded in reviving the German Baptist church. Through his efforts, Baptist witness spread not only throughout Hungary but also into Slovakia, Transylvania, and Serbia. The Austria-Hungary Association of Baptist Churches was organized in 1885. Beginning in 1893, two Hungarian Baptists, Lajos Balogh and Andreas Udvarnoki, initiated a movement that helped Hungarian Baptists establish their independence from the autocratic leadership of Meyer – who had tried to keep all Baptist work in Hungry under the control of his church in Budapest.

Political complexities associated with Romania's history contributed to four independent sources for the Baptist movement there. In 1856, Karl Scharschmidt, a disciple of J. G. Oncken, baptized converts of German ethnic heritage who had settled near Bucharest. In 1863, August Liebig organized them into a church, which still exists today, albeit as a Romanian congregation. German Russians from the Ukraine organized a church at Cataloi in 1869 (at the time within the Ottoman Empire). Constantin Adorian established another Romanian Baptist work in the Bucharest and Dogrogea area in the 1870s. Finally, a Hungarian-speaking Baptist ministry was begun in the Transylvania and Banat regions (which were then a part of Hungary). Mihai Cornya surfaced as a dynamic leader in this region and a significant catalyst for Baptist work. Between 1871 and 1910, more than one hundred churches were established in Transylvania, which eventually grew to have the largest number of Baptists in Romania. Labeled "Repenters," Baptists there have formed some of the largest Baptist churches in all of Europe.

General Identifying Characteristics of Continental European Baptists

Among the significant distinctives of the Continental European Baptist movement during the frontier phase of Baptist life was its non-Anglo identity. From the start, the movement was indigenous, at least among peoples of German ethnicity, and subsequent developments reflected the movement's easier fit by its rapid and widespread acceptance. Although Anglo and Anglo-American Baptists exercised assisting roles, they clearly did not hold the key positions of decision making among Continental Baptists. In some instances, leaders from German Baptist heritage attempted to exercise strong control over Baptist developments among non-German ethnic populations, but usually such domination was resisted.

Spiritual awakenings growing out of the Wesleyan revivals in England and the Great Awakenings in North America sometimes contributed to spiritual awakenings among state-church denominations on the Continent, especially among the Lutheran and Reformed churches. In addition, second and third waves of the Pietist movement (which had contributed to both the Wesleyan and North American revival movements) often created conditions favorable to acceptance of Baptist beliefs. Pietism promoted personal devotion, Bible study, prayer life, and spiritual introspection. These qualities created a bridge that facilitated transition into Baptist life. In addition, similar movements, such as those of the Stundists and Molokans, brought the same contextual phenomena to bear on the Baptist movements in Russia and Southeast Europe.

These developments took place in a political environment that tended to be conservative and reactionary. Consequently, popular frustration over pent-up desires for self-determination gradually built and finally began to erupt around the mid-nineteenth century. Although such forces took many directions, much of the working-class population found in Baptist belief and ecclesiology opportunities for religious self-determination. In addition, for many expatriates, especially those of German heritage, Baptist identity offered opportunities to personally shape one's religious life in ways that state-governed ecclesiastical traditions could not do in a foreign land.

Collectively, these factors produced a distinctive European Baptist identity that tended to be theologically conservative, focused heavily on personal piety, was self-assured in the face of challenges, and offered strong leadership roles for lay persons.

BAPTIST FRONTIERS IN AFRICA

Previous chapters have introduced the fundamental cultural and theological traditioning sources of African Baptist life. These included tribal modes of social organization; belief in a transcendent, distant, and supreme creator god; the multifarious and complex actions of intermediate deities; a multitude of spirits present in every aspect of nature; and traditional worship focused around divination and sacrificial offerings intended to placate those mediating beings. The overarching objective of these practices was to establish, maintain, or restore harmony among all elements of creation. To this culturally integrated religious foundation were added Baptist beliefs and practices that introduced new theological and cultural elements derived from European and North American sources. Consequently, the Baptist movement in Africa was forced to deal with issues surrounding the integration of Christianity with African cultures, theologies, and worldviews. That history was fraught with tensions between missionary and indigenous interpretations over the acceptability of a wide variety of beliefs and practices, including customs regarding appropriate dress, veneration of ancestors, and polygamy. Baptists' presence in Africa was further complicated by the fact that the movement's introduction occurred in the context of slavery and European colonization. Inevitably, the two phenomena colored African perceptions of those who arrived sharing Baptist beliefs and traditions.

Slavery and colonization had a major and abiding impact on Africa over the course of the nineteenth and twentieth centuries. Estimates vary, but between 1500 and 1860, probably 14 million Africans were taken out of the continent as slaves. This translated into huge human losses, which hailed long-term consequences reflected in factors like the redistribution of tribal populations, erosion of labor resources, and privation of needed genius and skills. The European colonial "scramble for Africa" further exacerbated the problem.[8] The Western race to control Africa reached its apogee with the 1885 Congress of Berlin and transformed the continent forever. The old tribal, family, and social customs on which African culture had been based were either destroyed or seriously disrupted. The French, English, German, Belgian, and Portuguese divisions of territories were artificial and tended to follow geographic, not tribal or cultural, boundaries. Many of Africa's postcolonial ethnic, religious, and tribal conflicts can be traced in part to this balkanization. These intrusions have contributed to a culturally diverse continent, and one whose divisions have inhibited attainment of many common goals important to the well-being of Africa's nations.

The evangelical revival in Britain and the religious awakenings in North America generated enthusiasm among Baptists to undertake missionary witness among non-Western peoples. David Livingstone's expedition to introduce civilization, commerce, and Christianity to the dark continent helped stimulate widespread interest in Africa and made it one of the lands on which Baptist missionaries and their sending agencies focused immense attention. In addition, Britain's growing presence on the continent furnished an expanding cultural foothold from which to launch mission work. A less noble but more prominent theme in mission literature of the period reveals distress over the growing French and Portuguese colonial presence in Africa. This raised alarms among some Baptists that Catholic influence would overtake the region. Countering the territorial expansion of competing denominations was a powerful motivator for both Protestant and Catholic missionaries in the nineteenth century. Each was convinced that conversion to the alternate form of Christianity was tantamount to eternal damnation.

Baptist Frontiers in Sierra Leone

Besides South Africa (treated in the British Empire section), Baptists initiated work in Sierra Leone, Liberia, Congo, Cameroon, and Nigeria during the nineteenth century. David George established Baptists' first known presence in Africa at Freetown, Sierra Leone, in 1792. He and most of his congregation left Shelburne, Nova Scotia, and joined other black settlers in establishing what William Wilberforce hoped would become a "bridgehead from where the trade in slaves could be attacked and the rest

---

[8] See Thomas Pakenham, *The Scramble for Africa* (Ashton-on-Ribble, U.K.: Abacus, 1992) for a careful study of these events.

of the continent reached for the gospel."[9] George visited England in 1793 and convinced the newly formed Baptist Missionary Society to assist. The society sent two missionaries to establish its work in 1796. But when one of them died the following year, the society's effort was discontinued. Even so, George's often-forgotten mission work in Africa was concurrent with the heralded endeavors of William Carey in India.

In 1855, T. J. Bowen (a Southern Baptist missionary en route to Nigeria) stopped in Freetown to ordain J. J. Brown and George R. Thompson — two members of the local Baptist community — as Baptist ministers. The same year, Southern Baptists decided to initiate mission work in Sierra Leone and employed first Thompson, then Brown as missionaries. Inadequate funding curtailed the effectiveness of this endeavor throughout the remainder of the century. Jamaican Baptists took great interest in Sierra Leone's fledgling Baptist community and gave support to the extent possible. By 1859, Baptists had organized churches at Freetown and Waterloo in addition to a school at Freetown.

Baptist Frontiers in Liberia

Lott Carey, a black Baptist from the United States, paved the way for Baptist work in Liberia. Serving as a missionary of the Baptist Board of Foreign Missions (Triennial Convention), he established Liberia's first Baptist church at Monrovia in 1822.[10] Both Sierra Leone and Liberia were beachheads for British and American attempts to rid themselves of freed slaves by resettling them in Africa. Although this recolonization effort never succeeded, it became the occasion for Baptists' earliest presence in Africa. Their visions for expansion were frustrated, however, by a high mortality rate among missionaries. The medical missionary Ezekiel Skinner is noted for his forty years of service, but most missionaries survived only a few years, many for only months.

The American Baptist Missionary Union (ABMU) supported ministries in Liberia until 1856. It preferred to appoint black missionaries, believing they were "by nature and constitution, better adapted to endure the trials of its climate."[11] This proved not to be the case. After assuming the ABMU mission, Southern Baptists continued their work until 1875.

---

[9] Lamin Sanneh and Gerald H. Anderson, eds., "George, David," in *Bibliographical Dictionary of Christian Missions* (Grand Rapids, MI: William B. Eerdmans Publishing, 1998), 238–9.

[10] See Leroy Fitts, *The Lott Carey Legacy of African American Missions* (Baltimore: Gateway Press, 1994).

[11] "Report on Missions in Africa," presented at the 68th annual meeting of the American Baptist Missionary Union as printed in *The Baptist Missionary Magazine* (July 1882), 182.

From then until well into the twentieth century, black Baptists in the West were the only supporters of Baptist work in Liberia. The Consolidated American Baptist Foreign Mission Convention and Jamaican Baptists sustained the effort during those years. In 1880, Liberian Baptists organized their first nationwide Baptist union, called the Liberian Baptist Missionary Convention. Black Baptists in the United States worked closely with this organization for the remainder of the century.

Jamaican Baptists were significant promoters of Baptist endeavors in West Africa. George Leile, a former slave from Virginia, fled to Kingston in 1782 after British troops withdrew from Savannah, Georgia. In 1791, he organized Jamaica's first Baptist church. The Baptist Missionary Society (BMS) began assigning missionaries to Jamaica in 1814, and through that connection, Jamaican Baptists convinced the society not only to begin mission work in West Africa but also to utilize West Indians in the effort. They hoped through this endeavor to end slavery and transform African society. Subsequently, the society's work in Africa and in the West Indies became closely linked.[12] From Jamaica, John Clarke and G. K. Prince were sent in 1841 to begin work along the Niger River. Stranded en route on the island of Fernando Póo, they came to recognize its potential as a strategic staging point for mission work into Sierra Leone, Liberia, and Cameroon. They proceeded to England and encouraged the BMS to establish a mission there.

Baptist Frontiers in Cameroon

In 1844, Clarke returned with missionaries Alfred and Helen Saker of England and Joseph Merrick and Alexander Fuller of Jamaica to establish a base in Clarence, a town on Fernando Póo (modern Bioku, Equatorial Guinea). A year later, Joseph Merrick moved to Bimbia, Cameroon, and began to minister among the Isubu people. The Sakers initiated Baptist work in Cameroons Town (modern Duala, Cameroon), which was the source of Cameroon's first Baptist Church (Bethel), in 1849. Their first convert, Thomas H. Johnson, later became the church's first African pastor. When the Spanish expelled Baptists from Fernando Póo in 1858, the entire operation was transferred onto the African mainland. This flourishing ministry was disrupted once again in 1884 when German occupation of Cameroon caused the Baptist Missionary Society to hand its enterprise

---

[12]   See Horace O. Russell, *The Missionary Outreach of the West Indian Church: Jamaican Baptist Missions to West Africa in the Nineteenth Century* (New York: Peter Lang Publishing, 2000), chapter 5.

over to the Basel Mission. But when Cameroon Baptists became dissatisfied with the new arrangement, German Baptists found it necessary to assume responsibility for the work in 1891.

Baptist Frontiers in the Congo

Exploration of the Congo Basin in the 1870s drew attention to the opportunities for missionary engagement in that region. With substantial support from the estate of the Baptist layman Robert Arthington of Leeds, England, the Baptist Missionary Society moved forward with a Congo mission in 1878. Among a distinguished group of early Baptist missionaries, George Grenfell became renowned for his exploration of the Congo River beyond the rapids below Kinshasa. Piloting an Arthington-supplied steamer named *Peace*, he charted 3,400 miles of the Congo River system. Consequently, BMS was able to establish a chain of churches and schools that included São Salvador, Lukolela, Bolobo, Yakusu, Leopoldville (Kinshasa), and Kimpese. The network of missions would eventually stretch over 1,200 miles.

The American Baptist Missionary Union (ABMU) agreed to take over the Livingstone Inland Mission's work in 1884. This enterprise extended for seven hundred miles and included seven centers of mission operations. Banza Manteke, Palabala, Vanga, and Sona Bata emerged as the primary bases of ABMU efforts. The initiative was significantly enhanced in 1886, when a revival movement occurred among the African people around Banza Manteke. More than a thousand persons embraced the Christian faith during this Pentecost of the Congo, although many would be forced to wait for years before they could meet the mission's standards for baptism.[13] William Mantu Parkinson was among the early Congolese to embrace Baptist beliefs. He was baptized in 1886. Congo's first Baptist church was organized in 1887 at São Salvador. From these modest beginnings, within a century, the Democratic Republic of Congo became one of the largest and strongest centers of Baptist traditions in the world.

Baptist Frontiers in Nigeria

Baptist work was first introduced into Nigeria in 1850 through the preaching of the Southern Baptist missionary Thomas J. Bowen. The focus of his ministry was in Yorubaland in the western part of the country. He organized Nigeria's first Baptist church in 1853 at Ijaye. Two years later, work was

---

[13] Wardin, *Baptists around the World*, 36.

established in Obomosho, but health problems forced Bowen to leave Yorubaland in 1859. On his way back to the United States, his ship stopped in Brazil, where he happened to encounter slaves speaking the Yoruba language. He attempted mission work among those peoples, but because he spoke no Portuguese slave owners were suspicious of his intentions. Bowen labored in Brazil for slightly more than a year before being forced to leave in 1860.

Although Nigeria eventually became one of Baptists' strongest communities, during the latter half of the nineteenth century, it did not seem very promising. Language barriers, health problems, Islam, and transportation difficulties were but a few of the challenges. The 1860–1 Nigerian civil wars stimulated an anti-Christian backlash from adherents of the kingdom's traditional religions, forcing Southern Baptists to abandon their work in 1872. Two years later, William J. David (a Southern Baptist Convention missionary) and W. W. Colley (a missionary of the Colored Baptist Convention of Virginia) joined M. L. Stone (a Nigerian preacher) in establishing a Baptist church in Ogbomosho. This soon became the center for Baptist work in the country. Tensions between missionaries and African leaders in Lagos led to a serious schism in 1888 and to creation of the Native Baptist Church. This became a decisive African initiative for assumption of control, support, and leadership over Nigerian Baptist church life.

Distinctives of the African Baptist Experience

In the nineteenth and early twentieth centuries, Baptists in Africa were not significantly different from Baptists in England and North America. Missionaries tended to reproduce the same organizational structures, worldviews, forms of worship, types of architecture, methods of education, and ways of proclaiming the Christian message they had known back home. Consequently, most Africans viewed Baptist traditions as foreign – the white man's religion. Missionaries tended to see Baptist faith and Western culture as part of the same fabric. However, over time, experiences like learning Africa's languages to communicate the gospel and translate the Bible, efforts to deal with deeply entrenched traditional African religions, and the need to make the Christian message more meaningful helped missionaries to grow in their comprehension of the necessity that Christianity adapt to the African context. Also, as African Baptists grew in their confidence to interpret the Bible and Baptist ecclesiology for themselves, they increasingly chose to express faith in terms that were meaningful for their own cultural experiences. Gradually, Baptist traditions that were genuinely

African began to emerge, although sometime this happened alongside and in tension with customs that more closely aligned with an Anglo-oriented Baptist heritage.

FRONTIERS OF BAPTIST GROWTH IN ASIA

The continent of Asia possesses such variety of cultures that some scholars question the value of the very designation itself, concluding that the name obscures more than it illumines. Other observers, however, insist that amid Asia's physical, geographical, linguistic, and cultural diversity, there is a unity of civilization that cannot be ignored. This unity amid diversity makes the Baptist story in Asia difficult to recount and evaluate. During the frontier phase, Baptist work was concentrated mostly in India, Ceylon (modern Sri Lanka), Burma (Myanmar), Thailand, Japan, and China. Baptist ministries flourished in Indonesia between 1813 and 1857, but Dutch control of the colony brought that to an end. Baptist work would not return there until the twentieth century. Baptist ministries were introduced into Korea near the end of this period but will be treated in a later chapter. The roots of most Baptist churches in Asia during the nineteenth century can be traced in some fashion to either Anglo or Anglo-American Baptist missionary endeavors. In each situation, regional history, customs, and relationships constituted major ingredients for the subsequent success or failure of Baptist work.

Baptist Frontiers in India and Ceylon

Robert Clive's victory at Plassey in 1757 inaugurated an era of British rule that gradually spread over the entire Indian subcontinent, reaching its full extent in 1849. As a consequence, India was transformed into a supplier of raw materials for Britain's global industrial machine and a market for its manufactured products. At the close of the eighteenth century, Indian society was built around the country's innumerable small villages that formed stable, close-knit, and rather self-sufficient communities. Those villages usually were governed either by a chief or council of elders, and their social structures were organized along caste lines. Over the course of the nineteenth century, however, British governors gradually transferred ownership of the villages to a body of tax collectors called zamindars. This change was inaugurated primarily as a way to collect the revenues used to finance Britain's colonial administration. However, the new system had a far-reaching impact on village life. Slowly, India's economic and social structures were transformed from the small village system to one controlled by a few large landowners. Under the new system village elders ceased to govern, village artisans lost their place in the market, and village unity began to disintegrate.

The development of an export economy caused farmers to shift production from food to cash crops. This required that railways be built to transport those raw materials to the growing port cities and then on to industrial markets. The result of those and associated changes was that, during the latter half of the nineteenth century, the social, economic, and political life of India was radically disrupted. A series of famines later in the century, together with periodic economic crises, served to further the concentration of wealth and land in the hands of a few landlords and moneylenders, augmenting the already-widespread poverty suffered by the masses. In the midst of the transitions, Baptists appeared in India – culturally aligned with the British and bearing a new theology that seemed quite foreign to most Indians. How might the worldviews of Anglo Baptists and those of the Indian masses ever find common ground?

Baptists' first missionaries, William and Dorothy Carey and John Thomas, arrived in India in 1793. Sent out by the Baptist Missionary Society, they eventually established Asia's first Baptist churches. In 1800, Krishna Pal, India's first Baptist convert, was baptized, but progress among the Hindu population was very slow and difficult. After fifty years of work in India, Baptists still numbered fewer than 1,500 adherents. In general, the churches they organized in Bengal (as well as most of North India) were dependent on missionary leadership, financial support, and protection for their survival. This arrangement tended to perpetuate Baptist identity as foreign, which made it difficult for most Indians to find their message appealing. The few who did become Baptists usually became social outcasts and gained the status of foreigner for themselves. Only those with little to lose were inclined to take up a challenge of this magnitude. The degree of opposition led to the establishment of Christian villages as havens for those driven from their homes. By 1844, seven such villages existed in the Kalinga region.

Baptists' greatest successes in nineteenth-century India occurred among tribal peoples, especially in Northeast India. American Baptists began ministries to the Assam tribes in the 1830s, the Meghalaya tribes in the 1860s, and the Naga tribes in the 1870s. These formerly animistic peoples became the core of a strong Baptist community in Northeast India. The first Baptist church in the Northeast was organized in 1845 at Guwahati, and the Baptist Association of Assam formed in 1851. Funding problems generated by the

American Civil War left Baptists of Assam on their own during the 1860s. This unexpectedly proved to be fortuitous. During this interval, Kandura, a member of the lowest caste in Assamese society, took up the challenge and became the means for extending Baptist ministries into the hills. "With the baptism of forty Garos and the establishment of the Rajasimla church in 1867, the number of Baptists in the region doubled almost overnight."[14] Today Baptists constitute a majority of the population in Nagaland and southern Mizoram.

In addition to Northeast India, Baptists became well established in southern India as a result of success among the Dalit communities and in northern Sri Lanka. Canadian Baptists initiated work among the Telugu tribes in 1836, followed by American Baptist missionaries in the 1840s. Telugu tribal areas extended from Orissa almost to Madras and four hundred miles inland. Beginning in the 1860s, the Telugus became more responsive to Baptist ministries, and significant growth began. Earlier, James Chater of the Baptist Missionary Society had moved from Burma to Sri Lanka and despite significant hardships was able to lay the foundations for Baptist work there. Using education as a means to introduce his ministry, he opened schools and translated the New Testament into Sinhala. Ebenezer Daniel succeeded Chater in 1830, continuing the educational work and extended his preaching into the villages around Colombo. Charles Carter served in the regions of Kandy between 1853 and 1891 and attained a wide reputation as a Sinhalese scholar. His accomplishments included a Sinhalese grammar and Sinhalese-English dictionaries. Unfortunately, lack of human and financial resources, together with the rise of a militant Buddhism, contributed to stagnation of the work in the latter half of the century.

India was among the regions of the world where nineteenth-century Baptists concentrated significant missionary effort. Although the percentage of Baptists to the overall population is not great today, one of the largest concentrations of Baptists outside North America is located in the corridor extending from Burma along the Bay of Bengal and southward to northern Sri Lanka. By the end of the frontier period, Indian Baptist churches were still strongly tied to and dependent on Anglo or Anglo-American Baptist missionaries, but some of Baptists' greatest successes had occurred when Indian Baptists themselves took responsibility for extending the ministry. Most of those early Baptists were either tribal peoples or outcasts of Indian

---

[14] Fredrick S. Downs, "Historical Reflections on the Changing Context of North East India," *American Baptist Quarterly* 15, no. 2 (June 1996): 105.

society, a reality that supplied an important context for development of Indian Baptist identity.

Baptist Frontiers in Burma

Burma (officially known as Myanmar since 1989) has a long heritage dating back at least to the Mon era in the late fourth century BCE. Centuries of cultural and political developments had shaped the region when Baptists began their first missionary endeavors there during the last years of the Konbaung dynasty. Established by a popular Burmese leader named Alaungpaya, the dynasty united the kingdom in the mid-eighteenth century by successfully expelling the Bago armies from northern Myanmar, reconquering Bago and southern Myanmar, and regaining control of Manipur. The capital was established at Rangoon during this time. When his son Hsinbyushin conquered Ayutthaya in 1767, China took a military interest in Myanmar. However, after four failed attempts at invasion between 1766 and 1769, the Chinese abandoned their expansionist designs. In January 1824, King Bagyidaw conquered Assam, thereby bringing Myanmar face to face with British interests in India. Three wars resulted in Britain's inexorable annexation of parts of Myanmar in 1826 and 1852, and in its final conquest of the entire kingdom in 1885. As a consequence, Anglo and Anglo-American Baptist missionaries experienced both the benefits and the hardships of ministry during these decades of struggle.

Charles Chater and Felix Carey became Baptists' first missionaries to Myanmar in 1807, when the Baptist Missionary Society sent them to Rangoon from the Serampore mission. Chater left in 1812 to begin work in Sri Lanka; Felix resigned in 1814 to serve the Burmese court. Just one year prior to this, Adoniram and Ann Judson had arrived and soon afterward established the American Baptist mission in Rangoon (an unimportant city at the time). In 1817, the Judsons started printing Baptist literature on a press donated by the Serampore mission, a venture that proved very successful. Believing the work might advance even more rapidly if relocated to Burma's seat of power, in 1824, they moved to the capital of the Burmese Court at Ava. Unfortunately, the move coincided with Britain's first war with Burma, resulting in Adoniram's spending the next year and a half in prison. When released, the Judsons moved south to British-controlled territories, residing first in Amherst (Kyaikkami) – where Ann and their infant daughter died – then to Moulmein (Mawlamyine), where Adoniram's most fruitful years of ministry occurred. Having demonstrated the value printing could have for Burmese Baptist work, Cephas Bennett was commissioned to establish the

American Baptist Mission Press at Moulmein in 1830. As a consequence, printing and literature distribution became an important part of early Baptist ministries in Burma.

The Burmese field was the first foreign mission venture for American Baptists, and they invested heavily in the enterprise. From their initial concentration in urban areas, they gradually expanded to the hill tribes, then to Thailand and China. Adoniram Judson created a script and literature for the Kayins (Karen) and employed Karen assistants and evangelists. This, together with publication of his Myanmar Bible in 1840, became the source of many converts. In 1852, the missionaries Elisha Abbot and Henry Van Meter extended Baptist ministries among the Karens in Bassein. Francis Mason, Josiah Cushing, and Jacob Freidays were instrumental in launching another significant work among the Kachin peoples in the 1870s. A major educational component of American Baptist work included establishment of Karen Theological Seminary in 1845, Rangoon Baptist College (later Burma Baptist College) in 1871, and a widely scattered system of schools for children. By the close of the nineteenth century, Burmese Baptist churches were organized into fifteen regional conventions united by the Burma Baptist Missionary Convention, which had been founded in 1865.

Baptist Frontiers in Thailand

Unlike many other areas of Baptist work in Asia, Thailand (formerly Siam) never experienced foreign colonization. The British gained a colonial foothold in the region in 1824, but an Anglo-French agreement in 1896 guaranteed the kingdom's independence. King Rama I, founder of the Chakri dynasty, moved the royal capital across the Chao Phraya River from Thonburi to Bangkok in 1782. The kingdom's third king, Nang Klao (1824–51), opened relations with Western nations and developed trade with China, and King Mongkut (1851–68) concluded treaties with European countries, thereby avoiding colonization and laying the foundations for modern Thailand. As with most Asian countries in the nineteenth century, Thailand was undergoing major social and economic reforms when Baptists began work there.

Ann Hasseltine Judson initiated the earliest known Baptist work among the Siamese. She took an interest in colonies of Siamese prisoners of war in Rangoon and Moulmein, Burma. Encouraged by Adoniram, she learned Siamese and translated several Christian tracts and a Baptist catechism into that language. Her preparations played a crucial role in the earliest Baptist work among the Thai people.[15] In 1828, Carl Gutzlaff of the Netherlands Missionary Society and Jacob Tomlin of the London Missionary Society began work in Thailand and wrote Adoniram Judson urging the Baptist mission in Burma to send missionaries. In 1833, John and Eliza Jones left Moulmein in response to that request and initiated ministries in Thailand, although government restrictions limited their labors to Bangkok. They soon discovered openness to their teaching among the expatriate Chinese. Boon Tee, Chek Peng, and Chek Seang-Seah became the first Baptist converts in Thailand. Recognizing the great potential for successful work among the Chinese in Thailand but sensing his own commitment to work with the Thai people, Jones urged the American Baptist Foreign Mission Society to send missionaries for that work. In 1835, William Dean arrived and took up the assignment, becoming Baptists' first missionary to the Chinese people. His ministry resulted in the organization of what became the Maitrichit Chinese Baptist Church in 1837. This was the first Protestant church to be organized in East Asia and the first Chinese Protestant church in the world.[16] Two charter members of that church, Tang Tui and Koe Bak, became Baptist preachers and effectively disseminated Baptist work in Bangkok and Hong Kong.

When China was opened to missionary work in the 1840s, however, Anglo Baptists turned their attention northward and largely neglected the Thai field for several decades. Thai (and especially expatriate Chinese) Baptist leaders continued the work under challenging conditions. Only after the closing of China in 1949 was attention again focused on Thailand. Although little can be concluded about Thai Baptist identity development in the nineteenth century, this foundation became important for the expansion of Asian Baptist work in the following period.

Baptist Frontiers in China

Unlike India and Burma, China was not occupied by European colonial powers and therefore was not subjected to the status of a colonial possession. This saved Chinese culture from some aspects of change. However, China was exploited in numerous ways, first by the Portuguese, then the Dutch, then the British. The golden age of Chinese trade occurred in the latter half of the eighteenth century, but that trade had minimal effect on the

[15] Alex G. Smith, *Siamese Gold: The Church in Thailand* (Bangkok: Kanok Bannasan, 1982), 12–13.
[16] Samuel Kho, *150 Years of Thankfulness: A History of the Maitrichit Chinese Baptist Church (1837–1987)* (Bangkok: n.p., 1987), 6.

country as a whole because it was limited mostly to a privileged group of Chinese traders known as the Cohong. However, everything changed in the nineteenth century. The Opium Wars of 1840–2 forced the opening of five treaty ports to Westerners, including Canton and Shanghai. The Taiping Rebellion in 1860 opened seven more ports. Russia took China's Maritime Province, and the first Sino-Japanese War cost China Korea. Throughout the century, world powers exploited China's internal weaknesses for their own benefit. Once again, Baptists entered an Asian country mostly as Anglo missionaries in the wake of Anglo cultural aggression. The fact that the right to preach, disseminate religious views, and erect churches was gained through unequal treaties attained through war tainted any message that Western missionaries might proclaim. Baptist missionaries seem to have had little understanding of how that context and their own cultural perceptions colored the faith experiences they sought to share.

Baptists vigorously pursued mission opportunities in China following the Treaty of Nanjing in 1842. American Baptist work was centered in the regions of Hong Kong and Swatow. Following its creation as a denom-ination in 1845, the Southern Baptist Convention adopted China with a special interest as one of its first foreign mission targets. For the next century, more Southern Baptist missionary resources were concentrated in China than in any other part of the world. Their work was centered mostly in the Canton (modern Guangdong) region of South China. The General Baptist Missionary Society established a mission at Ningbo in 1845 but was unable to sustain the work beyond 1854. Later, British Baptists began missions in Shanghai, then at Yantai. The work languished until Timothy Richard of the Baptist Missionary Society began his work in 1870. Greatly influenced by Hudson Taylor's mission philosophies, he longed to move inland beyond the reaches of Western influence, which he felt was inhibiting Chinese abilities to encounter the message Baptists wanted to proclaim on its own terms. Swedish Baptists began work in Shantung in 1899.

Baptist missionaries went to China with the vision of saving souls. Therefore, they initially employed techniques such as street evangelism, the renting of spaces for preaching services, and tours into the interior to distribute Bibles and tracts. These direct evangelistic approaches did not accomplish their purpose, however. In the context of forced treaties, missionaries, preachers, and Christianity itself were seen as symbols of the Western invasion. What Baptists offered was perceived as a threat to Chinese tradition and culture. Consequently, those individuals who became Baptist were considered by fellow Chinese as foreign – no longer

Chinese. Protected by treaty provisions, these converts usually lived in segregated groups and depended totally on missionaries.

Nineteenth-century Anglo and Anglo-American Baptists generally considered Chinese culture as demonic and incompatible with Christian faith. Experiences with practices like blind marriage, foot binding, corrupt legal systems, and superstitious practices convinced them that Chinese culture and religion required fundamental changes if the people were to become enlightened by God's truth. Missionaries tended to see Westernization and Christianization as essentially the same thing. Therefore, a clash of cultures was an often-unperceived but very real part of Baptists' message in nineteenth-century Chinese society.

In an effort to soften Chinese opposition, Timothy Richard led the way among Baptists in focusing on social work as a means for introducing their message. During the great famine of 1876–7, he developed a fourfold plan for approaching mission work. It included famine relief programs, instruction in Christian civilization, training for new and productive employment, and teaching spiritual truth.[17] His emphasis on the social dimensions of Baptist missions profoundly influenced the thinking of other Baptist missionaries. Eventually, education, medical care, social ministries, and relief efforts were offered as strategic methods for presenting the gospel.

A common thread through almost all Baptist missionary approaches was the need to extract Chinese converts from a hopelessly "heathen" culture and reeducate them into a new Christian culture. This had obvious consequences for Baptist identity within Chinese culture – the belief that the two were incompatible. For a potential convert, this meant a tough choice: being Chinese or being Baptist. Unless that person was in some sense an outcast from Chinese society, the possibility of not being Chinese did not exist; the possibility of not being Baptist did. For those who chose to become Baptist, the struggle over how to comprehend themselves as both Chinese and Baptist became a reality. Anglo Baptist missionaries had thereby introduced an identity that only Chinese Baptists could satisfactorily resolve.

Baptist Frontiers in Japan

Economically and culturally, Japan was unique from the other Asian countries into which Baptists entered during the nineteenth century. It achieved its Industrial Revolution without the severe social disruptions that occurred

---

[17] See Timothy Richard, *Forty-five Years in China: Reminiscences* (New York: Frederick A. Stokes Company, 1916).

in most other nations. This was because the old feudal regime and its traditional social and economic ordering had been gradually undergoing change throughout the period from the late seventeenth to the early nineteenth centuries. This had resulted in a precapitalism that was ready to blossom into a modern economy when Mutsu Hito seized power in 1868. A political revolt was ready to happen when the American fleet arrived in 1853, lighting the fuse for the Meiji Revolution. The emperor consequently had little difficulty overthrowing the old regime, because in reality he was only demolishing the facade of a system that was spent. The fact that this transformation took place without major social upheaval meant that Baptists did not have the same phenomena of social displacement to work with. There were no major cracks in the social fabric that would produce persons searching for new identity, as had been the situation in most other Asian contexts. Consequently, following an initial period of Christian growth after the 1873 rescinding of an edict prohibiting Christianity, the Meiji government recast national identity along lines based on state Shinto and emperor veneration. Subsequent Japanese suspicion of foreign ways rendered Baptist work in Japan frustrating and difficult.

The first known Baptist witness in Japan is associated with Jonathan Goble, who first visited the island as a sailor on Commodore Matthew Parry's 1853 expedition. Inspired by the experience, Goble returned to America, and in 1859, he secured appointment as a missionary to Japan by the American Baptist Free Mission Society. He initially centered his work in Kanagawa, where he completed a translation of the Gospels in 1864. In 1868, he moved to Yokohama. Nathan Brown was sent to Yokohama by the American Baptist Missionary Union in 1873 to work with Goble and formed Baptists' first church in Japan. Three years later, the First Baptist Church of Tokyo was organized. Australian Baptists established a mission at Hiroshima in 1874, but it was closed in 1877. An especially productive literature ministry was begun by Luke Bickel of the American Baptist Missionary Union in 1898. This mission to Japan's Inland Sea islands operated from the boat *Fukuin Maru*. By 1916, he reported work on sixty islands in cooperation with several denominations. Southern Baptist missionaries began work in 1889, focusing their efforts to the south and west of Kobe. By 1900, their eight missionaries had organized only two churches – in Moji and Fukuoka. The 1902 annual report voices their challenges:

Most of our preaching places are rented from people who are unfriendly to our work.... In one of our stations we were forced to change locations five times within six years. Each move involves a loss in the results of the work.... In each new place we have to go through the successive stages of opposition, idle curiosity, indifference, and then a slowly developing interest.[18]

Distinctives of the Asian Baptist Experience

In Asia, Anglo and Anglo-American Baptists encountered complex cultures, most with old and deeply ingrained traditions organized around advanced religious philosophies. In situations where social, economic, and political structures had been disrupted, leaving groups of people alienated and searching for meaning, Baptist missionaries sometimes appeared at the right time to gain an appreciative hearing for their message. This was most often the case among tribal peoples and expatriate ethnic groups. In many other instances, however, Baptists began their ministries in close proximity with colonial conquests. Although Baptist missionaries wanted persons to hear a message of eternal salvation available to all people, inability to distinguish Western culture from biblical principles of truth and the close association with colonial contexts obscured that communication for most Asians. Besides creating impossible cultural barriers for most individuals, this Anglocentric Baptist understanding created significant identity struggles for those who became converts. One way to resolve the conflict was by becoming Anglo (i.e., adopting an identity as a cultural foreigner or outsider). A preferable way, however, involved pioneering a theological trail that would allow Baptist identity to become appropriately redefined to fit Asian cultural forms. Anglo missionary control of Baptist beliefs, practices, and resources tended to make this impossible in the nineteenth century. Much of that endeavor would become the task of future generations of Asian Baptists.

FRONTIERS OF BAPTIST GROWTH IN LATIN AMERICA

Baptist traditions in Latin America initially drew from and built on cultural and theological sources that paralleled but were distinct from those of North America. In contrast to early North American Baptists' predominantly Anglo and Protestant traditioning sources, early Latin American Baptist identity was shaped chiefly in Iberian and Catholic contexts. Additional traditioning influences were derived from Latin America's Native, African, and numerous other ethnic populations. Furthermore, many of the issues associated with the other instances of early modern European conquest

[18] *Annual of the Southern Baptist Convention* (Asheville, North Carolina, 1902), 103.

(such as enslavement, cultural annihilation, and identity crises) that already have been discussed in relation to North American Native Baptists, African and African American Baptists, and Asian Baptists equally are applicable to the diverse Latin American Baptist communities. As in other locations, the unique convergence of these elements produced tremendous traditioning diversity among Baptists in Latin America. In the nineteenth century, their strongest unifying factors came from the organizational structures and resources supplied primarily by Anglo and Anglo-American missionary organizations. But even the firm hand of religious paternalism could not prevent schisms from occurring.

Culturally and religiously, Spain had been shaped by the Roman Catholic "reconquest" of the Iberian Peninsula. Uniformity of religious belief and war against heresy had produced a religious and political culture of inquisition and monarchical control. Portugal was characterized by a somewhat more moderate version of this same heritage. The Iberian system of conquest and Christianization was transmitted to the colonies, so that between 1492 and 1810, "the Church functioned as a political and economic institution and as the social and intellectual catalyst of conquest and colonization."[19] Consequently, Iberian Counter-Reformation Catholicism along with semifeudal social structures dominated most of Latin America's colonial period. Míguez Bonino describes this as a culture in which "obedience to the great king of Spain and submission to the King of Heaven were demanded as one single act."[20] Baptists initially found this cultural environment very difficult to penetrate.

But an exclusive Catholic franchise by Latin America's colonial administrations did not guarantee Christianization. From the beginning, the size and inaccessibility of Latin America's territories, together with insufficient numbers of priests, made a thorough Catholic evangelization nearly impossible. Legal declarations of exclusive toleration for the Catholic faith were not sufficient to ensure that Native and African (nor even Iberian) populations would become grounded in its theology and practices, despite the heroic evangelistic efforts of monastic missionaries. Among Native peoples, an inadequate catechization frequently resulted in a strongly syncretistic blend of primitive religious concepts with elements of Christianity. Among African populations, it produced distinctive religious expressions such as spiritism and voodoo. Even Latin American Catholicism itself exhibited

---

[19]   Richard E. Greenleaf, ed., *The Roman Catholic Church in Colonial Latin America* (New York: Alfred A. Knopf, 1971), 1.

[20]   Jose Míguez Bonino, *Doing Theology in a Revolutionary Situation* (Philadelphia: Fortress Press, 1975), 5.

great diversity of opinion, as evidenced by divisions among Galicanists versus Ultramontanists, liberals versus traditionalists, and *peninsulares* (natives of Spain) versus criollos (American-born Spanish). Therefore, although a dominant popular Catholicism among the Spanish and Portuguese populations made it difficult for Baptists to gain a foothold in Latin America, internal dissent and diversity of belief opened the possibility for alternate religious expressions. As colonies gained their independence over the course of the nineteenth century, one by one, doors slowly began to open for a Baptist presence.

As the Spanish and Portuguese colonial cultures gave way to a British neocolonialist and capitalist culture, Latin America's political and social structures began to shift. Criollos demanded more personal liberties, freedom of thought, political decision making, and economic opportunity. Enlightenment thought, the United States' revolt against England, and nineteenth-century liberal movements fed desires for change. Such conditions made Protestantism more welcome. Sometimes described as "the religion of the investors and developers and as the religion of democracy, progressivism, science, and culture," Protestant churches complemented the emerging culture of individualism, freedom, and enlightenment.[21]

As a consequence of their having been introduced under those cultural conditions, anti-Catholic attitudes were heightened among Latin American Baptists, fostering a strong counteridentity. Early Latin American Baptists tended to define themselves more clearly in the negative terms of being not like the Catholics than in the language of what they actually stood for. Brazil's first national Baptist pastor, Antônio Teixeira de Albuquerque, offers an example of this in his treatise titled "Three Reasons Why I Left the Church of Rome." His argument focuses on rejection of three things: the doctrine of transubstantiation, the requirement of a celibate clergy, and the practice of oral confession and absolution. He calls attention to religious ignorance, clergy misconduct, and superstitious practices as compelling reasons enlightened readers should leave the Catholic Church. Naturally, such arguments appealed most strongly to persons unhappy with Latin America's deeply intertwined ecclesiastical and political institutions. Efforts to exercise greater self-determination and assert more personal freedom during the decades following independence helped strengthen this dimension of Baptists' appeal.

[21] Rebecca S. Chopp, *The Praxis of Suffering: An Interpretation of Liberation and Political Theologies* (Eugene, OR: Wipf & Stock Publishers, 2007).

Baptist beginnings in Latin America during the nineteenth century generally followed a recognizable pattern. First, non-Baptist precursors made inroads into rather isolated sectors of a country, either as business representatives or as colporteurs. Often such individuals managed to introduce Protestant beliefs and practices, but their efforts were usually short lived. As the nineteenth century progressed, mission societies of various types introduced themselves. These efforts mostly occurred after a nation gained independence from its mother country and often were only temporary. Areas like Mexico, the Plate River, Patagonia, Chile, and Brazil were among the most significant of those regions. In many cases, more than one start was required for a mission enterprise to succeed. Finally, after midcentury, Baptists began building on those early experiences by introducing their own work. In most cases, congregations were launched by an Anglo or Anglo-American missionary, who would be assisted initially by national Baptist individuals who subsequently developed among the converts; then churches would be formed and organized into associations under direction of the missionaries; and eventually national Baptist leaders would begin to press for greater decision-making authority. In the nineteenth century, Baptists began work in Mexico, Brazil, Argentina, and Chile. Most other efforts in Latin America did not succeed until later.

Baptist Frontiers in Mexico

Beginning in 1827, numerous attempts were made to establish Protestant work in Mexico, but the country's first Baptist church was not formed until 1864 at Monterrey. James Hickey of Cork County, Ireland, was the founder of that work. Born in 1800, Hickey grew up to become a Baptist preacher in the region around Limerick. Economic factors forced his emigration to Canada, then to the United States in 1830. For the following three decades, he worked as a bivocational missionary in Pennsylvania, Maryland, Missouri, and Texas. In 1861, he immigrated to Mexico – in part because of his opposition to slavery – and became an agent of the American Bible Society.

John Westrup Sr. immigrated to Mexico in 1852 for business reasons and settled permanently in Monterrey around 1861. The following year, his wife, Bertha, of Baptist background, passed away. The Westrups's oldest son, Thomas, in deep grief, began a struggle of faith that eventually brought him into contact with Hickey. Out of those associations, the Christian Church of Monterrey (Baptist) was organized with Thomas Westrup as pastor and the brothers José and Arcadio Uranga among the members.

These three became pioneer leaders of early Mexican Baptist work, organizing six additional Baptist churches by 1869. Besides this, John Westrup, a brother of Thomas, had established three other Baptist churches in northern Mexico by 1879. His significant ministry tragically was cut short, however, when he was murdered while on a preaching tour later that same year.

Throughout the remainder of the nineteenth century, both the American Baptist Home Mission Society (ABHMS) and Southern Baptist Foreign Mission Board (FMB) continued supporting mission work in Mexico. Together they sustained about a hundred missionaries during that period. In addition, many national Baptist pastors emerged who led and expanded the work, including Pablo Rodríguez, Alexander and Francisco Treviño, Zeferino Guajardo, and Teófilo Barocio. Through their efforts, the number of churches grew to the point that two associations of churches were organized, one in Saltillo in 1884 and another in Monterrey in 1885. By the early twentieth century, Mexican Baptists were beginning to reflect the ethnic, political, and linguistic variety that was part of the general Mexican culture. These became the traditioning sources for Mexican Baptist life.

Baptist Frontiers in Brazil

The earliest Baptist presence in Brazil occurred as a result of the U.S. Civil War. In 1870, a group of Southerners immigrated to Santa Barbara d'Oeste in the state of São Paulo, where they hoped to continue the life they had known earlier. The land was favorable for the crops they were accustomed to raising, and slavery had not yet been abolished in Brazil. Among the colonists were Baptists, who organized a church in 1871. Soon they appealed to Southern Baptists' Foreign Mission Board for missionaries. As a consequence, William and Anne Bagby and Zachery and Kate Taylor were sent to Brazil. Antônio Teixeira de Albuquerque soon joined them and together they organized Brazil's first Baptist church for native Brazilians at Salvador, Bahia, in 1882. Because most of Brazil's population lived within one hundred miles of the coast or along the Amazon waterways, this location became strategic. From that center, Baptist work quickly spread southward to Rio de Janeiro, São Paulo, Campos, Espírito Santo, and Minas Gerais. At the same time, it spread northward to Maceó, Recife, Belém, and along the Amazon Basin. Z. C. Taylor, W. E. Entzminger, J. J. Taylor, and J. L. Downing established many of the missionary outposts in northeastern Brazil at this time. Soon, Brazilian Baptists emerged to lead and extend the work, including the Paranaguá family of Piauí, Tomaz de

Costa, F. F. Soren, Theodoro Teixeira, and Francisco de Miranda Pinto. The missionary Erik Nelson, of Swedish Baptist heritage, whose family immigrated to Kansas in the United States when he was a boy, moved to Brazil and established a string of Baptist churches along the Amazon River with the aid of his boat, *Buffalo*. In the south, the Bagbys, A. L. Dunstan, and Solomon Ginsburg experienced great success with their pioneering work. The Brazilian Baptist leaders José Alves, Francisco José da Silva, and Pasquale Giuliani were among the leaders who helped establish the work there.

Another significant source of Baptist heritage in Brazil came from immigrant communities. Baptists were among the German, Bulgarian, Latvian, Russian, and Hungarian populations that settled in Brazil in the late nineteenth and early twentieth centuries. As the American immigrants had done earlier, these groups organized Baptist churches reflecting their own ethnic characteristics. German Baptist immigrants settled in Brazil as early as 1882 and organized their first Baptist church in 1893 in Rio Grande do Sul. Frederick Leimann and Herman Gertner became noted early leaders of this Baptist community. The work was assisted by missionaries sent both from German Baptists in the United States and Baptists in Germany. A German Baptist church was organized in Linha Formosa in 1893 and pastored by Augusto Matschulat. Another church was organized in Porto Alegre in 1897 and pastored by J. Schwartz; it became the center of German Baptist work for the entire region, including Argentina, Uruguay, and Paraguay. Latvian Baptists began immigration to Brazil about the same time. By the end of the century, they had organized four churches in the states of Santa Caterina and Rio Grande do Sul. Arnald Gertner and Richard Inke were among their noted early leaders. Over time, the Latvian and Hungarian Baptist communities integrated into the Brazilian Baptist network of churches. German and Russian Baptist immigrants maintained their ethnic distinctiveness and organized in regional associations.

The dynamics of Baptist origins and early development in Brazil show close parallels to those described earlier for Baptists in the United States. Initially, they faced stiff opposition from the dominant religious community. As the work took root, appeals were made back home for leadership to be sent that could help strengthen and advance the enterprise. The early Brazilian Baptist movement was predominantly of Portuguese heritage, but many other ethnic Baptist communities existed as well. As with nineteenth-century Baptists in many other places, Brazil was receiving immigrants from numerous parts of the world. Thus, an ethnically complex and diverse Baptist movement emerged, rich in variations of conviction and practice. As with other parts of the global Baptist family, the communities were fertile with dreamers who envisioned faith communities that would express and address the spiritual and physical needs of people in their specific contexts. The blend of those dreams eventually breathed life into a plethora of Brazilian Baptist churches and organizations, producing one of the world's largest Baptist communities.

Baptist Frontiers in Argentina

Baptists had two short-lived beginnings in Argentina prior to the first permanent work being established in 1881: the first by the Scottish pastor James Thomas and the second by a group of Welsh immigrants in Patagonia. Paul Besson, founder of the first permanent Baptist church in Argentina, was a missionary of the Swiss Reformed Church in France when he became Baptist. In 1881, he came to be the pastor of a group of Swiss immigrants in Santa Fe Province, but he soon moved to Buenos Aires and started a new congregation there. In addition to founding two other churches, he also became noted for his struggle to secure religious freedom for Argentine Baptists. In 1878, German-speaking immigrants, some of whom were Baptists, began settling in parts of Argentina. They organized their first church in 1894, with many others being established in the ensuing years. Later Slavic Baptists immigrated, adding their ethnic distinctives to this already fertile ethnic mix. Southern Baptist mission work was first introduced in 1903 by the missionary Sidney M. Sowell. The mainstream of Argentine Baptist work would gradually develop in the confluence of these streams of Baptist beginnings.

Baptist Frontiers in Chile

Baptists in Chile have roots that date to the work of Oscar von Barchwitz, a Baptist pastor from Germany. Having immigrated to Chile, he became an agent of the Chilean government to recruit German settlers. By 1884, numerous German families had settled in southern Chile, among them some of Baptist heritage. Following a revival that broke out among the German colonists under the preaching of Philip Maier, a Baptist church was organized in Contulmo in 1892. Two additional churches were organized soon afterward. In 1888, the Scottish Baptist pastor William MacDonald settled in Chile. His ministries eventually became the driving force that gave rise to the Evangelical Baptist Union in 1908.

Distinctives of Latin American Baptist Work

Unlike Africa, where Anglo Baptist missionaries witnessed amid animistic tribal peoples, and Asia, where they struggled to convert adherents of competing major world religions, in Latin America, Baptists sought to convince adherents of another Christian group of their need to embrace a new version of the Christian faith. Nineteenth-century Baptists generally did not consider Catholic Christians to be Christian at all, and some still do not. Therefore, to convince a Catholic to become Baptist was the same thing as winning a soul from spiritual darkness. Baptists generally perceived Catholics as being legalistic, idol worshippers, superstitious, and bereft of any true Christianity.

Despite the significant differences in the nature of the religious challenges, the convert's identity issues were very similar. How could a person be Baptist and truly Mexican or Baptist and truly Brazilian? Although the distance between Anglo and Anglo-American culture and Iberian and Latin American culture was not as great as that of Africa or Asia, it was still significant. In many ways, nineteenth-century Anglo-American Baptist missionaries were inviting Latin American Catholics to join in a counter-identity similar to the one that sixteenth- and seventeenth-century Anglo Baptists had embraced against the Church of England. Until the American Revolution, being countercultural was a major part of Baptists' DNA.

For the most part, however, Baptist counterculturalism in Latin America was not homegrown. In the nineteenth century, it depended heavily on missionary resources, organization, and culture. Eventually, the essence of Baptist theology would have to be distilled by Latin American Baptists in their own context and authentically embodied within their own cultural identities.

FRONTIERS OF BAPTIST GROWTH IN THE CARIBBEAN

The first Baptist work in the Caribbean was initiated by freed black Baptists from the United States. They settled especially on the islands of Jamaica, Turks and Caicos, Hispaniola, and Trinidad. For those Baptists, the islands presented a new frontier of independent survival, self-determination, and promise. The first Anglo Baptist work on the islands came three to five decades later, under the auspices of the Baptist Missionary Society of Britain. When the two cultures of Baptists did finally meet, the results were a mixture of cooperative ventures and misunderstandings and divisions.

Baptist Frontiers in Jamaica

George Leile, a former Virginia Colony slave, began preaching in Kingston in 1782 and organized Jamaica's first Baptist church in 1791. John Rowe of the Baptist Missionary Society (BMS) opened a school for the children of slaves in Falmouth around 1814. Other BMS missionaries followed, including William Knibb, the noted spokesperson for emancipation of slaves. By 1841, Baptists had established at least one church in every parish of the island.

In 1842, Jamaican Baptists organized the Jamaican Baptist Missionary Society. Established initially to support Baptist mission work in Africa and Central America, the society went on to advance Baptist work in Cuba, Costa Rica, Haiti, Cayman Islands, and West Africa. In 1843, Jamaican Baptists established Calabar Theological College. The Jamaica Baptist Union was organized in 1849 to coordinate the work.

After seventy-eight years of work, the Baptist Missionary Society withdrew, depriving the region of much-needed human and financial resources. Jamaican Baptists faced the challenge and continued their effort in heroic fashion, although a weak economic base and the lack of trained leadership negatively affected the work. Horace O. Russell writes that, as a consequence, Jamaican Baptists developed "a new self-awareness and identity which led to the creation of institutions designed to nurture their life in terms of their own needs and not those of B.M.S."[22]

Baptist Frontiers in Bahamas

Frank Spence came to Long Island, Bahamas, as a slave of British Loyalists during the American Revolution. He began preaching and around 1780 organized a church in Nassau. Another former slave named Amos Williams arrived on New Providence from Silver Bluff, South Carolina, in 1788 and began a ministry that continued through the 1790s. Prince Williams and Deacon Sharper Morris arrived in New Providence in 1790 and later organized Bethel Baptist Church, the oldest continuous Baptist church in the entire Caribbean.

In 1833–4, the Baptist Missionary Society sent two Anglo Baptist couples to work in the Bahamas. Concluding that the churches lacked sufficient doctrinal and moral standards, major reform was instituted. This resulted in a division of Baptist work between the churches united with the BMS and

---

[22] Russell, *Missionary Outreach of the West Indian Church*, 251.

those that connected with the Native Baptists. Other divisions followed. When the former BMS missionary Daniel Wilshire returned to Bahamas to work independently, still other divisions resulted. Finally, in 1892, Wilshire and his followers were able to establish the Bahamas Baptist Union, which succeeded in producing a platform encouraging greater coordination of the work among these many and divided congregations.

Baptist Frontiers in Turks and Caicos

Sharper Morris visited the Turks Islands in 1830, hoping to moderate the persecution of Baptists there. On that visit, he baptized fifty converts. About five years later, a missionary couple with the Baptist Missionary Society helped organize the first Baptist church on Grand Turk Island. The Jamaican Baptist Union sent representatives to work with Baptists on the islands in 1849, and three new congregations came out of that effort. The BMS missionary J. Henry Pusey served on the island from 1880 to 1890. He helped develop strong leadership for the work and led in formation of the Turks and Caicos Baptist Union. When the BMS halted its work in 1892, the Jamaican Baptist Missionary Society gave assistance. During the twentieth century, Baptists became one of the largest religious bodies in the territory.

Baptist Frontiers in Trinidad

During the War of 1812, some American slaves managed to gain freedom by joining British regiments. After the war, they were given the opportunity to settle in the southern part of Trinidad near Princess Town. Many named their village after the company in which the soldiers had served, such as Third Company, Fifth Company, and Sixth Company. Some of those settlers were Baptists. In 1816, William Hamilton organized Trinidad's first Baptist church, the Fifth Company Church. John Law of the Baptist Missionary Society began work in southern Trinidad in 1845. He aimed to organize the work and root out what he interpreted as superstition and heathen customs. Once again, this created divisions. The churches that decided to cooperate with the BMS formed the Baptist Union of Trinidad and Tobago in 1860. In 1890, the St. Paul's Independent Baptist Missionary Society was founded, from which numerous independent Baptist bodies have emerged.

An independent tradition known as the Shouter Baptists existed in Trinidad and Tobago as well. Derived from Yoruba slaves transported to the islands, Shouter worship included chanting, hand clapping, bell ringing, and shouting that likely derived as substitutes for African customs and instruments. In the nineteenth century, they existed on many Caribbean islands and were known as Shakers (in Trinidad and Tobago called Shouters). In the early twentieth century, they were outlawed on some islands and began conducting their worship in secret. Theologically, they are similar to other Baptist groups but with views that associate Yoruba dance and music with biblical practices.

Baptist Frontiers in Dominican Republic

The Dominican Republic and Haiti coexist on the island of Hispaniola – the former being culturally Spanish and the later predominantly black and French speaking (or Creole speaking). The earliest Baptists were English-speaking freed blacks from America who settled at Puerto Plata on the northern coast. In 1843, William Littlewood of the Baptist Missionary Society organized a Baptist church within the black community. The church ceased to exist after the 1844 War of Independence but was reconstituted in 1852. The work survived into the twentieth century, when a stronger Baptist work was initiated with the aid of Haitian and other Baptist churches.

Baptist Frontiers in Haiti

Haiti is the second oldest republic in the Western Hemisphere, having declared its independence from France in 1804. Thomas Paul of the Massachusetts Baptist Missionary Society organized a church at Cap Haitien (Cape Haitian) in 1823 but did not remain very long with the work. In 1836, the black Baptist William C. Monroe of the Triennial Convention organized a church of English-speaking black Baptists but left the work the following year. The American Baptist Free Mission Society sent William M. Jones to Port-au-Prince in 1845. He and William L. Judd established Baptist work there and led the work for about twenty years. One of Judd's converts, Lucius Hippolite, a Haitian, became pastor of the church and continued the work for the following thirty years.

Between 1845 and 1885, the Baptist Missionary Society sent missionaries and then turned its work over to the Jamaican Baptist Missionary Society. Jamaican Baptists established work at Jacmel. The church there was led by the Haitian pastor Nosirel Lhérisson from 1894 until 1934. During his administration, the church grew to a membership of more than 2,000 with another 2,000 inquirers. Jamaican Baptists also sent George Angus to St. Marc and Daniel Kitchen to Port-de-Paix and then Cap Haitien. Jemima Straight undertook education work at Ste. Suzanne, and later Elie Marc, a French student studying in Boston, worked in regions around Trou-de-Nord. During most of the nineteenth century, Baptist work in Haiti was very weak. In many cases, it was characterized by halting starts. However, the most successful part of the work was that undertaken by Caribbean Baptists, and much of that success was accomplished by Haitian Baptists themselves.

Baptist Frontiers in Cuba

Some of the Cuban refuges in the United States during Cuba's Ten Years' War (1868–78) became members of Baptist churches. Albert J. Díaz was among them. In 1882, he returned to Havana and led in the organization of an independent church called Iglesia Getsemaní. In 1885, he was ordained as a Baptist minister by Florida Baptists. The following year, Díaz led his congregation to become Baptist. Additional concerns for Baptist work in Cuba originated among some Baptists working with refugees in Florida and among leaders of the Jamaican Baptist Missionary Society. Between 1886 and 1896, when Cuba gained its independence from Spain, Baptist work was initiated or extended in the cities of Havana, Cienfuegos, Regla, Batabanó, Guanabacoa, and Trinidad.

After the War of Independence (1895–8), the Southern Baptist Home Mission Board and the American Baptist Home Mission Society assisted Cuban Baptist work. In an agreement that would shape the future of Baptist work there, they decided that Southern Baptists would take missionary responsibility for the four western provinces, whereas American Baptists would assist the work in the two eastern provinces and the island of Puerto Rico.

Distinctives of Caribbean Baptist Work

With the exception of Cuba, the core of Baptist work in the Caribbean region rested with African American Baptists. Often assisted in significant ways by Anglo and Anglo-American Baptists, the basic identity formation was that of black Caribbean culture, with its obvious African cultural heritage. During the nineteenth century, Anglo and Anglo-American Baptist attempts to minister to these populations, though valuable in some ways, frequently precipitated divisions that seem largely due to differences in cultural understandings. Black Caribbean Baptists were predominantly preliterate and defined their Baptist identity through African cultural expressions that seemed pagan to those of Anglo heritage. This led to misunderstanding and division and to fragmentation of Baptist work.

In spite of the struggles, the stage was prepared for the next period when Baptists grew to constitute the largest Protestant denomination in Bahamas, Turks and Caicos, and Haiti, and one of the major denominations – along with the Pentecostals – in Cuba. The earliest Baptists in the Caribbean Islands came from the lowest economic classes, many being either slaves or freed blacks. Undeterred by their disadvantages, they succeeded not only in achieving a basic organization and leadership but also in providing much-needed social uplift to their adherents and to others as well.

CONCLUSION

At the close of the nineteenth century, Baptist churches existed in each of the inhabited continents. Their numbers in the countries addressed in this chapter were few, but they were taking root in increasing numbers of communities. By 1904, Continental Europe had about 124,000 Baptists, Asia and Oceania about 161,000, Africa about 10,200, and Latin America about 5,500. In most instances, they constituted only tiny minorities amid dominant cultures in which they were not welcome. This reality tended to reinforce a minority and countercultural identity. In general, the impulse that drove these Baptists was a fearless faith in God built on a firm confidence in the reliability of Scripture and the need to give expression to this through a supportive worshiping and witnessing community.

Much of the early impetus came through Baptist immigrants and missionaries. As a consequence, early Baptist church and denominational structures in Europe, Africa, Asia, and Latin America reflected heavily the influence of their British and North American sources. At times, those frameworks functioned adequately to support the advancement needs of local Baptist communities. Unfortunately, they also tended to betray their foreignness to local non-Baptist populations who resisted their intrusions. But despite those handicaps, these Baptists were beginning to dream of new and better things. In many instances, Baptists offered a faith option that nurtured dreams of personal liberties, freedom of thought, enlightenment, and choices in religious expression. Part of Baptists' success rested in the fact that they appeared at the right time in many cultures that were on the verge of embracing liberal freedoms. Baptists' discovered that their greatest opportunities for acceptance were to be found among the masses that were

Figure 6. Singers illustrate the very up-to-date methods and technologies employed by many Baptist congregations of India today.

Figure 7. A women's choir from Northeast India represents the many tribal traditions and long history of Baptists in India, Nepal, Myanmar, and Thailand. (Both photos courtesy of Benjamin Chan, area director of the American Baptist International Ministries for East Asia and India).

Figure 8. U Naw Baptist Church, Yangon, Burma's first Baptist church organized by Adoniram and Ann Judson in 1816 (author's photo).

Figure 9. First Baptist Church, Mawlamyine, Burma, organized by the Judsons in 1827 (photo courtesy Francisco Litardo, Central Baptist Theological Seminary, Shawnee, Kansas).

Figure 10. Ann Hasseltine Judson (1789–1826) Adoniram Judson Sr. (1788–1850), the pioneer American Baptist missionaries to Burma (both Judson engravings courtesy of American Baptist Historical Society, Valley Forge, Pennsylvania).

most oppressed by the existing sociopolitical structures and were hungry for a new vision of life. In Baptists' frontier phase, new dreamers were born. In the subsequent phase, they entered the process of confronting the powers of status quo entrenched in the existing political, theological, social, and ecclesiastical order.

GLOBAL OVERVIEW OF BAPTISTS AT THE CLOSE OF THE FRONTIER PHASE

When viewed globally, Baptists during the frontier age were overwhelmingly an Anglo cultural force. The strength of their movement continued to be found among the globally expanding Anglo population. Exceptions to this can be found among certain German-speaking peoples, where a slightly different cultural force was at work. Mission and evangelistic efforts attempted to extend Anglo and Anglo-American understandings of Baptist faith into a variety of other cultures and did succeed in some contexts. In a few cases, an Anglo Baptist theological understanding was blended with a non-Anglo culture sufficiently for that culture to develop

Figure 11. The Maitrichit Chinese Baptist Church organized in 1837 in Bangkok,
Thailand (author's photo)

its own Baptist traditions; the African American Baptist tradition is an
example. In many other cases, becoming Baptist meant losing one's Native
culture and attempting to live under an Anglo version of Baptist tradition.
In most instances when this was tried, the results were not satisfying. The
Native American Baptist tradition offers evidence of this experience.

As the overview presented in these chapters suggests, throughout this
period, the Baptist movement evinced an ever more complex traditioning
process. The interplay between power and dreams grew more intense as
Anglo and Anglo-American Baptists expanded their influence in the wake
of European colonial extension and as British and American societies began
to experience social, political, economic, and religious transformations. In
general, the Anglo Baptist community shared a dream for a world expressive
of its theology and values. Anglo Baptists differed among themselves over
issues like the extent of Christ's atoning work, open or closed communion,
methods for doing their work, and slavery. However, most were convinced
that at the core of the Anglo Baptist tradition was a divinely inspired
perception of the way life, church, government, gender roles, and all of

culture should be. That way was believed to be the best one for all people, everywhere, and at all times.

Armed with this understanding, how did Baptists of the dominant and power-holding Anglo culture perceive and address the dreams of non-Anglo populations, especially in colonial contexts? Indications are that they could not imagine any other dreams than the ones they entertained for themselves. Thus, power and dreams began their processes of interaction. In many instances, the culturally defined dreams of Anglo Baptist traditions were impossible for the non-Anglo. If social, political, and economic barriers excluded a person from ever attaining the culturally defined dream, what possibilities were left? For some it meant trying to become "white" while forever standing on the periphery of a dream they could never reach. For others it meant elevating the dream to an eschatological level – perhaps in a future life they might attain the dream of complete inclusion as fully empowered persons of God if they obeyed the religious rules in the present. For still others, attaining their dream resided in somehow adequately "Baptistifying" their culture so as to allow for coherence between who they were and what they believed God wanted them to be.

The same tension existed for many Baptist women. An impenetrable barrier stood between the realities of the lives they were forced to live and the culturally defined ideals of womanhood they were expected to attain. Some Baptist women found substitute ways to grasp portions of the dream while not appearing to violate the restrictive dictates of true womanhood. Missionary vocation and local church mission-support organizations offered one of numerous avenues for this.

In the end, however, Baptist teachings about the nature of God's liberating gospel planted the seeds for new interpretive traditions. The interpretive intentionality of nineteenth-century Baptist traditions could not prevail at all points. New Baptist dreamers were born whose voices began to address the matters relevant to their own contexts and apart from the interpretations the various Baptist authorities desired to impose. Consequently, the next phase of Baptist development would be characterized by growing tensions that emerged from a variety of primal traditions and influences, each with its own version of what being Baptist should look like.

PART IV

Age of Proliferating Traditioning Sources
Global Baptist Development Phase 3,
1890 to Present

The Baptist Church in Russia has proved her vitality. Not only has she survived the systematic and long-continued persecution of both Church and State, she has done more – has grown strong, and diffused herself throughout the vast Russian Empire: "from the glowing plains of Colchis to the bleak rocks of Finland" – from St. Petersburg, across the snow-covered deserts of Siberia, to Amur and Manchuria. If a man should travel from Odessa to Churbin – a month's journey by rail – he would find even in the latter remote town a little body of Russia's believers. As to the variety of the nations and tribes who up to the present time have embraced our Baptist faith in their land, they comprise: Russians (proper), Armenians, Tartars, Germans, Poles, Esthonians [sic], Livonians, Lithuanians, Letts, Finns, and Swedes.

Vasili G. Pavloff, Odessa, Ukraine
*The Rise, Growth, and Present Position of the
Baptist Body in Russia*, 1908

A BAPTIST PROFILE

On July 30, 1960, the Congo was granted its independence from Belgium. As would occur in numerous similar situations, many Congolese Baptists began to dream of a new day – one in which they would have greater choices over their own destinies. Ministerial ordination was symbolic of the problems that long had irritated these African Baptists. As did most other mission groups in Africa at the time, missionaries of the Conservative Baptist Foreign Mission Society (CBFMS) refused to ordain African pastors. Many believed that ordination required a level of education not available to Africans and, therefore, was a status that only missionaries could attain. Properly trained pastors (*wapastor wachungaji*) could administer the sacraments, but missionaries believed that ordained status would cause those leaders to become conceited and refused to extend to them that level of recognition.[1] With no expectation of an end to the control of African Baptist churches by foreign Baptist leadership, some Congolese Baptists broke with the missionaries and formed a committee that they hoped could gain legal recognition for Congolese rights to ownership and administration of Baptist properties. Previous attempts under colonial governors always had been decided in favor of the missionaries. Many Congolese Baptists hoped that a change of government would offer a new opportunity.

In the Kivu region, a considerable number of Baptists joined the Centre de Regroupement Africain (CEREA), convinced that the political party could offer the greatest hope of aid for peasant farmers, for the redistribution of wealth controlled by European settlers, and for their freedom from foreign domination. Building on their earlier efforts to gain greater control over Baptist resources, certain antimissionary Congolese attempted to leverage the situation to their advantage and have the new government grant them management over mission resources. Most missionaries seriously resisted the effort, convinced that African leadership did not have the ability to manage the properties and suspicious that their true motive was to seize the wealth and properties for themselves.[2] The result was typical of such efforts – a division occurred, with some African Baptists siding with the missionaries and others taking strong positions favoring the efforts of the nationalist Baptist group.

The Conservative Baptist missionary Don Nelson became convinced that, "under the veneer of deference and submission Africans had, in fact, been chafing under humiliating missionary domination; and this was behind the manifestation of hostility that, heightened by nationalistic fervor, was boiling over."[3] In a paper titled "Parallel Divergences," he sought to express the perspectives of both parties in the situation as he was able to decipher it:

Both [sides] feel their cause is completely justified and righteous. Both can quote scripture to prove their point.... Neither group can understand how the other can possibly be so blinded as to not see the error of its way....

The African is fighting the battle of human rights. Suddenly he wants recognition, respect and equality.... Anyone who stands in his way is obviously sinning because he feels himself to be a creature of God, created in the image of God and has every right to expect equality, recognition and respect as well as full authority over his own affairs.... He has been an inferior, treated with disdain and repeatedly told

---

[1] Jack E. Nelson, *Christian Missionizing and Social Transformation: A History of Conflict and Change in Eastern Zaire* (New York: Praeger Publishers, 1992), 61–3.
[2] Ibid., 92–4.   [3] Ibid., 97.

that in the final analysis he is extremely ignorant. Something deep within his soul throbs and surges for he knows these ideas are not true. . . .

To assure himself that he has equality, he demands more authority, higher pay, better housing. . . . Missionaries see this as only the lust . . . for filthy lucre. . . . [Missionaries, on the other hand,] oppose him because he capsizes our mission program. To jettison our sacred mission program really wasn't his primary objective. It was merely an unfortunate necessity as he leaped toward maturity. He cries for recognition [as a human being] and we can't see the high quality of his basic aims (however right they might be) because all we can see is the beautiful and holy mission structure which is crumbling before our very eyes. . . .

The present skirmish . . . is centered, we say, on a concerted effort on the part of Africans to destroy the divine principles of the authority of the Word of God and the autonomy of the local church. But alas, for him the independence of the local church is only an incidental as he hurries forward toward his goal of human rights – equality, authority over his own affairs. . . .

Our Conference meets and decides when, if ever, they [African Baptist leaders] can be ordained. Our Conference determines how their [African] children will be educated. We determine how and when and where we will have medical work. . . . To them [the Africans] it is obvious they are not free. They don't have a voice; they are not even consulted. . . . [4]

In these words, Nelson captures the conflicting dreams of parallel Baptist communities – one with most of the financial, organizational, educational, and physical resources (and therefore the power to control), and the other with only a dream for a better and self-determined life. What is described here, with a few modifications, would be repeated over and over in numerous locations during the twentieth century. Moreover, what is presented here as a conflict between missionaries and national Baptists also existed at other levels of Baptist life, where parallel dreams of variant Baptist communities using the same Bible and the same basic faith tradition and the same family name saw the world through very different sets of eyes. Nineteenth-century Anglo and Anglo-American Baptists never imagined that the cause they were promoting around the world could ever have developed culturally variant interpretations capable of bringing the Baptist movement to a crisis of identity. Each Baptist body was certain that the theological interpretative intentionality it employed was the right one and would be embraced in toto by those enlightened to its truth.

[4] Don Nelson, "Parallel Divergences," in Jack E. Nelson, *Christian Missionizing and Social Transformation: A History of Conflict and Change in Eastern Zaire* (New York: Praeger Publishers, 1992), 98.

CHAPTER 6

Baptists' Evolving Traditioning Sources in Africa, Asia, and Oceania

In general, Baptists were not prepared adequately to handle the array of alternate perspectives thrust on them over the course of the twentieth century. The major medical, technological, political, social, and scientific advancements of the twentieth century offered ideational possibilities Baptist theological frameworks were not proficient to negotiate. Changes in those fields radically transformed the ways much of humanity lived and perceived its world, producing ethical, theological, and organizational issues that many Baptists individually and corporately were not equipped to face. As the century progressed, clear differences appeared in the priority rankings given by distinct Baptist traditions to the varied matters of local and global concern. Those variations reflect obvious ethnic, income, social class, and regional discrepancies and suggest that a complex set of traditioning sources were at work within the Baptist movement, many of which had been concealed by the prevalent ways of conceptualizing Baptist identity.

Among the major topics of contention addressed by Anglo-American Baptists were evolution, biblical critical studies, feminism, the civil rights movement, faith and politics, sexual orientation, and medical research (such as cloning and stem cell). In general, such issues focused on ideological and technological shifts that threatened prevailing Anglo-American Baptist worldviews. African American Baptist struggles were more focused on questions of how to approach justice issues such as civil rights, housing discrimination, educational inequities, and health-care costs. Issues raised by technology did not seem as important as liberationist-oriented theological concerns. British Baptists wrestled with a growing secularism that was augmented by the horrors of two world wars, seriously declining membership, and identity issues over what it should mean to be Baptist in a society that increasingly questioned the relevance of religious faith altogether. Russian Baptists had major divisions over whether a Christian should cooperate with a communist government by obeying laws regulating religious activity.

Baptist women in various contexts tended to express more concern related to the theological issues surrounding equal opportunities in education and employment, family matters, and gender insensitivity in Baptist life. In Latin America, Africa, and Asia, Baptists seldom divided over the issues about which Anglo-Americans fought. This indicates something about the lack of relevance of those concerns in other cultural contexts. Anglo and Anglo-American Baptist theological divisions frequently were imported via missionaries into those contexts, especially through competing mission organizations created expressly as a consequence of differences back home. Many of the divisions that developed in non-Western regions grew out of disagreements with missionary leadership; the growing influence of Pentecostal practices in Baptist church life in some regions; and theologies that developed over particular local concerns, especially liberation theologies. As had been the case during previous phases, some Baptists reacted against innovation, others took more accommodating approaches, and still others grew confused by the ambiguity among Baptists over how to address the multitude of challenging issues that seemed to be surfacing.

Culturally, Baptists readily accepted the advantages of advancements in communications and transportation, which allowed them to be more connected and directly involved in distant parts of the world. At a personal level, most Baptists lived into the changes in worldview inculcated by the theories of relativity and quantum physics. At a theological level, however, they often chaffed and expressed concern. From a finely tuned machine operating according to natural laws that were discoverable by the human mind, the world was becoming more complex, doctrines more relative, and identity more uncertain. The consequent relativism of culture, morality, and authority generated much debate, conflict, and division among Baptists.

Two world wars, threats of nuclear annihilation, environmental contamination, global warming, energy shortages, economic crises, and terrorism caused many non-Western peoples to question the basic assumptions of Western culture. What had seemed self-evident and superior a century earlier had less appeal. Although on the one hand international corporations, popular music, and entertainment seemed to suggest an increasing cultural homogeneity, on the other hand, pluralism and diversity seemed to make local communities more aware of their ethnicity, uniqueness, and value. Increasingly, representatives of Western Baptist bodies came to be seen more as partners in ministry whose decisions and wishes might be questioned and overruled. With booming Asian economies, Western Baptist institutions found themselves sometimes seeking financial assistance from those who once had asked them for handouts. For some Baptists this required incredible adjustment and reassessment of long-held assumptions of cultural superiority, all of which were fraught with implications for the future of global Baptist traditioning sources.

When the twentieth century opened, Britain was the world's most powerful nation. But as the decades progressed, Britain's empire began to shrink and its economy to struggle. Japan, however, developed its industrial base at an incredible speed and rapidly expanded its empire throughout eastern Asia. That empire was lost during World War II, but Japan's economic prowess soon recovered and had gained the world's respect once again by the century's end. The United States also continued to develop as a world leader. World War II opened a new chapter in world history, with the United States and the Soviet Union emerging as leading world powers. The ensuing Cold War not only divided governments into spheres of influence and exerted pressure on the political policies of most nations, they also divided Baptists into similar spheres of thinking.

After World War II, most Asian and African countries gradually gained their freedom from European colonial control. The methods for achieving this varied widely, from nonviolent protests in India to armed rebellions in Kenya and Ghana. France was forced out of Indochina and Algeria, the United States granted independence to the Philippines, and all European countries gradually withdrew control over their colonial lands. In the end, Russia gave up the domination it exercised over the Eurasian republics.

By the early twenty-first century, global Baptists ministered in a very different world than the one they had known a century prior. Communications, transportation, and medical technologies had radically altered the daily lives of most of the world's populations. Europe, divested of its colonial empires, had achieved a lasting peace for the first time in centuries. China, with about 20 percent of the earth's population, had opened its doors to interaction with the modern world and in the process emerged as a new economic powerhouse. The Indian subcontinent, with 17 percent of the planet's population, had secured independence for the first time in centuries and was on its way toward becoming a major economic force as well. Africa, with nearly a billion people, had become a continent of truly independent new nation-states. Economically and in other ways, the world was experiencing a second wave of globalization, occurring at a time when the United States was largely unchallenged in its position of world influence and therefore carrying many Americanizing overtones. Consequently, those populations that felt threatened by the flood of changes taking place often focused their feelings around anti-Western or anti-American rhetoric. This especially became the case in the Middle East.

Globalizing economic structures widened the gap between the rich and the poor. Among other things, this has meant that the Baptist world has faced a growing divide between those who live with abundance and those who suffer abject poverty. This not only has generated differing spheres of experience but also is producing ever-widening varieties of traditioning sources that will require diverse theological perspectives. In addition, health issues (such as AIDS, SARS, and West Nile Virus) threaten to destabilize many regions of the world where Baptists are currently experiencing their principal growth.

A WORLD ALLIANCE FOR BAPTISTS

During the seventeenth and eighteenth centuries, many Baptist congregations grew in recognizing their need for greater cooperation with other Baptist bodies. Slowly, they formed regional associations of like-minded churches. In the nineteenth century, the need for even larger venues for collective effort resulted in the formation of organizations that were national in scope. In 1813, English Particular Baptists formed a Baptist Union as the first national organization for their work. The following year, American Baptists organized the General Missionary Convention. By the end of the nineteenth century, national unions and conventions of Baptists could be found around the world.

As the twentieth century opened, increasing numbers of Baptists perceived the need for a still larger fellowship of Baptist churches. Recognition of this need began to coalesce around issues and concerns that were greater in scope than any single national Baptist body could encompass. A series of Baptist congresses held between 1882 and 1914 offer one illustration of this growing interest. Those conferences originated in 1881 with a group of Baptist ministers in New York who envisioned a forum for "discussion of current questions – religious, social, political, or philosophic." Organizers decided that, rather than advocate particular Baptist positions, the meeting would offer an opportunity to exchange views so ordinary people could explore contemporary world problems. This, together with similar conferences in other parts of the Baptist world, accompanied what some have called the first wave of globalization, which was brought to an end by World War I.[1]

---

[1] Horace O. Russell, "Early Moves in the Direction of Greater Cooperation," in *Baptists Together in Christ, 1905–2005* (Falls Church, VA: Baptist World Alliance, 2005), 9–10.

Besides congresses, other developments helped move the initiative along. The 1891 union of General and Particular Baptists fueled interest in further collaborative efforts on the part of British Baptists. Also, the requests sent by overseas Baptist churches to the Baptist Union of Britain for assistance in finding pastors, the need expressed by Russian Stundists for Baptist intercession with the Russian government on their behalf, and British Baptists' desire to promote closer union with Baptists in the colonies contributed momentum to the movement. In addition, several Baptists in the United States began promoting the notion of a world gathering of Baptists. Finally, John Howard Shakespeare, secretary of the Baptist Union, was joined by Alexander Maclaren and John Clifford in convincing English Baptists to extend an invitation to Baptists of the world to join together at a meeting to be held in London on July 11–19, 1905. There the World Baptist Alliance was organized.

This gathering of Baptists was called an alliance to clarify its nature as a meeting, not a council. The body has no authority over churches or national Baptist unions but serves as a forum for collaboration. Its principal purposes include promoting sensibility of other Baptists and their unique qualities, facilitating Baptists' worldwide connectedness, providing encouragement for Baptists surviving in hard situations, and offering a united voice on matters of mutual concern (such as justice issues, human need, disaster assistance, and interfaith relations).

The Baptist World Alliance is reflective of the shifts in global Baptist life over the course of the twentieth century. Although the following statistics reflect only those Baptist bodies that are affiliated with the Baptist World Alliance, they do visualize important trends. In 1904, Baptists numbered about 6,188,000. Of that number, 395,000 were located in the British Isles; 5,450,000 in the United States and Canada; 42,300 in the Caribbean Islands; 124,000 in Continental Europe; 161,000 in Asia, Australia, New Zealand, and the rest of Oceania; 10,200 in Africa; and 5,500 in Middle and South America. The Baptist World Alliance statistics for 2007 show that, a century later, the Baptist distribution is roughly as follows: of a world total of approximately 53 million Baptists,[2] 789,500 were located in Europe (including the British Isles); 37 million in the United States and Canada; 257,000 in the Caribbean Islands; 5,265,000 in Asia, Australia,

[2] In 2004, the Southern Baptist Convention decided to withdraw from membership in the Baptist World Alliance. Claiming a membership of 16 million, the results would be significantly skewed should they be left out. Consequently, the numbers used here reflect the Baptist World Alliance statistics plus Southern Baptist Convention totals for the sake of this rough comparison.

New Zealand, and the rest of Oceania; 7,253,000 in Africa; and 2 million in Middle and South America. From a regional perspective, in 1904, 97 percent of all Baptists were located in the British Isles, the United States, and Canada. By 2007, that had shifted to 70 percent. Although these numbers obscure the ethnic makeup within each national Baptist grouping, they do illustrate that a major change is under way in global Baptist life. The following regional analyses will offer greater clarification.

AFRICAN BAPTISTS' EVOLVING TRADITIONING SOURCES

At the beginning of the twentieth century, the entire African continent, with the exception of Ethiopia and Liberia, was claimed by European powers. The major players were Britain and France. A second tier included Belgium, Portugal, and Germany. Spain and Italy were less significant contenders. Germany lost its African holdings after World War I, and Britain, France, Belgium, and South Africa took over those territories. The nature and extent of control exercised by these authorities varied greatly, however. In British West Africa, for example, Britain's primary interest was extraction of wealth and strategic advantage for the Royal Navy. No serious effort was ever made to colonize these regions. In other areas, however, colonial interests became more deep seated as settlement by European populations was promoted. Among the colonies that attracted sufficient settlers to make a lasting impact were British East India, Northern and Southern Rhodesia, and South Africa. France developed plans to settle Algeria, with intentions eventually to incorporate it as one of the nation's provinces – a goal that proved to be impossible.

In general, colonial occupying countries did not have sufficient personnel to administer directly the territories they had claimed. Consequently, it became necessary to exploit local power holders for assistance. This practice became radically disruptive to the traditional structures of African leadership, as many Native individuals and groups discovered opportunities to gain power within their local communities through cooperation with colonial administrators. In many cases, aspiring entities invented traditions to legitimize their claims to power, complete with appropriate ceremonies and artifacts.

The intellectual roots of African nationalism developed during the period between the world wars. Some African politicians and intellectuals began to recognize their positions of strength during World War I when conditions forced their colonial overlords to rely heavily on local populations for their own defense. The divisions and atrocities of the war shattered the myth of the superior European, giving insightful African voices a toehold from which to gain advantage against their occupiers. Although most European colonial administrations held firm during the period, the way was beginning to open for the post–World War II independence movements.

Africa's freedom movements began with Ethiopia in 1941 (Liberia, South Africa, and Egypt were already independent). Having been occupied by Italy in 1935, Ethiopian freedom fighters and British forces expelled Italian armies and declared Ethiopia's sovereignty in January 1941. Libya initiated Africa's postwar wave of independence movements in 1951. In the 1950s and 1960s, most of the rest of Africa gained independence. Portugal was the most reluctant of the colonial powers to grant independence to its colonies and did so only after years of bitter warfare that lasted until the mid-1970s. Following independence, most countries and cities that had been given names by colonial occupiers were renamed according to African traditions. In numerous cases, localities have been renamed more than once.

The Cold War era brought both benefits and liabilities to Africa. Among the benefits were the subsidies and other resources the United States and Soviet Union were willing to provide in exchange for total loyalty to the particular country's ideologies – communism or capitalism. The liability came in the form of often-brutal dictators who were kept in power by this system of patronage, although not every country followed this path. The end of the Cold War around 1989 had a significant impact on Africa's political environment. Economic aid shifted to governments that (at least ostensibly) promoted democratic freedoms and held free elections. Although this resulted in accusations of fraud and violence, the pressure was toward greater involvement of citizens in determining their nations' futures.

As noted in previous chapters, Baptists' presence in Africa at the beginning of the twentieth century was concentrated in the modern countries of Nigeria, Liberia, Congo, Cameroon, Malawi, and South Africa. Besides the indigenous sources that sprang up among European settlers in South Africa, most of the rest of Africa's Baptist movement had roots in European and North American Baptist missionary efforts. Prior to World War I, the major missionary agencies engaged in African Baptist work were the Baptist Missionary Society of Great Britain, the Mission Society of German Baptists, the American Baptist Missionary Union, the Southern Baptist Foreign Mission Board, the National Baptist Foreign Mission Board, the Jamaica Baptist Missionary Society, and the Lott Carey Baptist

Foreign Mission Convention. Since World War II, the number of missionary agencies has grown significantly. A new trend that is exerting a significant impact on Baptist ministries in Africa involves non-African Baptist churches and associations that partner directly with African Baptist entities for mutual development. In addition, over the past three decades, Africa has suffered major famines, brutal civil wars, genocide, and health crises. Baptist ministries have been initiated in response to each of these pressing human need situations.

West African Baptists

Early in the century, the West African region was under the colonial domination of Britain and France.[3] However, after World War II, nationalist movements emerged, the most noted being that led by Kwame Nkrumah of Ghana. In 1957, Ghana became the first colony south of the Sahara to gain its independence. By 1960, the French colonies had gained their freedom, and by 1974, all of West Africa had been liberated. In the early days of independence, numerous leaders arose offering creative and promising ideas for the region's future. Among these figures were Léopold Sédar Senghor, founder of the negritude movement; Cheikh Anta Diop, historian of Africa's ancient Pharaonic Egyptian civilization; Félix Hpuphouët-Boigny, proponent of pro-Western liberalism; and the work of Abdoulaye Ly, Joseph Ki-Zerbo, Adu Boahen, Kennety Dyke, and J. F. Ade Ajaya, who offered new insights into the devastating impact of colonization and the Atlantic economy on African societies. However, nationhood did not end the region's problems. Internal conflicts, corruption, and civil wars continued to trouble Nigeria, Sierra Leone, Liberia, and Côte d'Ivoire, and numerous military coups plagued Ghana and Burkina Faso. Some observers have blamed many of these difficulties on the artificial political entities established by European colonial powers that created countries along boundaries that followed geographical features rather than tribal territories. Consequently, historically rival populations were bound together in political entities difficult to govern and whose unity would require generations of national identity-building efforts. For varieties of reasons, many West African countries have failed to reach the economic potential their appreciable natural resources would warrant. This failure has

---

[3] For the purposes of this book, West Africa includes the following twenty-first-century countries: Benin, Burkina Faso, Cape Verde, Côte d'Ivoire, The Gambia, Ghana, Guinea, Guinea-Bissau, Liberia, Mali, Mauritania, Niger Republic, Nigeria, Senegal, Sierra Leone, and Togo.

generated repeated economic and political crises, social disruptions, numerous reform movements, and occasionally serious violence.

Prior to West Africa's independence movements, Baptists were mostly located in Sierra Leone, Liberia, Nigeria, Côte d'Ivoire, and Niger Republic. Since then, Baptists have gained some presence in each country of the region except Mauritania. Even so, 80 percent of those Baptists are located in Nigeria, with 2.5 million adherents in more than 9,555 churches out of a total of 2.7 million members in 11,676 churches for the entire region. Growth earlier in the century was mostly associated with the efforts of Anglo Baptist missionary efforts and the indigenous witness of Yoruba traders who were responsible for establishing Baptist congregations in Benin, Togo, Ghana, Côte d'Ivoire, Burkina Faso, and Niger Republic. Illustrative of that influence was Yoruba Baptist success in organizing several congregations at Abidjan and neighboring villages in Côte d'Ivoire during the 1930s. Those churches became part of the Nigerian Baptist Convention. Later in the century, African Baptists created missions organizations that, together with the work of local Baptist congregations, have been the major sources of West African Baptists' phenomenal growth. Those efforts have been assisted by Western missionaries and by direct partnerships with Baptist congregations and organizations from other parts of the world. Independence and pressing social needs led Baptists to give attention to educational, medical, agricultural, and housing needs. By the twenty-first century, increasing amounts of those ministries were being addressed through local partnerships between African Baptists and Baptist individuals, churches, and other entities from around the globe.[4]

Under colonial governments, West African Baptists were hindered by several problems. First, most of the work was Anglo-American in orientation and therefore unprepared to take on the challenges of ministry in French-speaking Catholic colonies. With a few exceptions (such as a limited amount of French Baptist–sponsored work), only after independence did Baptist missionary agencies move aggressively into those territories. In addition, Islam exercised a formidable influence, creating a strong cultural deterrent in many areas. The skill to minister effectively among those populations has often come from specialized mission bodies and African Baptist sources. Also, African American Baptist mission work – which was

---

[4] See, for example, William H. Duke, comp., and Barbara D. Jackson, ed., *Seeds of Hope: Liberian and Virginia Baptists* (Richmond, VA: Center for Baptist Heritage Studies, University of Richmond, 2002).

concentrated most heavily in Liberia and Sierra Leone – since the days of the colonization societies had been connected with the ruling elite, thereby cutting itself off from the indigenous populations.[5] This kept African American Baptists from taking a more active part in the spread of Baptist witness to other parts of West Africa.[6]

Baptists have also been the source for several African Indigenous Churches (AIC) in West Africa.[7] The first originated in the late nineteenth century through the influence of Christian Hayford and became known as the National Baptist Church. The son of a Methodist pastor, Hayford became a Baptist while residing in Lagos, Nigeria. Independent of outside help, he organized his first church in Cape Coast, Ghana, which soon spread into the interior as far as Atebubu and westward into Côte d'Ivoire. The church was characterized by "native effort, self-reliance and independence, and this brought it in line with nationalistic aspirations."[8] The church disappeared soon after Hayford's death in 1935.

Central African Baptists

The nations of Central Africa experienced some of the most brutal aspects of European colonialism, especially because of French and Belgian policies that prioritized the extraction of resources at minimal cost.[9] Consequently, little was invested back into local development. King Leopold II held the Congo as a personal possession and was notorious for his ruthless exploitation of labor, natural resources, and rubber production. His regime became an international scandal in 1905, and he was forced to give up his

---

[5] See, for example, Olu Q. Menjay, "'In the Beginning': Assessing Interactions between the Colonists and the Natives of Liberia," *American Baptist Quarterly* 23, no. 4 (December 2004): 391–407.

[6] Albert W. Wardin, ed. *Baptists around the World: A Comprehensive Handbook* (Nashville, TN: Broadman & Holman, 1995), 67.

[7] Differences exist among authors concerning how to designate these churches. The term *African Independent Churches* was introduced by Bengt Sundkler in *Bantu Prophets in South Africa* (London: Butterworth Press, 1948). Two decades afterward writers had come to prefer the designation *African Indigenous Churches*. Paul Makhubu, in *Who Are the Independent Churches?* (Johannesburg: Skotaville Press, 1988), suggested that African Instituted Churches or new religious movements of Africa would better fit the reality of this phenomenon in African religious life. Today the terms are used interchangeably in much of the literature treating the movement, although many scholars argue that there are subtle and significant differences that should be maintained, such as Steve Hayes, in "The African Independent Churches: Judgement through Terminology?," *Missionalia* 26, no. 2 (August 1992): 139–46.

[8] Deji Ayegboyin and S. Ademola Ishola, *African Indigenous Churches: An Historical Perspective* (Lagos, Nigeria: Greater Heights Publications, 1997), 45.

[9] In this book, Central Africa includes the countries of Cameroon, Central African Republic, Chad, Congo, Democratic Republic of the Congo (formerly Zaire), Equatorial Guinea, and Gabon.

personal control of the Belgian Free State to the Belgian government in 1908. The reputation of colonial administrations in French Equatorial Africa fared little better.

In the 1920s, political consciousness began to develop, aimed at addressing the human rights abuses. André Matsoua is among the best-known leaders in this campaign. His work inspired an African messianic movement called Matsouanism, centered in Lari, Kenya. In eastern Gabon, two rebellions broke out among the Awanji people in 1927–8, and in Oubangui-Chari the Mbaya people also revolted. Known as the Kongo-Warra War, the revolt lasted until 1931 and may have claimed as many as one hundred thousand victims. Popular protests often emerged as messianic movements, such as the Matswanist movement in French Equatorial Africa and the Kimbanguist movement in the Belgian Congo. Rapid urbanization in centers like Brazzaville, Libreville, Bangui, and Leopoldville created population concentrations that were impossible for colonial administrators to control. With far too little social investment and concomitant overextraction of wealth, freedom movements pressed for nationalization. In 1960, independence was achieved throughout Central Africa.

Political instability radiated throughout the region in the decades that followed. Riots, massacres, mutinies, assassinations, and coup d'états became characteristic of the area. Congo even experienced a Marxist-Leninist regime for a period. In the 1990s, civil war broke out in the two Congos. The unrelenting struggles, together with political instabilities, helped give birth to a system of warlords and local political factions brutally serving the interests of mining companies and neighboring countries (e.g., Uganda, Rwanda, Zimbabwe, Angola). By the early twenty-first century, Central Africa faced two major challenges: internally, massive social needs leading to despair, racism, and even genocide, and externally, the power of international economic interests. The wealth that armed gangs commanded from sales to international buyers enabled warring factions to equip themselves with weaponry that defied the abilities of fragile and often-corrupt governments to control.[10]

As this contextual overview illustrates, Baptist ministries in Central Africa during the period were shaped first by the strong economic interests of European colonial governments unwilling to tolerate anything that smacked of challenge, and then by a combination of massive human needs

[10] Catherine Coquery-Vidrovitch, "Central Africa," in *Encyclopedia of Twentieth-Century African History* (London: Routledge, 2003), 68–72.

and lack of public infrastructures capable of addressing them. This has been one of Baptists' most productive regions in Africa. By 2007, Baptists in Central Africa had established more than 4,726 churches with a total of more than 2.2 million members. At the beginning of the period, Western mission agencies were still dominant in the work, especially the Baptist Missionary Society (Britain), the American Baptist Missionary Union, the Foreign Mission Board of the Southern Baptist Convention, the Missionary Society of the German Baptists, Baptist Mid-Missions, and the Örebro Society of Sweden. By the end of the period, however, African Baptists controlled their own church bodies, and foreign mission organizations assisted through supporting roles. In addition to evangelism, Baptists had developed significant medical and educational ministries.

Political developments in the West significantly affected Baptist work throughout the century. For example, World War I ended German control of Cameroon. West Cameroon came under British control and East Cameroon under French control, thus dividing Cameroon Baptists into two camps. After 1919, no Baptist missionaries resided in the region until German Baptists were allowed to return in 1927. In 1940, the German Baptist missionaries were interned, and American Baptists of German heritage, through the North American Baptist Conference, took over the ministry. They were especially successful with institutional development – establishing hospitals, colleges, and secondary schools. However, most of the grassroots work was accomplished by Cameroon Baptists. For example, the Baptist church in Victoria extended work into the grasslands, training evangelists and making trips into the interior for preaching tours. In 1954, they organized the Cameroon Baptist Convention and the Bible Training Center for training ministers. The Paris Evangelical Missionary Society assumed control of Baptist work in French Cameroon in 1917. They imposed a constitution giving French leaders a dominant voice, something the Cameroonian Baptist leadership resented. Under Lotin Samé, an independent Native Baptist Church was organized, which became the Église Baptiste Camerounaise in 1945. In 1952, the Union des Églises Baptistes du Cameroun was formed by churches in cooperation with the Paris Evangelical Mission Society. The complicated interaction of local and international political developments, together with colonial versus indigenous control of the work, has produced a very complex traditioning process for Baptists throughout the Central African region.

Similar divisions occurred in the Democratic Republic of the Congo, where several Baptists groups separated from the churches controlled by

Western missionaries. In 1949, the Communauté des Églises Baptistes Autonomes separated from the Swedish Baptist mission to form an independent work. In 1953, the Union des Églises Baptistes du Kwilu formed an association of churches separate from Baptist Mid-Missions. In 1957, the Communauté des Fidéles Baptistes Protestants organized independently from the Norwegian Baptists mission. In the early 1960s, a similar division occurred between the Community of Baptist Churches of Eastern Zaire (consisting of Baptists loyal to the Conservative Baptist mission) and the Baptist Community in Kivu, which sought independent control of the work.

Early in the twentieth century, a Baptist-related African Indigenous Church (AIC) originated in Central Africa under the leadership of Prophet Simon Kimbangu. Originally orthodox, the movement known as the Church of Jesus Christ on Earth through the Prophet Simon Kimbangu eventually acquired characteristics that have caused some to question its Christian identity and much more whether it preserves anything Baptist. Regardless of how the movement might be interpreted today, however, its early history illustrates the magnitude of challenge authentically African expressions of Baptist faith encountered under Africa's colonial regimes.

Born in Kimbangu Village, in what became the Democratic Republic of the Congo, Simon Kimbangu grew up and was educated at Ngombe Lutete, one of the Baptist Missionary Society's (England) mission stations. Integral to the society's method for evangelizing converts was their removal from traditional African settings by housing them in the mission commune. The larger African community referred to such persons as *muntu mundele*, meaning "blacks living like the White."[11] Eventually, Simon married and had three sons, the youngest of whom led the Kimbanguist Church until his death in 1993.

In 1918, Simon began experiencing visions convincing him that he was being called by God to preach. Members of his home church wanted him as their evangelist, but BMS missionaries rejected the request. The visions continued. In April 1921, his call was intensified when a woman for whom he prayed was healed. "By this miraculous event . . . something strange and new happened that made people wonder and marvel. The seed was sown, and the occasion is what is generally called the 'Pentecost of Nkamba'."[12] Thus the Kimbanguist movement began.

---

[11] Ayegboyin and Ishola, *African Indigenous Churches*, 126.
[12] Welo-Owango-Welo, "The Impact of the Kimbanguist Church in Central Africa," *Journal of the Interdenominational Theological Center* 16, nos. 1–2 (Fall–Spring 1988–9): 126.

The rapid spread of the Kimbanguist Church brought alarm to both missionaries and colonial officials, and within six months, Simon was charged with insurrection and sentenced to death. Protests by some officials of the Baptist Missionary Society and the American Baptist Missionary Union succeeded in having King Albert of Belgium commute his sentence to life imprisonment. Simon died in prison in 1951. Between 1937 and 1957, thousands of his followers were deported, imprisoned, or killed. Only through United Nations intervention in 1957 were the persecutions stopped. The group was given legal status only months prior to Congo's independence from Belgium. Today adherents number more than 3 million.

Regardless of how the group might be classified doctrinally, it possesses many characteristics that are reflective of indigenous Baptist concerns. In addition to its focus on Bible study and prayer, the Kimbanguists place great emphasis on African music. More than 6,000 hymns have been collected in their *cantiques captes*, which are sung to the accompaniment of full orchestras often with highly trained musicians. Also, every member is expected to be involved in the activities of the church, in raising funds, and in publicity. Strict attention is given to morality, doctrine, the guidance of the Holy Spirit in the affairs of the individual believer and the congregation as a whole, the experience of suffering as part of the Christian life, and end times. In every dimension of daily life, literalist readings of the Bible are closely associated with the realities of African existence. Consequently, the church's teachings and practices are simple, easily comprehensible to Africa's masses, and highly relevant.

Baptists of Southern Africa

Southern Africa is made up of the countries most affected by South Africa's economic hegemony.[13] It is the area where white minority rule endured longest in Africa, and it includes some of the last African countries to gain their independence. Early in this period, as colonial rule took a firmer grip, black African populations became increasingly alienated from the land and from traditional social structures and customs. Despite efforts to resist colonial domination (such as the Bambatha Rebellion of 1906–8 and the Herero and Nama War of 1904–7), the entire region had been brought under colonial control by the start of World War I. Much of

---

[13] This book defines the region of Southern Africa and the Indian Ocean to include the following countries: Angola, Botswana, Lesotho, Madagascar, Malawi, Mauritius, Mozambique, Namibia, Réunion, South Africa, Swaziland, Zambia, and Zimbabwe.

the driving force for domination came from mining interests generated especially by the discovery of vast quantities of gold and diamonds. The need for labor fueled migration of populations to urban centers connected with the mining industries, and various land acts throughout the region restricted tribal African populations to ever-smaller portions of the land. This opened up major blocks of land for European settlers.

These radical shifts created major social disruptions, which colonial governments attempted to address through segregationist policies. Racist regulations were prompted by "settler fears of African competition, black class-consciousness, or of being overtaken by a black majority."[14] Such policies generated deep-seated resentments, especially among the disenfranchised black African populations. Over time, mission-educated Africans began to emerge as spokespersons for reform and independence.[15] Leaders like Patrice Lumumba of the Congo, Jomo Kenyatta of Kenya, Kwame Nkrumah of Ghana, Abel Muzorewa of Zimbabwe, and Desmond Tutu of South Africa raised voices of anticolonial critique.

World War II had a major impact on Southern Africa's outlook. The disruption of products that formerly had been supplied by European factories forced Africa to manufacture many of its own goods. In short order, manufacturing joined mining and agriculture as major components of the region's economy, opening up vast new possibilities for development. However, those shifts continued to augment migration toward urban centers as displaced peoples sought a means for survival. Because the potential workforce outstripped available jobs, unemployment and destitution resulted. Such conditions fed political protests, which were met with brutal suppression by colonial administrators. Repressive measures, in turn, augmented popular resistance to colonial government and added pressure for majority rule.

By the mid-1970s, most of Southern Africa had gained its independence, but internal struggles among rival political forces continued causing violence to escalate in several countries – Angola, Mozambique, South Africa, and Zimbabwe offer particularly notable illustrations of this. Finally, with the release of Nelson Mandela and the first nonracial elections in 1990, South Africa adopted a progressive constitution that moved it toward social, economic, and political stability. Zimbabwe, in contrast, moved in the opposite direction. At the close of the period, Botswana, South Africa,

---

[14] Lynette Jackson, "Southern Africa," in *Encyclopedia of Twentieth-Century African History* (London: Routledge, 2003), 511.

[15] For example, see Erasto Muga, *African Response to Western Christian Religion* (Nairobi, Kenya: East African Literature Bureau, 1975).

and Namibia experienced reasonably good economic conditions; most of the rest of Southern Africa faced serious financial troubles. To this has been added the staggering impact of one of the highest HIV/AIDS infection rates of any region in the world.

As this overview highlights, Baptist ministries faced huge human, political, and moral challenges in Southern Africa during this period. This region had received little attention from the larger Baptist missionary organizations prior to the age of independence. Except for the Foreign Mission Board of the National Baptist Convention, USA, other Baptist mission enterprises had concentrated their efforts mostly in West Africa. Consequently, Baptists of Southern Africa were forced to survive on their own. As a result, by the mid-twentieth century, they constituted only a very small minority that was concentrated in the Republic of South Africa.

One notable episode in Baptist life during the early decades of the period occurred in Malawi through the ministry of Joseph Booth. Born in Britain, Booth immigrated to New Zealand and then Australia before going to Nyasaland (modern Malawi) in 1892 to establish the Zambezi Industrial Mission at Mitsidi. Similar to fair-trade industries of the twenty-first century, industrial missions combined Christian witness with skills acquisition aimed at helping local peoples learn the dignity of work, gain the ability to support themselves, and achieve "civilization." The work was assisted first by British Baptists, and then by Australian Baptists. In 1897, Booth took John Chilembwe of the Yao tribe with him on a trip to America to assist him in gaining further education. While there, Booth became a Seventh Day Baptist and returned to Nyasaland under their support with the mission of establishing the Sabbath Evangelizing and Industrial Association. This mission focused its work around a coffee plantation that the association purchased as a means for providing the holistic development he envisioned. Crop failures doomed the venture almost from the start, and in late 1901, Booth returned to the United States as a result of health problems and political opposition.

Throughout his life, Booth stayed on the move, geographically and denominationally, uniting with several Baptist bodies and then with the Seventh Day Adventists. Probably a major reason for his behavior related to his vocal advocacy of human rights. In Africa, he quickly gained the ire of both mainline missionaries and colonial authorities because of his advocacy for better treatment of and more political rights for black Africans. As a result, he often was held responsible for the political discontentment that surfaced among those populations. He influenced several significant African Christian leaders, including John Chilembwe, Elliot Kamwana

Chirwa, Charles Domingo, and John L. Dube. In 1915, he was deported from Lesotho to England as an undesirable and passed the remainder of his life in obscurity.

When John Chilembwe completed his education in the United States, he returned to Africa as a missionary of the Foreign Mission Board of the National Baptist Convention (NBC). In 1900, he established the Providence Industrial Mission in Chiradzulu, Nyasaland, and was assisted by the missionaries L. N. Cheek and Emma B. Delaney. In 1913, he led in construction of a large church that became the pride both of Baptists in Nyasaland and black Baptists in the United States.[16] In 1915, however, Chilembwe was killed leading an African uprising against British rule, a cause for which he is highly honored in Malawi today. In 1926, the NBC was allowed to reopen the Providence mission under the leadership of Daniel S. Malekebu. As the century unfolded, it became one of the most successful of the NBC mission ministries, with churches, hospitals, and schools growing from its work. In 1945, Malekebu also led in formation of a national association of Baptist churches known today as the African Baptist Assembly of Malawi. Southern Baptists began work in Malawi in 1959 and organized a separate work that evolved into the Malawi Baptist Convention in the 1970s. These bodies, together with the Evangelical Baptist Church of Malawi, today number more than 2,500 churches with a total of almost 300,000 members.

From very small beginnings in 1900, Baptists in Southern Africa have grown to number more than 5,500 churches and almost 800,000 members. The Baptist Missionary Society (Britain), the Foreign Mission Board of the National Baptist Convention (United States), the Scandinavian Independent Baptist Mission, and the South African General Mission have been major contributors to the growth of Baptist work in South Africa, Malawi, Mozambique, and Zambia. Southern Baptists have contributed to thriving Baptist churches in Malawi, Zambia, and Zimbabwe, and Seventh Day Baptists have been major supporters of work there as well. A small indigenous Baptist presence exists in Madagascar, and in Mauritius and Réunion. In addition, Baptists have grown beyond their earlier ethnic limitations among mostly Anglo and German populations to include a wide variety of races, tribes, nationalities, and languages. Southern Africa also

---

[16] William J. Harvey III, *Bridges of Faith across the Seas: The Story of the Foreign Mission Board National Baptist Convention, USA, Inc.* (Philadelphia: Foreign Mission Board, National Baptist Convention, USA, 1989), 44–8.

has contributed to the growing number of African Indigenous Churches (AIC), many of which include Baptist in their name. Although mainstream Baptists often do not include AICs as part of their movement, greater attentiveness to indigenization has caused some naysayers to reconsider the issue for at least a few of those groups. The geographical, demographic, and cultural expansion of the Baptist movement in Southern Africa has forced Baptists to struggle both with questions of identity and with the burgeoning spiritual, political, social, medical, and economic issues of this region and beyond.

North and East African Baptists

Because so few Baptists are found in North Africa, North and East Africa are treated as one unit here, even though they are quite distinctive in many ways.[17] Like the rest of Africa, North Africa experienced colonial takeover and administration during the first half of the twentieth century. During that period, economic, cultural, and political transformation occurred. Modern economies developed, with industries, education, banking, and services adapted to fit the European systems from which they were modeled. Extractive economics demanded investment in infrastructures to transport raw materials and agricultural products, all of which brought major shifts to local social and cultural traditions.

After decolonization, the wealthiest, most skilled, and best-educated settlers departed, leaving the region dependent on the expertise and economic networks of the former colonial administrators. After independence, each of these countries joined the Arab League, but beyond that, a great degree of difference has developed among them over systems of government, alliances, policies, and ideologies.

Baptists have little presence or history in North Africa. Much of the history that does exist is connected with expatriate professionals or military personnel, and Baptist churches and ministries mostly left with them when they departed. Egypt offers a notable exception in the person of Seddik W. Girgis. Born into the Egyptian Coptic faith, he became a Baptist while working in Jerusalem, later studied theology in the United States, and was ordained. In the early 1960s, he returned to his hometown at Fayyoum,

---

[17] For the purposes of this book, North Africa includes the countries of Algeria, Egypt, Eritrea, Libya, Morocco, Sudan, Tunisia, and Western Sahara. East Africa includes the countries of Burundi, Djibouti, Ethiopia, Kenya, Rwanda, Somalia (including Somaliland), Tanzania, and Uganda.

Egypt, and began preaching. By 1963, he had established six churches. Today there are fewer than one thousand Baptists in Egypt, but even that number is significant considering the difficulties they face.

In East Africa, in contrast, Baptists have experienced phenomenal growth since the mid-twentieth century, although most of that has been limited to just three countries: Kenya, Rwanda, and Tanzania. Of the 8,248 Baptist churches and their 1.6 million members, almost 80 percent of the churches and 94 percent of members are located in those three countries.

Colonial rule came more slowly to East Africa than the rest of the continent, and though its effects were clearly felt, its hold was more tenuous. Germany and Britain had to rely heavily on African intermediaries for control, a practice that disrupted the traditional tribal lines of authority and social cohesion but also opened the eyes of perceptive African intellectuals to the weaknesses of colonial power holders. These somewhat unique dimensions of East Africa's development help explain the region's history of resistance to colonial rule – including armed revolts, the formation of separatist churches, millennial movements, and political assassinations, all of which constitute expressions of independence that found their fuller realization in the nationalist movements following World War II.[18] After gaining independence, one party systems of government emerged, in many ways reflective of the colonial governments they replaced – detentions without trial, patronage, control of media, and so on. After 1991, Kenya and Tanzania moved toward a multiparty political system, yet with previous ruling powers still entrenched. Socially, the former segregationist policies were ended, health care was improved, and educational opportunities were expanded. However, population growth, especially among black Africans, exerted great pressure on social services. Economic downturns, ethnic rivalries, and the impact of HIV/AIDS have been devastating for the region.

As noted earlier, acceptance of Baptist views and ministries in East Africa has been limited to certain groups. Significant growth has occurred among the more settled agricultural peoples of Kenya, Tanzania, Rwanda, Burundi, and Uganda, but little acceptance has occurred among the more nomadic populations. No Baptist churches exist in Sudan, Djibouti, Eritrea, or Somalia. In many cases, political realities, Muslim restrictions, and harsh living conditions have severely limited mission efforts. Some Baptist groups have engaged in extensive relief work in those countries, but no permanent presence has been developed.

[18] Robert Maxon, "East Africa," in *Encyclopedia of Twentieth-Century African History* (London: Routledge, 2003), 156.

In the three East African countries where Baptists are growing, the work of local Baptists churches has been decisive. In Tanzania, for example, churches utilize practices such as teaching, market preaching, revivals, and witnessing in villages and towns in combination with public reading rooms, medical clinics, and agricultural work to extend their ministries. Similar methods are employed by Baptist churches in Kenya, together with mission congregations and home Bible studies.

African Baptist Women

As with so many other discourses associated with global Baptist history, the roles, challenges, and activities of African women are too complex to treat adequately in the summary fashion required here. Perhaps a few observations could have value in introducing the topic to readers, however. That will be the objective here.

It is important to note that, historically, African women were able to utilize kinship bonds to assert their authority over certain aspects of life and society. Clan positions and decision making, practices of African religious cults that included female leadership, and village organizations that included women for adjudicating conflicts are a few of those activities. These social networks fed other informal women's associations that were the equivalent of credit pooling and labor assistance. Colonization significantly transformed those traditional avenues of connection and brought new challenges to Africa's women. Thrust into the context of emerging modern economies, African women had little opportunity for education or paid employment; therefore, the road to public life was long and hard.

African women played important roles in the struggles for independence, and some outstanding women leaders gained attention for their contributions during the struggle. However, after independence, those women did not receive the recognition their efforts deserved, nor did they gain improvement of status in the new African societies. Often the transition into nationhood meant a loss of political influence for African women. Caught between their desires to see the new African leaders succeed and their own need for political improvements, women's positions in society were often undermined. In Islamic contexts, women found especially difficult the "problematic coexistence of patriarchy, religion, and Western influence."[19]

---

[19] Philomina Okeke, "Women's Movements," in *Encyclopedia of Twentieth-Century African History* (London: Routledge, 2003), 600.

By the 1970s, African women were finding it necessary to organize around issues of daily survival. In contexts that were often unstable, patriarchal, and violent, women had few options to leverage social platforms for better treatment. Even government-sponsored reforms during the United Nations' Decade for Women (1975–85) were more cosmetic than substantive. Thus, African women "were forced to build their political platforms around the socially accepted roles they possessed in society."[20]

In a rare study of black Baptist women in Africa, Rachel Nyagondwe Banda offers important insights into the relationship between the Bible and culture in Baptist women's understanding of gender behavior in Malawi. Her analysis has the potential for much broader application as well. Banda raises questions concerning why African Baptist women have not actualized the freedom that Baptist teachings and polity regarding the individual would logically make possible. One inhibiting factor that she identifies is the missionary hermeneutic, which relegates women to a support role. She suggests that this is an Anglo-American cultural interpretive influence. Baptist women from patrilineal African societies also have kept women in subordinate positions. Even in those contexts, however, she sees change taking place toward greater freedom for women to assume more leadership in church life.

In cases where African women come from matrilineal African societies and encounter missionary Christianity, they are more inclined to keep the freedoms of their traditional culture while becoming involved in the life of a Baptist church. "Thus Baptist women in matrilineal societies show relative freedoms in their engagement in church and society, as opposed to women in the patrilineal societies."[21] Thus, she sees a missionary hermeneutic and a local hermeneutic at work. The missionary hermeneutic would limit women's voices to women's organizations. Many African women, especially those operating culturally out of a more matrilineal framework, have not been satisfied with such a role. When asked why they do not obey the biblical admonition that "women should be silent in Church," the local hermeneutic women respond, "because we see women leaders in the Bible."[22] Building on her own matrilineal heritage, Banda declares that Baptist Convention churches should ordain women who evidence divine giftedness for such ministry.

---

[20] Ibid., 602.
[21] Rachel Nwagondwe Banda, *Women of Bible and Culture: Baptist Convention Women in Southern Malawi* (Zomba, Malawi: Kachere Series, 2007), 191.
[22] Ibid., 193.

Although Banda's thesis does not reflect the views of all (or perhaps even a majority) of African Baptists, it does offer evidence that critical questions over womanhood and Baptist identity are surfacing in African Baptist life alongside the many other concerns African women face in modern culture. Obviously, Baptists also hold different interpretations of the issue as Banda's thesis indicates. However, the studied treatment she offers reveals an emerging new future for African Baptist women.

African Baptists' General Identifying Characteristics during the Age of Proliferating Traditions

For Baptists in Africa, twentieth-century political, social, and religious developments have meant several things. First, they have meant greater African control of Baptist work. Although Baptist missionary work has continued and even multiplied throughout the period, after the independence movements of the midcentury, non-African Baptist involvement has been more partnering than controlling in nature. Naturally, the party that owns the resources carries great weight, and clashes have continued to erupt on occasion between African Baptist leadership and non-African Baptist decision makers over differences of vision, purpose, priority, and deployment of resources. But African Baptist leaders exercise a stronger voice in deciding their own destinies than was generally the case before 1960.

Second, rapid growth has occurred among Baptist churches in Africa. From 10,200 members in 1904 to 7.3 million in 2007, African Baptists have experienced one of the fastest rates of growth among Baptists anywhere in the world. Consequently, two of the areas with the largest Baptist populations in the world are in Africa – Nigeria with 2.5 million members and Democratic Republic of the Congo with 1.9 million members. By far the largest growth has occurred among Africa's nonwhite populations and in countries not heavily affected by British settlement.

Third, Baptist work has become much more integrated into the native cultures of Africa. Although many elements derivative of Anglo and Anglo-American Baptist influence survives, increasingly the organization, music, and theology of African Baptists is reflective of African worldviews, cultural preferences, and priorities. So far, Baptists have not been at the forefront of those developing theologies that engage the complex questions of Christian faith and African experience. Theologians like Bolaji Idowu, Harry Sawyerr, C. G. Baeta, and Kwesi Dickson are among the twentieth-century thinkers who have laid the foundations of an African theology for Protestant churches in West Africa. John Mbiti has done similar work from the experiences of East African Christianity. These and other African thinkers have influenced the theological reflection of many Baptists as they seek answers for questions of faith in the hard realities of African life – questions not adequately addressed solely through Anglo Baptist theological traditions. The distinctive situation in South Africa generated a different body of theology that has focused on political protest rather than inculturation. Baptists' traditional focus on religious experience rather than theological reflection continues to be evidenced in African Baptist life. However, emerging generations of African Baptists show greater inclination to question the meaning of Baptist belief and thought in relation to African cultures.[23] This trend will likely grow stronger in the future with new generations.

Finally, with their growing maturity, African Baptist leaders are exercising an increasingly active voice in global Baptist affairs. Their willingness to advocate for African Baptist needs and perspectives in Baptist world forums is occasionally unsettling to some Western Baptist leaders who have been more accustomed to African deference in deciding major issues. However, these African voices are indicative of the growing complexity of global Baptist traditioning sources and the gathering challenges to many of the hereditary shapers of Baptist identity.

ASIAN BAPTISTS' EVOLVING TRADITIONING SOURCES

Asia encompasses about 30 percent of the world's land area and, with more than 4 billion people, contains more than 60 percent of the world's population. Asia's 5.3 million Baptists seem insignificant in that context because they constitute far less than 1 percent of the population. However, among Baptists globally, Asian Baptists constitute about 10 percent of the total. In 1904, there were about 3.2 times more Baptists in Europe than in Asia. In 2007, there were 6.7 times more Asian Baptists than European Baptists. Viewed from that perspective, the significance of the Baptist movement in Asia gains a different level of importance.

The world in which Asian Baptists ministered underwent tremendous change over the course of the twentieth century. In the nineteenth century, Baptists had experienced their greatest successes among smaller ethnic groups. However, during the twentieth century, the expansion of nation-states and increasing integration of economic relationships eroded the

---

[23] For example, see the Cameroonian Baptist David Tonghou Ngong, "God's Will Can Actually Be Done on Earth: Salvation in African Theology," *American Baptist Quarterly* 23, no. 4 (December 2004): 362–77; "The Trinity and African (Christian) Identity," *American Baptist Quarterly* 23, no. 4 (December 2004): 378–90.

autonomy of those groups and incorporated them into larger political, social, and economic systems. Politically, by midcentury, the Soviet Union and China controlled the vast territories of Siberia and Central Asia, South Asia had gained independence from colonial administrations, and modern countries had emerged out of the remnants of the Ottoman Empire. As with other continents, advances in transportation, communication, and global economics fueled the change. But, as a consequence, smaller ethnic groups gradually lost their distinctive cultures as they were absorbed into dominant populations – ethnic Russians dominated the institutions of power in the Soviet Union, ethnic Chinese did the same in China, the Burmans in Myanmar, to mention but a few examples. Tribal peoples generally lost the most as a result of these developments. The ancestral lands of less complex cultures were diminished as modern economic and political interests coveted their domains. In some cases, they remained caught as political refugees in the no-man's-lands of global politics.

The degree of economic development among Asian nations has varied greatly throughout the continent, calling for widely varying ministries among Baptists. On one end of the scale are countries like Myanmar, Cambodia, and Vietnam, with very low incomes; at the other end are Japan, Singapore, and South Korea, with highly developed economies. Prior to World War II, Japan was among the few countries of Asia to have developed a nationally owned, financed, and operated industrial base. Most other countries functioned under colonial economies organized around supplying raw material in exchange for manufactured products. After the war, Asian nations threw off colonial governments but adopted varying strategies for developing their economies. India and China adopted isolationist strategies that focused on self-sufficiency. South Korea, however, chose a path of international trade. Some governments opted for systems of state ownership and socialist economics, and others adopted private ownership and capitalist systems. By the end of the century, the economic successes of South Korea, Hong Kong, Taiwan, and Singapore had influenced other nations – especially China – to rely more on international economic relations and to pursue economic policies that included private ownership.

Economic shifts have been accompanied by population shifts. Migration to major industrial centers has been massive despite the fact that increasing mechanization has lessened the need for human labor. In most instances, the service sectors of those economies have offered the greatest new opportunities for employment. In many of the poorer countries, small, family-owned businesses have become major sources of survival.

Despite these developments, however, the majority of Asians still work in agriculture – usually farming small, ancestral plots of land. The income level remains low, however, motivating younger generations to risk the dangers of moving to the cities for a chance at a better life. The world of Asia's Baptists is changing, and so are the views, methods, and expectations of individual Baptists, as the following regional overviews will help to illustrate.

South Asian Baptists

Over the course of the twentieth century, colonial control over Asia gradually unraveled along the lines of a process that was initiated in India. The manner in which a culturally, ethnically, racially, and religiously diverse collection of peoples managed to unify in opposition to the organized power of colonial governments was by creation of imagined communities. Such ideological constructs allowed persons who had never thought of themselves in terms of a nation to find common ground around which to unite against a foe. Mohandas K. Gandhi played a key role in identifying and communicating the symbols that guided resistance against India's British overlords and resulted in nationhood. The Indian National Congress embodied those symbols and gave them visibility.

Because the imagined community of the Indian National Congress was very Hindu and North Indian in nature, other submovements soon emerged using the same processes to evoke other communities. Indian Muslims, for example, developed a separate but overlapping identification for themselves. Another community grew up around the Tamil language and culture. Many others also emerged, being built around still different cores of identity. This model was multiplied throughout the colonized world as an effective means for mobilizing resistance. They also became models employed by other groups that sought independence from the newly formed national governments once the colonial power was gone.

Part of India's independence included partition – Britain handed over power to two independent countries, India and Pakistan. Sri Lanka and Maldives secured their independence a few years later. Although the Indian National Congress was not happy with the division, the partition acknowledged that no federal system could be devised that gave sufficient assurance to Muslim activists that their interests would be protected in a government whose rhetoric united Hindu and nationalism so closely in its identity. Thus, Pakistan was born as a nation constructed of five disparate population groups located in two widely separated territories – East

Pakistan and West Pakistan, with India between – united by little more than a sense of Islamic unity. However, without a unifying political and institutional structure, the nation's leaders were unable to control the escalating violence. Hundreds of thousands of persons died in the struggles among Hindu, Muslim, and Sikh communities, including Gandhi himself.

Through the 1950s and 1960s, tensions mounted between East Pakistan and the seat of government in West Pakistan. Bengalis became alienated, feeling they were being exploited culturally and economically. Efforts of West Pakistan to impose Urdu as the national language of the Pakistans added to the suspicions, as did disproportionate allocation of the national budget, employment of Bengalis in government jobs, and appointment to high-ranking military offices. The differences finally resulted in the independence of East Pakistan in 1971 and the creation of Bangladesh (meaning Bengal Land).

Bhutan (one of the most isolated and least developed countries in the world), Maldives, and Sri Lanka, though significant in their own right, are overshadowed by the size, economies, and military might of the other three nations of the Indian subcontinent.

The identity of Baptists in South Asia has been shaped in part by the hard realities that underlie this series of monumental social, cultural, and political developments. The significance of the events for global Baptist life has long been overlooked by outside observers because the nation's 2.4 million Baptists are easily lost statistically in the 1.1 billion population of India. At less than 1 percent of the total population, these Baptists seem insignificant and unimportant. But collectively they constitute the largest community of Baptists outside the United States and are a growing voice within the global Baptist communion. A perusal of the two dozen unions and conventions that affiliate with the Baptist World Alliance from this region shows a rich diversity of ethnic and tribal traditioning sources with potential for major contributions to the vitality of the global Baptist movement.

From 1793 until independence, this region was one of the areas on which Anglo Baptists focused their greatest mission endeavors. Since India's independence, missionaries from the West have diminished in numbers as a result of governmental restrictions. Still, a wide range of Baptist missionary agencies have supported the witness of Indian Baptists in varied capacities. But, over the course of the twentieth century, Indian Baptists themselves have taken control of the work and continued to expand it with tremendous success.

From the earliest mission efforts, Baptists have experienced very limited success in winning adherents among the Hindu, Buddhist, or Muslim cultures. Their witness has yielded great receptivity, however, among the formerly animistic tribal peoples, especially in Northeast and North India. Today some of those groups possess generations-old traditions as Baptists. Many have matured to the point of organizing mission outreach that extends beyond their own tribal groups, so that they, too, are engaging in cross-cultural ministries.

The hill tribes of Northeast India offer good illustrations of India's Baptist traditions. The hill tribes had no written language when they had their first contacts with missionaries. Eventually, languages were reduced to writing and the first literature was made available. Usually that corpus of writings included grammars, Scripture portions, and learning tools. Among the Nagas in the territories of Garo Hills, Nagaland, and Manipur, missionaries established schools that trained teachers for the villages. Eventually, higher levels of education were added, including Eastern Theological College at Jorhat. In addition, medical ministries were gradually developed. Thus, Baptist identity came to those peoples in ways that helped stabilize, improve, and elevate their sense of personhood. Furthermore, education and numerical size enabled some of these Baptists to become politically, socially, and economically powerful in the region. Insurgencies in the northeast forced the removal of foreign missionaries in the latter decades of the twentieth century, which had some impact on the activities of Baptist churches. However, local Baptists made the necessary adaptations and have more than compensated for the losses.

Nazir Masih is illustrative of the thousands of Indian Baptists whose work is foundational for the growth that Baptists are experiencing today. In 1977, he gave up his position as a translator and distributor for Every Home Crusade to begin preaching in Chanigarth, located in Northwest India. Similar to J. G. Oncken of Germany, he had never heard of Baptists when he began his ministry, although he employed principles that were essentially Baptist in nature. Later, a Baptist pastor from the United States introduced him to Baptist doctrine, which Masih discovered were close to his own, and he decided to become Baptist. As one who understood the local cultures, possessed powerful organizational and communication skills, and commanded respect from the Indian peoples, Masih was able to gather a team of twenty-two evangelists who, by 1992, had organized 120 churches and 250 preaching points that collectively claimed twenty thousand members. He did this in a region where Baptists previously had experienced very little success.

The only truly successful Baptist ministry among Hindus also occurred through the efforts of Indian Baptists. In South India between 1925 and 1935, more than 30,000 Sudras became Baptist through the witness of a group of Baptists from Lait (outcast) background. During the same period, even greater Baptist growth occurred among the Dalits.

G. Samuel, pastor of the Hyderabad Baptist Church in South India, led that church to phenomenal growth. He helped organize the church in 1969. By the early 1990s, it had grown to more than 5,000 members, had established thirty-six new churches, and begun additional work in seventy-five area villages. Sumitra Borde and his nephew Pradeep Borde accomplished similar results in Maharashtra State in the 1990s.

As Baptist work grows and extends into new cultures, important new traditioning sources are born that broaden, revitalize, and complicate Baptist identity. Like elsewhere, India's tribal cultures have made their own adaptations to many Anglo Baptist doctrines and practices. For example, the churches "are organized into structures which superficially resemble those of Baptists elsewhere but which actually represent adaptation to the context. Local congregations, each with its own pastor, are grouped in various ways. There are mother-daughter complexes, or circles. The most important group is the association."[24] In Northeast India, the associations are further organized into regional unions – Assam, Garo, Karbi Anglong, Manipur, and Nagaland. In 1950, a larger association was formed called the Council of Baptist Churches of North East India.

In some areas, Baptists are the largest of the Protestant churches. This is especially true in several areas of Northeast India and among the Telugu peoples in Andhra Pradesh in the South. Baptists have a very limited presence in other regions of India and in Pakistan. Though their presence is very small, they do have thriving communities in Bangladesh and Sri Lanka. As of the mid-1990s, no Baptist church existed in Bhutan, but the Ao Baptist churches of Nagaland maintained several ongoing ministries in the kingdom.

As in India, most Baptists in Bangladesh are culturally connected to one of the many tribal groups. This has cause Bangladeshi Baptists to be divided both geographically and ideologically. Baptist work was first introduced to the region by William Carey in 1795, when the area was known as East Bengal. The Baptist Missionary Society (BMS) continued

---

[24] Frederick S. Downs, "Northeast India (Assam and Neighboring States): Baptists of Northeast India Historically Related to the American Baptist Churches in the USA," in Albert W. Wardin, ed., *Baptists around the World: A Comprehensive Handbook* (Nashville, TN: Broadman & Holman, 1995), 136.

ministries to the region over the centuries, focusing heavily in the twentieth century on medical, educational, and economic development ministries. In 1956, the BMS helped churches organize their own association called the Baptist Union of Pakistan (today Bangladesh Baptist Sangha). In the 1880s, Australian and New Zealand Baptists appointed missionaries for work in East Bengal. Besides establishing churches, they also engaged in medical and educational ministries. The work progressed very slowly but finally in 1920 was strong enough to form into an association known as the East Bengal Baptist Union (today the Bangladesh Baptist Fellowship). In 1957, Southern Baptists from the United States joined Australian and New Zealand Baptists in the mission. In addition, the Association of Baptists for World Evangelism (American Independent Baptists) and the Örebro Society (Swedish Baptist) have created other centers of Baptist work.

Baptists' presence in Pakistan began in 1954 through the work of Conservative Baptist missionaries in the Sindh Province. In their work, they discovered pockets of discouraged Christians in Jacobabad, Shikarpur, Larkana, and Dadu. They were mostly descendants of persons who had embraced Christian faith during the mass movements of the 1920s and 1930s. As a result of their work, the leader of a Hindu tribe called the Marwaris adopted Baptist beliefs. He and six family members were baptized and became the source of a revival movement that brought several hundred persons into the Baptist communion. In 1995, the Sindh Evangelical Baptist Association (formed in 1980) had about twenty-five churches with 1,500 members.

Baptists have a very limited presence in Sri Lanka, although a few Baptist individuals have been influential in the field of education and in the National Christian Council. W. M. P. Jayatunga, C. H. Ratnaike, S. J. de S. Weerasinghe, and W. G. Wickramasinghe have been noted among the leaders of the independent Sri Lanka Baptist Sangamaya. Most Baptists come from the Sinhalese peoples, and there is essentially no Baptist presence among the Tamils in the North.[25]

Baptist identity in southern Asia has been formed largely through the experiences of two types of adherents – the oppressed classes and indigenous tribal peoples. For both groups, Baptist ministries have offered social and spiritual liberation and hope for a better future. Since the mid-twentieth century, Baptist identity has been further shaped by struggles for independence and subsequent nation building. For Baptists, this has gradually

[25] Brian Stanley and Albert W. Wardin Jr., "Northeast India (Assam and Neighboring States): Baptists Historically Related to the Baptist Missionary Society, in Albert W. Wardin, ed. *Baptists around the World: A Comprehensive Handbook* (Nashville, TN: Broadman & Holman, 1995), 137.

generated impulses for the indigenization and contextualization of their faith and practices. This has found expression in more positive attitudes toward local cultures, development of more indigenous styles of worship, utilization of church architectural styles that are more expressive of local aesthetics, and approaches to evangelism that better communicate indigenous forms of thought and sensibilities. In India, Baptists have contributed to church unions that manifest Indian patterns of connecting. They have also created numerous Indian Baptist missions for extending Baptist witness and ministries to a growing population. Throughout this region, Baptist identity has raised awareness of the need to preserve freedom of religious practice for minority groups as well as for other persons.

Southeast Asian Baptists

Following World War II, France and Holland were not in a position to give immediate attention to their colonies in Southeast Asia. Consequently, real power passed into the hands of local leaders. For some this offered an opportunity to declare their independence. But the French were not prepared to cede their interests in Vietnam; neither were the Dutch willing to do so in Indonesia. Wars of independence ensued. In spite of internal complexities, Indonesia had secured its independence by 1949. Vietnam won its freedom from France in 1954 but immediately became a pawn of Cold War forces. Most other nations of the region secured independence with relatively less conflict.

By the time independence was won, Southeast Asian societies had undergone too much change to return to their precolonial traditions. Therefore, the new nations generally attempted to model their new governments along the lines of Western democracies. But colonial regimes had not equipped them with the skills needed to do so, and significant political and ideological conflict resulted. Religious differences often produced violent contests. Ethnic rivalries threatened the new states. In addition, the ideological forces of capitalism and communism added to the divisions. In most cases, the process of achieving stable independence followed a threefold pattern: a period of ruling military regimes that imposed "unity" and set a course for modernization, emergence of national ideologies that defined the character of the people, and rejection of Cold War models in favor of independently derived forms of government that seemed to work better in the Southeast Asian context. In most cases, this involved some type of synthesis between an authoritative form of government and limited democratic freedoms.

This model worked well for some nations – Thailand, Indonesia, Malaysia, and Singapore among them. In others, however, the outcome of authoritarian rule was not social and economic progress – Myanmar and the Philippines are examples. By the beginning of the twenty-first century, many Southeast Asian countries had begun to form greater regional ties for purposes of economic development, security, and common concerns. The Association for Southeast Asian Nations is the most notable example of this trend.

This region of peninsulas, islands, and archipelagoes supports a population of more than 568 million people. Baptists number about 1.8 million in about 8,700 churches – almost 3.5 percent of the global Baptist family. The majority are located in Myanmar. Baptist missionary outreach began in the region in 1813, when the Judsons located in Burma (Myanmar). But when China was opened to missionaries, Southeast Asia was neglected by Baptists until the mid-twentieth century. The mainland portion of Southeast Asia, which includes the countries of Cambodia, Laos, Myanmar, Thailand, and Vietnam, is dominated by the Thai and Austroasiatic peoples, who are mostly Buddhist. The maritime section, which includes Brunei, Indonesia, Malaysia, the Philippines, and Singapore, is predominately Austronesian and Islamic. Baptist growth has mostly occurred among tribal peoples and ethnic immigrant populations in each of these regions, but they have had to interpret their message into cultures heavily defined by Buddhism and Islam. This has shaped Baptist identity in these regions differently than that in the historically Christian and secularized cultures.

Indonesia is illustrative of Baptist development in Southeast Asia at the time that colonial control came to an end. Baptist work is multifaceted, with numerous independent theological and polity perspectives. A very old tradition of Baptist ministry in Indonesia dates back to Gottlob Brückner, who ministered in Java from 1814 to 1857, but no lasting Baptist presence was achieved. In 1951, Ais Pormes, an Indonesian who fled his native land, became Baptist; he was educated in Australia and the United States, then returned to Indonesia and organized the country's largest Baptist church in Jakarta. With the closing of China, Anglo Baptist missionaries gave increased attention to Indonesia, placing special focus on educational, publishing, medical, and student ministries. After a failed communist coup in 1965, large numbers of Indonesians embraced the Christian faith, and Baptists were among the denominations that experienced significant growth.

In addition, several young people from the Protestant Reformed churches of Minahasa left their old denomination to form a new, more evangelical church in 1951. Over time, they came to recognize that their beliefs and practices were essentially Baptist, so in 1971 they adopted that name. Their missionary vision motivated them to minister in surrounding villages and islands, thereby further extending Baptists' presence in the area.

Ernest Loong, a pastor from Hong Kong, established a Mandarin-speaking Baptist congregation in Jakarta in 1953. With a somewhat distinctive ecclesiological outlook, the Indonesian congregations of Chinese descent think of themselves as one church with multiple locations. Conservative Baptists, along with various independent Baptist groups from the United States and Australian Baptists, have also ministered with success in numerous locations among Indonesia's seventeen thousand islands. Particular success occurred among the Dani peoples of Irian Jaya in the 1950s and 1960s. Other Indonesian Baptists emerged independently as a result of Dutch Mennonite ministries, which were abandoned when the Dutch were forced out of Indonesia. Consequently, Indonesian Baptists reflect a complex amalgam of traditioning sources within the larger Baptist movement, with a wide range of perspectives on practices and doctrinal particularities.

Baptists in Myanmar continued to grow throughout the twentieth century in spite of several major disruptions to their work. The first upheaval occurred with the Japanese occupation in World War II. Another shock transpired with the expulsion of missionaries and the nationalization of Baptist properties in 1966. The tribal insurgencies also disrupted Baptist efforts among those peoples. Still, Baptists grew phenomenally. In 1963, on the eve of the nationalization of Baptists institutions, Myanmar had 216,000 Baptists. Today there are more than 1.2 million Baptists. Ten Baptist-related theological institutions have served as important centers for leadership development.

Baptists began work in the predominantly Roman Catholic country of the Philippines after the United States wrested control of the islands from Spain in 1898. Their presence has been widely varied, reflecting the missionary presence of basically every type of Baptist found in the United States – mainline, conservative, fundamentalist, independent, Seventh Day, Landmark, Primitive, and others. These, when wedded to the varieties of tribes and cultures in which they have taken root, have given rise to a disjointed collection of Baptists, some of whom have little toleration for other Baptists who may differ on sensitive topics. Collectively, however, Filipino Baptists are among the largest Protestant denominations in the country, numbering more than four hundred thousand members. Many of those churches have matured to the point that they now sustain overseas mission programs of their own.

After Anglo missionaries abandoned ministries in Thailand to concentrate in China in the nineteenth century, the Maitrichit Baptist Church in Bangkok was left to continue the work alone. A predominantly Chinese church, its work grew to include more than thirty-two churches and numerous missionaries. When communist rulers in China expelled missionaries in 1949, many of those missionaries relocated to Thailand to work among the populations of Chinese descent located there. In addition, Karen Baptists from Burma sent missionaries to work among the Karen peoples located in Thailand. In 1954, American Baptists joined this effort, assisting with medical, agricultural, educational, and evangelistic ministries. Baptist ministry has largely organized along the lines of ethnic identity – predominantly Chinese, Thai, Karen, and Lahu.

During the decades when Thai Baptists were bereft of significant assistance from the global Baptist community, they formed relationships with other Christian churches through the Church of Christ of Thailand (CCT). Organized by Presbyterians, the CCT functioned as a synod with presbyteries (called *pahks*). Chinese Baptist churches in Bangkok initially became part of the 7th Pahk along with Chinese Presbyterian churches of that region. Conflicts over ecclesiological decision making resulted in creation of the 12th Pahk in 1959, which was exclusively Baptist. This arrangement has allowed the Baptist, Presbyterian, and Disciples of Christ churches to cooperate closely in Thailand. When Southern Baptists entered Thailand in 1949, they chose not to become part of the CCT and developed an independent work. In 1971, they organized an independent association of churches known as the Thailand Baptist Churches Association. In addition, the Thailand Karen Baptist Convention was established in 1955, followed by the Philippine Baptist Mission in 1964 and the Lahu Baptist Convention in 1972.

In general, Southeast Asian Baptist identity prior to World War II was rooted in the Anglo Baptist cultures of the missionary-sending agencies. After the war, as nations won their independence, Baptist churches moved toward greater independence as well. Leadership was transferred to national Baptist leaders, organizational independence was granted, and increasingly financial independence was assumed as well. The need for trained leadership contributed to the creation of seminaries and the need for coordination of efforts led to the growth of denominational structures.

In many cases, governments nationalized the schools, hospitals, and orphanages operated by Baptist mission organizations. In other contexts (such as the Philippines), Baptist universities continue to play a significant role. In some instances, Baptist individuals have contributed to the political and business life of the region. Furthermore, churches in Singapore, Malaysia, and the Philippines are sending missionaries to other areas of the world, even to the West – where they usually work among the rapidly growing Asian American populations. In the past, many Asians had considered persons who became Baptist as being, in some sense, culturally deformed. A major hurdle in the pathway toward achieving a satisfying Asian Baptist identity resides in the theological pitfalls involved in any search for a biblical faith that is firmly rooted in the culturally distinctive issues relevant to the diverse peoples of this region.

East Asian Baptists

For the sake of manageability, this study speaks of East Asian Baptists in one category, but the challenges Baptists in this region face vary greatly. Efforts to indigenize their theology present very local and specific demands.

As the twentieth century opened, Anglo American Baptist missionary organizations continued to make their heaviest investments in this area of the globe, especially among the Chinese. With the close of China to missionary enterprises, efforts shifted to surrounding countries such as Japan, Hong Kong, Taiwan, and Korea. As the century neared its end, Baptists found nontraditional ways to continue ministries to Chinese populations, though usually not under the name *Baptist*.

During Baptists' period of expanding traditioning sources, East Asia was dominated by three major economic powers – Japan, Korea, and China. Two other economic giants whose political designation was troublesome during the period were Hong Kong and Taiwan. Each of those countries has had importance for Baptist growth in East Asia during the twentieth century.

Six major political developments had particular significance in shaping the region during this period: the First Sino-Japanese War (1894–5), the Russo-Japanese War (1904–5), World War II (1939–1945), the 1949 Communist Revolution in China, the Korean War (1950–3), and the Vietnam War (1959–75). The First Sino-Japanese War shifted regional dominance from China to Japan, demonstrating the success of Japan's modernization programs and the weakness of China's Qing dynasty. The Russo-Japanese War manifested the expansionist ambitions of imperial Russia and the empire's need for an eastern warm-water port. However, Japan consistently thwarted Russia's designs for the region, delivering repeated defeats. The victories elevated Japan's image as a world power and increased Russian popular dissatisfaction with their tsarist government, fueling the 1905 revolution.

The Second Sino-Japanese War was fought between China and Japan between 1937 and 1945. In that conflict, Japanese imperialist policies confronted China's emerging nationalism and goals for self-determination. After Pearl Harbor, the war merged into World War II. As Japan suffered defeat, the Communist Party of China under the leadership of Mao Tse-tung defeated the Nationalist Party of Chiang Kai-shek. The new government followed a rigorous isolationist policy from 1940 to the early 1990s, expelling all foreign powers, including missionaries. The lone exceptions were Hong Kong, which continued by treaty as a British protectorate until 1997, and Taiwan, where Chiang Kai-shek fled with the remnants of his government. China's former Nationalist Party controlled Taiwan until democratic elections were held in the early 1990s. The political status of the republic continues to be a source of dispute.

During the Cold War, the northern portion of Asia was dominated by communist governments – the Soviet Union and the People's Republic of China. Much of the southeastern region was dominated by Western powers, symbolized by treaties such as the Central Treaty Organization (CENTO) and the Southeast Asia Treaty Organization (SEATO).[26] The Korean War, the Vietnam War, and the Soviet-Afghanistan conflict represent the ongoing clashes between these two forces. The end of the Cold War in the 1990s terminated Soviet aggression in the region. China, too, abruptly shifted its policies to allow capitalist economic development to flourish under the control of a communist government.

Japan emerged from World War I as one of the big-five nations of the new world order. The nation's steps toward democratic government became sidetracked by economic and political pressures that emerged during the Depression, after which Japan became increasingly militarized. Gradually, Parliament became more responsible to the emperor than to the people, and finally Japan's imperial ambitions brought it into conflict with the United States and to military defeat in 1945.

---

[26] CENTO, an acronym for the Central Treaty Organization, a pact among Iran, Iraq, Pakistan, Turkey, and the United Kingdom, was adopted in 1955. Its original name was the Middle East Organization (METO), but it was popularly referred to as the Baghdad Pact. The treaty was terminated in 1979. The Southeast Asia Treaty Organization (SEATO) was a collective defense treaty established by the Southeast Asia Collective Defense Treaty, which was sometimes referred to as the Manila Pact. Its primary aim was to halt the spread of communism in Southeast Asia.

During the Cold War, and especially the Korean War, Japan came to be seen as an important ally to the United States. The 1951 Treaty of Peace with Japan established conditions for Japan's independent future. Between 1951 and 1990, Japan underwent rapid development, emerging as a major world economic power. That "miracle" came to a halt in 1991 with a serious economic downturn that changed the conditions of employment for Japan's younger generation, making vocation more temporary than had been the case for the older generation of Japanese.

Following the Russo-Japanese War, Korea in effect became a protectorate of Japan. In 1910, Japan annexed Korea, setting up transportation and communication networks that enhanced Japan's ability to exploit the nation while offering little benefit to the Korean people. Gradually, Korea's population was pressed into forced labor and resistance efforts were suppressed. These policies reached their height between 1937 and 1945, when Japan attempted to eradicate Korea as a nation, forcing Shinto worship, not allowing schools to teach the Korean language or history, and destroying all remnants of Korean culture. During World War II, Koreans were forced to support Japan's war effort.

The inability of the Soviet Union and United States to agree on a unified provisional government, together with the serious tensions of the Cold War, resulted in a divided Korea. After the Korean War, South Korea, under United States protection – and amid internal political struggles and several dictatorships – became a democracy, whereas North Korea, under the Soviet Union, became a communist state. Economically and religiously, the two nations developed along very different paths.

Baptist missionary effort in China continued to be strong at the opening of the twentieth century, even though its work was widely interpreted as an arm of Western imperialism by the Chinese masses. Although missionaries suffered insults, the greatest pain was borne by those Chinese who chose to become Baptist. Referred to as "running dogs of the foreigners," they became the easiest targets for the frustrations many Chinese felt toward the death of the Qing dynasty and the ineffectiveness of the new republican government. As communist revolutionaries emerged offering hope for relief, Baptists with their strong ties to the West increasingly became alienated from the "new" China.

Already by the 1920s, some among missionary and Chinese leadership were sensing the urgency of developing national leadership for Baptist work. The Baptist leader Gideon Chin developed the comprehensive five-year movement, which treated Christianity as a way of life. The plan's aim was to apply Christian principles in economic, medical, and educational matters as a way of improving the quality of life of the masses of Chinese people. In 1925, following political turmoil, Baptist churches in the South of China declared their independence from foreign administration and graduates of several Western-styled Baptist colleges in China formed the Ling Tong Baptist Council. Such efforts helped some areas of Baptist work become more genuinely Chinese in nature.

Following the 1949 revolution, Baptist schools and hospitals were nationalized. In an effort to salvage a position for Christian faith in the new Marxist regime, the three-self movement was formed by Chinese Christian leadership in 1951. This program employed earlier mission goals of self-government, self-propagation, and self-support as a means for Chinese Christians to declare independence from Western ties. China's new government supported the initiative but also demanded loyal political support from church leaders. In 1958, a policy was initiated to reduce the number of churches, eliminate denominational identities, and limit the teaching of religion. During the Cultural Revolution (1966–76), numerous Christian leaders were imprisoned, and most of the remaining churches were closed. Many in the West believed that Christianity had been eliminated totally from China. The Baptist World Alliance no longer listed Baptist statistics for China. However, in 1979, China changed its religious policies, and more contact with the outside world was permitted. With that development, it became apparent that thousands of house churches had been formed during the thirty-year period since 1949 and that Christianity had grown phenomenally during that era. The winter had passed. A new hope was dawning.[27]

Baptists no longer work under that name in China; they relate to a post-denominational Christianity. Although many of China's churches function much like Baptist churches, they do not bear that or any other denominational label. The churches function under restrictions that are difficult for many Western Baptists to understand, yet the churches are growing.

In the nineteenth century, Hong Kong and Macao served as bridges for Baptist missionary endeavors aimed toward the Chinese Empire. The first Baptist churches in the entire Pacific Basin were organized there – Queen's Road in 1842 and Tie Chiu in 1843. Until 1949, Baptist efforts were focused toward the mainland, but Hong Kong still received some attention. After 1949, however, things changed dramatically. Several former missionaries in China relocated to Hong Kong. The population began to grow rapidly,

---

[27] The words of a song based on Song of Songs 2:10–12, popular among many Chinese Christians following the Cultural Revolution.

and Baptist work among groups of refugees was initiated. This, together with educational, medical, and evangelistic work, has contributed to rapid growth. By 2007, Hong Kong and Macao had at least ninety-six Baptist churches with more than seventy-three thousand members. From the center in Hong Kong, tenuous relationships were maintained with Baptists in interior China, especially with the Swatow-speaking Christians.

In Japan, Baptist work has been slow and often heavily dependent on mission support. Moreover, numerous Baptist missionary organizations have launched work in Japan, many holding an ecclesiology that discourages cooperation with other Baptist groups that differ from their own. The result has been a highly fragmented Baptist presence in Japan. Although Japanese leaders administer the work of the major Baptist bodies, they have generally found it difficult to find a true home within Japanese culture. However, in some cases, Baptists have established a positive image among many Japanese, especially because of their educational institutions and the role they have played in helping modernize Japan.

An ongoing challenge has been the need to express Christian thought in terms more indigenous to the Japanese context. Post–World War II efforts to do this are illustrated by Kazo Kitamori's *Theology of God's Pain*. He understood Japan's postwar experience in terms of pain and shame. Traditional Western theologies treated the issue in ways that seemed to alienate Japanese people from the God of the Bible by treating the experience of pain and suffering as ontological concepts. Kitamori sought theologically to reconstruct that understanding, interpreting it as constituent of the relationship between the Father and Son, and therefore between God and errant humanity. Pain, therefore, was understood as part of the fabric of relationship rather than as an aberration. Furthermore, numerous seemingly simple reconstructions such as Christ being interpreted as the rice of life rather than the bread of life were explored, demonstrating how even the subtleties of culture could aid or obscure identity. Although Baptists have not been at the forefront of such theological efforts, attempts to contextualize Christian thought into Japanese realities have benefited Baptists in varied ways.

The experiences of Baptists in South Korea have contrasted sharply with those of Japan, particularly since the Korean War. The nature of their origins and development has kept them more united and less dependent on foreign Baptist support for survival and extension. In 1889, a Canadian independent missionary named Malcolm C. Fenwick began a nondenominational mission work in Korea. To avoid friction with the Presbyterian and Methodist missions, he focused his work in Manchuria, Khan Island,

and Siberia. His methods were modeled closely along the lines of those he detected in the book of Acts, and thus were highly indigenous. In 1906, he organized the Church of Christ of Korea. Demoralized and disorganized after the period of Japan's occupation of Korea, in 1949, leaders of Fenwick's churches sought affiliation with a like-minded body of churches in America. Subsequently, they affiliated their churches with the Southern Baptist Convention and became the Korean Baptist Church. That work furnished the core from which most Korean Baptist work has flourished in the past five decades. In 2007, Korean Baptists numbered almost eight hundred thousand in more than 2,500 churches.

Korean Baptist identity was born during a period of transition between the Chosen dynasty and Japanese occupation – a time when many Koreans were seeking new answers to basic life questions. The result was a close connection between modernization and Western Baptist values such as education, freedom, and progress. This has meant that Korea, different from other Asian countries, was attracted to Western values rather than viewing them as being signs of colonial domination. Becoming Christian for many Koreans was a way to assert one's identity, especially in opposition to Japanese colonial values. The Korean War augmented South Korea's openness to a Western worldview through the forces that promoted freedom and democracy. Thus, Baptist (and other) churches promoted a religious identity formation that accompanied the development of a Korean worldview that preserved the values progressive Koreans were embracing.[28] Minjung theology, though not specifically Baptist, was expressive of this perspective.

In the late twentieth century, Korean Baptists reached a new level of maturity through missionary outreach and church growth. Hundreds of Korean Baptist missionaries now extend Baptist witness to other countries and have become one of the significant missionary forces in modern Baptist life. Also, some of the largest Baptist churches in the world are located in Korea. Billy Kim, formerly the senior pastor of the Suwon Central Baptist Church near Seoul, South Korea, is illustrative of Korean Baptist development during this period. In 1960, Kim began the church with ten members. By 2008, the church had grown to more than twenty thousand members. Because of his capable leadership and global outreach, Kim was elected president of the Baptist World Alliance, guiding that organization through challenging adjustments in the period between 2000 and 2005.

[28] Young-Gi Hong, "Korean Protestantism to the Present Day," in *Blackwell Companion to Protestantism* (Oxford, U.K.: Blackwell, 2007), 216–21.

When he retired after forty-five years of ministry, his retirement celebration was attended by the president of South Korea and the mayor of Seoul, indicators of his status in South Korean life.

Baptists of the Middle East

Although their existence has been tenuous and complicated, Baptists have maintained a small, and sometimes prominent, presence in the Middle East. Dwarfed by Judaism in Israel, Orthodox Christianity in Cyprus, and Islam elsewhere in the region, Baptists have been a strong minority in Lebanon and have survived in small communities in Israel, Jordan, Syria, and Iraq. In general, however, opportunities for Baptist witness in this region have been closed. Some educational and medical ministries have existed on occasion, but with heightened terrorist activities in recent decades, those have either been seriously curtailed or terminated altogether.

Many Baptists in the region face social and religious discrimination and, in repeated instances, security concerns as well. Most ministries have to be done discretely and usually only humanitarian efforts are allowed. Naturally, this requires an identity that some Baptists in the West find difficult to imagine or accept. With no possibility of being boldly evangelistic or demanding religious freedom in any significant way, many Baptists must employ concepts of witness that focus on modeling the meaning of faith rather than publically announcing or promoting it.

Asian Baptist Women

Virginia Fabella summed up the theological challenge of multitudes of Asian Baptist women when she wrote, "Asian women cannot speak of religion and cultures without speaking of poverty and multiple oppressions. Neither can they speak of liberation from poverty and oppression without speaking of 'spiritual' liberation."[29] In many instances, Asian Baptist churches are culturally traditional in their interpretations of the roles of women in church and social life. Consequently, many Baptists would not embrace Fabella's statement at face value. However, the theological truth expressed in her statement remains relevant to the reality experienced by many Baptist women. As new generations of Asian Baptist women gain greater opportunities for education and employment, there is a greater

---

[29] Esther Byu, "Women's Movements," in *A Dictionary of Asian Christianity* (Grand Rapids, MI: William B. Eerdmans Publishing, 2001), 899.

need for Baptists to prepare themselves to help those women and others negotiate the issues of identity and faith.

Although not specifically Baptist, Asian women's theologies are paving the way for such realities. Taking the pain and suffering of many Asian women as their starting point, those theologies seek to help women discover a biblical identity that liberates rather than enslaves, motivates rather than discourages, and gives hope rather than encouraging mere endurance. Numerous organizations offer opportunities for building solidarity and networks of supportive relationships.

In Asian Baptist life, women's organizations similar to those in traditional Anglo-American Baptist bodies exist. As noted in other contexts, these offer opportunities for the development of leadership, management, and planning skills. They offer much needed support for churches and mission endeavors and for development of Baptist women's identities. However, as global cultures transform the traditional roles of women, Asian Baptists will find themselves increasingly challenged to develop more adequate theologies of womanhood. Some Baptist communions of Nagaland and South Korea stand out as notable examples of the theological advances that need to be occurring in the arena of women's emancipation today.

Asian Baptists' General Identifying Characteristics during the Age of Proliferating Traditions

Baptists in Asia largely have had to forge their identities from the position of cultural outsiders. This is especially significant in societies where "face" is highly important. To some extent, all persons harbor concerns for what the important others in their lives think of them, regardless of their culture. But many Asian societies have a particular way of understanding face that makes this an especially important element of their culture. Western Anglo cultures have tended to place great value on the self-reliant individual. Western Baptist theology has embraced that cultural quality to a significant degree and has inculcated it into its value systems and identity. This integration has become so thorough that most could not imagine "Baptistness" apart from certain understandings of individual freedoms. In a parallel fashion, most Asian cultures have incorporated some variation of the concept of face. To find a home in many Asian cultures, Baptists either already have or must develop an identity that suitably values face.

Asian societies tend to place great importance on social relationships (i.e., the individual in the context of important others) that stands in contrast to Western individualism. Face involves "how important or unimportant one is in a community. Do you have a good or bad name? Do you make a good or bad impression?"[30] Although the interpretation of face varies among Asian cultures, preserving face is important in each one of them, and how that is appropriately achieved is essential for each. In Chinese culture, for example, Confucian teaching has instilled the value of caring for one's own family and community before giving to strangers. A Baptist theology of stewardship somehow needs to interpret giving in the context of this cultural understanding. Furthermore, to Chinese culture, Western individualism seems immoral. In that setting, staying in close contact with parents and living in harmony as family is of paramount importance, even for married couples. These two values, together with related cultural standards, have important implications for the Chinese understanding of what a Baptist faith community should be. The ecclesiological dimensions of this cultural interpretation must and will influence the way Chinese Baptists comprehend their identity. The way Asian Baptists interpret a wide variety of faith experiences within specific cultural settings will be distinctive and will sometimes contrast with the way Anglo and other Baptists would define aspects of ecclesiology from within their own contexts. However, each set of experiences and interpretations has important contributions to make to an emerging global concept of what it means to be Baptist, and each should be appropriately honored.

The concept of face is but one of many cultural qualities that are pregnant with possibilities for the enhancement of Baptists' identity globally. Several others include concepts of shame versus guilt, social ranking versus egalitarianism, variations in how departed loved ones are to be honored, and the nature of the ways friendships are formed. In addition, Asian Baptists have a long history of being Baptist in religiously pluralistic societies. They have developed some admirable skills for addressing that reality. Careful reflection on that aspect of Asian Baptists' experiences offers possibilities for assisting the larger Baptist family in adjusting to a similar reality, which is often new to them.

Asian cultures challenge the purveyors of a Baptist theological intentionality with yet another body of traditioning sources that is on the verge of making its voice heard among the larger family of Baptists. Although Asian Baptists often seem conservative to Western Baptists, tendencies to interpret that quality as meaning that we can all fit under an Anglo-defined Baptist rubric would almost inevitably lead to further misunderstandings and conflict.

---

[30] Dick Worley, *Serve Christ Always: Memoirs of Dick and Charlotte Worley* (n.p.: published by the author, 2005), 243.

OCEANIAN BAPTISTS' EVOLVING TRADITIONING SOURCES

As the globe has grown smaller through advances in transportation and communications, even the remotest parts of Oceania have become integrated into the world community in ways never imagined early in the twentieth century. Traditionally divided into Australasia, Melanesia, Micronesia, and Polynesia,[31] the area includes more than ten thousand islands and about 33 million inhabitants, including Australia's 21 million people.[32]

During the twentieth century, the islands attracted increased attention because of their strategic value among world powers. Much of the political concern of the smaller islands has centered on issues surrounding colonial control, problems faced by Native peoples because of expanding populations, the impact of outside economic interests, and rising standards of living. Over the centuries, intertribal mixing has greatly transformed the ethnic makeup of island inhabitants, although many indigenous people continue to identify themselves by their home island or their mother language. Traditional Polynesian culture has especially valued aesthetic creativity, complex social etiquettes, hereditary aristocracies, and elaborate religious rituals. Micronesian cultures are more culturally heterogeneous and value fishing and interisland trade. Melanesian cultures have tended to be patrilineal and have organized around a local "big man" with his network of relatives who build influence and wealth through ceremonial exchanges of goods.

World War II brought massive change and an increasing need on the part of most island communities to interact more with Western society. Disruption to traditional patterns of life has affected islanders in a multitude of ways, including the proliferation of mystical cults, resistance to assimilation, epidemics of diseases, poverty, unemployment, and the breakdown of family structures. Following decades of colonial administration – principally by Australia, New Zealand, France, Britain, and the United States – since the 1960s, the islands have gradually gained their independence.

[31] This book uses the following definitions for distinguishing the parts of Oceania: Australasia includes Australia and New Zealand, although New Zealand is also culturally and linguistically part of Polynesia. Polynesia includes French Polynesia, Cook Islands, Samoa, and Tuvalu. Melanesia includes New Caledonia, Solomon Islands, New Guinea, Vanuatu, and Fiji and is culturally and racially distinct from Polynesia. Micronesia is also distinct and includes Guam, Kiribati, Marshall Islands, Federated States of Micronesia, Nauru, Northern Mariana Islands, Palau, and Wake Island.

[32] Indonesia, Taiwan, and the Philippines are generally not included in this grouping because their cultures and peoples are more closely connected to Asia than to these islands.

The widely scattered islands have long been the object of missionary concern. Given the wide diversity of cultures and the vast areas over which their relatively small communities have been scattered, evangelization has not been easy. However, by the beginning of the twenty-first century, most of the indigenous populations had embraced Christianity, which was mostly accomplished by the efforts of Christian islanders themselves.

Outside of Australia and New Zealand, Baptists had very little presence in Oceania, and even within those countries, their numbers have been small in comparison to the Anglican, Methodist, Presbyterian, and Roman Catholic churches. In much of the rest of Oceania, there was no Baptist presence at all before World War II. Since then, Baptists have experienced a steadily growing presence in the region, with most of their numbers concentrated in Australia, New Zealand, and Papua New Guinea. In 2007, Baptists throughout the entire region totaled about 1,500 churches with 250,000 members.

Australian Baptists

By 1890, each of Australia's six colonies had gained responsible government status, thereby possessing the freedom to manage most of their own political affairs while remaining part of the British Empire. In 1901, a federation of the colonies was enacted, making the Commonwealth of Australia a Dominion of the empire. By 1942, most remaining constitutional links to the United Kingdom ended with Australia's adoption of the Statute of Westminster. Finally, the 1986 Australia Act ended all British roles in Australian government. This developmental history is important for understanding Australian Baptist life, because its union structures still reflect an earlier political outlook. In 1926, the Baptist Union of Australia was created along the lines of a federal charter, giving a form of coherence to the independent state unions (see the previous chapter) that functioned much like the nation's governmental structure at that time. Each state union retained its autonomy, and the union served an advisory function and helped coordinate Baptist educational, mission, publication, and evangelistic efforts. The greatest source of common identity among Australian Baptists has been their foreign mission work. The various independent state foreign mission societies were united in 1913 under a board now known as the Australian Baptist Missionary Society, which in 1995 had 129 missionaries serving in twelve countries and among Australian Aboriginal peoples. A second significant ministry focus for Australian Baptists has been educational work. Since 1891, Baptist colleges have been established in Melbourne, Brisbane, Sydney, Adelaide, and Perth.

The threat of invasion by Japanese forces during World War II motivated Australia to form closer alliances with the United States, a connection that continued throughout the century in various forms, especially the Australia, New Zealand, United States Security (ANZUS) Treaty.[33] Those ties have helped fostered some cooperative partnerships between Australian Baptists and selected Baptist churches and other entities in the United States. Strict and Particular Baptists, Seventh Day Baptists, Baptist Mid-Missions, the Baptist Bible Fellowship, the Association of Baptists for World Evangelization, and the American Baptist Association (Landmark) also are among the Baptist bodies present in Australia, but none in large numbers.

In 1973, Australia abandoned the white Australia policy, allowing immigration from non-European regions of the world. Consequently, a rapid transformation occurred in Australia's demographic and cultural makeup, and has affected the national self-image. Since the 1970s, Australia has taken steps to forge stronger ties with other Pacific Rim nations while maintaining ties with traditional allies. This has been a challenge for Baptist witness but has transformed Australian Baptists into a more diverse community. Since the 1970s, charismatic practices have influenced worship and leadership styles in most churches. Diversity of theological traditions has increased, mostly from different state and ethnic influences, but in general, Australian Baptists have tended to be conservative.

Religiously, Australia has experienced significant changes as well. In 2006, 64 percent of the population identified itself as Christian, 19 percent as nonreligious, 5 percent as non-Christian religions, and 12 percent declined to answer. However, most polls indicate that the actual participation in church life is less than these statistics might seem to suggest. Only about 8 percent of the population attends church on a weekly basis. Since World War II, Australian Baptists' greatest challenge has been that of appealing to a population that has become highly secularized and often indifferent to the claims of religious faith. In 2007, Australia had about seventy thousand Baptists of all types in about one thousand churches.

New Zealand Baptists

In 1901, New Zealand chose to become a Dominion on par with Australia and Canada rather than become part of the Commonwealth of Australia.

---

[33] The ANZUS Treaty obligates Australia and New Zealand and, independently, Australia and the United States to cooperate on matters of defense in the region of the Pacific Ocean.

In many ways, New Zealand gained national consciousness through its participation in World War I, during which, among other things, it took Western Samoa from Germany and administered the islands until their independence in 1962.

The global Depression of the 1930s had a major impact on New Zealand's political, social, and economic life. With no social safety net in place, many of the unemployed found their only means of survival through relief work programs. The experience led not only to the election of New Zealand's first Labour government but also to the establishment of a full welfare state with free health care; education; and assistance to the elderly, disabled, and unemployed.

World War II increased New Zealand's role in international affairs. Internally, the nation's economy underwent major shifts. Prior to the war, New Zealand's economy had been based on trade relations connected to Britain. Britain's decision to join the European Economic Community in 1973 had major implications for New Zealand and not only forced it to find new markets but also caused a reexamination of its national and global identity. New Zealand still retains strong but informal ties to Britain. By the late 1940s, almost 70 percent of the population lived in urban areas.

These changes have produced social, political, and intellectual shifts that require adaptations in Baptist ministries. Carey Baptist College was established in Auckland to help address the denomination's needs for leadership trained to better handle those developments. With declining denominational loyalty, Baptists have found themselves forced to rethink their purpose, mission, and forms of worship. An increasingly materialistic and secular culture requires that Baptists engage issues with greater insight and depth of understanding than ever before.

In addition to radical shifts in the European populations, postwar New Zealand experienced changes in the Maori populations as well. Many moved from rural settings to the cities to pursue new employment and new ways of life. By 1990, more than 80 percent of the Maori population was urban but suffered discrimination. Protest movements have helped raise awareness of Maori culture and combat racism. In addition, a relaxation of immigration restrictions has allowed more Asians to immigrate, thus diversifying the population somewhat. As a consequence, Baptist life has become more multicultural. In addition to Maori work, New Zealand Baptists also support ministries among Chinese, Korean, and Pacific Islander immigrants.

Today, New Zealand Baptists number more than 245 churches with more than twenty-five thousand members. Most are middle class, ecumenical in spirit, and cooperate with the government to provide social services that benefit the larger community. Baptists have had less success in reaching New Zealand's working classes.

Other Oceanian Baptists

In most of the remainder of Oceania, Baptists' presence has been very limited. In the mid-1990s, Fiji had about fourteen churches; Guam, eight; the Northern Mariana Islands, one; Samoa, six; and the Solomon Islands, thirty-five. The one significant exception was Papua New Guinea, which had 263 churches with more than eighty thousand members in 2007. Under Australian control after World War I, the island was inhabited by numerous tribes with various languages and dialects. During World War II, Australian army chaplains identified this as a mission outreach possibility, and Australian Baptists began ministries there. Between 1949 and 1977, when the Baptist Union of Papua New Guinea was organized, Baptists grew to more than fifteen thousand members. As young people have moved to the coastal towns for employment, they have spread Baptist witness to other areas of the island. Recurring revivals have extended and deepened the faith of those Baptists. Indigenous witness has been supplemented by educational, medical, and literature ministries offered by international missionary organizations.

Baptist Women of the Oceania Region

As in other regions of the world, the contributions of Baptist women in Oceania were essential to the establishment, development, and support of Baptist churches. Their most noted accomplishments were made in areas like Christian education, missionary organizations, and children's work. As those ministries suggest, women often have been relegated chiefly to supporting roles. Only occasionally have they been inducted into higher positions of leadership and decision making in church life. In the 1960s and 1970s, that imbalance began to change in Australia and New Zealand. As movements for women's liberation grew in the general society, Baptist women also began to demand greater opportunities for participation in all areas of church life, including pastoral leadership. As the more dominant Anglican community wrestled with the issue, the question of ordination of women was introduced into Baptist churches as well.

The issue began to surface among Australian Baptists in the 1960s, with fierce debates over the idea. Christy Hayward is illustrative of those who favored women's ordination, arguing, "It is just plain foolishness to permit women to work with men in some fields of Christian work and deny them the right to become 'first class Christians' at the ministerial level."[34] On the other side, it was argued that allowing women to lead would "leave a corrupted Baptist church."[35] By the mid-1960s, women were being given opportunities to serve as full-time deaconesses but not yet as ordained pastors. The first women to apply to the Candidates' Board for ordination were urged to seek recognition as deaconesses instead. But the matter continued to agitate.

In 1974, Edith McKay was elected president of the South Australian Union, the first woman to hold such an office. Gradually, other women were elected to equivalent offices in other unions. In 1977, the Victorian General Council endorsed women's ordination in principle, which brought forth demands for recognition of counterviewpoints. But the way was opened for Marita Munro to become the first woman to be ordained by Australian Baptists. During the 1980s, progress was slow but continued. Between 1991 and 2004, fourteen women were ordained in Victoria. Finally, other state unions also voted to allow women's ordination and increasing numbers of women joined the ranks of ministers serving Australian Baptist churches.[36]

Baptist women in New Zealand were not allowed to participate in Baptist Union assemblies until 1908. In addition, Baptist church pastorates, diaconates, and committees were the exclusive domain of men. But as social forces supportive of women's liberation from culture-bound role interpretations mounted, Baptists began to change their views as well. In 1984, Dame Vivian Boyd became the first woman to serve as president of the Baptist Union of New Zealand. In the late twentieth and early twenty-first centuries, numerous women have trained for pastoral ministry, but as of 2008, only eleven had held positions as senior pastors. Many others have held positions as chaplains, assistant pastors, and educators. At the local level, women have experienced greater opportunity to serve as deacons, elders, and worship leaders. Yet many still feel that Baptists' predominant attitudes about women have been prejudicial and oppressive.[37] For cultural reasons, the small number of Polynesian and Melanesian Baptists have steadfastly resisted changes in gender boundaries.

[34] *Australian Baptist*, November 2, 1960, 10, cited in Ken R. Manley, *From Woolloomooloo to "Eternity": A History of Australian Baptists* (Milton Keynes, U.K.: Paternoster, 2006), 2:731.

[35] *Australian Baptist*, November 9, 1960, 11, cited in Manley, *From Woolloomooloo to "Eternity,"* 2:731.

[36] Manley, *From Woolloomooloo to "Eternity,"* 730–6.

[37] See Scott Higgins, "Breaking through the Stained Glass Ceiling? Women's Participation in Leadership in Australian Baptist Churches," report prepared for *Baptists Today* (2008).

Figure 12. Matondo gathering at Kinkosi, Democratic Republic of Congo, in 1928 – on this occasion, 228 persons were baptized (photo by Viola L. Smith, courtesy of American Baptist Historical Society, Valley Forge, Pennsylvania).

Figure 13. Lott Carey (1780–1829), born into slavery in the United States, earned his freedom and established Liberia's first Baptist Church in 1822 (courtesy of American Baptist Historical Society, Valley Forge, Pennsylvania).

Oceanian Baptists' General Identifying Characteristics
during the Age of Proliferating Traditions

The general ethos of Baptist life in Australia and New Zealand during this period was characteristically British, with some American influences after midcentury. In the rest of Oceania, there was variety. Generally, Baptists shared a widespread Protestant sentiment that God's providence had created and blessed their nations or peoples, thereby tying faith and group identity together in a theological package. They tended to value most highly four core commitments: the Bible as supremely authoritative, liberty of conscience, justification by faith alone, and moral integrity.

Baptists emphasized education and made significant investments from their limited resources to support such endeavors. They also formed and supported missionary societies and other efforts aimed at evangelism and social improvement. Publications also were important, and numerous denominational papers were maintained. Unfortunately, cross-cultural ministries often were tainted by an implicit racism. The superiority of British culture was simply assumed by the mainstream of Baptists, ensuring attitudes of inferiority toward indigenous and Asian peoples, who were often approached in a paternalistic fashion. This contributed to the failure of many well-intentioned ministry efforts. This problem plagued a high percentage of the early missionary endeavors in the Pacific Islands as well. Such attitudes began to change during the latter half of the twentieth century as Baptists grew in awareness of the cultural dimensions of their theological systems, of indigenous issues, and of boundaries between religion and science.

After the 1970s, new groups of Baptists began to emerge – especially in Australia and New Zealand. Korean, Indonesian, Chinese, and Pacific Island congregations have begun to appear, and as they have grown, they also have begun to challenge traditional denominational priorities. In addition, Pacific Islander, Aboriginal, and Maori Baptists, as they mature, question the normative character of Anglo Baptist assumptions, demanding that their own cultural traditions be given weight in theological constructs and denominational identity. In the Pacific Islands, wheresoever the Baptist faith has been embraced, that faith and the adherent's traditional culture have tended to become closely integrated. Although true to the islanders' historic cultural patterns, this also has proved a problematic union at times, as when military coups have seriously disrupted traditional culture.

For Oceanian Baptists of the Anglo traditions, the twenty-first century brought new identity challenges. Among them were the widespread anti-institutional attitudes that fostered antipathy toward ecclesiastical institutions in general. Anglo-Oceanian Baptists also were pummeled by seemingly insoluble theological and ethical divisions surrounding questions over sexuality, social justice, and gender roles that threatened the continued loyalty of the faithful on the one hand and their total alienation from the larger society to which they needed to relate on the other hand.

CHAPTER 7

Baptists' Evolving Traditioning Sources in Latin America, the Caribbean, Europe, and Eurasia

The themes treated in Part IV have intentionally inverted the traditional Western ordering of Baptist history, which usually is cast as flowing from Europe (especially Britain) to North America, then to the mission fields of Africa, Asia, and Latin America. Although substantial evidence exists to support that arrangement, this schema also tends to obscure the fact that the Baptist world is changing dramatically. In many instances, the mission fields have come of age and are rapidly emerging as mature, vibrant, and fertile centers of Baptist life. This chapter brings four of those worlds together in an uncommon coupling to accentuate the significance and nature of those developments.

At the dawn of the twentieth century, modernism seemed to be gaining ground against the established traditions of philosophy, government, and religion. In Europe, modernism became the entrenched worldview of intellectuals and was hailed as the key to solving humanity's most obstinate problems, such as poverty, disease, unemployment, and crime. Numerous widely embraced movements – like liberalism and neoclassicism – looked positively to the Enlightenment as the source from which their intellectual systems had evolved. These mental frameworks tended to emphasize particular applications of rationality as a means for undermining many long-established assumptions about reality. Thus, appeal was made to Enlightenment thought as a basis for fighting superstition, intolerance, and confessionalism. Freedom, democracy, reason, capitalism, the scientific method, and religious tolerance became the core virtues of this new world, and Western societies were considered the epitome of this unprecedented standard of human achievement.

Following World War II and the rise of postmodernist philosophies, those virtues became vices in the minds of many people. Sterile reason, mechanistic lifestyles, consumerism, environmental damage, failure to heed traditional wisdom, and recognition of the destructive potential of Enlightenment reason evoked a reaction. Michael Foucault, Jacques

Derrida, Richard Rorty, Jean-François Lyotard, Emmanuel Levinas, Max Horkheimer, and Theodore Adorno are among the many postmodernist philosophers who questioned the assumptions, methods, and conclusions of modernism and opened the way for new foundations on which to base thought and the pursuit of truth.

Cultures, like those of Western Europe, that imbibed heavily of modernism emerged from the twentieth century with a significantly different outlook on the world from that of the cultures that had been less shaped by those thought forms. Secularism, skepticism, utilitarianism, and materialism often characterized the former societies in ways that were far less pronounced among the latter ones. For instance, the cultural ethos of Latin America and the Caribbean engaged modernist perspectives quite differently than did Europe and North America. That variance contributed not only to the rather different results that Baptist ministries experienced in those continents over the course of the twentieth century but also to subtle but important distinctives in their identities as Baptists.

LATIN AMERICAN BAPTISTS' EVOLVING TRADITIONING SOURCES

The transition from colonial rule to independence among Latin American nations often left caudillos (charismatic authoritarian leaders) in charge of governments. In some cases, those leaders offered a temporary solution to chaotic political conditions. In other instances, they gave opportunity for the ruthless ambitions of self-serving dictators. In this world, two factions tended to predominate – liberals, who promoted public education, land reform, and personal freedoms, and conservatives, who wanted to preserve the privileged position of the Catholic Church and the economic status quo with its benefits to the wealthy. As the twentieth century dawned, the conservative factions prevailed in much of Latin America. In that context, Baptists' core convictions identified them among supporters of the liberal agenda, even though theologically they were not liberal. Usually politically insignificant, Baptists spoke of the need to challenge the status quo and encouraged adherents to dream of new societies for Latin America that would be characterized by personal freedoms and economic betterment. This appeal found acceptance among a few. But their tendency to focus so heavily on personal betterment suggested to the more reflective persons among the underprivileged that Baptists offered a dream that was totally other worldly and not socially reforming, thereby leaving the dispossessed to live on in intolerable conditions while awaiting a better life after death. In many instances, Baptists did seek to address personal need through educational, orphanage, and medical ministries. However, evangelism was frequently the driving purpose even for those efforts, which ultimately betrayed an underlying otherworldly restraint that was bound up in accepting a systemic status quo for the present life.

Politically, the big-stick policy of Theodore Roosevelt established the tone for international relationships with Latin American countries during the early decades of the century. This policy essentially declared not only the "right" of the United States to oppose European intervention in the Western Hemisphere (the Monroe Doctrine) but also the "right" to intervene in the domestic affairs of Latin American governments should they be unable to maintain order and national sovereignty for themselves. This policy governed U.S. actions on numerous occasions up to World War I – for example, independence of Panama from Colombia in 1903; a two-year occupation of Cuba from 1906; and the U.S. Marines' occupation of Honduras in 1911, Nicaragua in 1912, Haiti in 1915, and Dominican Republic in 1916. Those actions generated resentments among those populations and fueled the power of numerous dictators willing to cooperate with U.S. policies. The fact that Baptists' presence in Latin America at that time was associated closely with U.S. missionary organizations necessarily colored local citizen's perceptions of them in light of government actions. For those Latin Americans who were dissatisfied with existing conditions, the possibility of something better helped cast Baptists in a more favorable light. For many others, the political context augmented the view that Baptists were agents of imperialism. This outlook stood in stark contrast to that of Anglo-American Baptists, who tended to interpret their nation's military actions as politically liberative and their missionary efforts as carrying light to a darkened humanity that should be appreciative of the opportunities it was receiving.

World War I gave a boost to Latin America's economies but set the stage for the disastrous depression that came after 1929. This renewed the caudillo tradition in the form of military dictatorships. Franklin Roosevelt's good-neighbor policy helped improve relations between the United States and many Latin American nations. Following World War II, Latin America generally moved toward democracy, but the advance was also hindered by numerous instances of return to military regimes and the emergence of powerful drug cartels in certain regions of South and Central America. Nicaragua, Paraguay, Guatemala, Haiti, Bolivia, Uruguay, Chile, and Argentina each had periods of brutal dictatorships, with campaigns of terror and death squads. Fearful of communist infiltration, the United

States acted secretly to topple left-leaning governments in Guatemala in 1954, Chile in 1973, and Nicaragua in 1984.

By the mid-1980s, most Latin American nations began replacing military regimes with democratically elected governments. This was seldom an easy accomplishment amid economic crises, corruption, and the ravages of poverty. Liberation theologies sought both to empower the oppressed masses and to challenge the larger Christian world to take a new look at the Bible from the perspective of those who suffer as a consequence of policies and systems that benefit a few at the expense of the multitudes.

Over the course of the twentieth century, amid political and economic transitions, Baptists developed steadily growing ministries in Latin America that usually were sustained initially through missionary efforts. By the twenty-first century, however, most Baptist work was maintained and governed by local Baptists who had advanced to the point of initiating cross-cultural missionary enterprises of their own. Before World War I, Baptist churches in Latin America were concentrated in the five countries of Argentina, Chile, Brazil, Cuba, and Mexico and the U.S. commonwealth of Puerto Rico. By the end of the century, they had established a presence in each of the Latin American countries. In most contexts, they were growing at remarkable rates and in many instances had transitioned from the status of outsiders to cultural insiders. Moreover, the Baptist movement in Latin America has been wonderfully varied ethnically. Black Baptists from the Caribbean islands have spread into Belize, Honduras, Nicaragua, Panama, Guyana, Colombia, Venezuela, and beyond. German Baptists in Chile, Argentina, Uruguay, and Brazil have contributed to the Baptist movements in those countries and elsewhere. The first residents of Guyana to become Baptists were from Chinese ancestry; the first in Suriname were from Java. In the complex and varied populations of Latin America's megacities can be found English-speaking, French-speaking, Korean-speaking, German-speaking, Spanish-speaking, Portuguese-speaking, Japanese-speaking, and Chinese-speaking Baptists, in addition to many others. Furthermore, numerous indigenous tribes throughout South and Central America have embraced a Baptist identity. Although the greatest numbers of Baptists have come from the less privileged classes, increasing numbers can be found in the middle classes and a few among the wealthy members of Latin American society.

South American Baptists

Baptists have experienced significant growth in South America since the mid-twentieth century, increasing from about 250,200 in 1965 to almost

1.8 million in 2007. But the greatest concentration of growth has occurred in Brazil, where Baptists number almost 1.1 million, constituting more than 60 percent of Latin America's Baptists and forming one of global Baptists' largest constituencies. Prior to World War I, Argentina and Chile were the only Spanish-speaking countries in South America where Baptists had succeeded in establishing sustainable work. Even in those locations, their numbers were exceedingly small. Only since World War II has the Baptist movement taken root in other areas of the continent. In most cases, national Baptists lead and sustain the work, frequently with various forms of international missionary assistance. Furthermore, in many countries, Baptist churches have matured to the point of sustaining mission programs of their own that reach out to distant regions of the world, including Europe and North America.

In 1907, Brazilian Baptists organized a national association called A Convenção Batista Brasileira (the Brazilian Baptist Convention). At the local, state, and national levels, this body of Baptists has organized according to patterns reflective of the Southern Baptist Convention in the United States. To a surprising degree, the cultures of most Baptists in Brazil have been very compatible with those of most nineteenth- and twentieth-century Southern Baptists, allowing the two to work together in great harmony. From the beginning of Baptist work in Brazil, talented Brazilians were involved in leadership of the ministries, but in the early decades, missionaries held many of the convention's leadership posts. As the twentieth century progressed, however, Brazilian Baptists increasingly assumed both administrative leadership and financial support for the work. By the end of the century, the Brazilian Baptist Convention's foreign mission board supported 132 missionaries who served in ten countries of South America, four countries of Africa, several countries of Europe, and the United States and Canada. The convention's home mission board supported more than 450 missionaries who were active in extending Baptist ministries throughout the nation. In addition, most local churches interpreted a part of their mission as including the organization of congregations that they helped to develop into mature, self-sustaining churches.

Such growth has demanded trained leadership, which has necessitated the development of educational institutions. Three seminaries were established by Southern Baptists, initially organized according to American models of theological education and the source of most Brazilian Baptist leadership training during the first half of the twentieth century. In the late 1950s, a different, more local model was developed by Brazilian Baptists that minimized investment in costly real estate and maximized the utilization of available talent for professional training. This system of *faculdades* quickly caught on and was multiplied by numerous state conventions, regional associations, and even local churches. By the end of the century, Brazilian Baptists had created and sustained more than forty such educational institutions throughout the country. In addition, Brazilian Baptists have sponsored other schools around the country that provided education for students from the prekindergarten through the senior high levels.

After midcentury, Brazilian Baptists struggled with differences over Pentecostal practices. As the Pentecostal movement gained increasing popularity among the same population groups Brazilian Baptists were reaching, some Baptists recognized that the music, animated worship services, physical involvement in worship, and similar practices were very indigenous to much of Brazilian culture. However, most Baptist worship was reflective of the more orderly and subdued worship styles of American middle-class Baptists of the era. The result was division. In 1967, the National Baptist Convention of Brazil (CBNB) was organized by several former Brazilian Baptist Convention churches that blended a long-held Baptist tradition with certain Pentecostal practices. In 2007, the CBNB numbered 2,831 churches with almost four hundred thousand members.

Other controversial issues affecting Brazilian Baptists have included differences over liberation theology, women in ministry, styles of worship, and types of music used in worship. In addition, varieties of Baptists in the United States and Europe have organized alternate Baptist bodies adding to the variety of Baptist traditions found in Brazil today.

Baptist witness and investment in the Spanish-speaking countries of South America have lagged behind that of Brazil. However, since World War II, the situation has changed dramatically. A growing Baptist presence could be found in every South American country at the dawn of the twenty-first century, with the largest communities found in Argentina, Venezuela, Bolivia, Chile, and Colombia. In most cases, although the total number of members among those churches is much smaller than those of Baptists in Brazil, the rate of growth has equaled or surpassed that of Brazilian Baptists.

The sources of Baptist life in South America are widely varied. Baptist foundations in Bolivia, for example, were laid by Canadian Baptists. In Chile, they came from a Scottish Baptist minister. In Colombia, a political refugee who became Baptist while living in Cuba initiated the work. In Guyana, the National Baptist Convention in the United States and the Lott Carey Foreign Mission Convention were significant contributors to development of Baptist witness among the large black population; a member of the Baptist church in Canton, China, began work among Chinese immigrants; and still other sources initiated Baptist ministries among the East

Indian populations. In Peru, the Irish Baptist Foreign Mission planted the first Baptist churches. In addition, Brazilian Baptists and Argentine Baptists have contributed to furthering Baptist work in surrounding South American countries. In most of those nations, Southern Baptist missionaries have at some point contributed to Baptist development. Many other Baptist mission organizations have been active as well. Consequently, the work is varied and evidences a complex combination of traditioning sources at work.

Baptist identities in Latin American contexts have been shaped by a variety of influences, including their status as a Protestant minority in predominantly Catholic cultures, their position as economically lower- and lower-middle-class constituents, their appeal to a wide variety of ethnic groups with distinct cultures and needs, and their history of suffering persecution. In most instances, Baptist ministries were introduced through missionary entities from either the United States or Europe. However, despite the external origins of their witness, local Baptists assumed leadership of the work as the twentieth century progressed. Today, in most cases, the grassroots work is accomplished by local Baptists, sometimes with support from missionaries, but with decreasing amounts of such outside aid. As the work has become more indigenous, gradual modifications have enabled it to fit better into the cultures where it has taken root.

Central American Baptists

In September 1903, messengers from a number of Baptist churches in Mexico met in Mexico City to organize the Convención Nacional Bautista de Mexico (CNBM, National Baptist Convention of Mexico). This action began the transition of Mexican Baptist work from missionary to national control. Baptist ministries were seriously disrupted by Mexico's revolution, which lasted from 1910 to 1917, with numerous churches, schools, and members being lost to the violence of that period. Among the restrictions imposed by Mexico's postrevolutionary socialist government were nationalization of church properties, permission for only native-born Mexican citizens to lead services, and limitation of church activities to the church's property. Working within those parameters, Mexican Baptists began to rebuild.

With little missionary assistance, Mexican Baptists extended their ministries and enlarged their organizational structures throughout the 1940s. After World War II, other Baptist groups from the United States entered Mexico, establishing additional Baptist bodies alongside the CNBM. In

1993, the convention was able to register with the Mexican government, thereby gaining the benefits of legal status. By 2007, the CNBM recorded 1,550 churches with more than 150,000 members.

Little Baptist work existed in the rest of Central America prior to World War II, with the exception of Jamaican Baptist ministries among English-speaking black populations and American Baptist work among Spanish-speaking people in Nicaragua and El Salvador. Since then, a variety of Baptist mission organizations have established ministries in every country of Central America. Most of this work is controlled by national Baptists, often with some assistance from various mission bodies and through part-nering relationships with individual churches and associations in North America. In 2007, Baptists numbered more than 1,200 churches with more than 110,000 members. Outside of Mexico, Baptists' largest and strongest work is in Guatemala, Honduras, and Nicaragua.

Latin American Baptist Women

Women have constituted an essential element of Baptist work in Latin America from its initial stages. A very familiar pattern for new church starts has included the coalescence of a nucleus of dedicated women who form the backbone of a congregation's early life, followed by a period of formal organization, at which time men fill the prime positions of congregational leadership. Women usually share a voice in church business meetings and generally exercise roles in public worship, especially in music. But women are usually not given positions of true power in the church's governance. It is far more common for women to do much of the support work. Without the dedicated service of committed Baptist women, the educational, mission support, fund-raising, evangelistic outreach, social programs, and mainte-nance needs of most congregations could not be sustained. In São Paulo, Brazil Baptists' *adensamento* programs of the 1980s and 1990s, women were crucial in church planting efforts. They commonly became the avenue for accessing the women and children of the community from which the initial core of congregants would be formed. Through their influence and build-ing on their networks of relationships, greater numbers of men gradually became attracted to the work. Consequently, it has been usual for these Baptist churches to be family and neighborhood based, at least initially. However, although women were commonly the key recruiters for bring-ing others into the church, after the congregation was formally organized as a church, without exception, a male pastor was called and women's involvement in decision making beyond a certain level became restricted.

During much of the twentieth century, the church work of Baptist women in Latin America paralleled that of Baptist women in North America and Europe (treated in earlier chapters). Women's missionary societies became the primary venue for accomplishing mission education, support, and activities. Through such organizations, women developed leadership skills, which afforded them opportunities to lead other women. But as Latin American society undergoes changes, so do the roles and expectations of women in general. Education and economic necessity increasingly have thrust Baptist women into public spheres. As women exercise more leadership in secular contexts, Baptist churches are challenged to help them bridge the gaps of theology and worldview that are thereby created. Baptists' historic affirmation of the equality of all persons before God, together with the concerns raised by women's movements in the broader society, have led some Baptists of Latin America to reconsider their attitudes regarding women's roles in the church. A few Baptist faith communities have begun to explore and implement the possibilities for greater involvement by women in ministry, including women's ordination for pastoral leadership. Among many Latin American Baptist bodies, such practices are unthinkable. A few Baptist churches, however, already allow women equal access to ordination and pastoral leadership. Baptist women in Latin America continue to work within the unique challenges and opportunities of their own contexts, and the way forward is often filled with frustrations. But one thing is clear: gender roles are changing and Latin America's Baptists, like others, will need to deal constructively with that reality.

CARIBBEAN BAPTISTS' EVOLVING TRADITIONING SOURCES

Over the course of the twentieth century, European nations gradually gave up their colonial interests in the Caribbean as the United States expanded its influence in the region. Expressive of Theodore Roosevelt's policies, the so-called banana wars asserted American economic and political interests throughout the basin. Fidel Castro's defiance of U.S. interference in Cuba resulted in prolonged tensions between those two governments and in the decades-long imposition of economic and political sanctions, which have continued into the twenty-first century. Since the mid-twentieth century, the United States has been militarily involved in the Dominican Republic, Granada, and Haiti, in addition to Panama and Nicaragua. In most instances, communist threat was cited as the compelling reason for the interventions. As the century progressed, the Caribbean grew in strategic importance for the United States, as about half of that country's crude oil and many other goods passed through the basin on their way to U.S. ports. Conversely, as Caribbean nations grew in their political and economic independence, and as they sought to strengthen their participation in a global market, the United States also became more strategically important in their affairs.

Assessment of Baptist development in the Caribbean during the twentieth century is difficult because of the region's wide diversity. The particularities of colonial rule, culture, language, and dates of independence, and the subsequent political, economic, and social developments, have created very complex and contextually specific patterns of growth. Furthermore, interisland connection has tended to follow colonial cultural models, with significant impact on identity development. Political and linguistic traditions also have shaped patterns of identity. Spanish-speaking islands have experienced a double identity – united on the one hand with similar island cultures and on the other hand with Latin America in general. English-, French-, and Dutch-speaking islands have tended to be more insular. In general, the region can be culturally divided into four major categories: Hispanic plus Haiti, the British West Indies, the French Antilles, and the Dutch Antilles. In some countries, following liberation, black populations have dominated and ruled, whereas in others, blacks have been treated as second-class citizens and segregationist practices have prevailed. Thus, a social stratification based on color has developed in many Caribbean societies. Such differences have significantly affected Baptist ministries. One consistent characteristic throughout the region, however, has been the struggle for self-determination.[1] This spirit can be found among Baptists as well. Efforts have been made to introduce greater cooperation among the fragmented Baptist bodies of the region, especially through the work of the Caribbean Baptist Fellowship, organized in 1970.

Jamaican Baptists

In the 1880s, Jamaica gained a small degree of self-government as a British Crown colony. During the following decades, a middle class of low-level public officials emerged, although colonial administrators prevented the local population from advancing to major offices. The economic depression

---

[1] For a careful analysis of Caribbean culture and development, see Gad Heuman, *The Caribbean: Brief Histories* (London: A. Hodder Arnold Publications, 2006).

of the 1930s precipitated the colony's first major social transformations through revolts that helped introduce both organized labor and multiparty systems of government. In 1962, Jamaica gained its independence from Britain but retained status as a member of the Commonwealth of Nations.

In the 1970s, Jamaica pursued socialist political policies along the lines of those in Cuba. Those policies were radically altered during the 1980s by a national agenda that sought to develop closer ties with the United States together with economic privatization. Throughout the century, the Jamaican population remained in flux as citizens joined migrations looking for employment in the banana and sugarcane fields of Central America, Cuba, and the Dominican Republic. Later in the century, the United Kingdom became a major destination for emigrants. Then, after the mid-1960s, the United States became the favored objective, with about twenty thousand Jamaicans immigrating to the United States each year. The major population shifts spawned ministry needs among Jamaican Baptists located both in the islands and in the United States.

Emigration, insufficient leadership, and controversy contributed to a decline in Jamaican Baptist membership during the first half of the twentieth century. After World War II, greater assistance from the Baptist Missionary Society, Canadian Baptists, and Baptists in America helped strengthen the work and turn the tide of losses. Still, emigration has continued to be a challenge. Educational institutions like the United Theological College of the West Indies have helped supply needed leadership, and a circuit system by which churches voluntarily share pastors and cooperate in ministries has helped improve the situation. But in 2007, membership was roughly the same as it had been in 1995, despite a vigorous pace in the number of baptisms.

Jamaican Baptists are divided into at least seven major denominational bodies. Yet a sense of common heritage exists, formed around "the legacy of a new psyche given to freed slaves by the Christian faith, a personhood rooted in equality before God given in Jesus Christ."[2] Persons shaped by that heritage have contributed two prime ministers, two presidents of the Senate, and other leaders to Jamaican government in recent decades. In July 2007, the Jamaican Baptist leader Neville Callam was elected general secretary of the Baptist World Alliance, highlighting the level of achievement this regionally influential Baptist tradition has attained.

---

[2] Horace O. Russell, "Jamaica (1793)," in Albert W. Wardin, ed., *Baptists around the World: A Comprehensive Handbook* (Nashville, TN: Broadman & Holman, 1995), 305.

Bahamian Baptists

At the dawn of the twentieth century, Bahamian society reflected the rigid racial stratification inherited from British colonial practices. This structure was based on assumptions of the superiority of European culture and inferiority of African traditions. Those attitudes not only influenced Bahamian Baptist perceptions of their human and religious identity but also manifested themselves in society through such realities as inequitable distribution of wealth. Even though persons of African heritage constituted the majority of the Bahamian population, they were deemed morally and intellectually inferior. Thus, when the National Baptist Convention, USA (NBC) began work among the black Baptist populations of the Bahamas in 1925, the residual effects of slavery manifested through notions of racial inferiority stood as a major challenge for both Baptist bodies. Throughout the 1930s and 1940s, the NBC gave encouragement to Bahamian Baptists, especially via their ministries of education, literature, and visitation. This support assisted Bahamian Baptists as they matured to the stage of organizing the Bahamas Baptist Missionary and Educational Convention in 1935.

In 1973, the Bahamas gained independence from Britain. Subsequently, the nation underwent significant social and political transitions in which black Bahamians gradually won greater voice in leadership and society. Under the Bahamian colonial traditions, black citizens had suffered discrimination, but throughout the period, they had found strength and hope through Baptist ministries. As a consequence, Baptists today form the largest denominational family in the Bahamas, numbering almost one hundred thousand out of a total population of slightly more than three hundred thousand in 2007. In addition, they have experienced significant advancements in education and in social standing. In 1992, the black Baptist Hubert Ingram was elected prime minister of the Bahamas, serving in that position until 2002. Afterward, he continued to be an important voice in Bahamian politics and was reelected prime minister in 2007. Advancements of this type inspire aspirations for even greater achievement by a communion long denied its voice in the islands' circles of government.

Haitian Baptists

Haiti has suffered significant political upheaval over the course of the twentieth century. From 1915 to 1938, Haiti was occupied by U.S. military forces. The Duvalier family governed as dictators between 1957 and 1986, a period marked by a private army and death squads. In 1990, the former priest Jean-Bertrand Aristide was elected, then deposed by a coup in 1994. With U.S. support, Aristide was returned to power in 1995 and was reelected in 2000. However, in 2004, he was removed from office with international assistance after months of popular opposition. As this history demonstrates, Haiti's culture has been filled with conflict, replete with French and American interventions and with oppression by dictators. Baptist ministry has flourished despite this sociopolitical context of instability and volatility.

The American Baptist Home Mission Society began work in Haiti in 1923, building on foundations laid by earlier Haitian Baptists. At the time, about 1,200 Baptists and eight pastors were scattered throughout the country, with a concentration in the north led by Elie Marc and another in the south led by Nosirel Lhérisson. The society's work was centered in the north around Cap Haitien. In 1947, a seminary was organized at Limbé, followed by the Good Samaritan Hospital at Cap Haitien in 1953, an Eye Center also at Cap Haitien in 1989, and the North Haiti Christian University in 1994. Through these and other institutions, together with about 650 churches, Haitian Baptists have undertaken medical, educational, and evangelistic ministries that have flourished as the century has unfolded. In 2007, Haitian Baptists of all types numbered about 250,000. Haitian Baptists minister in a culture that is divided between old-line Duvalierists and populist supporters who seek reform. The people struggle with economic and social disorder and little hope for a better future, a reality further exacerbated by a devastating earthquake on January 12, 2010 that left 230,000 people dead, 300,000 injured, and more than 1 million homeless. Under those conditions, the masses survive amid unemployment, hunger, and powerlessness. Haitian Baptist churches (with limited external help) heroically sponsor ministries that attempt to alleviate suffering to the degree possible and offer a message of hope to those who find little basis for optimism.

Puerto Rican Baptists

In 1898, Puerto Rico came under the direction of U.S. military forces, resulting in major changes to the island's way of life. Civilian government replaced military rule in 1900, and the island came to be administered via a governor appointed by the president of the United States. The arrangements allowed for open commerce between Puerto Rico and the United States. However, from that point, tensions emerged between those Puerto

Ricans who preferred that the island become a U.S. state and those who wanted national independence. This division continued throughout the century. In 1917, Puerto Rico became a U.S. territory.

The American Baptist Home Mission Society began work on the island in 1898 amid the unfolding conditions. By 1900, American Baptists had appointed five missionaries to Puerto Rico, and they organized their first church at Río Piedras in July 1899. Manuel Lebrón, who had assisted the work from its inception, became Puerto Rican Baptists' first ordained pastor and helped spread Baptist work to neighboring towns. At the same time, Baptist ministries gained acceptance in the south of the island as well. In November 1899, a Baptist church was organized at Ponce and spread Baptist witness to the surrounding region. A theological seminary was organized on the property of the Ponce Baptist Church in 1907, which eventually became part of the interdenominational Evangelical Seminary of Puerto Rico, located at Río Piedras. This school has served as an important institution for leadership training since 1919. In 1902, an association of Baptist churches was organized, which eventually became recognized as one of the affiliated regions of the American Baptist Churches, USA.

Following World War I, the Puerto Rican economy improved dramatically, largely because of sugar exports. This enabled major improvements to the island's infrastructure, development of commerce, and the general standard of living. However, the Great Depression brought an abrupt end to that prosperity, which was further worsened by several devastating hurricanes that added to the suffering of islanders during the ensuing decades. After World War II, the conditions produced by those losses prompted massive migrations to the continental United States. Consequently, Baptist life on the islands has reflected the ups and downs of fluctuating economic conditions and their losses from emigrating members.

In 1948, Puerto Ricans were allowed to vote for their own governor. Under new leadership, programs to encourage industrialization and land reform were inaugurated limiting the control of sugarcane interests. In 1950, Puerto Rico gained the right to draft its own constitution and assumed the status of commonwealth. Although this status was desirable for some citizens, other Puerto Ricans continued to press for independence. Disappointed that nationalist dreams seemed to be losing political ground, uprisings began to occur. In subsequent decades, political differences over the preferred status of Puerto Rico with the United States have continued to animate the nation's political life. Deteriorating economic conditions also have agitated the island's population and have created further division.

After World War II, other Baptist missionary organizations began to work in Puerto Rico, including Southern Baptists and Conservative

Baptists. In 1995, Baptists associated with those varied traditions totaled 128 churches with about twenty-five thousand members. As these cultural developments would suggest, the identity of Baptists in Puerto Rico has been formed around a unique blend of Latin American, Caribbean Island, and U.S. traditions. The affiliation of the Convention of Baptist Churches of Puerto Rico with the American Baptist Churches, USA, together with the Hispanic Caucus, have challenged the Baptists of that communion to expand their perceptions of what it means to be Baptist in a multicultural world.

Cuban Baptists

Cuban history during the twentieth century can be divided into roughly two equal parts – a period of American economic domination and a period of anti-American policies. During the first half of the century, Cuba's political and economic life was dominated by American influence, and Baptists from America were heavily engaged in Cuban ministries during that era. After the Spanish-American War, American Baptists and Southern Baptists agreed to divide the work in Cuba and Puerto Rico. Southern Baptists assumed responsibility for leading Baptist missionary efforts in Cuba's four western provinces and helped to organize the Western Baptist Convention of Cuba in 1905. American Baptists were assigned the eastern half of the island and all of Puerto Rico; they led in organizing the Eastern Baptist Convention the same year. A sizable Haitian population in the region motivated the formation of a Haitian Baptist Convention in 1940 in the province of Camagüey, Cuba. Both American and Southern Baptists invested heavily in educational, publication, and evangelistic ministries. Free Will Baptists and the Baptist Bible Fellowship also launched missionary programs later during the period.

The 1959 Cuban Revolution radically altered the island's status in the West when Fidel Castro's government socialized Cuban institutions, ended American corporate domination, and formed close ties with the Soviet Union. These actions resulted in a break in U.S.-Cuban relations and in a sustained U.S. effort to isolate Castro and encourage anti-Castro forces. At the time of the revolution, most Baptists came from Cuba's working classes. Some supported the government of Fulgencio Batista, and others were active participants in the revolution. Frank País was among the latter. A noted Baptist teacher, País joined the ranks of leaders promoting the revolution, was killed during the conflict, and gained the status of a national hero. After the revolution, some Baptist missionaries and pastors decided to leave Cuba, though others stayed. In 1961,

Baptist schools were nationalized, although churches and seminaries were allowed to remain open. In 1965, forty-eight Baptist leaders were arrested and sentenced to prison. During the late 1970s and 1980s, Castro's policy of internationalism led to Cuban involvement in support of revolutionary movements as far flung as Ethiopia, Algeria, Nicaragua, and Angola.

As a result of Castro's policies, Cuban Baptists were forced to become self-governing. Although Baptist agencies from abroad were allowed to continue support of special ministries, the responsibilities for organization, support, and administration of the work rested in the hands of Cuban Baptists. In 1989, an association of Baptist churches called La Fraternidad de Iglesias Bautistas de Cuba was formed by several churches that had been excluded from the Western Baptist Convention. La Fraternidad differed from the convention churches by its involvement in political concerns, practice of open communion, more open policies related to baptism, and ordination of women as pastors.

Since the end of Soviet assistance in 1991, Cuba has faced serious economic challenges. Internal efforts to bring change to Cuba's government since then have been unsuccessful. Deteriorating conditions have motivated hundreds of Cuban citizens to seek to leave the island, which has resulted in significant Cuban populations in the United States, especially in southern Florida. In the midst of these challenges, however, Baptists in Cuba have experienced significant growth. "Churches are full, attracting many young people as well as some professionals. In some areas attendance has doubled. . . . Local congregations are organizing hundreds of house churches."[3] In most instances, Cuban Baptists are conservative theologically and hold to practices reflective of an earlier time. But as the twenty-first century begins, churches are gradually awakening to a more Cuban way of doing things, including the adoption of Cuban styles of music and a growing interest in engaging contemporary theological concerns. In 2007, Cuban Baptists numbered almost six hundred churches with about forty-seven thousand members.

Other Baptists of the Caribbean

Baptists also exist in lesser numbers in other regions of the Caribbean Islands, especially Antigua, Barbados, Bermuda, Cayman Islands, Dominican Republic, the Leeward Islands, Netherlands Antilles, Trinidad and

---

[3] Ibid., 296.

Tobago, the Turks and Caicos, and the Windward Islands. In 1995, Baptists in those regions totaled about two hundred churches with a membership of around fourteen thousand. The largest of the Baptist communions is found in the Dominican Republic. In general, the Baptists of these islands reflect similar historical patterns and identity issues as those already discussed in relation to other Caribbean islands.

Caribbean Baptist Women

Caribbean cultures long have been characterized by migrations, as shifting economic, political, and environmental conditions have required populations to keep moving to survive. Those realities have made life in the region subject to "permeable boundaries and multiple identities." Consequently, Caribbean cultures are characterized by "continuous redefinition of the self and of one's relationship to society."[4] This underlying reality of life is important for understanding the faith, struggles, ministries, and dreams of Caribbean Baptist women.

Today's Caribbean culture is a complex mixture of Native, African, Asian, and European ethnic populations, bound together in societies that include African oral traditions; the linguistic diversity of English, Spanish, French, and Dutch written and spoken traditions; Creole and numerous other local dialects and customs; and a rich diversity of history that includes colonial domination, popular resistance, and continued struggles to discover a stable place in a changing world economy with limited resources for doing so. As this scenario suggests, Caribbean Baptist women are culturally diverse to a degree that makes more traditional Western categories of public (male) and private (female) interpretations of gender distinction less helpful. However else the histories of Baptist women in the Caribbean might be conceived, they must give serious consideration to the grassroots realities of these women who contribute to their families, churches, communities, and societies in a multitude of ways. Underlying issues demanding consideration relative to these women's identities include such realities as interregional women's employment; the interplay of race and culture in national Baptist life; the impact of colonial political, religious, and cultural traditions; and the roles of Caribbean Baptist women in providing continuity within Baptist communities of faith. Significant scholarly endeavors

---

[4] Consuelo López Springfield, ed., *Daughters of Caliban: Caribbean Women in the Twentieth Century* (Bloomington: Indiana University Press, 1997), xi.

are needed to secure the names, stories, and contributions of those women who have modeled Baptist ministry within this context.

EUROPEAN BAPTISTS' EVOLVING TRADITIONING SOURCES

The twentieth century opened with great promise for European nations, and Baptists shared that optimism. European powers dominated the globe through their colonial empires and reaped the economic benefits of that system. Europeans were preeminent in science, envied for their cultural refinements, and respected for their military might. But the thirty years between 1914 and 1945 would change things dramatically. After World War II, Europe's colonial empires gradually dwindled into oblivion. The continent's collective political power was diminished and its moral influence exhausted. Amid ruined economies, European nations were forced to rebuild their infrastructures, their means of production, their social and cultural life, and their self-confidence. By the end of the century, many European countries had achieved each of those objectives.

The atrocities of those years, however, left lingering scars that were slow to heal, and not the least of these related to deep-seated questions of theology, morality, and human nature. How could masses of people be so easily manipulated into serving the causes of fascism, communism, and exterminations? How could Europe's educated elites be induced to support such objectives? How could the church so easily have become complicit in the ventures? Perhaps these questions were less bothersome to those who won the wars than to those defeated by them, but questions of God's providence and goodness lived on and a multitude of theologians wrestled with those issues.

During the half century after the war until the 1989–91 reforms that ended the Cold War, Europe experienced major transformation. From a divided continent living under the threat of nuclear annihilation, Europe emerged with greater unity than ever before. From decolonization, Europe focused its energies toward economic integration and cooperation, creating new avenues for creativity and production, now more as partners in a globalized world rather than colonial masters. Living and witnessing through those changes brought gains, losses, challenges, and victories to Baptists.

At the dawn of the twenty-first century, European Baptists had significant constituencies in the United Kingdom, Sweden, northern Germany, Hungary, Romania, Moldova, and Ukraine. In contrast, they were notably absent in the traditionally Catholic countries of southern Europe, the

Balkans south of the Danube River, and the Muslim-dominated republics of Central Asia. Early in the twentieth century, Baptists were growing robustly in many areas of Europe, but the thirty years between 1914 and 1945 witnessed a serious shift in that trend. Although Europe's overall population was larger, Baptists ended the century roughly the size they had been shortly after World War I. Baptists in the United Kingdom and northern Europe have experienced persistent decline, with all the frustration and identity issues that accompany such loss. Some gains have occurred among Baptists in central and southern Europe, but southeastern Europe has experienced the most dramatic growth. As the twenty-first century opened, European Baptists were experiencing some of their greatest gains in former Soviet-bloc countries, especially Russia, Ukraine, Moldova, and Romania.

Baptists in the British Isles and Ireland

England entered the twentieth century in a position of strength and prosperity. Two world wars, economic depressions, loss of colonial holdings, and global economic and political shifts caused periods of decline in economic activity, but major adjustments have helped the nation realign itself to new world circumstances. This had renewed Great Britain's prosperity as the twenty-first century began.

Following conflict and war, the Irish Free State was created in 1922, which became a republic in 1949. Six counties in the northeast of the island were separated in 1920 to form Northern Ireland, which remained part of the United Kingdom but was ruled locally as a devolved government. Violence and inability to achieve effective power sharing resulted in periods of direct rule from London in the latter half of the century. Wales and Scotland also remained part of the United Kingdom under devolved governments, although the powers of each government differed somewhat.

During the twentieth century, Ireland continued to experience extensive emigration of its population, even after independence. The 1950s and 1980s were periods of especially high migration, despite government efforts to counter it, which included joining the European Economic Community in 1973. Improvements in Ireland's economy and greater job opportunity since the mid-1990s have enabled many Irish to build prosperous lives at home.

After World War II, the demise of the British Empire terminated the extensive exodus of population from Great Britain to other parts of the world. In contrast, Britain began to attract new ethnic groups from former colonial lands, especially the Caribbean Islands and the Indian subcontinent. Following Soviet perestroika and the lifting of restrictions in former East European countries, significant immigration from that region has occurred as well. In a very general sense, these shifts set the rough parameters for Baptist developments in the British Isles and Ireland during this phase of Baptist life.

The twentieth century was a time of great struggle for British Baptists. At the dawn of the century, Baptists possessed an optimistic spirit and core values that seemed to connect well with aspirations held by the rest of society. At that point, they were growing in respectability and seemed to be on course for a grand future. The vision and aspirations of J. H. Shakespeare reflected this outlook and were embodied in the union's organizational structures. At the end of the century, things looked quite different. British society had changed. The committed churchgoer had "'become, just slightly, an oddity' in a predominantly secular culture."[5] For English Baptists, increasing numbers of new adherents were from Africa, the Caribbean, or the Indian subcontinent. The ordination of women began to change the face of the clergy, and Protestant influences from America were increasingly introduced. Although English Baptists embraced some aspects of American religious influence, they have not bought fully into Americanization and have generally stayed away from the more apocalyptic millennarian theologies that have been attractive to large numbers of Baptists in America. This and related challenges have required English Baptists periodically to rethink what it means to be a Baptist community.

Tragedies of war, imperial reversals, shifts in worldview, and economic changes were among the factors that transformed the religious outlook of many English. Such changes affected all denominational bodies in England, and Baptists were among them. Declining membership motivated Baptist leaders to restructure their organization, deal seriously with questions of theology and patterns of religious practice and belief, and ecumenical cooperation. In 1906, Baptists in England and Wales numbered about 411,000 in 2,811 churches. By 1991, the numbers had declined to 160,000 in 2,121 churches. Although these figures are not absolutely comparable because of certain inconsistencies of reporting, they help quantify the magnitude of the challenge. At some point, such losses easily generate systemic discouragement, which contributes to further decline. To their credit, English Baptist churches and leaders did not give in to what seemed

---

[5] Ian M. Randall, *The English Baptists of the 20th Century* (Didcot, U.K.: Baptist Historical Society, 2005), 523.

a hopeless effort but continued to search for new and creative ways to carry on Baptist witness.

English Baptist struggles to articulate a new vision for what it means to be Baptist in a changed social context has involved four major dimensions, including questions related to ministry, shaping the spirituality of the churches, Baptists' voice in public affairs, and changing configurations of interchurch relationships.[6] In 2002, churches of the British Baptist Union entered into a new form of organizational life intended to "create a stronger sense of both a national and transnational Baptist community."[7] The significant changes inaugurated through this endeavor were possible in part because of new freedom allowed by "an indifference to denominational values." As one observer noted, "Interdenominational co-operation between the like-minded is strengthened and denominational labels become less important. Today, homosexuality is far more likely to divide Protestants from one another than episcopacy or infant baptism."[8] English Baptists search for the means to build stronger relationships in the midst of a postdenominational society in ways that remain appropriately faithful to their Baptist traditions. In addition to the union, other Baptists have diverse interpretations of the Baptist tradition, which they seek to keep alive in varieties of ways as well. Among them are the Strict and Particular Baptists, Gospel Standard Strict Baptists, Grace Baptist Assembly, Reformed Baptists, Seventh Day Baptists, and independent Baptist churches.

Somewhat in contrast to the English situation, Baptists in Ireland experienced slow but steady growth throughout the twentieth century, increasing from 18 churches at the beginning of this period to about 113 churches and almost nine thousand members in 1995. The Baptist Union of Ireland is divided into two associations, the Southern Association for the Republic of Ireland and the Northern Association for Northern Ireland. Now separate, pre-1895 they were part of the Baptist Union of Great Britain and Ireland. However, membership in the associations is very uneven. Ninety-four churches and 8,153 members of the union are located in Northern Ireland. This is indicative of Irish Baptists' greater success among Scotch-Irish populations of the north than among the traditional Catholic culture of the south. Still, by the end of the twentieth century, the few Baptists located in the Irish Republic were integrated politically

---

[6] See ibid., chapter 12, for details in each of these areas of development.   [7] Ibid., 530.
[8] Gerald Bray, "English Protestantism to the Present Day," in *The Blackwell Companion to Protestantism* (Oxford, U.K.: Blackwell, 2007), 106.

and culturally, whereas Baptists in Northern Ireland were challenged by political turmoil between forces that sought to preserve Protestant privilege against a Catholic minority.

Irish Baptists have tended to be more conservative and less inclined toward ecumenical engagement. However, an important component of their identity has revolved around mission involvement. In 1991, about 150 Irish Baptists were serving as missionaries through a variety of missionary organizations. The Irish Baptist Foreign Mission (organized in 1924) supported missionaries in France, Belgium, Peru, and Spain. In addition to many other ministries, Irish Baptists also maintained the Irish Baptist College in Belfast, an institution whose mission is focused on ministerial training.

Churches of the Baptist Union of Scotland (BUS) were influenced in a more conservative direction by the Keswick movement, premillennialism, and holiness doctrine earlier in the twentieth century. This conservatism has been reflected in periodic reactions to modernism and resistance to ecumenical connections. Reaction against growing ecumenical ties led some BUS churches to withdraw and create a network of Reformed Baptist churches. Scottish Baptists have also been plagued by several other divisive controversies, including the charismatic movement, women in ministry, and divorced pastors.

Baptist strength in Scotland has been concentrated along the corridor between Glasgow and Edinburgh. In the twentieth century, they experienced their greatest appeal among working- and middle-class persons. Since midcentury, the fastest-growing congregations have been characterized by an emphasis on preaching, charismatic renewal, informal worship styles, and team ministries.[9] Distinct from the practice of most English Baptist churches, Scottish Baptists required believer's baptism for membership and practiced life appointment for deacons. The union also did not accept women as candidates for ministerial training, although a local church was free to call anyone it wished as pastor. In 2007, the BUS had 176 churches and 13,769 members, which reflected an increase in churches but a decline in membership since 1900. It was typical for Baptist churches in the British Isles to have a significantly greater worship attendance than the number of actual members. Although traditional Baptist identity remained strong, survival rather than denominational distinctiveness increasingly constituted the major issue confronting Scottish Baptists.

---

[9] David W. Bebbington, "Scotland (1750)," in Albert W. Wardin, ed., *Baptists around the World: A Comprehensive Handbook* (Nashville, TN: Broadman & Holman, 1995), 190.

The twentieth century began well for Baptists in Wales. Riding a wave of growth, they entered the century with more than one hundred thousand members, the largest portion located in the south. A widespread revival in 1904–5 brought additional growth. The revival was largely led by laity and often included anticlerical sentiments. However, by 1907, it had vanished with few long-term effects. During the remainder of the century, Welsh Baptists have mostly experienced a slow decline. By 1991, they had diminished to a total of 729 churches and 37,463 members.

As the century drew to a close, Welsh Baptists faced several major hurdles. One was a significant change in the nation's economy and society, which forced migrations and introduced a more secular culture that no longer looked to the church for its center. Second was the continued decline of Welsh Baptist churches to the point that aging members could no longer offer programs capable of reaching new generations. Also, although only about 25 percent of the population still spoke Welsh, about 70 percent of Welsh Baptist churches continued to conduct worship in that language. Those characteristics demonstrated the magnitude of the gap between those churches and their contemporary world, offering bleak prospects for the future vitality of their ministries.

Baptists on the European Continent

Baptists on the European continent have cultural and historic traditions that are distinct from those of the British Isles and Ireland. The degree of diversity requires that those Baptists be divided somewhat into the regions of major cultural influence, although accomplishing this is not an exact science. In a very broad sense, five major cultural regions might be identified. Central and central-eastern Europe were forged culturally by the late medieval Holy Roman Empire, and later, most sections also were further shaped by the Austro-Hungarian Empire and its history. Religiously, this region was formed around Roman Catholic traditions. Northern Europe and the Baltic region were culturally shaped by Nordic traditions, especially those associated with Sweden. Originally Catholic, the area became predominantly Lutheran during the sixteenth century. The region herein designated as Eurasia was culturally related to Russian traditions and history, and religiously centered on Orthodox Christianity. Southeastern Europe, centered in the so-called Balkan countries, was culturally dominated from the late medieval to the modern period by the Ottoman Empire, and it possesses a mixture of Catholic, Orthodox, and Islamic religious traditions. Finally, Southern Europe was culturally shaped by the Latin heritage and religiously rooted in Roman Catholic traditions.

In a very general sense, the following treatment of Baptist developments in Continental Europe during the twentieth century is organized around the foregoing cultural groupings. This organizational model offers clues as to why Baptists have experienced greater success in some regions than in others.

Baptists in Central Europe

At the start of this period, Baptist life in Central Europe was mostly concentrated in Germany and the Netherlands. The more Catholic cultures of Austria, the Czech Republic, Slovakia, and Poland were, and continued to be, resistant to Baptist ministries. World War II devastated Baptist work in those areas. Besides deaths, displacement, and loss of property, a large part of Europe's Baptist population found itself under socialist regimes that often inhibited Baptists' freedom to conduct the ministries with which they were most adept. The result was a postwar world very different from the one that Baptists had known at the beginning of the century. In the western portions of Central Europe, Baptists faced a secular culture strongly influenced by materialistic values. In the eastern portion, they faced a population significantly shaped by the atheistic values derived from decades of communist governments. A reunited Germany now offers Baptists a strategic position of strength from which to extend their ministries throughout Europe, if their message can find the appropriate roots within those cultures.

At the opening of the twentieth century, German Baptists were strongly characterized by the influences of J. G. Oncken and his associates. Their doctrine and practices included a few Lutheran emphases, influences from a Moravian Brethren spirituality, and Pietist elements. Those qualities, together with their unique cultural and political contexts, distinguished them from Anglo Baptists. Among other things, they were less inclined toward political engagement, strongly emphasized a personal piety that placed high value on personal conversion and witness, accentuated the Bible as the source of all belief and practice, and tended to be very provincial in outlook. Many of their distinguishing qualities reflected their minority status and the heavy discrimination they had endured throughout much of the century.

Under the Weimar Republic (1919–33), German Baptists received more favorable treatment than they had under the old German Empire. By 1930, they had gained the same legal status as other religions and were free to practice their faith openly, to evangelize publically, and to participate in public life – although they still suffered popular discrimination. Thus, German Baptists were just beginning to taste the first fruits of acceptance when the Third Reich was inaugurated in 1933. Hoping to conserve the gains they had made, Baptists sought to focus on their evangelistic endeavors and avoid conflict with Nazi authorities. This required compromises, some of which proved to be embarrassing after Germany's defeat in 1945.

In 1934, the Baptist World Alliance met in Berlin to commemorate the one hundredth anniversary of German Baptists' beginning. This was a moment of great achievement for this minority church and an opportunity to display to all Germans the significance of Baptists globally. It was also preempted by Hitler's government as a propaganda opportunity and touted as a demonstration of "the religious toleration of the German nation." World Baptists were divided on the matter. Some concluded that Hitler was not a threat and returned home to speak favorably of the new Germany (at least for a brief period of time). Others, however, felt that German Baptists were ignoring reality and turning a blind eye to burning moral issues in Germany. By 1936, the harsher face of Nazi intentions began to emerge in the form of strongly anti-Christian policies. Yielding to political pressures, in 1938, the Pentecostal Elim Congregations were accepted into the Union of Baptist Congregations (organized in 1849), followed in 1942 by the Plymouth Brethren. The combined churches were called the Union of Evangelical Free Church Congregations, a title German Baptists retained after the war.[10]

The partition of Germany after World War II resulted in a division among German Baptists as well. Very different political and social conditions produced different worldviews, sets of values, and emphases among the divided communions. Although some contact between the two Baptist bodies continued during the period of divided Germany, they grew apart. Between 1969 and 1991, two separate Baptist unions existed for the two Germanys. Since the fall of the Berlin Wall, the separation has been healed. Previously, few of the Baptists from eastern Germany who had moved west had become part of union churches, a further indicator of the differences a generation of culturally and spiritually distinct traditions had produced between the once-united Baptist communions.

---

[10] See Gunter Balders and Richard Pierard, trans., "Germany (1834)," in Wardin, *Baptists around the World*, 200–3.

The decades from 1960 into the twenty-first century have produced a radically different social order in Germany. Secularization, multicultural-ism, religious pluralism and indifference, and shifting values characterize that world. German Baptists have responded in a variety of ways, including focused mission projects, new forms of evangelism, new styles of worship, educational opportunities for church members, and greater engagement in political and social concerns.[11] Charismatic practices influenced the wor-ship styles in some churches. The question of women's roles in pastoral ministry was faced and agreement was reached that it should be a matter for each local church to decide for itself. In 1984, the Union of Evangelical Free Churches in Germany issued a statement confessing its failures during the Nazi regime. We "are humbled by having been subordinated often to the ideological seduction of that time, in not having shown greater courage in acknowledging truth and justice," expressed the heart of German Baptist regrets.[12]

In 2007, the Union of Evangelical Free Churches in Germany and the English-speaking International Baptist Convention had a total of 910 churches and 90,167 members. Special groups of Baptists within the union have been formed to accommodate the particular needs of differing tradi-tions among the body's membership. Of particular importance have been large numbers of German Russians who have immigrated to Germany since the relaxation of border restrictions. As the only recognized Protes-tant body in Kazakhstan and much of Central Asia, persons of German ethnicity who were resettled under Soviet administrations frequently affili-ated with Baptist churches, including many from Mennonite and Lutheran heritages. Those Baptists have distinctive traditions, including nonuse of alcohol and tobacco, separation from worldly activities, simplicity of attire, and particular worship practices unique to their traditions. Such groups have been especially challenged by the materialism and secularism of the society in which they now find themselves. For the most part, they have not joined the existing union but have formed their own unions so that the Baptist movement in Germany is divided into several autonomous bodies. A few Baptist bodies in the United States have exploited some of the young unions as opportunities to gain a foothold in Germany to

---

[11] Erich Geldbach, "The Religious Situation in Germany: Past and Present," *American Baptist Quarterly* 23, no. 3 (September 2004): 238–57.

[12] From a confession of failure by the Evangelical Free Church Congregations in Germany read before the Congress of the European Federation, Hamburg, Germany, 2 August, 1984.

promote their own agendas. German Baptists sponsor work in more than twenty languages in about 150 municipalities, indicative of the magnitude of challenge they face in a globalized culture.

Despite their early-seventeenth-century geographic connections to Baptist beginnings, the Dutch Baptist movement today dates only to the mid-nineteenth century and to the witness of persons associated with Oncken's movement from Germany. Dependent on German, English, American, and Scandinavian Baptist institutions for ministerial training, Dutch Baptists have received influences from many Baptist traditions but are indigenous to Dutch culture. At the beginning of the twentieth century, Baptists of all types in the Netherlands totaled twenty-four churches and about 1,600 members. But throughout the century, Dutch Baptists have experienced steady growth. By 2007, they numbered more than eighty-five churches and 12,000 members.

Like most other West European countries, the Netherlands has experienced serious decline in religious affiliation, with more than half the population describing themselves as not belonging to any church at the end of the century. Dutch Protestant religious institutions have gone through serious upheavals over issues of modernism, theological revision, and social issues, which have produced three broad church groupings – the Dutch Reformed Church, the Kuyperian neo-Calvinists, and Lutherans. The Lutherans formed one organization with the Calvinists in 2004 to form the Protestantse Kerk in Nederland (PKN). Disillusionment among the youths of reorganized Protestantism has been an important source of growth among evangelical churches in recent decades. Programs catering to the spiritual needs of those young people have been an important source of Baptist growth since shortly after World War II.

Baptists in Germany and the Netherlands constitute about 1,000 of Central Europe's approximately 1,200 churches and about 130,000 of its approximately 140,000 members. Besides those two constituencies, the next-largest body of Baptists is found in Poland, where Baptists have experienced a radically changing situation over the course of the twentieth century. After independence in 1918, Poland included two major ethnic Baptist groups – German and Slavic. In 1922, the Union of Slavic Baptists was organized in Poland, which included churches of Polish, Russian, Ukrainian, Belarusian, and Czech ethnicity. By 1939, the Slavic union reported 7,700 members. In 1928, German Baptists had formed a separate Union of the Baptist Churches of the German language, which had thirty-eight churches and about 8,000 members by 1939. After the war,

German migrations and Russian annexation reduced the Baptist communion in Poland to about 1,500 members. They remained a tiny minority in a dominant Catholic culture under Communist control until the 1990s. Persecution, exclusion, and isolation contributed significantly to the formation of Baptists' identity throughout that period. Since 1991, membership in Poland's larger Baptist churches has included professionals, whereas smaller churches mostly appeal to agricultural and unskilled laborers.[13]

In Austria, the Czech Republic, Slovakia, and Switzerland, Baptists continue to constitute a small minority in predominantly Catholic cultures (except for Switzerland, where the few Baptists are located in predominantly Protestant cantons). Of special significance was the relocation of the International Baptist Seminary from Rüschlikon, Switzerland, to Prague in 1993. As a consequence, Prague increasingly has developed into an influential center for Baptist leadership training (especially for Eastern Europe) and will likely benefit Baptist identity development as well as numerical growth in the Czech Republic and beyond.

Baptists in Northern Europe

The dominant and established Lutheran churches of Northern Europe experienced significant change in the twentieth century reflective of the kinds of social, cultural, and religious shifts noted earlier throughout the rest of Western Europe. Among the major challenges confronting these traditional church communions were disestablishment, secularism, orthodox-liberal theological controversies, the role of women in ministry, and religious pluralism. In most Nordic countries, Lutheranism claimed an overwhelming majority of members, but attendance has remained very low. In Norway, for example, as the twenty-first century opened, 88 percent of the population identified as Lutheran, but only 3 percent of the population attended church regularly. In Sweden, the numbers were roughly the same.

Baptists were the earliest of the free churches to appear in Scandinavia but have remained a small minority in these traditionally Lutheran societies. Prior to World War I, they constituted a vital part of the global Baptist movement, especially among the Swedish, Latvians, and Estonians. Since 1927, however, they have experienced persistent decline as a result of

---

[13] Konstanty Wiazowski and Albert W. Wardin Jr., "Poland (1858)," in Wardin, *Baptists around the World*, 207–8.

migrations of populations, communist leaders who were hostile toward religious groups in the Baltic regions, and the same ideological forces that were challenging all Christian groups in the postwar Western world. In 1927, Baptists in the Baltic and Scandinavian countries totaled about 95,000 members. By 1995, that number had declined to about seventy-five thousand. About two-thirds of the Baptists in this entire region are located in Sweden. Although Lutherans constitute the overwhelming majority of the population in Denmark, Baptists are the largest non-Lutheran Protestant group in that country.

Latvian Baptists illustrate the challenges Baptists in the Baltic regions faced over the course of the twentieth century. Before World War I, they numbered ninety churches and about 8,000 members, but the war caused severe disruptions, church closings, and banishment of leadership. Latvia gained its independence in 1918, and Baptists enjoyed full freedom as a consequence. However, emigrations (especially to Brazil) and losses to Pentecostal churches contributed to decline. Controversy over the ministry of William Fetler caused a schism in the Latvian Baptist Union that lasted from 1923 to 1934. But despite the hardships, by 1940, the number of Latvian Baptist churches had grown slightly to 104 with almost 12,000 members.

During World War II, Latvia was first occupied by the Soviet Union, then by German forces, then again by the Soviets. That series of events proved devastating to Baptist work. Their seminary was closed, churches were destroyed, leaders were deposed, and many Baptists fled in desperation. By 1945, membership had declined to 4,500.

With glasnost, Latvian Baptists have experienced renewal. Theological education has been revived, publication work reestablished, and churches reopened. The ministries of Vadim Kovalev are illustrative of this regeneration. From his base as a Baptist pastor in Riga, Kovalev founded the Latvian Christian Mission with the objective of providing food, shelter, and spiritual guidance, especially to Latvians and Russians in Riga, but also to needy persons throughout the former Soviet Union. Addressing those basic needs of Latvia's population at that critical juncture has helped build foundations of trust and familiarity on which future Baptist ministries can be built. In addition, by the end of the century, significant Latvian Baptist communities also existed in Brazil, Canada, and the United States.

Lithuanian Baptists experienced similar struggles under communist rule, but with even more devastating effects. By 1992, they had only 160 members. Having reorganized themselves, the Baptist Union of Lithuania registered 384 members in eight churches in 2007. Although very small, the numbers reflect an amazing will to rebound following a half century of incalculable hardships.

Swedish Baptists illustrate the development and challenges Baptists have faced in Scandinavia during the twentieth century. When World War I began, Swedish Baptists had 635 churches and more than 54,000 members. However, two significant schisms disrupted their work. Around 1913, tensions began to develop in the union over Pentecostal practices that had emerged among some Baptist churches. Lewi Pethrus, pastor of the Filadelfia Baptist Church in Stockholm, was among the first Baptists leaders to embrace the movement, and in 1913, his church was excluded from the union as a result. This church became the center for a developing Pentecostal movement in Scandinavia. In the 1930s, a second division occurred. In the late nineteenth century, John Ongman, pastor of Filadelfia Baptist Church in Örebro, organized the Örebro Mission. This mission developed a program of cross-cultural ministry independent of the union, and after 1913, it inclined toward Pentecostalism. After Ongman's death, leaders of the Örebro faction withdrew from the union and established a separate work, which continues today. A significant focus of Örebro ministry has been foreign mission work, especially in Africa, Asia, and Latin America. In 1991, the Baptist Union, the Free Baptist Union, and the Örebro Mission had a total of 722 churches with about 50,000 members.

In Norway, Baptists began this period mostly as a church of the working classes, but by the end of the century, they had become primarily a church of the middle class. They have focused their resources on educational, missionary, and youth ministries, and they have been active in ecumenical efforts. Two of their leaders, Arnold T. Ohrn and Josef Nordenhaug, have served as secretaries of the Baptist World Alliance. Thus, although they are a small group with only sixty-four churches and about 5,500 members, their global influence has superseded their numerical size.

Baptists in Southeastern Europe

Southeastern Europe is one of the continent's most ethnically diverse areas and Baptists here reflect that reality. At the beginning of the twentieth century, the small and scattered Baptist presence in the region owed its existence mostly to German Baptist witness and Baptist colporteurs employed by the British and Foreign Bible Society. Baptists in the United States and Northern Europe had no serious involvement in the area until after World War II, and in many cases, they had no access until the liberation of the republics from Soviet domination after 1991. During the forty years of regional communist governments, local Baptists had to survive without much outside help. The means they employed for achieving this varied greatly, but in every case, Baptists in those countries had to accommodate to restrictions most other Baptists could hardly comprehend. Some Baptists chose to run the risks of secret religious activities, concluding that any cooperation with communist authorities was unacceptable. However, many other Baptists felt that a degree of cooperation was the only possible route for maintaining a witness. As one Baptist leader stated during those decades, "While we have the freedom to preach the gospel and to make converts and baptize them, we are happy; and we are prepared to accept the restrictions. While the door is open wide enough for us to do this, we will not push it in case it should come back in our faces and what we have should be lost."[14] Many, if not most, Baptists accommodated their beliefs to socialist political systems, with the exception of policies promoting atheism. Most were loyal to their countries even if resentful of their oppressive rulers.

With that domination over, Baptists in southeastern Europe face new challenges. The relationship between the secular state and church remains one of distrust and caution. Also, structures for mature theological education are lacking, although creative approaches are being employed to address this need. More serious are the tensions between some of the dominant religious communities and the Baptist minorities. Such conditions have prompted efforts to establish networks of cooperation that can unite and strengthen those Baptists in their mission.[15]

Of the eleven countries constituting this region, only Hungary and Romania have developed sizable Baptists communities.[16] When the twentieth century opened, Hungarian Baptists were hopelessly divided between Baptists of German heritage organized under Henrich Meyer and Hungarian-Slovak Baptists organized through the ministries of Lajos Balogh and Andreas Udvarnoki. The latter group of churches applied for and received state recognition in 1905, but in so doing, they gained certain disabilities through state interference in church affairs. This placed Meyer's

---

[14] Dean R. Kirkwood, *European Baptists: A Magnificent Minority* (New York: Houghton Mifflin Company, 1972), 142–3.

[15] Parush Parushev and Toivo Pilli, "Protestantism in Eastern Europe to the Present Day," in *The Blackwell Companion to Protestantism*, eds. Alister E. McGrath and Darren C. Marks (Oxford, U.K.: Blackwell, 2007), 160.

[16] This study includes the following countries in the designation Southeastern Europe: Albania, Bosnia, Bulgaria, Croatia, Greece, Hungary, Macedonia, Romania, Slovenia, Serbia, and Montenegro.

group in the vulnerable position of being unrecognized. Efforts to resolve the division continued until 1920, when the two bodies finally united in one union. That same year, a seminary was organized in Budapest. Under the direction of leaders such as Imre Somogyi, Hungarian Baptists had doubled in membership by 1940.

Between 1947 and 1989, Hungarian Baptists chose to pursue a mediating position in relating to communist authorities. To the degree possible, they cooperated with officials, seeking to preserve the maximum degree of liberty for ministry obtainable. At the same time, they refused to become propagandists for the government. In spite of significant hardships imposed by Hungarian communist officials, they managed to preserve a vibrant witness. By 2007, the Baptist Union of Hungary had grown to 365 churches and 11,805 members.

As in Hungary, Baptist ministry in Romania began as a work among German settlers in the late nineteenth century. Ministries to ethnic Romanian populations had their roots in the early twentieth century, with the efforts of Jegalia Adorian. After World War I, Adorian guided Baptists to organize the Baptist Union of Romania. German Baptists in the country already had an association, and in 1920, Baptists of Hungarian heritage in Transylvania and the Russian-Ukrainian Baptists in Bessarabia formed their own unions. Therefore, at that stage, it appeared that Baptist witness would take its shape along ethnic lines. As the century progressed, however, German emigration largely ended that dimension of Baptist life in Romania.

By 1930, Romanian Baptists had grown to 45,000 members. Characterized by strict moral codes, they experienced periodic problems with government leadership, especially during the years of fascist control between 1938 and 1944. During the early years of communist rule, Romanian Baptists enjoyed a period of relative freedom. By the mid-1950s, however, communist authorities had initiated policies intended to limit religion. Baptist suffered harassment, threats, imprisonment, and other discrimination. Yet they managed to thrive. Since the overthrow of the communist regime in 1989, Romanian Baptists have resumed vigorous evangelistic and educational ministries. By 2007, they were the largest of the Baptist communions in southeastern Europe, with about 2,000 churches and more than 110,000 members.

Small but growing Baptist congregations are scattered among the remaining nine countries of southeastern Europe. Totaling 122 churches and 6,358 members in the mid-1990s, most were tiny, isolated, and struggling as insignificant minorities in cultures that were often suspicious of and hostile to their presence. Those conditions have exerted powerful shaping influences on the identity and outlook of Baptists in those regions.

Baptists in Southern Europe

Six countries and the French-speaking areas of Switzerland constitute Southern Europe for the purposes of this study.[17] Essentially every one of the dominant cultures of the region has not been responsive to Baptist work. Despite significant missionary effort, Baptists totaled only about thirty-five thousand adherents by the mid-1990s. Even though the region became more open to the possibility of Baptist witness over the course of the twentieth century, people abandoning their traditional Roman Catholic faith heritage have inclined more toward secularism than toward embracing an alternate form of Christian belief. One major problem for Baptists rests in the fact that no strong indigenous movement comparable to that of Johann Oncken in Germany has ever materialized in Southern Europe. Consequently, Baptists have tended to be viewed as outsiders. Though small, the largest of the Baptist communions to survive in the region have emerged in Spain, France, Italy, and Portugal.

The early foundations for Baptist work in Spain, laid by the American Baptist William Knapp and the Swedish Baptist Eric Lund, were largely exhausted by 1900. Emigration and persecution left Baptists with only ten churches and 115 members in 1896. Southern Baptist Convention (SBC) mission efforts in the 1920s helped revive the work, and by 1930, Spain had about 1,000 Baptists in twenty-one churches. But the Great Depression caused SBC Baptists to reduce support at a critical stage in development, before the work was self-sustaining. Consequently, Baptists were in a weakened state when the dictator Francisco Franco came to power. By 1939, only one Baptist church functioned with normalcy. Discrimination and persecution led Spanish Baptists to seek greater freedom under the leadership of José Cardona. A division occurred among Baptists in 1949 over issues related to funding and resulted in the formation of a second Baptist union in 1957. By 1958, Baptists had grown to 2,200 members and forty-two churches, despite the persecution they endured.

Baptists secured additional freedoms during the 1960s, and after 1980, they enjoyed full rights with other religious organizations. Although this relieved some of the stresses experienced by Spanish Baptists and served

[17] These countries include Belgium, France, Italy, Malta, Portugal, Spain, and French-speaking Switzerland.

to improve the Baptist image in Spanish society, it has not ushered in significant growth. Baptist ministries in Spain were fully in the hands of Spanish leaders by the end of the twentieth century, and in 1995, Baptists totaled about 14,000 members in 169 churches.

Baptist witness in France began as an indigenous movement in 1820, when a small Bible-study group in the northern village of Nomain embraced Baptist beliefs. The Baptist General Convention in the United States sent missionaries in the 1830s with the intention of strengthening and extending the work. A small church was organized in Paris and a theological school established near Nomain. The intent was for the school to provide trained leaders who might expand the work. By 1838, French Baptists had seven churches and about 150 members. Initially, Baptists suffered discrimination, but during the 1880s and 1890s, they were granted freedom and experienced significant growth as a result. Noted leaders included Philemon Vincent, Ruben Saillens, Paul Besson, and Charles Ramseyer. By 1900, they numbered thirty churches and more than two thousand members that were scattered throughout the north and in Paris, Lyons, Marseille, and Nice. Much of the work was located in rural areas, and French Baptists at the time reflected a more agrarian identity as a result.[18]

In the 1890s, tensions developed between Saillens and Vincent that caused a division among French Baptists and cost them precious momentum. Despite the setback, the French Baptist Union was formed by the Saillens faction in 1907. In 1911, the Vincents organized a competing union – the Baptist Evangelical Mission of Paris. Churches of that union suffered devastation during World War I. Following the war, divisions continued to fragment French Baptist work. Tabernacle Baptist Church in Paris withdrew and became independent in 1921. That same year the Association Evangélique des Églises Baptistes de Langue Française formed a separate union along fundamentalist theological lines. Since World War II, other Baptist denominations have organized additional independent work, producing nine separate Baptist bodies with a total of nine thousand members and 172 churches.[19] During the last decades of the twentieth century, Baptists in France focused greater attention on urban work. The work has found greatest acceptance among settlers from former French colonies

---

[18] Michel Thobois and Albert W. Wardin Jr., "France (1820)," in Wardin, *Baptists around the World*, 274–5.

[19] Sébastien Fath, *Une autre manière d'être chrétien en France: Socio-histoire de l'implantation Baptists (1810–1950)* (Geneva: Éditions Labor et Fides, 2001).

in Southeast Asia and Africa, thereby shaping French Baptist identity in unique ways, including significant ethnic diversity.

Baptists' first church in Italy was organized at La Spezia in 1867 through the efforts of an English Baptist named Edward Clarke. Giovanbattista Dassio became Italian Baptists' first native pastor, serving the La Spezia church. After Italian assumption of control over the Papal States in 1870, British Baptists established a church in Rome. Later, Oswald Papengouth of Russia planted another Baptist center in Naples. In 1922, Southern Baptists launched a mission program to enlarge, strengthen, and support the Baptist work in Italy. By 1939, Italian Baptist leaders had assumed responsibility for most of those ministries. In 1956, the Christian Evangelical Baptist Union of Italy was formed as an autonomous Italian Baptist cooperative.

During the twentieth century, Italian Baptist work was hampered by the frequent emigration of its members. But, as had been the case in many other areas of Southern Europe, after World War II, Italian Baptists discovered receptive populations among ethnic groups residing in the country, including Americans, Germans, Chinese, and Spanish. In addition, they have been open to ecumenical experiments, especially with the Waldensian-Methodists. By the mid-1990s, Italian Baptists numbered more than five thousand members in 102 churches.[20]

Baptist work in Portugal has been closely connected to Baptists in Brazil from its inception early in the twentieth century. João de Oliveira, a native of Portugal, became Brazilian Baptists' first foreign missionary in 1911 and began serving in Portugal the same year. He organized numerous churches, engaged in publication ministries, and was persistent in service despite monumental challenges. Amid hardships, successes, and disappointments, Brazilian Baptists persisted in their support. Beginning in the 1960s, Southern Baptists also assisted the effort through communications, publication, educational, music, and evangelistic ministry support. By the mid-1990s, Portuguese Baptists collectively had 5,500 members in almost a hundred churches.

European Baptist Women

World War I took most Europeans by surprise. It also thrust European cultures into processes of change, the results of which few could have imagined, and set in motion reforms that continued throughout the century

---

[20] Franco Scaramuccia and Albert W. Wardin Jr., "Italy (1863)," in Wardin, *Baptists around the World*, 277.

and beyond. Among the most enduring shifts were those that occurred in the social roles, status, and identity of women. Feminine identity transformation was a major element of the cultural context forming European Baptist women's identity during the period. Furthermore, Baptists' ability to adequately advance the theological underpinnings that could aid their members in negotiating those changes was one indicator of whether new generations of Europeans would find Baptist beliefs relevant for their future.

World War I required both women and men to make adjustments and sacrifices on a scale few had experienced before as a society. Among other things, women took up the positions absent males had left to advance the war effort. Many did so anticipating that proving their abilities would be rewarded with the full rights of citizenship when the war was over. In that hope, most were disappointed. A prevailing attitude among men was that the vote should be given only to those who paid for it with the "tax" of blood. Many women felt that they should have a voice in governments that affected their lives profoundly during both war and peace. Fearing that gender distinctions were being challenged, many policy makers promoted marriage as "a means of re-domesticating the female war worker, of re-socializing the traumatized veteran, and of replacing lost population."[21] Marriage and family as the foundation of society became themes of many postwar institutions, including most Baptist churches. Although creating a happy marriage and raising well-adjusted children was held up as the ideal for women, most married women's actual experiences were far from the model held up to them. Hard work, exhaustion, and lack of resources left them with little time to accomplish the ideals that the new science of psychology held before them as their duty. However, the pressure to return to motherhood and domesticity and to give up the demand for more just social structures that would allow the actualization of human potential for women could not turn back the clock. Most European Baptists took conservative positions toward the new roles of women in society, usually doing so in the belief that they were preserving biblical teachings about gender roles. However, social forces were at work that spoke to inner longings of Baptist women and to those of the wider society. Transformations were taking place, sometimes imperceptibly, sometimes with great leaps, but efforts to preserve a status quo that maintained male supremacy could not forever resist the pent-up demands for liberation.

---

[21] Ann Taylor Allen, *Women in Twentieth-Century Europe* (New York: Palgrave Macmillan, 2008), 22–3.

World War II came too close on the heels of the first war for purveyors of nineteenth-century views of womanhood to reestablish their ideological hold on society. Wartime emergency demanded women's return to the workforce, which marked a fundamental change in the status of women that would continue to unfold throughout the remainder of the twentieth century. Women's full-time employment, gradual movement into traditionally male jobs, and concomitant changes in family life became permanent trends after the war. Immediately following the devastations, the need for stability and nostalgia for better times fostered a period of more conservative social values. But European women felt they were receiving contradictory messages about themselves. At the same time they were being forced out of their wartime jobs and being expected to return to domestic "bliss," postwar culture promoted individualism, personal ambition, and progress. Baptists often continued to hold up more traditional ideals as models for women and families, but economic and social realities pressed members to live out their lives in ways that differed from the familiar traditions of old. The nineteenth-century mission societies women had organized and promoted earlier lost their appeal and gradually declined in membership. Many Baptist women's organizations found it necessary to shift their focus to meet the needs of a new breed of Baptist woman. New stresses, uncertainties, and ambivalences demanded new approaches and new answers.

As the twenty-first century dawned, many women still aspired to "'emancipation' from the condition of femininity," whereas "few men assumed that masculinity was a condition from which anyone needed to be emancipated."[22] Such social dissonance has motivated forces that continue efforts to redefine the prevailing assumptions about human identity, purpose, and fulfillment. As those forces press toward a more equitable social organization that allows greater personal fulfillment for all persons, Baptists will continue to face challenges that require the development of biblical theologies and practices that are adequate to support the God-given drive of each person to become all that God intends her or him to be. Among European Baptist women, leaders are emerging whose voices will help point the way for Baptists into that new day.[23]

EURASIAN BAPTISTS' EVOLVING TRADITIONING SOURCES

The geographical territories that today constitute the Commonwealth of Independent States (CIS) began this period in Baptist history struggling

---

[22] Ibid., 150–1.   [23] This is an area of much needed research in Baptist studies.

with a host of questions concerning the relationship between Orthodoxy and Russianness. They ended the period wrestling with the same issues once again but in a new political context. Between them stood seventy years of communist rule that significantly shaped the identity and practice of the more than three hundred thousand Baptists living in the region.

The emancipation of Russia's serfs in 1861 initiated social, political, and intellectual transformations that also carried important consequences for religious life as well. Moreover, the late nineteenth and early twentieth centuries constituted a time of industrialization, with accompanying economic and occupational changes. At the same time, the Bible became widely available in Russian for the first time. In the wake of those shifts, public debates surfaced that tended to support one of two positions: the belief either that spiritual revolution was necessary as the way to deal with the political and cultural crises of the time or that a return to the Russian Orthodox Church was the only way to restore the nation's traditional moral and political ideals. In 1905, Tsar Nicholas II approved an edict that allowed adherents of Orthodoxy to convert to other religious bodies if they so chose. From then until the Soviet-imposed restrictions of 1929, dissenting groups like Baptists became highly visible on the nation's cultural and political scene.

In that context, Baptist convictions began to spread in varieties of ways, including through migrant workers, itinerant preachers, and by word of mouth. Most Baptist converts were peasants who gathered in local homes for worship and Bible study. Church buildings did not replace homes as places of worship for some time after 1905, but from that point, Baptists did begin organizing their work. In that context, Baptists were "at once insiders and outsiders in Russian society, for they were Russians who had chosen what was perceived as a non-Russian path."[24] In that world of change, they offered what they believed were the best answers to modern challenges. Their choices put them "on the front line of experimentation with the possibility for cultural and political pluralism in Russia."[25] Despite both imperial and Soviet efforts to limit their activities, Russian Baptists considered witness and worship basic human rights. Their actions based on that belief produced at least three significant results: they expanded the boundaries of public life, promoted the possibility that a person could be both Russian and non-Orthodox, and opened the potential for being at once Baptist and socialist.

[24] Heather J. Coleman, *Russian Baptists and Spiritual Revolution, 1905–1929* (Bloomington: Indiana University Press, 2005), 3.
[25] Ibid., 4.

Russian Baptists

When the Bolsheviks came to power in Russia in 1917, Baptists were among those who believed a better day had arrived. Existing in two major groups, by 1928, Baptists had grown to about two hundred thousand members, five thousand congregations, and about 1,200 churches. The Baptist World Alliance had great hopes for Russia, looking forward to the day when it would become "the most Baptist country in the world, outside America" and "mark a turning point in the history of Europe."[26] Unsuccessful efforts were made by the alliance to effect a union between the Russian Baptist Union and the All Russian Union of Evangelical Christians (also known as Pashkovites). Then, in 1928, Joseph Stalin introduced a five-year plan intended to fully implement communist goals such as industrialization, collective farms, and state control of the means of production. Baptists' optimism soon met a new and harsh reality when the Soviet government terminated freedom of preaching and of religious association. In the 1930s, churches were closed, the Russian Union was dismantled, and pastors were sent into exile. The All Russian Union of Evangelical Christians managed to survive but lost all of its buildings. During World War II, the German Baptists were relocated to eastern republics, and many others fled to the West at the end of the war. By 1945, Russian Baptists were in a dismal state.

In 1944, Baptists and Evangelical Christians were allowed to form the All-Union Council of Evangelical Christian-Baptists. The organization was intended to bring all churches that practiced believer's baptism into one body. No Evangelical church could register with the government unless it was part of this group, and even then registration was limited. In 1945, Pentecostals joined the council, followed by Oneness Pentecostals in 1947 and Mennonite Brethren in 1963. Jakov Zhidkov was president of the council until his death in 1966, and Aleksandr Karev was general secretary until his death in 1971. Efforts were made to offer some theological training to leaders through correspondence courses and to administer Baptist work through the eleven senior presbyters of the republics, as well as through the numerous deputy and regional presbyters in the various districts of each republic.

In the early 1960s, a schism developed among Baptists between those who supported the work of the All-Union Council of Evangelical Christian-Baptists and Reformed Baptists (*Initsiativniki*), who felt the council

---

[26] J. H. Shakespeare, *Baptist World Alliance, Second Congress* (Philadelphia: Harper and Brother Company, 1911), 235.

was collaborating too closely with government authorities. Gennadii Kryuchkov became president of the new Baptist union, and Georgi Vins became its secretary. Both spent time in prison for their actions. In 1979, Vins was released from prison through the intervention of U.S. President Jimmy Carter (a Baptist) and deported to the United States. Government oppression produced a theology of suffering among the Reformed Baptists that strongly equated travail with the witness of a true Christian. The divisions between the two Baptist bodies did not end with Mikhail Gorbachev's reforms and continue today. The Union of Evangelical Christians-Baptists of Russia was established for the Republic of Russia in 1979.

In the year 1988, new freedoms were given to Baptists in Russia. Since then, they have been allowed to evangelize openly, organize new congregations, construct buildings, and educate leaders. In 1989, Pentecostals withdrew from the All-Union Council, leaving its total membership at about 204,000 members in 2,260 churches. In 2007, the Union of Christians-Baptists of the Russian Federation numbered 80,000 members in 1,309 churches.

Ukrainian Baptists

Following the Bolshevik Revolution, Baptists in Ukraine formed the All-Ukrainian Union. From 1918 until 1928, they experienced freedom to carry out their ministries and witness unhindered. But, as had happened in the Republic of Russia, they suffered persecution and severe restriction during the 1930s, before gaining some relief in the 1940s. Being part of the All-Union Council, they had their own senior presbyter, deputy presbyters, and regional presbyters. In 1992, they formed the independent Union of Evangelical Christians-Baptists. Since glasnost, the Ukrainian Union has experienced explosive growth. In 1993, the unions had 1,301 churches with 106,581 members. In 2007, that number had grown to 2,863 churches with 151,030 members. When all Baptist traditions are included, the numbers are further augmented, making Baptists collectively the largest Protestant body in Ukraine today.

Other Eurasian Baptists

Baptists form significant communities in several other CIS republics. In the mid-1990s, the largest of these communions included Moldova, with 17,800 members in 225 churches; Kazakhstan, with 14,545 members in 203 churches; Belarus, with almost 10,000 members in 135 churches; and the

Republic of Georgia, with 9,000 members in thirty-four churches. Because of their unique contexts while under communist rule, Baptists in the CIS reflect the standards of Baptist life that were common to the nineteenth century. Candidates are seldom accepted for baptism earlier than their teen years; discipline is rigorously exercised; and alcoholic beverages and tobacco are strictly prohibited, as are dancing, movies, and cosmetics. These have become distinguishing characteristics for most Baptists in this region of the world. However, as the social, economic, cultural, and intellectual life of the republics continues to change, questions surface concerning how CIS Baptists will adapt to the inevitable pressures such changes bring to the lives of their members and to the communities in which they minister.

Eurasian Baptist Women

Following the Bolshevik Revolution, Russia's communist government mandated that gender equality be practiced in politics, education, employment, and family life. After 1945, those policies were extended to Eastern European satellite states as well. But what Soviet governments actually achieved was the integration of women into the world of men, not true emancipation. Women were thrust into the challenges of combining family responsibilities and paid work that resulted in overwork, coercion, and oppression.[27] In the world of politics, women gained the rights to vote and hold office, and women's faces did begin to appear in greater numbers in local politics, but at the level of the powerful politburo, almost no women could be found. Women who gained elected positions in government discovered that those representatives "met chiefly to approve decisions that had already been made by the party leadership."[28] Although a few individual women managed to gain prominence in political circles, the advancement of women as a group did not occur. Women did play important roles in protest movements, especially in Eastern European states, but their contributions often were relegated to the quiet courage of the lesser-known people.

In family life, women's rates of literacy and educational attainment improved dramatically, but for most, the dream of gender equality was never attained. Women assumed a majority of the household duties along with the additional demands of employment outside the home, and they did so with fewer conveniences than women in Western societies. Household appliances and convenience foods were lacking, which made shopping,

---

[27] Allen, *Women in Twentieth-Century Europe*, 97.   [28] Ibid., 98.

cooking, cleaning, and child rearing even more time consuming. The lack of adequate housing for young couples, low-paying jobs, unsupportive husbands, and lack of child care, together with domestic expectations, contributed to dramatic rises in divorce and rates of abortion.

Although not often addressed in Baptist literature, such problems haunted Baptist women as well as other women in Eurasian society during the twentieth century. In addition, Baptists in the region tended to hold a very conservative social ethic that made extra demands of women. The expectations that women would not value fashion, jewelry, cosmetics, or things of the world were often the least of the women's problems. Domestic expectations, the penalties of their religious convictions on educational and employment opportunities, and lack of voice in so many of the decisions about how their lives would be shaped were of much greater impact. Many older women conformed to expectations in part because they had little choice. Newer generations of Eurasian Baptist women face a different world and changing possibilities that will demand alternate and more insightful responses on the part of Baptist leadership.

ONE COMMUNION, DIFFERENT WORLDS

This chapter has explored the Baptist movement as it evolved within four distinct settings over the course of the twentieth century – Western Europe, the Caribbean Islands, Latin America, and countries of the former Soviet Union. At the beginning of the period, Western Europe was the center of the world's dominating colonial powers. Confident of their achievements and mission, the nations of Europe tended to view their own cultures as superior to and beneficial for the inferior civilizations that were under their control. The nature of the relationships with their colonies was basically economic and extractive. They were sources of the raw materials needed to keep the wheels of industry turning and furnished ready markets for the manufactured products European factories produced. The greatest financial benefactors from this arrangement were Western European societies. As an empowered society sure of the rightness of its cause, the intellectual forces of modernist philosophies had the impact of offering the mental framework needed to grasp that world. Increasingly, the natural world became the focus of research, because comprehending that world was considered the key to managing and improving the human situation. Notions of the divine slowly came to be viewed as a product of human thought manipulated by religious institutions to control persons for their own ends. Attitudinally, this fueled secularist and skeptical convictions. In that world, Baptists seldom ranked among the power holders or decision makers. More often, their adherents came from the ranks of the working classes – the workforce needed to keep the industrial economy running. Although perhaps dreaming of a better world for themselves, they also had a vested interest in keeping the system going, because it was the source of their livelihoods.

As the century progressed, wars, economic shifts, and loss of colonial holdings greatly diminished the confidence and control of European nations. Yet commitment remained strong to the belief that intelligent insight into the natural world offered the best hope for managing and improving humanity's condition. For European Baptists, this meant living and seeking to witness in a world where the supernatural seemed out of place and intellectually lacking, especially among the dominant cultures. In most contexts, Baptists had the benefit neither of acceptance as an institution of the dominant culture's historic traditions nor of having a large following that commanded impressive resources. This chapter has shown that, in most Western European contexts, Baptists experienced their greatest acceptance among marginalized groups who did not share fully in the dominant cultures and therefore were disposed to seek empowerment from a different source. In those settings, Baptists experienced very slow and difficult growth under conditions that supported development of a strong countercultural identity – the voices of an alternate worldview often at odds with the interests and concerns of dominant cultures. Where they did exist as part of a dominant culture, finding inroads for their message in those contexts became increasingly difficult over time.

In the Caribbean Island cultures, empowerment has not been part of the majority population's experience. Their histories on the whole have been chapters in the stories of colonial domination – pawns of the policies of outside cultures that have held power over them. Unable to survive in isolation and needing protection from more powerful nations, Caribbean peoples have found it necessary to survive on the margins. Baptists have experienced their greatest acceptance in this context, where few presume to be in control of their world and where modernist philosophies have made little impact on the thinking of the masses. In these settings, ample room has existed for the divine, especially when purveyors of the message have been relevant to local cultures. Caribbean Baptists' long history of effective indigenous witness has resulted in several of those island nations becoming hosts to the densest Baptists-per-capita ratios of any region of the world. In some contexts, Baptists constitute one-third to one-half of the total population. As a consequence, Baptist identity in Caribbean cultures has tended to be that of a struggling second-class group. Although forced to

Figure 14. William L. Judd and the Haitian Baptist leader Lucius Hipolite in 1847, a work sponsored by the Baptist Free Mission Society (courtesy of American Baptist Historical Society, Valley Forge, Pennsylvania).

Figure 15. Cuban Baptist Pastors during a Baptist convention held in Baracoa, Cuba (date uncertain) (courtesy of American Baptist Historical Society, Valley Forge, Pennsylvania).

deal with issues of inferiority and marginalization, the experience has had a different effect than the ones that characterize small Baptist communities isolated in a much larger dominant population. One of the strengths of being an unempowered majority is the self-confidence afforded individuals within a larger social context. Often such conditions produce a will to change society along with the force of numbers to compel reform over time. In notable instances, Caribbean Baptists are doing just that, and they are gaining recognition of their right to participate as equal partners within the global Baptist family.

As with Western Europe, Baptists in Latin America have generally possessed a minority identity, but not within a secular culture. Because Christian beliefs still carry great value for most of Latin America's population, Baptist identity has focused on convictions that their views on the Bible and their church practices are the right ones. Consequently, Latin American Baptists have tended to reject ecumenism and to distrust non-Baptist influences. Catholic and Pentecostal practices frequently have been sources of controversy and generally avoided by Baptists. For instance, displaying a cross in the church can be interpreted as a Catholic custom and be

Figure 16. Worship at the Central Baptist Church, Moscow, 1989 (courtesy WCC/Peter Williams).

Figure 17. Baptist Church of Bucha, near Kiev, Ukraine (author's photo).

perceived as a threat to Baptist identity. Too much of certain types of emotional expression in worship might be viewed as Pentecostal and therefore not Baptist.

Modernist philosophies had an impact in Latin America, but one that differed significantly from that experienced by Western European cultures. As former colonies with mostly nonindustrial economies at the dawn of the twentieth century, Latin American societies characteristically generated two opposing political tendencies – a political liberalism that supported personal freedoms and economic innovation and a political conservatism that sought to maintain an economic status quo beneficial to the wealthy and to privilege the Catholic Church. In that context, modernism tended to take not a secularist turn (at least not for the masses) but one that supported liberal social and economic agendas. Because Baptists often were in agreement with those objectives, they more readily found adherents. However, the fact that Baptists tended to be purveyors of particular theological beliefs and church practices and not social reformers meant they could find a place among those seeking liberal (later called democratic) reforms, even though they seldom entered the ranks of political leadership. This was especially true of Baptists in Brazil, which became one of the major centers of global Baptist life.

In the countries of the former Soviet Union, Baptists faced yet another kind of cultural context that forged a somewhat different identity. Large portions of those territories had been shaped culturally by Slavic customs, Orthodox Christianity, and tsarist policies. The cultures that developed under the Soviet Union's domination mediated modernist philosophical assumptions through authoritarian regimes that promoted an atheistic materialist worldview. In that setting, Baptists initially hoped for a recognized place of acceptance within the new society. When that proved impossible, they developed a survivalist identity that had overtones of a persecuted remnant. Many Soviet Union Baptists continued to nurture hope of finding toleration within the Soviet system by cooperating with authorities to the extent possible. Others despaired of any such hope and attempted to go underground. Although the path to acceptance was a hard one, the common experience of suffering earned Baptists at least some sense of belonging within those societies. Reaching back to old traditions, Orthodox Churches in many former Soviet republics have attempted to reunite church and government in ways that would deprive non-Orthodox churches of their full place in the newly emerging nations. True to their tradition, Baptists have fought for full religious freedom and separation of church and government. From a faithful remnant, a new Baptist identity is emerging as builders of a new society characterized by religious liberty. In that new identity, however, the truly redeemed will live distinctive lives (as defined by local Baptist moral codes) that set them apart from the society at large.

As these societies continue to move beyond modernism into whatever an emerging postmodern era might become, their cultural contexts will reflect that reality somewhat differently. Postcolonial reinterpretations will demand different responses from those who ruled and those who were ruled. Postcommunist societies will require different types of responses from those cultures that were bound by the system and those that never experienced communist rule. Baptist identities that have been shaped by different twentieth-century contexts must enter a postmodern world, which will require important reconsiderations of what it means to be Baptist. Can interpretations of Baptist identity that were largely forged by premodern Anglo Baptist experiences prove adequate for the wide variety of Baptist contexts that have emerged? Baptists' traditioning sources have significantly expanded over the past century. Those sources will necessarily demand authentic expression if Baptist witness is to remain relevant in its many contexts. Is the course of interpretive intentionality in which the few attempt to define Baptist identity for the many a productive one, or is a new approach needed? Developing global Baptist experiences suggest that something more complex, diverse, and multicultural is required if the name *Baptist* is to have continued meaning or appeal. To achieve this, new forums for wider Baptist interaction, together with education toward greater appreciation of difference, will likely be necessary.

CHAPTER 8

Baptists' Evolving Traditioning Sources in North America

Religious life in North America was shaped principally by five major factors during the age of proliferating traditioning sources: immigration, war, economics, inventions, and social changes. Each of these elements brought important innovations to Baptist constituencies, worldviews, and ways of life – both benefiting and challenging their development and creating new traditioning sources that contributed to reformulations of Baptists' identity.

Both the United States and Canada experienced massive immigration in the last decades of the nineteenth century, which continued in a more controlled fashion throughout the twentieth century. Until World War I, many of those immigrants settled on the rapidly developing western frontiers, triggering conflicts with Native populations. The magnitude and ethnic diversity of immigration challenged Baptist resources. Greatest attention was given to ministry among persons of European heritage, although some Baptists invested sporadically in work among Native populations as well.

Canada was brought into World War I in 1914 by virtue of being part of the British Empire. The magnitude of losses forced the government to legislate military conscription, an act that generated major reactions among French Canadians. The United States entered the war in 1917 as part of a moral crusade to end the evils of war. For both the United States and Canada, World War I unleashed social and political forces that continued to transform those nations long after the hostilities ceased. The postwar years brought a spurt of prosperity to the U.S. economy and, to a lesser extent, to Canada as well. Baptists, among other denominations, began to dream of expanding their work and launched major development campaigns to finance the efforts. The stock market crash of 1929, combined with the Dust Bowl in the U.S. Midwest, ended the Roaring Twenties and introduced a decade-long economic slump that affected both countries. Baptist organizations, some of which had overextended themselves during the decade of prosperity, suffered great hardship. Mission programs were reduced or curtailed. Members migrated to other regions of the country seeking employment. And some Baptist individuals became bitter and disillusioned by the seemingly unending hardships, losses, and unanswered prayers.

Canada's connections to Britain once again brought the country into the conflicts of World War II ahead of the United States. The demands of war gave women a new role in the workforce that proved to be permanent launching social transformations that would continue throughout the remainder of the century. The magnitude of destruction experienced by European nations catapulted both North American countries into positions of greater influence in world affairs, especially the United States, which emerged as one of two world superpowers. At home, the United States experienced major social change as a result of the civil rights movement, the 1960s sexual revolution, and the social upheavals related to the Vietnam War. Canada underwent similar transitions with the Quiet Revolution and the emergence of Quebec's nationalism.

Perestroika introduced a period of economic expansion and optimism that helped win acceptance of the North American Free Trade Agreement among Canada, Mexico, and the United States. September 11, 2001, shattered that optimism when the United States suffered terrorist attacks, leading to military involvement in Afghanistan and Iraq.

As the twenty-first century dawned, the ethnic and religious diversity of both the United States and Canada continued to increase. Hispanics constituted nearly half of U.S. population growth in 2004–5, and the Asian American population increased by 421,000 (3 percent) during that period. African American, Amerindian, Alaska Native, Native Hawaiian, and Pacific Islander populations also increased significantly. As of 2005, Hispanics constituted 15 percent of the total U.S. population, blacks (including African Americans, African immigrants, and blacks of Caribbean origin) totaled 14 percent; Asian Americans, 5 percent; American Indians and Alaska Natives, 2 percent; and Native Hawaiians and Pacific Islanders, less than 1 percent. Collectively, these ethnic groups totaled almost 35 percent of the U.S. population. Canada also experienced major increases in minority populations. Between 1996 and 2001, discernible minorities grew by 24.6 percent in contrast to a 1.3 percent increase for other parts of the population. In 2005, minorities constituted about 14 percent of Canada's total population. The three largest ethnicities were Chinese, South Asian, and blacks.

These political, economic, and demographic shifts have challenged North American Baptists with changes of titanic proportions. From their significantly rural ministry settings at the beginning of the twentieth century, Baptists in the United States and Canada found themselves in countries that were mostly urban and industrial by the twenty-first century. However, the majority of their churches were still located in rural and small-town contexts. Population shifts after World War II increased the number of churches in the urban and suburban locations, but cultural shifts since have greatly challenged traditional Baptist identity. Religious pluralism, new theologies, ecumenism, secularism, gender equality, sexuality, diversity issues, medical advances, communications, and human need have been among the issues forcing change on Baptists.

Canadian Baptists

By the early twentieth century, Canada had completed its federation and taken steps to ensure its authority over the western territories. At this point, Canadian identity adhered to the tradition of a self-governing colony of the British Empire. However, participation in World War I fostered a greater sense of autonomous identity. The Great Depression, which persisted for more than a decade, took center stage during the 1930s and influenced political and social developments, with a profound impact on religious life as well. Among the major developments created by the economic crisis was Newfoundland's decision in 1934 to relinquish responsible government and become a Crown colony. A U.S. military presence in Newfoundland during the war led to developments that many Canadians feared might result in the colony choosing to become part of the United States. This possibility was terminated in 1949, when after much debate, Newfoundlanders voted to become a province of Canada.

Canada played a significant role in World War II. Legislation generated by war needs, especially conscription, added to tensions between French and English Canadians that persisted long after the war had concluded. In the 1960s, Quebec took steps to modernize its economy and moved away from the old order in which the Catholic Church had a central role. At the same time, nationalists pressed for Quebec's independence. The status of Quebecois continued to simmer through several governments until 2006, when it was recognized as a "nation" within Canada, defined as a cultural recognition that did not imply sovereignty or legal change of status within the federation.

Over the century, relations between Canada and the United States became strained at times and more cordial at others. The North American Free Trade Agreement was adopted in 1989 amid the concerns of both the Canadian and the U.S. public. As in many other Western governments, economic turmoil led Canada to take steps that affected social welfare programs but improved the government's financial situation. Other challenges have included demands for self-government by several Native peoples; the security of the U.S.- Canadian border after the September 11, 2001, terrorist attacks in New York; and environmental issues. As Canada seeks to clarify its identity and as various ethnic groups seek to define themselves in relation to the federation, Baptists in Canada find themselves challenged in new ways as well.

Early in the twentieth century, Canadian Baptists confronted immigration patterns that threatened political traditions associated with a Christian Protestant society and modernism. In those struggles, a divide emerged between the nature of urban and rural ministries. Urban society demanded ministries focused on the dispossessed and non-Protestant – a social gospel concept of ministry. Temperance movements, the Sunday-school movement, and similar missions were developed to address the challenges of cities. Rural religious life, however, focused increasingly on resisting the intellectual challenges of modernity. In that environment, the church's mission centered on independent theological education and missions to Native peoples, both in Canada and abroad. As the century progressed, denominational schools tended either to become more rigid in their own identities apart from developments in the larger secularized society or lose their denomination-focused identity. Social ministries kept some relevance alive until the 1960s, but eventually even that connection seemed no longer important.

As the century drew to a close, Anglo-Saxon Canadian ethnicity had become less dominant, and notions of a Christian nation were unsustainable. In the new environment, Baptists have found their growth mainly in two sources – non-European immigrant populations and elements of the populations formed in the earlier Canadian Protestant traditions. Canadian Baptist Ministries churches have programs in thirty-two languages, one of the significant being its Chinese work. Today, Baptists increasingly find themselves among those Canadian Protestant elements that struggle toward a coherent identity, still think themselves a theological colony, and wonder how they can be relevant.[1]

Consistent with the previous observations, early in the century, Baptist universities in Canada came under attack for modernist teachings. Acadia was able to weather the challenges, but McMaster suffered the brunt of Baptists' version of the modernist-fundamentalist controversy. The

---

[1] Darren C. Marks, "Canadian Protestantism to the Present Day," in *The Blackwell Companion to Protestantism*, ed. Alister E. McGrath and Darren C. Marks (Oxford, U.K.: Blackwell, 2007), 197.

so-called Matthews controversy in 1910 opened a sixteen-year struggle that ended with division in the Ontario/Quebec Convention. T. T. Shields of Jarvis Street Baptist Church became a noted leader of the fundamentalist elements, which were defeated. In response, he led the formation of the Union of Regular Baptist Churches of Ontario and Quebec in October 1927. Earlier that year, he had led in founding the Toronto Baptist Seminary. Shields served as president of both organizations. Within a year, one-seventh of the original convention had departed.[2] Similar events transpired in relation to Brandon College in western Canada.

As noted in Chapter 3, Canadian Baptists had formed regional unions by the dawn of the twentieth century. However, a century of effort was required before a permanent national union could be organized in 1944, the Baptist Federation of Canada. Among the inhibiting factors were distances; significant differences among the three basic regions – Maritime, Central, and Western; and the autonomous nature of local Baptist churches, associations, and unions. But with organization of the federation, Canadian Baptists gained an efficient means for coordinating the larger work of the regional unions. Prior to that, many Canadian Baptist churches had cooperated in mission ministries through the Canadian Baptist Foreign Mission Board, organized in 1912 – later renamed the Canadian Baptist Overseas Missions Board and still later Canadian Baptist International Ministries. Thus, after World War II, Canadian Baptists had two parallel coordinating bodies, the first for missions and the second for other ministries. To further unify their work, in 1995, the federation and mission board merged to form Canadian Baptist Ministries (CBM). This federation coordinates the common work of four regional bodies – Baptist Convention of Ontario and Quebec, Baptist Union of Western Canada, Convention of Atlantic Baptist Churches, and L'Union d'Églises Baptistes Françaises au Canada. This body represents two-thirds of Baptists in Canada, with a membership of 173,100 and 1,336 churches in 2007. In addition to CBM, at least thirteen other Baptist denominational bodies exist in Canada; at the close of the century, they totaled about 100,000 members in approximately 1,000 churches.

Canadian Baptist Women The nineteenth-century Canadian Baptist focus within women's education was on domestic roles. This fit the dominant Western pattern that considered the private sphere the appropriate

---

[2] Harry A. Renfree, *Heritage and Horizon: The Baptist Story in Canada* (Eugene, OR: Wipf & Stock Publishers, 2007), 216–24.

domain for women. This influence was evidenced in the twentieth century through the types of ministries women assumed in the church. Almost universally, mission was the acceptable "public" domain for women, and Canadian Baptist women excelled in that area. Hannah Maria Norris had opened the path for this in 1870, when she initiated the organization of thirty-three local missionary-aid societies in Maritime Baptist churches to help support her work in Burma. Gradually, central committees were set up to connect the societies. Soon, this type of effort was spread to other regions. In the 1870s and 1880s, four women's missionary societies were organized in the Baptist Convention of Ontario and Quebec. By the end of the 1880s, societies existed in western Canada as well. When the Canadian Baptist Foreign Mission Board was created in 1912, women's societies refocused their energies from the local boards to the united mission effort.

Two world wars and the Great Depression created added ministry needs that Canadian Baptist women stepped up to address. They did this while suffering losses to their ranks brought about by the modernist-fundamentalist controversies. Medical supplies, food parcels, and other assistance were provided to mission stations, Canadian troops, and persons suffering from the ravages of war.

In 1951, four societies united to form the Baptist Women's Missionary Society of Ontario and Quebec. The society's purpose was to share in the evangelization of Canada and other lands, to keep the cause of missionary vocation before children and young women, and to support missionary work and training. Through those ventures, Baptist women in Canada developed important ministry and leadership skills, which they applied for the benefit of their churches, communities, and the world beyond. Still, Baptist women's ministry opportunities beyond the activities already described were very limited. They were generally free to do support work but not to participate fully in ministerial leadership or decision making. This attitude is illustrated by a decision of the Baptist Convention of Ontario and Quebec in 1929 regarding women's ordination. Delegates at the meeting determined that, though women's work was "unspeakably valuable," there was no need "for beginning a practice that is so entirely new to us as a people."[3] However, that view would change by the end of the century.

Jennie Johnson, a black woman minister, was the first woman ordained in Canada. Pastor of Prince Albert Baptist church in Chatham, she was ordained in 1909 by churches of the Free Baptist Convention. However,

[3] Ibid., 251.

prejudice against ordination of a woman forced her to leave the work. As the century progressed, the roles and rights of women in the broader society began to affect Baptists. Whether or not they liked it, women began to enter the public sphere, even Baptist women. In the 1960s, membership in the mission circles and the number of circles began to decline. By 1980, participation in the women's missionary groups of the Ontario and Quebec convention had dropped from 11,400 in 1955 to 8,000. The number of groups had declined from 535 to 368. In subsequent years, the declines continued. Leaders have identified the reason as "the vast movement of women into the work force."[4]

As women's opportunities in the larger world grow, Canadian Baptists are being forced to reconsider the historic limitation placed on women's participation in leadership and pastoral ministries. Evelyn Richardson expressed that dream in a 1987 address, "Our heritage . . . is marked by women whose faith took Jesus' words seriously. 'This is impossible for man, but with God all things are possible.'"[5]

U.S. Baptists

This period of U.S. history opened with the Spanish-American War, which marked the beginning of the nation's rise to international power. A spirit of optimism and crusades against moral vices predominated during the early decades of the century and was barely interrupted by World War I, the crusade fought to end all wars. Returning to isolationist policies following the war, the crusades to conquer vice continued. In 1920, the Eighteenth Amendment to the Constitution prohibited the manufacture, importation, and exportation of alcohol. In general, Baptists made abstinence from alcohol a mark of identity and prohibition a major political issue. Even after the repeal of the Eighteenth Amendment, Baptists in many parts of the country fought to prohibit the sale of alcohol in local counties and municipalities, especially in the South. However, the perception that Protestant Christianity was being overrun by non-Protestant immigrants and atheistic modernist heresies led many Baptists to support the Immigration Act of 1924 restricting immigration and to call for legislation preempting public school curriculum content that would challenge traditional views of the Bible.

4 Dorothy Neal, "Report of the Baptist Women's Missionary Society, in the *Yearbook of the Baptist Convention of Ontario and Quebec* (1979–80), 182.
5 Evelyn Richardson, "Report of the Woman's Missionary Auxiliary," *Yearbook of the Baptist Union of Western Canada* (1986–7), 83–84, cited by Renfree, *Heritage and Horizon*, 325.

A number of developments in the 1920s and 1930s contributed to a growing uneasiness among many Baptists that the world was changing, and not for the better. The red scare following the Bolshevik Revolution alerted many Baptists in America to the presence of communism, eliciting apocalyptic and sometimes vitriolic responses. The Scopes trial in 1925 symbolized what many Baptists perceived as the attack of science against the Bible. Theories of evolution, along with critical and literary analyses of biblical content, caused many Baptists to feel that the foundation of their faith was being attacked. Some responded by adopting doctrinal statements that stated what their adherents were required to believe about the Bible and the teachings of science. Equally devastating were the experiences of the Great Depression, which spawned massive unemployment, foreclosures, migrations, and a sense of helplessness. The New Deal policies of Franklin D. Roosevelt affected the economic and political life of the nation through the introduction of massive new social and welfare programs for the first time in U.S. history. These consequences shaped U.S. Baptists in significant ways, some positively and others negatively.

Baptists were generally supportive of the United States' declaration of war following the Japanese attack on Pearl Harbor in 1941. Amid heavy sacrifices and loss of life, the war changed the American landscape in many important ways. Nuclear weapons had been developed and deployed, and they threatened human existence. Women had been mobilized to assist in the war effort. Having tasted the freedom of public life, many were not content to retreat to the private sphere of domestic roles that deprived them of opportunities for personal fulfillment. Black Americans who had fought sacrificially against the racist policies of Hitler were not prepared to return home to the limitation that racism in the United States continued to impose on them. Also, the internment of thousands of Japanese Americans during the war caused many to question what it meant to be American. The dominant Anglo-American culture had led the majority simply to assume that real Americanness meant being white, Anglo-Saxon, and Protestant. That definition perpetually excluded persons of many ethnic backgrounds from the possibility of genuine American identity. This realization propelled civil rights activities to new levels following the war.

After World War II, industrialization hastened the migration of populations from rural to urban areas. This had a major impact on Baptists, whose strength traditionally had been among rural populations. For the most part, Baptists in the United States were not prepared to deal with secularism, materialism, religious pluralism, social transformation, and ideological challenges associated with urban cultures. People were beginning to perceive the world in ways that Baptist theologies were not equipped to comprehend. For many Baptists, the only way to engage that world was through ideological opposition, patriotism, and accepting the benefits its technology offered.

The war forced the United States away from its traditional isolationist policies and toward increasing international involvement. The Cold War between the United States and the Soviet Union, together with U.S. participation in the United Nations, contributed to that growing involvement, stimulating America's global economic, political, cultural, ideological, and technological influence. Many Baptists in America became profoundly committed to fighting communism, both abroad and at home. Often, popular beliefs about conditions in countries under communist governments were unfounded, leading many to view their world through the lens of fear and misinformation.

The 1960s became a watershed in U.S. social and cultural life. In 1960, John F. Kennedy was elected the first non-Protestant U.S. president. A revolution occurred in youth culture, sexual attitudes, civil rights for African Americans and others, and young Americans' reactions against the Vietnam War. Major shifts occurred in ideas of family, gender roles, societal institutions, morality, and religion. Technological and communications advancements in the 1980s and 1990s furthered this transformation through the more egalitarian exchange of ideas made possible by the Internet, cell phones, and other developments. The cumulative impact of the interconnectedness fostered by economic, political, communications, and technological progress is often called globalism. But such developments have not been causes for celebration by all people. For a variety of reasons, some individuals, groups, and nations have employed terrorist tactics as a means both to protect their traditional values and to advance other esteemed causes that they feel are being lost or compromised by an irresistible onslaught of global change.

At the beginning of the twenty-first century, many Anglo Baptists in America faced a world that seemed less friendly and secure than the one thought to have existed when the nation was founded in 1776. That world seemed less Christian, more competitive, and more restrictive of Baptist activities in the public sphere. The emerging world prompted many Anglo-American Baptists to define more carefully the parameters between what might or might not be considered a Baptist stance on many issues. Some of those Baptists felt their only hope lay in organizing confessionally acceptable schools and universities and in creating Baptist megacommunities that would secure an often-beleaguered religious worldview against cultural developments that seemed uncontrollable. The public actions of many black and minority Baptists often came to be viewed more positively by the general population than those of numerous Anglo-American Baptists. Although the perspectives and public engagement of Anglo-American Baptists have varied widely, the types of reactions displayed by a few (generally those with greatest access to widespread public media) have led many in the larger culture to perceive all Baptists as protectors of the old order, purveyors of prejudices, and determined to leverage political power to legislate their own religious views on the general public.

Although Baptists in the United States appear to be widely diverse and disconnected, most can be organized into just a few major groupings based on a combination of their theology, organizing principles, culture, and ministry methods. In general, Baptists can be identified today either as of the Ecumenical Mainline family of Baptists, the Free Will/General family of Baptists, the Primitivist family of Baptists, the Independent Fundamentalist family of Baptists, the Conservative Evangelical family of Baptists, the Landmark family of Baptists, Reformed (Calvinistic) family of Baptists, the National (African American) family of Baptists, and families of Baptists identified by ethnic heritage.[6] Many of the Baptist bodies included here are relatively small, but because their collective missionary endeavors have spread them around the world, they are treated summarily for the benefit of those who encounter them in often-unexpected places and need introductions to their basic identities.

Anglo-American Baptists

The Ecumenical Mainline Family of Baptists
In general, the Ecumenical Mainline family of Baptist churches values cooperative relationships with different Baptists, as well as with other Christian denominations and entities. They are willing to evaluate Baptist belief and practice in light of the theological convictions and perceptions offered through the insightful critiques of those outside the Baptist fold, but they also affirm and defend Baptist faith traditions in light of those critiques. They do this from a firm confidence that, though Baptists have unique and valuable insights to offer the world, they are not the exclusive embodiment of Christ's revelation to humankind. This means there is a willingness to live in community amid differences of views while being

---

[6] These categories are adapted from those used in Albert W. Wardin, ed. *Baptists around the World: A Comprehensive Handbook* (Nashville, TN: Broadman & Holman, 1995), 367–71.

faithful to their own convictions. Ecumenical Mainline Baptists believe that God is actively engaged in the world as well as in the church, and that God intends for the church to be involved appropriately in addressing the world's needs as well. Consequently, the church is called on to speak prophetically and act on issues of social justice and human oppression (spiritual, mental, or physical) that stand in the way of a person's receiving God's good news of hope.

Of the Baptist bodies included in this category, only the American Baptist Churches USA (ABC-USA) has membership in the National and World Councils of Churches, and therefore meets the strict criteria of Ecumenical Mainline. On that basis, some would not include the Alliance of Baptists and Cooperative Baptist Fellowship (CBF) in this classification. They are included here because of their similarities on several key characteristics. Other interpreters might choose to classify them differently.

The American Baptist Churches USA   The American Baptist Churches USA (ABC-USA), historically has been a predominantly Anglo-American Baptist denomination that, by the late twentieth century, had no ethnic majority of members – a mixture of Anglo-American, African American, Asian American, Hispanic, Native American, and other ethnic groups. The earliest of the Baptist traditions in the United States, prior to creation of the Northern Baptist Convention in 1907, the ABC-USA possessed a very loose sense of denominational connectedness. The principal source of such unity as did exist came from three societies: the American Baptist Missionary Union, the American Baptist Home Mission Society, and the American Baptist Publication Society. Efforts to create a more centralized denominational structure met stiff resistance. In the twentieth century, that resistance gradually changed, but only at great cost in churches and members. American Baptists[7] began the century with great optimism

---

[7]   The denomination known as ABC-USA today began as a lose affiliation of autonomous local Baptist churches in the English colonies of North America. Their primary organization of connection was through regional associations. In 1814, the first U.S. nationwide organization was formed – the General Baptist Missionary Convention of the Baptist Denomination in the United States of America for Foreign Missions (GMC) – and Baptist churches throughout the country began forming a common mission around its work in addition to the work of their local associations. Within a decade the GMC's work had expanded also to include home missions and publications. In 1826, the GMC decided only to focus on foreign mission work and divested itself of the home mission and publication work, resulting in creation of the American Baptist Home Mission Society and the American Baptist Publication Society. After Baptists in the South withdrew to form their own denomination – the Southern Baptist Convention (SBC), the GMC in 1846 changed its name to the American Baptist Missionary Union (ABMU). American Baptists still had no central organizing body, only three independent societies gave any sense of national coherence to their identity and

and growth. Over the course of the century, however, the denomination faced several serious problems, including secularism, patterns of immigration that were unfriendly to Baptist ecclesiology and methods, and several divisive theological movements. In an effort to deal with those and other challenges, Baptists in the North organized the Northern Baptist Convention in 1907. In 1950, Northern Baptists reorganized their work and gave their denomination a new title – the American Baptist Convention. In 1972, American Baptists decided to restructure their denomination once again, this time under the title the American Baptist Churches in the USA.

Creation of the Northern Baptist Convention was, in many ways, a major turning point for this Baptist communion. It was the first time Baptists in the North had accepted a regional identity. It also signified a shift from a single-ministry society approach to a more unified convention approach. Equally important was the creation of an executive committee to coordinate the work of the whole denomination. However, many Baptists in the North were not happy with the shift. In the 1920s, many fundamentalist Baptists in the North identified "excessive denominational machinery"[8] as one of the grievances they felt remained unaddressed by fellow Baptists and a major reason for their withdrawal to form independent organizations.

Prior to the divisive eruption of fundamentalism as an identified movement in the Northern Baptist Convention in the 1920s, a number of incidents foreshadowed its coming. As early as 1893, William Bell Riley – who later became a noted fundamentalist leader – expressed public concern over the doctrinal views of professors at the University of Chicago (a school started by Baptists in 1890). In 1909, T. O. Conant presented the paper titled "Recent Tendencies to Change Denominational Practices," in which he strongly defended traditional interpretations of scriptural authority, baptism, and ecclesiology.[9] Prior to this, in 1900, Ira Price had presented

work. In 1907, the first centralized organizational structure was created under the name the Northern Baptist Convention (NBC). This is the source of the name Northern Baptists. In 1950, the NBC changed its name to the American Baptist Convention and restructured its organization. In 1972, the denomination was restructured again and changed its name to the American Baptist Churches in the U.S.A. Since then this body of Baptists has been popularly known both as American Baptists and as Northern Baptists. I often use the term Northern Baptist to refer to the organization between 1907 and 1950 and American Baptist for the period before and after these dates, although American Baptist pre-1907 and post-1950 are very different organizations.

8 For example, see Earle V. Pierce, "Northern Baptist Foreign Missions – Part II," *Watchman-Examiner*, August 26, 1943.

9 T. O. Conant, "Recent Tendencies to Change Denominational Practice," in *Proceedings of the Twenty-Seventh Annual Session of the Baptist Congress, New York, 1909* (Chicago: University of Chicago Press, 1909), 112–25.

a paper with a similar tone at the American Baptist Publication Society's meeting in Detroit, Michigan.

Two Baptist seminary professors came under fire during this volatile time. George B. Foster published *The Finality of the Christian Religion* in 1906, which suggested that the New Testament was more reflective of the apostle Paul's teachings than those of Jesus. This became a significant factor in the decision of more than 225 churches in southern Illinois to withdraw from the Northern Baptist Convention and unite with the Southern Baptist Convention. Walter Rauschenbusch, professor of theology at Rochester Theological Seminary, wrote *Christianity and the Social Gospel* in 1907, criticizing the church for forsaking the message of Jesus in favor of a Hellenized message about Jesus.

In a series of regional rallies, leaders such as William Bell Riley, John Roach Stratton, Frank M. Goodchild, and J. C. Massee awakened interest in the fundamentalist Baptist cause. These leaders led attacks in three major areas: Northern Baptist Convention colleges and seminaries, foreign missionaries, and the American Baptist Board of Publications. A committee appointed to study the colleges reported to the 1921 Northern Baptist Convention that the charges that had been made were largely inaccurate. A committee appointed to examine the conduct, policies, and practices of the American Baptist Foreign Mission Board reported only five or six missionaries with doctrinal problems, which the convention decided to allow the Foreign Mission Board to address. The American Baptist Publication Society tried to serve the needs of the broadly based constituencies of the Northern Baptist Convention. In 1925, Riley announced the creation of the Baptist Bible Union, which would offer only a fundamentalist line of church literature.

Another major concern raised by Northern Baptist fundamentalists was over the adoption of a confession of faith – preferably the New Hampshire Confession of 1833. At the Indianapolis convention in 1922, Nelson Bell Riley made a motion for the Northern Baptist Convention to adopt this confession with a premillennialist understanding of the last article. The convention rejected Riley's motion in favor of one affirming that "the New Testament is the all sufficient-ground of faith and practice, and we need no other statement."[10]

The conflict between the Northern Baptist Convention and fundamentalist Baptists resulted in the creation of the General Association of Regular Baptists in 1932, a split from the Northern Baptist Convention. This group

---

[10] *Annual of the Northern Baptist Convention*, vol. 15 (Indianapolis, Indiana, June 14–20. 1922), 133.

has been characterized by its strong independence and emphasis on fundamentalist principles. In 1947, a second group withdrew from the Northern Baptist Convention for reasons of doctrine and polity and formed the Conservative Baptist Association of America, which also gave strong emphasis to local church autonomy.

In 1947, Northern Baptists created a committee to study denominational structure and find ways to make it more efficient, democratic, and responsive to the needs of local churches. In response to the committee's recommendations, the name of the Northern Baptist Convention was changed to American Baptist Convention, and denominational structures were modified to promote greater coordination of the denomination's work. In that context, the decision was made to bring all of the convention's program agencies together in one place at Valley Forge, Pennsylvania. Among the goals of centralization was the hope that being physically located together would generate a greater sense of cooperation.

Following recommendations made by the Study Commission on Denominational Structure (SCODS) produced in 1968, the American Baptist Convention was renamed the American Baptist Churches in the USA, governed by a general council, with ministries organized around three major boards: international ministries, national ministries, and educational ministries. A major reason for this reorganization was to give voices to laity, women, minority groups, and others who had remained perpetually underrepresented in denominational decision making.

Early in the century, several influential thinkers brought a significant reputation to the domination through their scholarly achievements; among them were William Newton Clark, Augustus H. Strong, Walter Rauschenbusch, George B. Foster, Shailer Matthews, and Harry Emerson Fosdick. Membership in the American Baptist Churches in the USA has remained more or less stable since around 1928; today it stands at about 1.4 million members in 5,750 churches.

Cooperative Baptist Fellowship   The Cooperative Baptist Fellowship (CBF) is one of three significant splits that have divided the Southern Baptist Convention (SBC) since 1979. Reasons for the splits are rooted in events that go back several decades in Southern Baptist life. Since early in the twentieth century, Southern Baptists experienced tensions between members of more moderate and progressive convictions and those of more fundamentalist and exclusivist convictions. The differences reached a crisis in the late 1970s, when a fundamentalist faction in the SBC began concerted efforts to gain governing control of the convention.

Having been excluded from voice in the SBC for more than a decade, in September 1990, a group of Southern Baptists met in Atlanta. Their intention was to consult on the state of the SBC and how they should respond. Organizers were overwhelmed when more than five thousand persons showed up. Out of that meeting the Cooperative Baptist Fellowship was organized.

The CBF has attempted to preserve many distinctive Baptist features, including soul competency, local church autonomy, freedom of the believer (under Christ and the guidance of the Holy Spirit) to interpret Scripture, freedom of religion, and the conviction that God can call women to vocational ministry. A central value of the CBF is world mission. Understanding that the world has become more global and less bound by the traditional national boundaries, the CBF has embarked on approaches to mission that focus on people groups rather than national boundaries. The CBF likewise has broken down the distinction between home mission and foreign mission. In 2007, CBF churches totaled seven hundred thousand members in 1,854 churches.

Alliance of Baptists Organized in 1987 as a response to developments in the Southern Baptist Convention, they announced several goals, like valuing individual freedom to interpret the Bible, local church freedom to decide matters of faith and practice, theological education based on open inquiry and responsible scholarship, servant models of leadership, and commitment to actions that proclaim God's good news in Christ. The alliance also takes seriously the interdependence of Baptists with the larger people of God and therefore chooses to work cooperatively with non-Baptist denominations and others toward common goals. In 2007, the alliance had 125 churches and a theology school in Richmond, Virginia, among the entities that cooperated in its mission.

The Conservative Evangelical Family of Baptists
Each of these Baptists bodies, at different times and for different reasons, broke away from the American Baptist Churches in the USA (under different names). In the case of Seventh Day Baptists, the schism occurred in the late seventeenth century, even before a national or regional coordinating body existed, and then did not form a new denomination but became an American expression of one that already existed in England. Southern Baptists became an independent denomination in the nineteenth century as a result of severing relations with the American Baptist foreign and home mission societies over issues related to slavery. The Baptist General

Conference and North American Baptist Conference were originally ethnic Baptist groups with distinct organizations within the Northern Baptist
Convention (now ABC-USA) who decided in the mid-twentieth century to
separate and form completely independent Baptists denominations. Conservative Baptists originated as a protest movement within the Northern
Baptist Convention over liberal theology and formed their own organization in 1948.

The label of Conservative Evangelical identifies the fact that these Baptist
bodies have tended to reject Ecumenical Mainline theological inclusivism
and to prefer the conservative side of modern theological and social debates.
They also employ the use of confessions of faith as national bodies to establish clear boundaries of membership on the issues they consider essential.
Unlike strict fundamentalists, however, they cooperate with other evangelicals with whom they may differ on certain points.

Seventh Day Baptist General Conference   The Seventh Day body of Baptists
organized their first church in the United States out of a schism within the
Baptist church at Newport, Rhode Island (today ABC-USA) in 1671 (see
Chapter 2). In the nineteenth century, Seventh Day Baptists became very
involved in foreign mission ministries, especially in China, Burma, Poland,
Malawi, and Mexico. In the twentieth century, they became involved in the
Ecumenical movement, and for almost seventy years, they were members of
the World Council of Churches, withdrawing from membership in 1976.
They also have been advocates for human rights and peace initiatives. In
1995, Seventh Day Baptists had about five thousand members in sixty-eight
churches.

The Southern Baptist Convention   The twentieth century was a period of
remarkable growth for Southern Baptists. In 1900, they numbered slightly
more than 1.5 million members in 18,873 churches. By the year 2000,
Southern Baptists claimed about 16 million members in forty thousand
churches and constituted the largest Baptist denomination in the world.
Geographically, they expanded from a denomination located mostly in the
Southern United States to a nationwide denomination with a network of
missions that included a large portion of the globe. Organizationally, they
grew from three general boards and no standing committees or continuing
commissions to four general boards, seven commissions, several standing
committees, the Woman's Missionary Union Auxiliary, six institutions, and
one foundation. Changes in 1996 modified that structure to five boards,
six institutions, an executive committee, and two councils.

In 1925, partly as a consequence of a funding drive called the Seventy-Five Million Campaign, the Southern Baptist Convention's Cooperative Program was developed. The program provided a means for apportioning monies sent from the local church to support state conventions and the ministries of the Southern Baptist Convention (SBC). Also in that year, struggles over the question of evolution precipitated the SBC's adoption of its first confession of faith as a denomination – the 1925 Baptist Faith and Message. In 1963, a second Baptist Faith and Message was adopted as a result of the Ralph H. Elliott Genesis controversy. The confession was intended to affirm Southern Baptists' concerns over biblical authority. In the year 2000, the SBC adopted a third version of the Baptist Faith and Message.

The SBC suffered several major divisions over the course of the twentieth century. In the 1920s, fundamentalism emerged as a challenge through the work of J. Frank Norris. Several separatist, fundamentalist Baptist denominations resulted from these conflicts and the related doctrinal differences associated with fundamentalists' agendas. Also, several Landmark Baptist schisms occurred in the first half of the century. A more divisive controversy arose in the 1970s, when a fundamentalist-oriented constituency organized to take over the SBC. As control of the SBC shifted, those who experienced exclusion from leadership withdrew to form alternate church bodies, such as the Alliance of Baptists, the Cooperative Baptist Fellowship, and Mainstream Baptists. At the close of the century, support for Calvinist theology began to appear, creating further sources of friction and occasional controversy.

Baptist General Conference of America   Originally known as the Swedish Baptist Conference, the Baptist General Conference of America (BGC) originated in 1856 and was loosely connected with the American Baptist Churches in the USA, especially through the work of the American Baptist Home Mission Society. After World War I, the BGC began developing in an independent direction because of its maturing work and differences with American Baptists (Northern Baptists at that time), especially over ecumenical involvement. In 1944, a definitive break was made. Bethel College and Seminary in St. Paul, Minnesota, are important centers of its educational ministries.

North American Baptist Conference   Originally known as the German Baptist Conference, the North American Baptist Conference was created in 1851 to encourage the development of German-speaking Baptist work in the United States. Although a distinct body, it related closely with American Baptists through the Home Mission Society and the Publication Society. The conference's work was focused especially in the upper Midwest and in Canada, where German immigration was heavy. After several decades of growing estrangement, in 1938 the General Conference became independent, and in 1946, it reorganized as the North American Baptist Conference. In the United States, the North American Baptist Seminary in Sioux Falls, South Dakota, and in Canada, the Edmonton Baptist College and Edmonton Baptist Seminary have been centers for its educational ministries.

Conservative Baptist Association of America   The Conservative Baptist movement is a fellowship of autonomous congregations that separated from the American Baptist Churches in the USA (at that time the Northern Baptist Convention) in 1947 over differences in biblical interpretation, views on Baptist theological traditions, and certain policies of the American Baptist Foreign Mission Society (ABFMS). The Conservative Baptist Association of America (CBA) originated as a fellowship among American Baptist (Northern) Churches, and after two decades of disagreements with the ABFMS, it decided to organize the competing Conservative Baptist Foreign Mission Society in 1943 (after 1994, known as CB International). When the convention rejected a competing mission agency within its structure, CBA churches withdrew to form their own network. Eschewing traditional denominational structures, the CBA attempted to preserve local church autonomy through connectional patterns that kept their agencies independent.

Between 1957 and 1964, the CBA experienced a division by those within its ranks who sought to guide the movement into a more thoroughgoing fundamentalist posture. In 1961, about two hundred churches separated to form the World Conservative Baptist Mission (after 1966, known as Baptist World Mission). Cross-cultural mission has been a major focus of CBA churches, with work in forty-six countries. The churches contribute to the support of three seminaries – Western Conservative Baptist Seminary in Portland, Oregon; Denver Seminary in Colorado; and Conservative Baptist Seminary of the East in Dresher, Pennsylvania.

Free Will/General Family of Baptists
This family of Baptists originated slightly earlier than the larger Particular or Regular Baptist bodies (see Chapter 2) and has been most distinguished by its theology of atonement and human freedom to choose. Since the

eighteenth century, Regular and General Baptists have grown closer on the two issues as revivalistic theologies placed greater emphasis on human choice rather than on God's effective calling. However, the question of whether a believer can fall from grace has continued to divide the two Baptist families. Also, Free Will/General Baptists tend to give associational bodies greater authority in the life of local churches than do the Regular Baptist traditions.

National Association of Free Will Baptists   The National Association of Free Will Baptists (NAFWB) originated in 1935, when the General Conference of Free Will Baptists in the South and the General Co-operative Association of Free Will Baptists in the West united. This union occurred in the wake of a merger by many New England Free Will Baptists with the Northern Baptist Convention (today ABC-USA). The denomination has focused its efforts on educational, missionary, and evangelistic ministries, and it supports several four-year colleges in addition to missionaries in nine countries. In the mid-1990s, the NAFWB included about 230,000 members in 2,500 churches.

Original Free Will Baptists   The Original Free Will Baptists (OFWB) united with the National Association of Free Will Baptists in 1935, but withdrew in 1961 over issues of church government, educational philosophies, and publication ministries. In 1991, the OFWB had about 33,000 members and supported several institutions, including foreign mission programs in five countries.

General Association of General Baptists   The General Association of General Baptists grew out of the Liberty Association of General Baptists formed in 1824 and centered in Ohio, Indiana, Kentucky, Tennessee, Illinois, and Missouri. In 1870, churches within the movement formed the General Association of General Baptists and later added a Home Mission Board, Foreign Mission Board, college, and publications to their ministries. Today, the association has about 73,000 members in 816 churches.

Separate Baptists in Christ   True to their eighteenth-century heritage, the few remaining Separate Baptist churches, located mostly in Kentucky, are largely rural and served by theologically untrained pastors who derive their support from secular employment. By the end of the twentieth century, they had about 7,000 members in eighty-four churches and one missionary couple serving in Côte d'Ivoire.

Other Free Will Baptist Associations   Numerous independent Free Will Baptist associations exist; the largest ones are located in North Carolina, Tennessee, Indiana, Oklahoma, and West Virginia. Collectively, they number more than 21,000 members in 286 churches. Also, the United American Free Will Baptists, one of the very few black Free Will Baptist associations, was organized in 1899 in North Carolina.

The Primitivist Family of Baptists
The Primitivist family of Baptists is most characterized by rejection of missionary and educational institutions and opposition to a theologically trained ministry. These convictions are deeply rooted in theologies of God's sovereignty that take a negative view of human initiative in matters of faith. Being responsive to God's leadership is considered a concern of the will, not the mind. Therefore, human initiatives to shape thought in activities of faith serve only to thwart God's sovereign activity. Other distinctives often include rejection of Sunday schools, use of musical instruments in worship, the addressing of ministers as elders, foot washing as an ordinance, and rural culture.

These statements of theological position should not be taken to mean that Primitivist Baptists are static in belief and practice. The groups do change their opinions at times, and those changes often lead to new groupings of Primitive Baptists. Because this family of Baptists consists of very independent associations, the number of separate Primitivist Baptist bodies is quite large. Those treated here represent only a few of the larger ones. Their heaviest concentrations have tended to be located in the Appalachian South and a few other places to which populations from that region have migrated.

Most Primitivist Baptist associations are small and widely scattered. The Central Baptist Association is an example of this. Extending from central Indiana to central South Carolina, the association unites thirty-five churches and 3,300 members in a fellowship concentrated in the Appalachian Mountains of eastern Tennessee and southwestern Virginia. The General Association of Baptists, often called the Duck River and Kindred Association of Baptists, consists of a group of seven Missionary Baptist associations united around the Duck River Association of Tennessee. Centered mostly in middle Tennessee and northern Alabama, this Baptist denomination has about 11,000 members in approximately one hundred churches (and is not Primitive Baptist).

Regular Baptists in Kentucky were part of the Baptist movement in the eighteenth century that combined to form the United Baptists. However, the group retained the name *Regular* as a statement of its theology and practice. They are moderate in their Calvinist theology but agree with Primitive Baptists in rejecting missionary, educational, and other denominational institutions. Three types of Regular Baptists can be identified – Old Regulars, Regulars, and Enterprise Baptists. The Old Regular Baptists emphasize preaching by inspiration, not preparation; lined singing in worship without musical instruments; foot washing; and preaching limited exclusively to ministers of their communion. Women are excluded from any leadership roles and reject modern fashions in their attire. Regular Baptists are much like the Old Regulars, except they allow more innovation in their worship practices and in the lifestyles of members. Hymnals and musical instruments are allowed, and members can dress like the general population as long as modesty is observed. Enterprise Baptists have had association with Regular Baptists in the past, but they no longer do. They are more open to novelty in worship and lifestyle than the other Regulars.

Baptist churches that bear the name *Primitive Baptist* are the largest of the bodies that constitute the Primitivist family of Baptists. They vigorously oppose missionary, Bible, and tract societies; theological training; colleges; and Sunday school education. They also value an untrained and unpaid ministry, rejection of musical instruments in worship, simplicity in church buildings, and foot washing as an ordinance. Emphasizing a rigid Calvinist theology, Primitive Baptists reject evangelistic and missionary efforts as interfering in God's sovereign election. Collectively, they number about forty thousand members in about 1,159 churches today, and they can be identified in three groups – Absoluters, Old Liners, and Progressives.

Landmark Family of Baptists

The Landmark family of Baptist churches organizes around the conviction that, though true Christians might be found in other denominations, the only true churches are Baptist churches. They believe that Baptists originated during the time of Christ and have maintained a line of succession to the present. Therefore, non-Baptist bodies are mere human organizations, not true churches. Also, those Baptists who do not practice those principles are considered apostate. Because non-Baptist churches are not "true" churches, no act performed by them can be accepted as legitimate. The baptism of persons coming from other churches cannot be accepted. Ministers of other churches cannot be allowed to preach from their pulpits. Their churches often include the title "Missionary Baptist" as part of their identification to distinguish them from Primitivist Baptist churches.

Their greatest strength is in Mississippi, Louisiana, Texas, Arkansas, Oklahoma, and a few other locations where members from those regions have migrated.

The American Baptist Association (ABA) and Baptist Missionary Association (BMA) are major fellowships for many independent Baptist churches of Landmark theological conviction in the U.S. South and Southwest. The ABA was formed in 1924 by the merger of the state Landmark associations in Texas, Mississippi, Arkansas, Oklahoma, Louisiana, Florida, and Missouri and the Old General Association. Disagreements over leadership between Ben Bogard of Arkansas and other leaders, including W. J. Burgess, D. N. Jackson, and M. E. Childers, in the 1930s and 1940s eventually erupted into a schism that gave birth to the Baptist Missionary Association of America in 1950. The ABA supports five colleges and seminaries in Arkansas, Texas, Oklahoma, and Florida, and it maintains missionaries in thirteen countries. Membership at the dawn of the twenty-first century stood at about 250,000 in 1,700 churches.

Known as the North American Baptist Association between 1950 and 1969, the Baptist Missionary Association is strongest in Texas, with significant constituencies in Arkansas and Mississippi. Theologically, BMA united around a militant fundamentalism and the basic tenets of Landmarkism. They support missionaries in six countries and a seminary at Jacksonville, Texas. At the end of the twentieth century, they had 228,000 members in 1,364 churches.

In addition to the two major Landmark bodies, numerous independent Landmark Baptist associations and churches are scattered throughout the U.S. South and parts of the West. Many of these follow the principles of T. P. Crawford, whose gospel mission movement promoted a militant local church independence that rejected mission boards and insisted that churches give direct support to missionaries who function without any supervision from a mission agency. The fierce independence of these churches makes reliable numbers difficult to obtain.

Separatist Fundamentalist Family of Baptists
This family of very independent-minded Baptists militantly opposes theological liberalism and dissociates itself, not only from other Baptists who embrace views they consider liberal but also from like-minded fundamentalist Baptists who have relationships with liberal Baptists. Generally, they strongly endorse such theological positions as biblical inerrancy, premillennialism, and a dispensational interpretation of Scripture. Although most separatist fundamentalist Baptists are found in small congregations, in the

South, a few of their affiliated bodies constitute some of the nation's largest churches. These institutions center heavily on the pastor, whose charismatic leadership in many cases spawns complexes of church schools, colleges, and special needs organizations that become separate societies unto themselves. Their ministries are advanced through aggressive evangelism that maximizes use of the media, especially television, radio, and publications.

The Fundamentalist Baptist Fellowship of America   The Fundamentalist Baptist Fellowship of America (FBFA) originated in 1920 as a conference preceding the annual meeting of the Northern Baptist Convention (now ABC-USA) in Buffalo, New York. It continued as a special interest group within the NBC until the 1940s, with the purpose of holding the convention to conservative standards. In 1946, the fellowship's name was changed to Conservative Baptist Fellowship (CBF). During that period, separate mission societies were formed and other Conservative Baptist bodies emerged. In the 1950s, the CBF became militant in its separationist demands and began attacking leaders of the Conservative Baptist movement. In 1955, the CBF withdrew all cooperation with other Conservative Baptist bodies and adopted premillennial and pretribulation rapture doctrinal requirements. In 1961, it organized an independent missionary organization known today as Baptist World Mission, and in 1967, it changed the name CBF to Fundamentalist Baptist Fellowship of America (FBFA). Also in 1965, tensions in the CBF produced another schism, known as the New Testament Association of Independent Baptist Churches.

General Association of Regular Baptist Churches   The first major schism to occur after the formation of the Northern Baptist Convention occurred in 1932, when representatives of twenty-two churches met in Chicago and organized the General Association of Regular Baptist Churches (GARB). Adamant about Calvinist and fundamentalist doctrines, GARB churches reacted against modernist views, unequal representation of conservatives in NBC decision-making processes, and local church control over mission work. The term *Regular* conveys the view that they are the trustworthy heirs of true Baptist belief and practice. The GARB churches subscribe to the 1833 New Hampshire Confession of Faith with a premillennial interpretation and practice strict separation from any association or entity that has ties to liberal or ecumenical bodies, including Billy Graham's association. It supports foreign and domestic mission endeavors through organizations like Mid-Missions and Evangelical Baptist Missions. At the end of the century, they had about 136,000 members in almost

1,500 churches. In 1990, a schism occurred within GARB ranks when some who felt the association was weakening its strict separatist stance withdrew to form the Independent Baptist Fellowship of North America.

World Baptist Fellowship and Related Baptists   Several denominations of the Separatist Fundamentalist family of Baptists originated in the South at the same time the FBFA, GARB, and CBA were emerging in Northern Baptist life. The first of these grew from the ministries of J. Frank Norris, who was the pastor of the First Baptist Church of Fort Worth, Texas, from 1909 to 1952, and simultaneously pastor of Temple Baptist in Detroit from 1935 to 1948; he commuted between the two churches by air during the early days of commercial air travel. In the 1920s, Norris became increasingly fundamentalist in his views, and he grew dissatisfied with the positions of Southern Baptist Convention leaders, theological educators, and churches. In 1932, he led in the organization of the Premillennialist Baptist Missionary Fellowship, which was chartered as the World Fundamentalist Baptist Missionary Fellowship and has been known as the World Baptist Fellowship (WBF) since a schism within the group in 1950. Disillusioned with Norris's dictatorial leadership style, a number of pastors withdrew in that year to form the Baptist Bible Fellowship International (BBFI). In 1984, the WBF suffered another division when a group left to form the Independent Baptist Fellowship International (IBFI). Ministries of the WBF are centered at the Bible Baptist Seminary in Arlington, Texas. The BBFI's association centers on its headquarters and Baptist Bible College, both located in Springfield, Missouri. First Baptist Church of Hammond, Indiana, and Thomas Roads Baptist in Lynchburg, Virginia, have roots that go back to this organization, although both have developed into independent fellowships of their own. With missionaries in many parts of the world and associated congregations throughout the United States, these fellowships collectively had about .75 million members in approximately 4,300 congregations at the beginning of the twenty-first century. First Baptist Hammond recorded about 20,000 members, and Thomas Road Baptist, leader of the independent Liberty Baptist Fellowship, numbered 24,000 in 2006. In 1996, Jerry Falwell and his church became affiliated with the SBC. Because of their heavy use of media, these churches have shaped much of the public's image of who Baptists are and what they believe, even though they encompass only a small portion of the total family of Baptist denominations and churches. The Southwide Baptist Fellowship is formed around the ministries of Highland Park Baptist Church of Chattanooga, Tennessee. Under the ministry of Lee Roberson, who was pastor from 1942 to 1983, the church became one of the largest Baptist churches in the United States, claiming 57,000 members and sixty chapels the year Roberson retired. In 1946, he helped found and served as president of Tennessee Temple University. In 1960, he led in organizing Baptist International Missions, Inc., which by the end of the century had more than 500 missionaries working in sixty countries.

Reformed (Calvinistic) Family of Baptists

The Reformed (Calvinistic) family of Baptists focuses on recovering Particular and Regular Baptists' seventeenth-century theological roots as a means for reconstituting what its founders consider Baptists' seminal identity. Most endorse the First London Confession of Faith (1644), the Second London Confession of Faith (1689), and/or the 1742 Philadelphia Confession of Faith as their doctrinal standards. They tend to moderate between the superficial modern evangelical methods of evangelism and the hyper-Calvinistic predestinarian fatalism of some Primitivist Baptists. Most value disciplined education, reject premillennialism and Landmarkism, practice church discipline, and promote evangelism and mission when "properly" conducted. Major bodies associated with this Baptist family include Reformed Baptists, Sovereign Grace Baptists, and a few Strict Baptists (see English Baptists). At the end of the twentieth century, they numbered about 16,000 members in 403 congregations.

National (African American) Family of Baptists

At the 1894 annual meetings of the Baptist Foreign Mission Convention of the United States of America, the American National Baptist Convention, and the National Baptist Education Convention of the USA in Montgomery, Alabama, motions were made that the three conventions be merged into one. A joint committee was appointed to study the proposal and bring a report the following year. On September 28, 1895, a meeting convened in Atlanta, attended by more than 500 delegates, completed the merger that had been envisioned a year earlier. The resulting organization was the National Baptist Convention, USA (NBC). This convention was created with three boards – foreign mission, home mission, and education. In 1897, the Education Board was entrusted with responsibility for the NBC's publication work.

When the headquarters of the NBC Foreign Mission Board moved from Richmond, Virginia, to Louisville, Kentucky, some of the original members withdrew and formed the Lott Carey Foreign Mission Convention. The issues surrounding this withdrawal in 1897 were connected to loyalties for the old Foreign Mission Convention that had been headquartered in Richmond. Most of the persons who withdrew to form the Lott Carey Foreign Mission Convention were among the better educated of NBC's members from Virginia, North Carolina, and the District of Columbia. In 1905, the Lott Carey Convention and the National Baptist Convention reconciled, although each has maintained its separate existence. Today they continue to function as independent organizations, although most members have dual affiliations.

In addition to the National Baptist Convention, USA, eight other identifiable black Baptist denominations currently exist in the United States. They are the National Baptist Convention of America, organized in 1915; the Lott Carey Baptist Foreign Mission Convention, organized in 1897; the National Primitive Baptist Convention, USA, initially created in 1865 but formally organized in 1907; the United Freewill Baptist Church, originated in 1870 but formally organized in 1901; the National Baptist Evangelical Soul Saving Assembly of the USA, created in 1920 and formally organized in 1937; the Free for All Missionary Baptist Church, Inc., organized in 1955; the Progressive National Baptist Convention, Inc., organized in 1961; and the National Missionary Baptist Conference of America, organized in 1988.

Reverend E. C. Morris served as president of the National Baptist Convention, USA, Incorporated,[11] until 1922. After the loss of the publishing operation in 1915 (because of a schism that resulted in creation of the National Baptist Convention of America), a new board was created, the Sunday School Publishing Board of the National Baptist Convention. The Foreign Mission Board, however, became the center of the convention's focus rather than publications. L. K. Williams became president of the NBC in 1924 and served until 1941. In the following year, D. V. Jamison was elected president and served until 1952. In 1953, J. H. Jackson became president and held the office for a record twenty-nine years.

Jackson promoted a conservative social agenda and was a strong voice of opposition to Martin Luther King Jr. He succeeded in blocking the participation of the NBC in the civil rights movement. Partly for that reason, in 1961, King left the NBC and became one of the leaders of the newly organized Progressive National Baptist Convention. Jackson's successor, Dr. Theodore J. Jamison, was a strong civil rights advocate who

---

[11] After loss of the publishing board, NBC, USA reorganized and legally incorporated as a way of guaranteeing ownership and control of the convention's properties. As a result it has often been referred to as the Incorporated Convention.

had participated in marches and other activities integral to the civil rights movement. On his election in 1982, Jamison pledged support for social action. In 2007, the National Baptist Convention, USA, was the largest of the black denominations, with about 8.5 million members in 33,000 churches.

The National Baptist Convention of America, originally called the National Baptist Convention, Unincorporated, came into being in 1915 as the result of a division in the National Baptist Convention, USA, related to the publishing arm of the Education Board. The dispute involved a faction led by R. H. Boyd, secretary of the Publishing Board. Following the division, both the National Baptist Convention, USA, Incorporated and the National Baptist Convention, Unincorporated, claimed to be the original parent body. Today, both groups claim the founding date of 1880, although no unified national Baptist convention existed at that time. R. H. Boyd was succeeded by his son Henry Allen Boyd in 1922. A nephew, T. B. Boyd Jr., who directed the work of the publishing house from 1959 to 1979, succeeded Henry Allen. Since 1979, the publishing house has been headed by T. B. Boyd III. In 2007, the National Baptist Convention of America was the second largest of the major black Baptist bodies in America, with a national membership estimated at 3.1 million members in 12,336 churches. In 1988, the National Baptist Convention of America experienced another division, also related to differences over ownership of the publishing concern. As a result of the division, the National Missionary Baptist Convention of America was created. In 2007, that body had about 400,000 members in 300 churches.

The Progressive National Baptist Convention, USA, Inc. came into existence in 1961 as the result of a conflict within the National Baptist Convention, USA. Inc. Disagreements surfaced within the NBC in 1957, and ten pastors were expelled from the National Baptist Convention for challenging the presidency of J. H. Jackson in court on his ruling that an amendment setting a four-year limit on tenure was invalid. Jackson's opponents – feeling that the president was autocratic in his leadership – organized themselves around the candidacy of Dr. Gardner C. Taylor. Included in this faction were Martin Luther King Sr., Martin Luther King Jr., Ralph Abernathy, Benjamin Mays, and many other clergy committed to King's social agenda. At the 1960 convention in Philadelphia, the Nominating Committee presented Jackson's name for another term, and he was declared elected, whereupon Jackson's opponents protested. The next year, in Kansas City, Missouri, physical confrontations erupted between the Jackson faction and the Taylor team. Reverend L. Venchael Booth assumed leadership of the opposition and called for a meeting in November 1961 at his church, Zion Baptist Church, in Cincinnati. With thirty-three persons present representing black Baptists from fourteen states, the delegation voted to start a separate convention. The Progressive National Baptist Convention, organized out of that meeting, became actively involved in the civil rights movement; was supportive of the black power movement; and gave great emphasis to black political development, economic development, education, and strengthening the black family. It is the smallest of the three national Baptist conventions, with approximately 2.5 million members and 1,200 churches.

The National Primitive Baptist Convention, USA, organized in 1907, was an outgrowth of the antimission movement that was strong in the Midwest during the nineteenth century. Originally characterized by a heavy Calvinist emphasis, the body has moderated its Calvinism over the years. The denomination had 616 churches in 1991.

Some black Baptist churches affiliate exclusively with the American Baptist Churches, USA, and others with the Southern Baptist Convention. However, many churches have dual or triple or even more alignments with a variety of Baptist denominational bodies. Consequently, the same members are likely being counted simultaneously by two or three different organizations, thereby making the total number of black Baptists less than the total of the membership of those denominations.

Baptist Families of Ethnic Heritage

Major Twentieth-Century Ethnic Baptist Sources   The history of Baptist identity in the United States becomes very complex when considered from the perspective of ethnic origin. Numerous denominations of Baptists originated as ethnic bodies that later became part of the American mainstream. Other ethnic groups are more recent arrivals in the United States or have physical characteristics that have made mainstreaming more difficult. For those Baptists, ethnicity has continued to be a very important part of their identity. Among the major ethnic Baptists of European heritage in the United States at the beginning of the twentieth century were German Baptists, Swedish Baptists, Czechoslovakian Baptists, Hungarian Baptists, Polish Baptists, French Baptists, Romanian Baptists, Russian Baptists, Danish Baptists, and Norwegian Baptists.

As the twentieth century unfolded, those sources of Baptist life declined while Hispanic, Asian, and Caribbean sources became more significant. Among Latin Americans, Baptists of Mexican, Central American, and

Brazilian heritage have been most significant. Among Asian Americans, Baptists of Korean, Chinese, Japanese, Philippine, and Southeast Asian heritage have formed churches in significant numbers. Caribbean sources that have contributed significantly to the Baptist communion in the United States include large numbers of persons of Haitian, Jamaican, Puerto Rican, and Cuban heritage.

When viewed collectively, an incredibly large portion of Baptists in America have ethnic identities of some sort. Their members include significant numbers from African, European, Hispanic, Asian, and Amerindian cultural heritages, which make Baptists in America a widely diverse body representing believers from many parts of the globe or from ethnic identities that have become part of the social fabric of the United States. Such diversity not only needs to be understood by all Baptists but also should lead Baptists to seek better understanding of and relationship with fellow Baptists of diverse cultural traditions.

Native American Baptists Native Americans were inspired partly by African American civil rights initiatives to demand their own rights following World War II. However, rather than seek assimilation into the larger society, Native peoples generally sought the right to separate from the dominant culture and practice their traditional ways unfettered by governmental restrictions. Self-determination and respect as an independent people became their goal.

Over the course of the twentieth century, U.S. government policies regulating Native peoples moved from assimilationist to policies aimed to revitalize traditional Indian cultures, and then back to assimilationist. Assimilation was the general policy until John Collier became commissioner of Indian Affairs in Franklin Roosevelt's administration. Although he did not adequately involve Native peoples in his decision, Collier opposed the assimilationist policies. The 1934 Indian Reorganization Act granted tribes more freedom for self-government, promoted Indian culture, and restored religious freedom. However, the U.S. government kept the power to approve and veto decisions made by tribal councils. Far from perfect, the act marked a turning point for Native peoples.

In the 1950s, U.S. policies shifted again. The goals once more became assimilation through compensation and efforts to encourage relocation away from reservations to urban centers. Although the policies were terminated in 1958, the poverty and perceived lack of a satisfying future on the reservations, coupled with inadequate economic and educational opportunities, fostered urban migration for the remainder of the century.

Relocation tended to undercut traditional tribal identities but also "provided the setting for renewal of pan-Indian movements and the new militancy that demanded the right to self-determination."[12]

Early in the century, Baptist work among Native Americans followed familiar nineteenth-century patterns. As had been the case in the previous period, the greatest acceptance of Baptist beliefs occurred when Native persons led in those patterns' dissemination. The Iowa in Oklahoma offer an illustration of this. After being forced to settle in Indian Territory, the Iowa and Otoe tribes went through a process of attempting to adapt to a new and strange land in which tribal traditions did not seem to be working very well. In 1915, the Baptist evangelists G. L. Phelps and Robert Hamilton conducted so-called tent revivals among the nearby Sac and Fox tribes. Robert Small, an Iowa Indian, attended one of the services and concluded that the religion might be good for his people. He asked the evangelists to come to the Iowa peoples, and they agreed to do so. In 1921, the promised revival services finally were held.

In the interim, several Iowa children had studied at the Chilocco Indian School, accepted Christian faith, and started attending a nearby Baptist church. On visits home, they had shared their new faith with tribal members, thereby preparing the way for the preaching of Robert Hamilton. Those developments resulted in the organization of the Iowa Indian Baptist Church, which initially had twenty-six members. In 1924, church members constructed a church building with money the Iowa members themselves had collected. Frank Kent, an Iowa and charter member of the church, became its pastor, later decided to attend Bacone College in Muskogee, Oklahoma, and then went on to become a Native American Baptist pastor and leader himself.[13]

As this set of events illustrates, many dynamics were at work: loss of ancestral territorial contexts, adaptation to a new setting, and the need for new medicine that would work in this new place. For some members of the tribe, the new medicine was discovered through Baptist beliefs. A new grouping under a new set of beliefs and traditions challenged and changed older tribal structures and ways. New leaders emerged, selected on a different basis from that of the old traditions. The transition into Baptist identity carried the seeds for a future far more complex than either

[12] Susan Hill Lindley, *You Have Stepped Out of Your Place: A History of Women and Religion in America* (Louisville, KY: Westminster John Knox Press, 1996), 409.
[13] Joshua Grijalva, *Ethnic Baptist History* (Miami: META, 1992), 51.

the evangelists or the Iowa Baptists could ever have imagined. This story would be multiplied hundreds of times and among numerous tribes.

In the 1950s, attempts were made by the Baptist Convention of Oklahoma to disband the Indian association and assimilate their churches into the Anglo-American Baptist associations. In a demonstration of the fact that becoming Baptist did not mean abdicating Native identity, many Indian Baptist churches refused. In 1959, the Creek-Seminole-Wichita Baptists adopted a statement that declared that their records were "not part of the Baptist General Convention of Oklahoma and were not to be included in its report."[14] Eventually, Anglo-American leaders of the Oklahoma Baptist Convention recognized Native American Baptists' rights as autonomous Baptist bodies and accepted Indian associations on the same terms as non-Indian associations.

In the 1960s, as greater numbers of Native Americans began to reassert their distinctive existence and seek cultural revitalization, the issue of religion began to surface in new ways. For some Native persons, Indian religion could mean only the traditional tribal religions of a people. For others, it was important to somehow incorporate Christian faith into tribal culture. Furthermore, events of the previous three centuries had blurred the traditional boundaries to the point that recovery of a tribe's authentic religious customs proved impossible. In that sense, a broad Indian spirituality emerged for some alongside other expressions of religious faith among Native Americans. Thus, in Indian Baptist life, a complex of attitudes developed regarding how ethnicity and faith should intersect. For some Indian Baptists, being Baptist according to missionary definitions became primary, and elements of culture and faith that had been labeled "pagan" were to be avoided at all costs. Other Indian Baptists saw value in the Christian faith they had embraced but realized that new generations of Native Americans (needing connection with their cultural roots) could not relate to a missionary religion. Consequently, those Baptists searched for ways to embody their Christian faith in the flesh of Indian culture. Traditional Anglo-American Baptists and "assimilated" Indian Baptists tended to see this as heresy.

Diversity of belief has long been part of Native American traditions, together with intertribal and intratribal tensions over these matters. Sometimes open hostilities have erupted as a consequence. In new ways, Indian Baptists face similar struggles today. Managing the identity issues of being both Indian and Baptist has never been easy, but developments in the

---

[14] Ibid., 56.

concluding decades of the twentieth century and opening decade of the twenty-first century have further complicated that struggle. The hope of many Native Baptist leaders is that, with less interference from Anglo-American Baptist authorities, solutions that truly work for those who are Native and Baptist can be found.

Hispanic Baptists   Persons of Spanish-speaking heritage have come to constitute a significant portion of the U.S. population over the course of the twentieth century. In 1950, fewer than 4 million of the 150 million U.S. residents were Hispanic, about 2.5 percent of the population. By 2005, that number had grown to about 43 million of the population of 281 million, or about 14.4 percent. Persons of Hispanic heritage have become not only an important part of the general population but a significant and growing portion of Baptist churches as well. Among the American Baptist Churches in the USA, for example, in 1995 about 2.8 percent of the denomination's membership was Hispanic. In 2005, that number had grown to about 3.5 percent. In 1993, the total number of Hispanic Baptists in the United States was about 108,450 in more than 1,205 congregations. In 2006, that number may have exceeded 550,000 in more than 5,000 congregations. At the beginning of the twenty-first century, the greatest numbers of Hispanic Baptists were concentrated in the states of California, Texas, Florida, and New York.

Baptist ministries among newly arrived Hispanic populations have been challenged by such matters as the "undocumented" status of significant numbers of persons; low levels of education; high mobility; and the disproportionate numbers employed in low-skill, low-wage jobs. This has meant that ministries giving attention to health care, employment, legal concerns, and education along with spiritual support have been very important. Over time, Hispanics tend to experience improvement in income, wealth, and home ownership, ascending to middle- and even upper-class status and looking for a very different type of focus from Baptist ministries.

Hispanic immigration since the 1950s has differed in several important ways from that of many previous immigrant groups. First of all, because large numbers of Hispanic immigrants are undocumented, many concentrate in low-skilled service, agricultural, or production jobs, where they receive low wages and often experience discrimination because they have no legal recourse to challenge the abuses. Also, Hispanic immigration has continued at high levels for longer periods than that of most previous immigrant groups. Consequently, the challenges of integration into the broader culture of the United States are prolonged. In addition, economic conditions in the United States since the mid-1970s have increased demand for skilled labor at the very time that many young Hispanics have arrived with less-than-average educational levels, which has augmented their numbers in low-income sectors of the society. Finally, geographically, Hispanics have scattered more widely across the country than most prior immigrant groups, which complicates traditional social structures in unpredictable ways. These characteristics have meant that the ministries of Hispanics to Hispanics have been essential. At the same time, finding the resources and leaders capable of providing such ministries has been a major challenge for Baptists.[15]

Initiatives taken by Hispanic Baptists to minister among Hispanic peoples are illustrated in the history and work of the Hispanic Baptist Convention of Texas. Growing out of the efforts of several Mexican Baptist churches, the Convención Bautista Mexicana (CBM) was organized in 1910 to "foster fraternal relations among the churches, associations, and other Mexican Baptist bodies of the State, with the object of cooperation in the evangelization and education of the youth and the publication of Christian literature within its territorial limits."[16] In the 1940s, Hispanic Baptists of the CBM began to establish their own institutions, including the Bible Institute of Bastrop, the Mexican Baptist Children's Home, the Valley Baptist Academy, and the Mexican Baptist Bible Institute (MBBI). The MBBI is known today as Hispanic Baptist Theological School, with students from throughout the United States and more than a dozen Latin American countries. In the 1960s, the CBM decided to work cooperatively with an Anglo-American Baptist body, the Baptist General Convention of Texas (BGCT). Besides bringing greater coordination to Baptist work in Texas, the arrangement allowed for the sharing of personnel, resources, and ministries. Since the 1970s, ministries of education, housing, and health care, in addition to evangelism and church planting, have formed an important dimension of the convention's work. In the 1990s, CBM changed its name to the Hispanic Baptist Convention of Texas to acknowledge the fact that there were persons of other Spanish-heritage cultural groups present among its members.[17]

---

[15] Committee on Transforming Our Common Destiny: Hispanics in the United States and National Research Council, *Multiple Origins, Uncertain Destinies: Hispanics and the American Future* (Washington, D.C.: National Academies Press, 2006).

[16] Constitution of the Convención Bautista Mexicana (1910); see William Bricen Miller, "Texas Baptist History" (Th.D. dissertation, Southwestern Baptist Theological Seminary, 1931), Appendix B, 544.

[17] Albert Reyes, "Unification to Integration: A Brief History of the Hispanic Baptist Convention of Texas, *Baptist History and Heritage* 40, no. 1 (Winter 2005): 44–56.

In addition to the work in Texas, Hispanic Baptist congregations exist in practically every state. Most Hispanic Baptist work in the United States is smaller and more informally connected than that of the Hispanic Baptist Convention of Texas. Hispanic Baptists in the American Baptist Churches, USA (ABC-USA), for example, have the National Hispanic Caucus, which connects its membership on issues of mutual concern. Its members have a voice in matters of the denomination through the caucus as well as a structure for advancing work of particular Hispanic concern. The ABC-USA-related Hispanic members have tended to derive primarily from Puerto Rico, Cuba, Mexico, and Nicaragua. Southern Baptists, who also have a large Hispanic membership, have tended to garner more of their members from Mexico and Central and South America.[18]

Asian American Baptists   The Chinese Exclusion Act of 1902 barred Chinese immigration but did not end U.S. needs for cheap labor. Consequently, other Asian groups stepped in to fill the gap, especially Japanese, Korean, and Philippine laborers. As Anglo populations continued to demand restrictions on Asian immigration, local laws were passed institutionalizing racist treatment. For example, in 1906, California outlawed marriages between Anglo-Americans and Asians, and in San Francisco, Japanese and Korean students were ordered to be segregated from Anglo-American students. The resulting San Francisco school incident contributed to a gentleman's agreement between the Japanese and U.S. governments that Japan would restrict Japanese immigration and that the United States would work to prevent discriminatory practices against Japanese people residing in the country. One important outcome of this was the practice of restricting Japanese immigration to family members of those already living in the United States. This transformed the Japanese immigrant community into a family-based community.

Between World War I and the end of World War II, several pieces of legislation were passed with major impact on Asian American communities. The Asiatic Barred Zone Act of 1917 extended the measure of the Chinese Exclusion Act to essentially all Asian peoples from the Middle East, South Asia, and Southeast Asia. The Johnson-Reed Act of 1924 extended the exclusions to all East Asians, Southeast Asians, and South Asians, thereby ending Japanese and Korean immigration. Because the Philippines was a U.S. territory, the previous acts did not include Filipino immigration. As

---

[18] William H. Brackney, "Hispanic Baptists," in *Historical Dictionary of the Baptists* (Toronto: Scarecrow Press, 1999), 209.

a consequence, Filipino immigration grew dramatically during the 1920s and early 1930s. The Tydings-McDuffie Act in 1934 granting independence to the Philippine Islands also abruptly ended Filipino immigration. The most controversial of all anti-Asian legislation was the 1942 Executive Order 9066, which resulted in the internment of about 120,000 Japanese, including 77,000 American-born citizens, along with the seizure of their assets. Considered a wartime necessity by some, the same treatment was not extended to German Americans or to Italian Americans.

Naturally, Asian American Baptists were seriously affected by each of the developments, although the specific effects varied with a particular ethnic group, the time frame, and individual policies. This history, together with cultural characteristics and other factors, combined to produce quite distinctive identities among Baptists of Asian heritage. This is illustrated by the nature of First Chinese Baptist Church's ministries, which fluctuated according to the fortunes of such things as U.S. immigration policies, discrimination, and Anglo-American Baptist attitudes. A few Anglo-American Baptist leaders spoke out against the injustices suffered by this Chinese Baptist community, but many others either ignored the situation or supported the policies of the exclusionists.[19] Consequently, what it means to be Baptists in that context differs from that of the Anglo-American Baptist. Another illustration of unique ministry challenges is found in the history of the Japanese Baptist Church of Seattle. In efforts to meet the needs of different generations of Japanese immigrants, the Japanese Baptist Church included both a Japanese-language and an English-language ministry. During the years of internment, the Japanese pastor Shozo Hashimoto was interned with his members. Pastor Emery Andrews of the English-speaking congregation decided to relocate near the Minidoka Relocation Center in Hunt, Idaho, to continue ministering to his "beloved Japanese."[20] Ethnicity yielded very different consequences in this case, with the result that Japanese American Baptists underwent experiences that shaped them differently from Anglo-American Baptists during the twentieth century. Some Anglo-American Baptists were more understanding than others of the discrimination suffered by Asian Americans, but unique experiences mean that each has come to the Baptist communion today from a different angle of view, with different memories of the past, and with varied theological perspectives that need to be addressed.

---

[19] Lawrence Jay, "Baptist Work among the Chinese in San Francisco (1848–1888): The Early History of the First Chinese Baptist Church," *American Baptist Quarterly* 21, no. 3 (September 2002): 322–36.

[20] Kathleen Yukawa, "One Hundred Years of History of the Japanese Baptist Church of Seattle," *American Baptist Quarterly* 21, no. 3 (September 2002): 315.

In 1965, the Hart-Celler Act changed the nature of Asian immigration to the United States. Whereas earlier Asian immigration had consisted mostly of poor and working-class people, more recent immigration has tended to come from the ranks of the educated and skilled professionals. In many instances, the newer Asian American Baptist has been able to assimilate more easily into Anglo-American Baptist congregations, except for the physical characteristics that differentiate them. Repeated experiences of being stereotyped by ethnicity have led many Asian American Baptists to prefer ethnically identified Baptist churches, in part because there they can maintain cultural identity, find full acceptance, and enjoy social status and position that they generally have not enjoyed in the dominant culture's Baptist churches.

In Baptist life, Asian Americans often find themselves dealing with a combination of three or more syndromes that complicate their identity as Baptists – model minority, middle minority, and forever foreigners.[21] Model minority is the experience of fitting into Anglo-American cultural expectations. The educational, professional, and economic successes experienced by many Asian Americans lead some Anglo-Americans to assume that they are assimilating into traditional Anglo-American cultural norms, thus making them a model minority. Among Baptists, this often translates into model Baptists, as many Asian American Baptists reflect practices that are familiar to and supported by Anglo-American Baptists. This preserves harmony as long as Asian American Baptists remain quiet about areas of experience that do not fit easily into traditionally dominant Baptist interpretations.

Asians as a middle minority reflect the function of serving as a buffer between dominant power holders of American traditions and those minorities on the other side who exercise less voice. This phenomenon of the wider American culture is often reflected in Baptist life as well, causing Asian Americans to feel instrumentalized at times to preserve a buffer that protects traditional powers of dominance.

Finally, the forever-foreigner syndrome identifies the frustration of being judged by physical features, which keeps the Asian American from ever fully assimilating into the dominant culture and consequently from being considered one of "us." These syndromes accentuate the reality that Asian American Baptists have dimensions of identity that differ in important ways from Anglo-American, African American, and Native American experiences and must be voiced along with each of those sets of identities. Asian

---

[21] Tan, *Asian American Theologies*, 37–45.

American Baptists include traditions associated with Japanese American Baptist leaders like Fukumatsu Okazaki, Yoshigoro Akiyama, Yosaburo Nakayama, and Masahiko Wada; with Chinese American Baptist leaders like Dong Gong, Fung Seung Nam, Jitsuo Morikawa, and Lawrence Jay; with Korean American Baptist leaders like Changsoon Kim, Won Yong Kang, John Kun So Park, and Peter T. Cha; and with hosts of Vietnamese American, Indo-Chinese American, Filipino American, and other Baptist leaders.

Baptist Women in America during the Age of Proliferating Traditions

Ratification of the Nineteenth Amendment in 1920 was a milestone for women's rights and a turning point for American society. Although the amendment did not resolve discrimination against women, it opened a new chapter in the struggle. This and several other major developments seriously influenced women's involvement and roles in Baptist life. Advances in science introduced other sources of authority into public life that challenged age-old sociopolitical and religious traditions. Some of the new venues were more open to women's leadership than had been the case with the traditional institutions of American culture. Consequently, growing numbers of women discovered that religious organizations were not their only vehicles for public life. Furthermore, pluralism, greater emphasis on individual choice in religious life, and society's diminished expectation of religious involvement as a requirement for respectability served gradually to siphon off the talents and energies women once offered to the church.

In U.S. Baptist life, the changes tended to meet with two very different kinds of responses. In some circles, a slow but gradual progress toward women's inclusion among the ranks of decision makers and leaders occurred. Access was gained to ordination and to positions as senior pastors, deacons, denominational leaders, and members of significant committees. In other instances, and especially among more conservative Baptist bodies, reactions set in that actually diminished women's freedom to exercise significant leadership among their ranks.

Anglo Baptist Women   In the mid-twentieth century, many denominations began consolidating the independent women's missionary societies into the existing denomination's agencies in ways that were initially detrimental to women's roles of leadership. Elizabeth Miller describes this experience for women in the American Baptist Churches in the USA (ABC-USA) in an article titled "Women in the American Baptist Churches: A Perspective on the Past Thirty Years." In the article, she points out that "the staff of the women's missionary societies was fully involved in the decision-making of the denomination.... [They] were highly participatory in their approach and they encouraged and trained women in local churches."[22] Through the mission societies and their related programs, women helped new immigrants, assisted persons in understanding one another across racial lines, supported and administered hundreds of missionaries across the United States and throughout Asia and Africa, and trained and developed women to lead at all levels of American Baptist life. Their work clearly demonstrated American Baptist women's administrative insights, skills, and effectiveness.

After years of prompting, the boards of the women's foreign and home mission societies agreed to merge their work with the American Baptist Foreign Mission Society and the American Baptist Home Mission Society. Although some women expressed concern over the new arrangement, most anticipated that women would share in the administrative and decision-making processes of the societies and supported the integration. Miller states, however, that women were disappointed in the end. "The societies did not recruit and develop women on their staffs.... They did not identify women with potential and give them an opportunity to gain experience in supervisory positions.... By the end of the 1960s women began to look around and ask, 'Where have all the women gone[?]'"[23]

As American culture changed, the women's mission societies also changed – they worked more cooperatively with other American Baptist mission organizations until 1955, when the boards, staffs, and programs of the women's societies merged with those of the older societies (home and foreign). Long prior to merger talks, however, women leaders of the foreign and home mission societies sought a national forum in which to provide more mission education and to coordinate fund-raising in local churches. In 1921, that desire resulted in representatives from women's home and foreign societies forming the Committee of Conference. This group coordinated educational and fund-raising work with local women's societies, reorganizing in 1937 into the National Committee on Woman's Work (NCWW). The NCWW "gradually enlarged its scope to cover all phases of unified missionary effort among Baptist women."[24]

---

[22] Elizabeth Miller, *Women in the American Baptist Churches: A Perspective on the Past Thirty Years* (New York: Ministers and Missionaries Benefit Board of American Baptist Churches, 1986).
[23] Ibid.
[24] Eleanor Hull, *Women Who Carry the Good News* (Valley Forge, PA: Judson Press, 1975), 84–5.

The group handled the same tasks – coordinating and providing literature distribution and fund-raising among local churches – that after
1951 became the core work of the National Council of American Baptist
Women. When the denomination was restructured in 1972, American
Baptist Women became an independent entity related administratively to
the Board of Educational Ministries. On July 29, 1990, the council's name
was changed to American Baptist Women's Ministries. A sister organization, American Baptist Women in Ministry, was created to serve the
distinctive needs of women in vocational ministry. The two organizations
aimed to promote a full range of women's ministries among ABC-USA
churches and beyond.

American Baptist Churches in the USA began ordaining women as
early as 1882, although the numbers remained very low. By 1920, only
sixteen women had been ordained into ABC-USA ministries. In the 1960s
and 1970s, some ABC-USA women became more vocal in demanding
equal treatment; as a result, the denomination adopted a resolution in
1965 advocating the equality of women and men and the ordination of
women. Still, the autonomous nature of Baptist churches permits national
leadership only to influence, not to dictate, the choice of pastoral leadership
by a local church. By 2005, only 410 women served as pastors, about 10
percent of the denomination's total.

The Southern Baptist Convention (SBC) ordained the first woman in
1964, but it was 1972 before a woman actually served as pastor of an SBC-
affiliated church. By 1986, there were at least 232 ordained SBC women,
although very few were serving as pastors of churches. A major power
struggle in the SBC during the 1980s brought a more fundamentalist leadership to the denomination, with the ordination of women being one of the
divisive issues. In 1984, the SBC's national convention meeting in Kansas
City, Missouri, adopted a resolution that endorsed "the service of women
in all aspects of church life and work other than pastoral functions and
leadership roles entailing ordination."[25] This effectively excluded women
from ordination to pastoral positions. The denomination's Home Mission
Board (today the North American Mission Board) terminated assistance
to mission churches with a woman pastor.

In 2005, 102 women served either as pastors, copastors, or church planters
in churches associated with the Alliance of Baptists, the Baptist General
Association of Virginia (BGAV), the Baptist General Association of Texas
(BGCT), and the Cooperative Baptist Fellowship (CBF). Although this

---

[25] "Southern Baptist Convention Resolution Opposing Ordination of Women," *Annual of the Southern Baptist Convention* (Kansas City, Missouri, 1984): 68–9.

marked progress for women in positions of significant leadership in Baptist life, the percentages still were very low: 22 percent of Alliance Baptist churches, about 5 percent of CBF churches, around 1 percent of BGAV churches, and much less than 1 percent of BGCT churches had female pastors. In other positions of leadership where national Baptist leaders have had more direct influence, the inclusion of women in leadership positions sometimes has been greater. On the governing boards of their national bodies in 2007–8, the Alliance of Baptists had 45 percent women, the BGCT had 24 percent, the CBF had 38 percent, and the SBC had 8 percent.

The Original Free Will Baptists (OFMB) entered the twentieth century with a very open attitude toward the ordination of women as pastors. Between 1780 and 1920, at least seventy women pastored OFWB churches. However, in the 1950s, attitudes began to change, and although no official declaration was made against female ordination, few women were given leadership positions. In 2005, the OFMB's processes for ordination were revised, however, with the stipulation that all potential ministers, regardless of gender, would be given serious consideration for ordained leadership.

The first woman to be ordained by Seventh Day Baptists in the United States was ordained in 1885. Since then, at least fifteen other women have been ordained. In 2005, the Seventh Day Baptists had four women pastors, constituting about 3 percent of their total ministers.[26]

Baptist Women in Ministry (BWIM) was launched in 1964 as an organization among Southern Baptist women to assist and promote women in hearing and responding to God's call to full-time Christian service. As a significant resource of information and support, the BWIM seeks to "draw together women and men, in partnership with God, to illuminate, advocate, and nurture the gifts and graces of women."[27] They preserve and report essential statistical information concerning the state of women in Baptist ministry across the broad spectrum of Baptist denominations in the United States.

Black Baptist Women   Among all Baptists in America in the twentieth century, Black Baptist churches demonstrated the greatest public commitment to systemic community uplift and social reform. Thousands of little-known black women contributed significantly through the organizations that were

---

[26] Eileen R. Campbell-Reed and Pamela R. Durso, *Assessing the State of Women in Baptist Life, 2005* (Atlanta: Baptist Women in Ministry, June 2006), 2–3.

[27] See for example Pam Durso, "Q&A: Baptist Women in Ministry Leader Pam Durso," interview with Associated Baptist Press staff, *Associated Baptist Press*, February 1, 2010, http://www.apbnews.com/content/view/4789/104.

associated with the local church, such as mission societies, educational endeavors, and benevolent activities. But of equal importance was the involvement of black women in organizations not connected to churches. Secular beneficent and similar entities often became attractive to black women because opportunities for leadership in those bodies existed when many black Baptist churches denied them such openings. Some of those women capably and creatively might have filled the ranks of ordained ministry leadership had the possibility existed. Because it did not, they often found other venues for employing their talents.

Nannie Helen Burroughs was one such person. Sometimes called a trailblazer, Burroughs wedded church and career into a ministry that, though not an ordained ministry position, was transformative in American society. In 1900, she was elected to serve as the corresponding secretary of the Women's Convention of the National Baptist Churches, USA. She held that position for more than fifty years. Susan Lindley observes, "Her relationships with male Baptist leaders were seldom submissive and thus frequently stormy, but time after time she could count on the women's financial and moral support."[28] That support enabled her to achieve incredible feats during the century, among the most noted being the founding of the National Training School for Women and Girls in Washington, D.C. From those two platforms, she empowered and guided black women into political action.[29] In *Righteous Discontent*, Evelyn Higginbotham explores Burroughs's contributions in the context of a broader women's movement among black Baptist churches in the late nineteenth and early twentieth centuries.[30]

Black Baptist women have been challenged on two fronts – race and gender. During the first half of the century, the issues of race took precedence over those of gender. Black male ministers often have been content to allow women to remain in the background and serve under their direction but resistant to accepting them as full peers. At the close of the twentieth century, most African American Baptist denominations showed little support for the ordination of women. A Baptist Women in Ministry (BWIM) survey indicated that 57 percent of Progressive National Baptist pastors and 74 percent of National Baptist Convention, USA, Inc., pastors were opposed to the ordination of women for their churches. Official statistics

[28] Lindley, *Women and Religion*, 394.
[29] Dormetria La Sharne Robinson, "Nannie Helen Burroughs: The Trailblazer," *American Baptist Quarterly* 23, no. 2 (June 2004): 155–78.
[30] See Evelyn Brooks Higginbotham, *Righteous Discontent: The Women's Movement in the Black Baptist Church, 1880* (Cambridge, MA: Harvard University Press, 1993).

of the National Baptist Convention of America and the National Baptist Convention, USA, Inc., for the year 1997 indicated that no church within the conventions had a female pastor. At the dawn of the twenty-first century, increasing numbers of black women have begun to voice the gender issue, insisting that full human dignity demands gender as well as racial equal opportunity.

Native Baptist Women   As Native Americans who are Baptist continue their reaffirmation and rediscovery of tribal cultures, women's participation will be essential. Baptist women's engagement in that process will surely vary, and sharp differences will occur. But central to the process will be Baptist women's efforts to ensure the recovery of respect shown for women that existed in traditional tribal culture and the valued roles they filled in religious leadership and ritual in Native Baptist traditions and practices. Selective adaptation has been a characteristic of Native cultures for millennia. How might the images of the Cherokee Corn Mother or the Tewa Pueblo Blue Corn Woman and White Corn Maiden and images of other traditions be used to inform Native cultural identity for women who are Baptist and embrace the biblical values of that tradition?

Nancy Lurie records the story of a Winnebago woman named Mountain Wolf Woman whose life spanned from 1884 to 1960.[31] Mountain Wolf Woman retained traditional Indian customs, including becoming a medicine woman and practicing tribal ceremonies, and she still identified herself as a church member. Somehow she had made the two identities fit. For some observers, the worlds were incompatible, making Mountain Wolf Woman not truly Indian for some interpreters and not truly Christian for others. However, Mountain Wolf Woman had managed to so blend the two identities that when she died, "she was mourned at a traditional Winnebago wake and at a peyote meeting, and was then buried at the mission cemetery after Christian services."[32] Indian women who are Baptist will have distinctive ways to accomplish this but might find in such persons models for relevant faith identity development.

Hispanic Baptist Women   Ada María Isasi-Díaz writes that the guiding criterion for the way Latinas (U.S. women of Hispanic heritage) approach the Bible is need. Latinas struggle for survival, and that reality supplies the lens

---

[31] Nancy Lurie, ed., *Mountain Wolf Woman, Sister of Crashing Thunder: The Autobiography of a Winnebago Indian* (Ann Arbor: University of Michigan Press, 1961).
[32] Lindley, *Women and Religion*, 411.

through which the Bible is read and interpreted.[33] About 30 million people of Hispanic heritage live in the United States, and almost 50 percent of them are women. They come from a wide variety of backgrounds, educational levels, ages, and employment. About half of these women were either born in the United States or to a U.S. citizen, and the other half either immigrated or found their way into the country without documentation. A fact of life for many Hispanic women is the struggle for survival. As a group, Hispanic women have less education than non-Hispanic women, earn less than other women, are more likely to work in low-paying and blue-collar occupations, and are twice as likely to live in poverty. On average, Hispanic women are younger than other women and bear significant domestic and child-rearing responsibilities in addition to subsistence employment. Surviving amid heavy life demands with limited resources is the average Latina's reality. Isasi-Díaz summarizes the accompanying identity issues that Hispanic women face in the following overview:

Society questions our reality, how we understand it and deal with it. Society alienates Latinas and marginalizes us because our cultural values and understandings are different. We are not willing to participate in society on the terms of the dominant culture because those terms are oppressive for us. . . . Anyone, including biblical persons, who has gone through situations similar to ours serves as an encouragement to us to believe in ourselves and our communities. All such persons and examples help us know that we are not imagining things; that though we are often rendered invisible by those who have power, we do not cease to exist.[34]

Stereotyped images of Hispanic male machismo and female *hembrismo* tend to relegate Latinas to a shadow world of invisibility. In that image, men are authoritarian, domineering, violent, and promiscuous. Women are docile and submissive to male authority. Far from reality, this image is often held by non-Hispanic interpreters and creates an identity that Latinas find difficult to overcome in the U.S. public arena. Hedda Garza laments that so little attention has been given to invisible Mexican American women to correct the prevalent racist stereotypes of them.[35]

Among Hispanic Baptists, women have tended to experience many of the same limitations as Native, African American, and Asian American women, but with identity challenges that are distinctive from the Latin

---

[33] Ada María Isasi-Díaz, *Women of God, Women of the People* (St. Louis, MO: Chalice Press, 1995), Introduction. Available online at http://onlinebooks.library.upenn.edu/webbin/book/lookupid?key=olbp40789.

[34] Ibid.   [35] Hedda Garza, *Latinas* (Albuquerque: University of New Mexico Press, 2001), 31.

culture in America. These women have contributed sacrificially to their churches (most often in supporting roles) without much recognition by the larger Baptist community. The names, stories, and contributions of these women in Baptist history are almost impossible to find. One area in which Hispanic Baptist women have been visibly active in Baptist life has been in the missionary support organizations that were the vehicles of ministry for so many Baptist women in the nineteenth and twentieth centuries. The Hispanic Baptist Missionary Union of Texas is illustrative of that work. Yet the majority of Latina Baptists live, work, and contribute in ways that are inadequately publicized. To what role models can young Latina Baptist women look for inspiration and to better their lives? Who will inform them of the benefits that could accompany the investment of life and talents in behalf of the church and larger society? In addition to ethnic, gender, and minority issues, Latina Baptists' identity development must also struggle with reality as "invisible" women.

Asian American Baptist Women   Nikki Toyama describes the Asian Pacific Islander tradition of serving tea. Serving tea is the woman's role, and girls are taught the details of this ritual from an early age: "Stir the pot this way, hold your wrist just so, serve the most important guest first."[36] This act performed in the United States brings together gender, culture, and stereotyped roles in confusing ways that create identity questions and self-doubt. As Toyama and other Asian American Christian women point out, "Misogyny runs deep in Asia," and finding one's identity as a woman in cultures where females are often not valued is a major identity issue for Asian American women. In Confucian culture, for example, women were considered not only inferior but also of a different nature from men. One Confucian saying summarizes the tradition's view of women in the declaration: "A man's talent is considered a virtue; a woman without talent is virtuous." When united with traditional Anglo-American Baptist interpretations of women's roles, the resulting model carries great destructive potential for Asian American Baptist women's self-perception.

Asian women tend to be smaller than most Western women, and therefore experience life differently from others, often in subtle ways that most don't consider – such as using support railings in public transportation

---

[36] Nikki A. Toyama and Tracey Gee, eds., *More Than Serving Tea: Asian American Women on Expectations, Relationships, Leadership, and Faith* (Downers Grove, IL: InterVarsity Press, 2006), 17.

Figure 18. Nannie H. Burroughs, corresponding secretary for the Women's Auxiliary of the National Baptist Convention (photo courtesy of the Library of Congress).

that are too high to reach, shopping in clothing stores that do not have sizes small enough in styles that older women wear, and the like. Perceived flaws of gender and ethnicity are constantly reinforced by the often unvocalized messages communicated everywhere, everyday – even in church

Figure 19. Helen Barrett Montgomery, advocate for women's education, a New Testament translator, president of the Woman's American Baptist Foreign Mission Society, and president of the Northern Baptist Convention (courtesy of American Baptist Historical Society, Valley Forge, Pennsylvania).

life. Being woman, Asian, American, and Baptist when combined create identity issues that Asian American Baptist women must address uniquely and that require awareness from other Baptists, who could help best by listening and learning.

Although Asian American Baptist women have contributed to their churches, communities, and denominations in sacrificial and transformative ways, Baptist history often fails to recognize their important contributions. Consequently, these women suffer gender stereotypes that limit their leadership opportunities, a lack of role models that can inspire and empower, and self-doubt generated by cultural and church traditions that devalue their contributions. Much work is needed to bring into historical focus the contributions of women like Yoshiko Mizukami, Yoshi Okazaki, Sumi Okazaki Kashiwagi, Hoshiko Yabuki, Carolyn Yabuki Shimabukuro, and countless other women of the many Asian American cultures represented in Baptist life whose achievements should be added to the ranks of those whose traditions unite to make the global family of Baptists both what it is and what it could become.

CONCLUSIONS

The world of North American Baptists changed significantly during the twentieth century. The many innovations not only transformed the cultural context of the dominant Anglo Baptist communions but also altered the communions themselves in significant ways. Immigration changed the context of Baptist ministries and transformed the composition of Baptists themselves. As long as cultural diversity was marginal, the dominant Baptist culture's identity could remain intact and assimilationist philosophies of ministry could continue. But as the amount and degree of diversity grew, the pressures for recognizing new traditioning sources escalated.

This chapter has attempted not only to present indicators of the diverse traditioning sources that have been at work in North American Baptist life throughout this period but also to expose gaps where serious historical research and interpretation needs to be undertaken. The voices of these new traditioning sources must be admitted into the processes of decision making that shape public understanding of who and what North American Baptists are in the twenty-first century.

GLOBAL OVERVIEW OF BAPTISTS AT THE CLOSE OF THE AGE OF PROLIFERATING TRADITIONING SOURCES

The Baptist movement is regarded by many as geographically North American and European and culturally as Anglo. Although sheer numbers still support that impression, trends suggest that a very different reality is emerging. At the beginning of this period, Anglo and Anglo-American cultural definitions were still dominant in Baptist life. Exceptions existed, but the full impact of non-Anglo primal sources in Baptist life still had gained very little notice and were mostly viewed as corrupted expressions of forms more perfectly portrayed in male-dominated Anglo Baptist churches. Most descriptions of Baptists reflected a patriarchal and Anglo culturally shaped theological intentionality for the source of such coherence as the movement was thought to have possessed. By the close of the period, however, that situation was showing clear signs of change. Baptist identity was starting to lose some of its traditionally Western, Anglo, and male character as believers from many cultural contexts, ethnic perspectives, and women received its message and translated it into modes that fit their worldviews and met their spiritual needs.

What Allan Anderson has observed of Protestantism in general is also true of Baptists in particular: any discussion of globalization of the Baptist movement must also consider the "'localization' of indigenous and independent forms" of Baptist identity.[37] The greatest new growth among Baptists today is occurring in developing countries, and the global Baptist movement is being immensely affected by several major elements, including popular reactions against any religious forms perceived as colonial in nature, the rise of sometimes-militant expressions of national identity, and a growing desire for more contextually and culturally relevant forms of Baptist expression. Collectively, this means that the already-complex Anglo Baptist body of interpretive tradition continues to become far more complex in its traditioning sources, which creates possible new fault lines of identity and connection.

In Africa, as in Asia, Latin America, Eurasia, and Oceania, Anglo and Anglo-American Baptist missionary effort cannot be dismissed for its importance in introducing Baptist beliefs and practices into the regions. The stories of the often-heroic and sacrificial endeavors by missionaries merit an important place in Baptist annals of history. But missionaries were not the only Baptists who made heroic sacrifices, and ultimately it was the work of African Baptists and indigenous revivals that were most responsible for the Baptist growth that occurred there. As the century progressed, African Baptist churches often incorporated more popular culture into their worship, including African symbols, rhythms, and oratory. The more successful churches have given greater opportunities to women and youths than the more traditional patriarchal and elder-oriented ones. Yet tensions often surface between Baptist constituencies that desire to make their churches more African in character and those reluctant to change Western traditions.

Many similar forces are seen at work within Baptist life in Asia. Despite the initial and continued roles of missionaries in many Asian contexts, wherever local Baptists have failed to lead the way in developing the work beyond its initial introduction, the Baptist movement has remained weak and "foreign." Even in societies where Baptists possess a great deal of continuity with Western, Anglo traditions, the Baptist movement has taken on a distinctive form that has creatively and selectively transformed foreign

[37] Allan Anderson, "The Future of Protestantism: The Non-Western Protestant World," in *The Blackwell Companion to Protestantism* (Oxford, U.K.: Blackwell, 2007), 470.

symbols into forms that fit local worldviews. South Korean Baptists provide good examples of this.

At the beginning of this period, Latin America was predominantly Catholic. Often seen popularly as representative of colonial oppression, many reacted against the Catholic faith. Baptists often experienced their initial growth in Latin America in the wake of that reaction. As a consequence of initially developing in that environment, Baptist identity during much of the twentieth century was heavily shaped as an anti-Catholic movement. Míguez Bonino provides a description of Protestantism in Latin America that offers insight into the Baptist movement there as well. He speaks of three faces of Latin American Protestantism – the liberal face, the evangelical face, and the Pentecostal face.[38] The first face reflects the concerns of an older, ecumenical Protestantism with the kinds of concerns expressed by liberation theology. The second face reflects the Pietistic, often premillennial, and fundamentalist focus of evangelical Christianity. The third face reflects the otherworldly, spiritual focus of Pentecostalism. To some degree, each of these elements can find expression among Latin American Baptists, although the second face is probably the most recognized one. For the most part, Baptists in Latin America tend to be both politically and theologically conservative, but they seriously value theological education and give major energies and resources to developing educational programs accessible to church leaders. Clearly, the Pentecostal movement has exerted an influence on Baptist life in worship styles, music, and concepts of spirituality. Because Baptists have tended to come from the lower and working classes, the concerns of liberation theology have also been matters of interest for Baptists as well.

Anglo and Anglo-American Baptists often find themselves struggling in a rapidly changing world that asks hard questions and makes increasing demands. Their distinct voices and institutions of authority of the past do not command the same attention today, leading some to despair at the signs of aging and obsolesce. Yet Anglo Baptists have much to offer the world, but not in the same manner as in the past. Paternalistic patterns of relating and witnessing must yield to more egalitarian and partnering patterns. A postcolonial world means that power, authority, decision making, and identity must be shared. In secular cultures where Baptists often find themselves less appreciated than might have been the case a century

---

[38] Míguez Bonino, *Faces of Latin American Protestantism* (Grand Rapids, MI: William Eerdmans Publishing, 1997).

ago, they need the encouragement, witness, and insight of Baptists of all ethnicities, genders, nationalities, cultures, and life conditions.

During the eighteenth and nineteenth centuries, Baptist women came to be acknowledged as spiritual leaders through their work in voluntary societies associated with the church. Their feminine piety came to be valued as essential for the church's well-being. However, feminine piety could be properly cultivated only when women kept their proper place. Twentieth-century wars required that Baptist women as well as others took up a different place in the public workforce. But after the wars, Baptist churches generally pressed for women to return to the domestic sphere and interpret themselves primarily as wives and mothers. That expectation did not fit the realities of life for many women, nor could it adequately allow for individual need for creative expression and pursuit of interests. This has led to struggles among many twentieth-century Baptists in quest of theological understandings that allow women fuller participation. Some Baptists have responded by closing the circle more tightly against possibilities of female empowerment and leadership. Others have inched their way toward fuller inclusion, often amid condemnation and misunderstanding. Baptists will continue to be challenged to rethink deeply entrenched notions of theological anthropology that privilege some and deprive others.

The Baptist movement began in Britain, spread to and was shaped significantly by experiences in North America, and then dispersed throughout the globe from both centers. Baptists' growing edge today is found in other continents, and the diversity and spirituality of the movement in those contexts should be recognized and valued. As Baptists deepen their roots in the multitudes of world cultures, the rich variety of interpretative traditions already evident will continue to multiply, thus accommodating the need for contextually relevant expressions of Baptist belief and practice in each local situation. Baptists globally need to grow in their awareness of and appreciation for this diversity amid commonalities. One of the most recognized needs among global Baptist communities is for theologically trained leaders. Yet the stream of religious education cannot be a one-way flow. Western seminaries and schools of theology tend to be built around the cultural and theological assumptions of the entities that founded them, often infected with underlying attitudes of a colonialist and paternalist past. The same is true of many other Western educational institutions. The need exists for a theological education that is responsive to local contexts and does not blindly imitate the methodologies, content, and agendas of past models.

One of the strengths of Baptists has been their ability to adapt to local contexts through their autonomous churches and institutions that allow for differentiation without hierarchical controls. Their weakness has often been found in the bitter rejections, denunciations, and refusal to form cooperative relations with those who are different. In light of the developments outlined in the chapters of Part IV, Baptists seem to be positioned at a strategic juncture that requires wise decisions. The path that is chosen will likely determine the movement's relevance to many who are on the edge of identity formation. Are the prevalent systems of interpretative intentionality capable of hearing the voices of those who differ? Will the voices of primal traditions have the skills and patience to work out the tensions bound up in the varied elements of their struggles for identity as Baptists? The future of the movement may well rest in that balance.

PART V

Beliefs and Practices

In many cases, people just need to experience a woman pastor. Lack of experience tends to reaffirm previously held notions and opinions on the topic. I have had church members tell me "I did not vote for you when the vote was taken, but I would vote for you now." They just needed a chance to see it, hear it, and experience it. When the myths are dispelled, people are able to see that I am just a person who has been equipped and called by God to be a pastor – and I happen to be female.

Traci Bunn Powers
Portsmouth, Virginia, 2008

A BAPTIST PROFILE

In 1893, Helen Barrett Montgomery joined Susan B. Anthony in sharing a dream for bettering the conditions faced by multitudes of women in her day. That year she formed a chapter of the Woman's Educational Union (WEIU) in Rochester, New York, dedicated to serving poor women and children. An advocate for women's education, she became the first woman elected to any public office in Rochester, serving on the Rochester School Board for ten years. She advocated for creation of kindergartens, vocational training in schools, and health education. She also raised funds to enable women to study at the University of Rochester and to assist missionaries in starting Christian colleges for women in other countries where none existed.

Montgomery's interests in social reform, education, and improving opportunities for women and children prompted her to become the first woman to translate the New Testament from Greek into English and have it published by a publishing house. Drawing on her background as a student of Greek, she completed the Centenary Translation of the New Testament to make it plain for average readers, most of whom could not understand the standard King James Version.[1] The translation was published by the American Baptist Publication Society in 1924. Among the distinguishing features of her translation was the inclusion of section titles to aid the reader in following the subject matter treated by the ensuing verses. She

---

[1] Helen B. Montgomery, "Introduction," *Centenary Translation of the New Testament*, trans. Helen Barrett Montgomery (Philadelphia: American Baptist Publication Society, 1924), Introduction.

also interpreted some of the passages she translated in ways that enlarged the roles of women in the church.

Montgomery was in significant ways at the forefront of Baptist women who dreamed of a better day for women in Baptist life and in the larger society. Although she was never ordained, she was licensed to preach by Lake Avenue Baptist Church of Rochester, New York, in 1892. She served as president of the Woman's American Baptist Foreign Mission Society for ten years, wrote several books preserving and advancing the work of women missionaries, was president of the National Federation of Women's Boards of Foreign Missions, and was elected president of the Northern Baptist Convention (today American Baptist Churches in the USA) in 1921. Her vision, courage, ability, and achievements inspired generations of Baptist women to become more than their social contexts told them they could be. Expanding the frontiers of what it means to be Baptist, Helen Barrett Montgomery pointed toward a future in which gender alone would not define the limits of what a person could become.

CHAPTER 9

Baptists' Beliefs and Practices

Helen Barrett Montgomery shared numerous core values and beliefs with many other Baptists of her day. She shared their belief that the Bible was an authoritative revelation of God's truth, faith in Jesus as the Christ and her Savior and spiritual guide through life, confidence in the mission and methods of Baptist churches for engaging God's work in the world, and conviction that God calls faithful believers to act on those beliefs by living sacrificially for the sake of persons in need. The same convictions that united her with many fellow Baptists also distinguished her from some other Baptists and even alienated her from still others. Her belief in the Bible's superior authority would not allow her to elevate any human authority above that of Scripture. She was convinced that the Bible, when properly understood, gave women the same human freedom of being as men, and therefore the full potential for participation, decision making, and leadership. Some Baptists viewed her as a woman who had stepped out of her place. For them, Montgomery's beliefs and actions were unbecoming of feminine piety, and therefore certainly not biblical or Baptist. However, Baptist ecclesiology gave them no power to silence her or to exclude her from the Baptist fold. Purveyors of a particular theological intentionality could use their influence to convince their particular Baptist communities to exclude her and keep her from speaking at their gatherings, but other Baptist communities were free to give her a public voice and advocate her views as authentically biblical and Baptist.

Helen Barrett Montgomery illustrates the challenge of declaring almost any statement of belief and practice as *the* Baptist position. Statements can be associated with particular communities of Baptists at specific times in history, but almost every statement would either be challenged by or nuanced differently by some other body of Baptists. The best we can do is talk about certain tendencies in Baptist belief and polity. But, although Baptists are usually people of strong faith convictions, they are also adamantly insistent that no other authority or spokesperson preempt their own consciences. When elevated to a global scale, responsible freedom of conscience exercised in Christian community and informed through personal relationship with God by faith in Christ through the illumining power of the Holy Spirit and guided by the Bible's revelation would be the closest statement possible of what Baptists believe. This chapter seeks to offer intelligent discourse on what that means.

BELIEFS AND PRACTICES: A GLOBAL OVERVIEW

As has been observed throughout this book, the Baptist movement constitutes a loosely connected fellowship of Baptists whose histories, interpretations, cultural backgrounds, and contexts differ in significant ways. This means that even commonly stated beliefs and practices are not always understood the same way in differing contexts. Frederick Downs illustrated this with his observation that Baptists in Northeast India are organized into structures that on the surface resemble those of Western Baptist associations but in reality have been adapted to the local contexts.[1] In the past, many culture-related differences could be ignored simply because geographical distances and Euro-American cultural dominance allowed interpretative distinctions to be subsumed under the metanarratives that seemed to substantiate Anglo Baptist definitions. Postcolonial realities challenge such approaches. The views, concerns, interpretations, and experiences of specific Baptist communities seek to exercise shaping voices in defining Baptist beliefs, practices, and identity. What has thus far been shaped by a largely Western, Anglo, and male Baptist population will continue to be reshaped in the twenty-first century and beyond as new hands help mold the images identifying who and what Baptists are.

The Bible and Confessions of Faith

Baptist tradition places the Bible as the centerpiece of authority in matters of faith and practice for the believer. Several other elements such as personal experience, the insights of a believing community, the wisdom of religious tradition, the mystical intuitions of spiritual illumination, and the sagacity of enlightened reason all have a place in Baptists' discerning processes, but the Bible as the reliable and true record of God's revelation is held to be the

---

[1] Frederick S. Downs, "Northeast India (Assam and Neighboring States)," in Albert W. Wardin, ed., *Baptists around the World* (Nashville, TN: Broadman & Holman Publishers, 1995), 136.

believer's single best guide for knowing and doing God's will. The central witness of the Bible is to Jesus as the Christ who Baptists believe is the living Word (the One who embodies and imparts God's being through human personality). As a tangible agent that leads the believer to Jesus Christ, the Bible is often spoken of as the word of God. In this sense, Baptists speak of the Bible as being inspired, although the larger family of Baptists does not have a common view of how that inspiration is to be understood. Some Baptist communions insist on belief in a particular method of inspiration, but most do not. In general, however, Baptists regard the biblical revelation as being a sufficient record of God's revelation, to the point that all teaching and practice must be in harmony with the Scriptures.

Baptists' general agreement on the Bible's revelatory sufficiency does not ensure singularity of views on the many issues they confront. Wide differences can and usually do exist among Baptists on any given issue because of differences in how the Bible should be interpreted relative to each one. Although Baptists usually value the insight and guidance of qualified ministers, teachers, and scholars, no human authority is considered adequate to interpret the Bible dogmatically for any other believer. Therefore, Baptists have historically invested heavily in educational efforts that would assist each person in her or his efforts to interpret the Scriptures responsibly.

Baptists do not have a common creed that specifies what each adherent must believe and practice, and often Baptists are very resistant to any such effort. Part of the reason for this resides in Anglo Baptist roots as dissenters from a state church system that required subscription to legislated doctrinal statements. Early Baptists were convinced that such requirements were hindrances to authentic biblical faith, because genuine faith was believed to be a matter of individual conviction formed out of personal relationship with God. The Bible was the sole and ultimate authority for truth, so no creedal statement could be allowed a level of importance equal to that of the Scriptures. However, throughout their history, many Baptists have created and sometimes adopted confessions of faith as official expressions of their particular communions' agreed-on standards for the matters treated by that statement. Some Baptist bodies have used these confessions in a creedal fashion, treating them as declarations to which adherents must subscribe to be held in good standing with that communion. Other Baptists have used such confessions more loosely as expressions of general belief but not binding on the conscience of any individual believer. Still other Baptists have rejected any confessional statement, holding that the Bible alone is a sufficient foundation for the beliefs and practices of believers.[2] A few other Baptists have produced confessions because they were required to do so by political authorities (e.g., some Scandinavian Lutheran countries). In an effort to nuance the distinction Baptists have traditionally made between creeds and confessions, Leon McBeth has suggested that a creed "prescribes what members must believe" and a confession "affirms what a group of Baptists, large or small, believes at any given time and place."[3] Although some have found that distinction to be helpful, others have felt that it only begs the question. In any case, this differentiation is often a very sensitive issue for Baptists.

God and Salvation

Beliefs about God, humanity, the Bible, and salvation constitute the starting point for Baptist theology. Concepts as diverse as the church, civil government, individual freedoms, and how to relate with persons holding significantly different views ultimately are shaped on the anvil of Baptist beliefs about humanity's basic dilemma and how to resolve it. Historically, most Baptists have accepted classic Trinitarian definitions of God's nature, where God is understood as being the originator of all created being. Originally in perfect harmony with God, the creation, and humanity in particular, lost that harmony through willful disobedience. The overarching purpose of human history, therefore, is the restoration of harmonious relationship between human beings and God, which will ultimately culminate in God's perfect reign over all that exists. Basic to this theological system is the belief that human beings will experience different eternal states on the basis of their status with God during life.

Often referred to as salvation, most Baptists believe that harmonious relationship with God is possible through a process of regeneration (experiencing a transformation of life) by faith in Jesus as God's agent of reconciliation (restored relationship). Baptists have differed, however, in their understanding of how that restoration is effected. Particular atonement Baptists embrace a more Calvinistic view that emphasizes God's sovereign election – meaning that God has already determined who will and will not be restored to harmonious relationship. Regeneration, therefore, is totally dependent on God's unearned and prevenient grace. The human recipient

---

[2] For examples of Baptist uses of confession of faith, see Albert W. Wardin, "Baptist Confessions: Use and Abuse," *American Baptist Quarterly* 21, no. 4 (December 2002): 468–83.

[3] H. Leon McBeth, *The Baptist Heritage: Four Centuries of Baptist Witness* (Nashville, TN: Broadman & Holman Publishers, 1987), 66–7.

is merely a passive receiver of God's reconciling work. These Baptists believe that Jesus' atoning work was accomplished only for the elect (those previously chosen by God). The outcome is already decided. General atonement Baptists embrace a more Arminian view that emphasizes the importance of human choice. They believe that God's work of reconciliation through Jesus, the Christ, offers hope for any human being willing to accept the regeneration God offers. Proclamation of the Bible's message about salvation helps persons understand the reconciliation God is offering all people and gives them opportunities to experience a transformed life now and harmonious relationship with God for eternity. Baptists generally believe not that death ends a person's existence but that life continues in a spiritual dimension forever. These convictions are powerful motivators for evangelism and missionary endeavors. Having experienced a transformed life for themselves, many Baptists believe that God intends them to offer the same possibility to other people. Consequently, what some non-Baptists experience as being an obtrusive proselytism, most Baptists perceive as caring actions borne of a deep concern for other people's eternal well-being.

For Anglo and Anglo-American Baptists, this soteriological formulation has a strongly individualistic and otherworldly focus. In the early twentieth century, the Social Gospel movement associated with the Baptist theologian Walter Rauschenbusch attempted to awaken corporate and this-worldly dimensions of biblical teaching on salvation, but many Baptists reacted against that theology and denounced it as compromising the spiritual nature of regeneration. For some other Baptists, however, God's deliverance from the oppressive forces of this life is equally emphasized along with the future spiritual liberation. Both African American and Native American Baptist formulations of soteriology have reflected this. It is also emerging as an important element of soteriology for at least some African Baptists. David Tonghou Nong, a Cameroonian Baptist theologian, explains:

We must understand the triune God, creation, and humanity in terms of the salvific relationship that the triune God set in motion. . . . The acid test for faithful Christian theological reflection will not be faithfulness to received dogma but whether it has served the soteriological purpose. This method holds that the closest we can come to knowing how God wants us to act in a particular situation is how God has already acted in God's eternal movement to give life to humanity and the rest of creation. This is the only way we can participate with God in God's life-giving activity to promote the attainment of meaningful life for humanity and the rest of creation. This means that Christian mission and evangelism will not so much be based on asserting the *a priori* superiority of Christian religion and mouthing lifeless doctrinal positions (as has often been the case) but it must actually be seen promoting the soteriological function of the faith.... The soteriological contribution of the faith must be susceptible to assessment in order to verify whether what is said is what is happening so that salvation should not remain a fabulous ghost.[4]

Since the mid-eighteenth century, most Baptists have tended away from doctrinal positions heavily focused on God's election and have given greater emphasis to human choice. However, after having chosen salvation, Baptists have tended to support the concept of the eternal security of the believer. This means that a person who accepts God's offer of regeneration enters into a relationship with God that is so transformative that the individual can never lose that state of relatedness. Not all Baptists agree with this view. General and Free Will Baptists especially disagree, holding that a person always has the freedom to choose unity with or alienation from God. Baptists in tribal contexts often have found the whole concept of individualistic-focused processes of choice to be confusing. A realistic theology of salvation in those Baptist communities might look quite different from anything discussed here.

Beliefs about soteriology form the basis for Baptists' convictions regarding the church. Originating in the context of a state church tradition, Baptists insisted that Christian faith had to be a matter of individual choice, not legislative action. Consequently, a biblical church could never consist of all the people living in a geographic area, but only those who responded to the presentation of God's offer of salvation through choosing to believe in Jesus as the Christ and being baptized as a proclamation of that choice. This is what Baptists mean by "believer's church" and "believer's baptism." They understand the church to be a fellowship of believers united through their faith in Jesus as the Christ. In theory, this means the church is a fellowship of regenerate persons (those who have experienced a transformation of life through faith in God). In reality, Baptists have had to acknowledge that creating such a church is unlikely in this world. Consequently, they sometimes have employed the Reformed concepts of a visible church and an invisible church to distinguish the actual historical institution (which is subject to imperfections and failure) and the company of those truly regenerate (who constitute the people of God and might be found in any and all ecclesiastical bodies and possibly even outside them). Landmark Baptist theologies tend to place much greater emphasis on the visible aspects of the Baptist church, whereas more ecumenically minded Baptists value Baptist

---

[4] David Tonghou Nong, "God's Will Can Actually Be Done on Earth: Salvation in African Theology," *American Baptist Quarterly* 23, no. 4 (December 2004): 374.

forms and traditions while acknowledging the biblical legitimacy of other ecclesiastical forms and traditions.

The Church Ordinances

Historically, most Baptists have regarded two acts of the church as holding special status – baptism and the Lord's Supper. Again, derived from their early context, Anglo Baptists thought that many people viewed the sacraments of the state churches in a superstitious fashion, as somehow conveying a "magical" power that operated apart from faith. Rejecting such notions, early Baptists defined those special acts as ordinances, meaning that they possess symbolic value as expressions of and aids to faith but possess no operative power in and of themselves. However, not all Baptists agree with that interpretation. Especially in British Baptist life, a sacramentalist theology exists among some Baptists who assert that baptism and the Lord's Supper should not be interpreted as "magic" but should be understood as more than "mere symbols." Baptist sacramentalism holds that the two acts, when correctly observed, embody God's promises to humanity in a special and mysterious fashion that unites symbol and the thing symbolized in ways that should not be trivialized as simply "symbolic."[5]

Baptism

Baptism has historically been one of the most controversial aspects of Baptist doctrine, and two distinctives of Baptist belief about this act have generated most of the discussion – who should be baptized and how. From their beginning, Baptists have argued strongly that baptism should be administered only to persons who are capable of making conscious and willful commitments of faith in Jesus as redeemer (divine agent for restoring harmonious relationship of the individual and God) and testify to a conversion experience (a process of entering into a state of harmonious relationship with God through trusting in Jesus' power to reconcile or justify). Persons able to offer evidence of a transformed life based on that faith experience are candidates for baptism, which Baptists have traditionally identified as believer's baptism. Baptists do not practice infant baptism for several reasons. First, because baptism is understood as a symbolic act rather than a sacrament that communicates some benefit to the

[5] For fuller details of this theological position, see Anthony R. Cross and Philip E. Thompson, eds., *Baptist Sacramentalism* (Bletchley, U.K.: Paternoster, 2003); Stanley K. Fowler, *More Than a Symbol* (Bletchley, U.K.: Paternoster, 2002).

recipient, Baptists have historically held that the rite has no benefit for the infant. Infant children are often dedicated, which means that special prayer is offered for the child and parents, and the faith community covenants to assist in guiding the child's development into a physically, mentally, socially, and spiritually healthy adult, but no baptism is performed. Only after a child matures sufficiently to perceive alienation from God and the need for reconciliation, experiences spiritual transformation through faith, and then seeks baptism as expression of that experience and commitment is she or he baptized. Most Baptist churches in the West do not connect this with a specific age. However, among Baptists in the Commonwealth of Independent States, a person must be at least fourteen years old before being considered for baptism. This practice may derive from communist prohibitions against religious education of children and youths.

As these descriptions suggest, most Baptists view the essence of salvation to reside in the faith of the believer, which opens the possibility for God's reconciling activity, not in the baptismal act itself. Therefore, although baptism is considered an important act of faith that the regenerate believer should seek, it is not an essential act for experiencing God's reconciling activity. Therefore, most Baptists hold that a child who dies prior to achieving consciousness of alienation from God and the need for reconciling faith (called the age of accountability), and thus not having received baptism, is accepted by God in a special state of grace. In the seventeenth century, some strongly Calvinist-oriented Baptists argued that only the elect, whether adult or infant, are "regenerated and saved by Christ through the Spirit," and that their salvation is assured even if they "are incapable of being outwardly called by the Ministry of the Word." "Others not elected... neither can nor will truly come to Christ; and therefore cannot be saved."[6] A few Baptists adhere to this doctrine in the twenty-first century, although most do not. Most Baptist confessions of faith do not address the question of unbaptized infants at all. An exception is found among English General Baptists, who issued *A Brief Confession or Declaration of Faith* in 1660, a confession also used by Free Will Baptists in the United States. Article 10 explains:

All children dying in infancy, having not actually transgressed against the Law of God in their own persons, are only subject to the first death, which comes upon them by the sin of the first Adam, from whence they shall be all raised by the second Adam; and not that any one of them (dying in that estate) shall suffer for Adam's sin, eternal punishment in Hell (which is the second death) for of such

---

[6] *Second London Confession of Faith*, chapter 10, sections 3–4.

belongs the Kingdom of Heaven . . . not daring to conclude with that uncharitable opinion of others, who, though they plead much for the bringing of children into the visible church here on earth by baptism, yet nevertheless by their doctrine that Christ died for some, shut a great part of them out of the Kingdom of Heaven forever.[7]

The earliest Baptists did not immerse (baptize by putting the candidate's entire body under the water) but poured water over the recipient's head. By the 1640s, however, most had adopted immersion as the correct method of baptism, and subsequently, the manner of baptism became a serious issue for most Baptists. The *First London Confession of Faith* from 1644 states that "the dispensing of this Ordinance the Scripture holds out to be dipping or plunging the whole body under water."[8] Although this confession did not speak for all Baptists, all known Baptists were adhering to this practice by the mid-seventeenth century. The practice took on increased significance in the nineteenth century, when the Landmark Baptist movement made this a distinguishing mark of the only true church. As a consequence, baptisms administered by any other denomination, even if by immersion (called alien immersion), were not considered true baptisms. This meant that persons seeking membership in a Landmark-oriented Baptist church had to be rebaptized before being accepted. In many cases, even baptisms performed by non-Landmark Baptists were not acceptable. Many, but not all, churches of the Southern Baptist Convention also were influenced by this theology and embraced variations of this view of baptism.

Ecumenical conversations induced some Baptists to give serious consideration to how their theology of baptism related to that of other Christians. They acknowledged that refusal to accept any other form of baptism administered by another Christian denomination based on its traditions was tantamount to declaring that its members had not been baptized. The *Baptism, Eucharist, and Ministry* (BEM) document of the Faith and Order Commission or the World Council of Churches advanced this discussion by acknowledging that salvation is a process. Some view baptism as the beginning of that process (infant baptism) and confirmation as the individual's acceptance of the faith on a personal basis. For Baptists, baptism

---

[7] See J. Matthew Pinson, *A Free Will Baptist Handbook: Heritage, Beliefs, and Ministries* (Nashville, TN: Randall House Publications, 1998), 135. Also see *A Treatise of the Faith and Practices of the Original Free Will Baptists* (adopted by the National Association of Free Will Baptists, November 7, 1935), article 6, paragraph 3, available in Pinson, *Free Will Baptist Handbook*, 149–212.

[8] *The Confession of Faith, of those Churches which are commonly (though falsly* [sic] *called Anabaptists* (London: Matthew Simmons, Printer, 1644), article XL, available in William L. Lumpkin, *Baptist Confession of Faith* (Valley Forge, PA: Judson Press, 1959), 167.

marks a faith commitment, but clearly there were processes that preceded this commitment and growth in faith that continued afterward. The BEM states, "When one who can answer for himself or herself is baptized, a personal confession of faith will be an integral part of the baptismal service. When an infant is baptized, the personal response will be offered at a later moment in life. In both cases, the baptized person will have to grow in the understanding of faith."[9]

The theological concern for these Baptists has been to express their convictions that believer's baptism by immersion is their understanding of New Testament practice while acknowledging the possibility that other legitimate interpretations and traditions are possible. Furthermore, these Baptists have not wanted to trivialize baptism by forcing potential members to undergo a rite for church membership that loses the connection to its biblical purpose. Some Baptists have chosen to address this difference by focusing on the faith of the individual believer. In such cases, Baptist churches that practice open membership are willing to receive persons from other denominational communions who might not practice believer's baptism by immersion as long as that person's understanding of baptism and confirmation represents a sincere commitment to Christ. However, many Baptist churches refuse to grant such recognition and insist on believer's baptism by immersion as an absolute prerequisite for church membership.

The Lord's Supper

Traditionally, most Baptists have understood the Lord's Supper as being a memorial meal, celebrated as a reminder of the abiding need to remember and reflect on the reconciling work that Christ accomplished on behalf of the believer. As with baptism, this act of worship has generated tension at two points – who should be included and how often should it be celebrated. Since the seventeenth century, some Baptists have insisted that the Lord's Supper should be shared only among those persons who have received believer's baptism by immersion. This position is referred to as closed communion. For these Baptists, communion became closely associated with church discipline, and only persons in good standing with their local church were allowed to participate. In contrast, other Baptists viewed the Lord's Supper as an aid to faith and an observance intended for all believers. For them, all persons who consider themselves true believers in Jesus Christ regardless of their Christian communion should be allowed to share in the

---

[9] *Baptism, Eucharist, and Ministry*, Faith and Order Paper No. 111 (Geneva: World Council of Churches, 1982), 4.

meal. This belief became known as open communion. Today, most Western Baptist churches practice open communion, although significant enclaves of Baptists do not – especially those of Landmark convictions. Globally, Baptists vary widely on this practice, with those outside Europe and North America tending to be more restrictive regarding who is invited to join in the local church's communion observance.

The earliest Baptists probably celebrated the Lord's Supper weekly. Over time, however, most Baptists rejected this practice, believing that too-frequent observance diminished the significance of the celebration for the believer. Today, the frequency of observance varies widely. Many Baptists celebrate communion monthly, some only every three months (quarterly), and a very few only annually. In the Baptist tradition, spiritual spontaneity has been highly valued and anything suggestive of routine or ritual has been resisted as characteristic of dead religion. Because preaching has been considered the high point of worship, communion has had a different meaning for Baptists than for those traditions in which it has been the focus of worship. By the end of the twentieth century, however, a few Baptists had begun seriously to reconsider the role of visual, symbolic, and ritualistic practices in worship. For some Baptists, the Lord's Supper was coming to be seen as a visual proclamation of the gospel message and therefore an important part of weekly worship.

Church-State Relations

Anglo and Anglo-American Baptists have a strong tradition supporting the concept of keeping church and government separated. Often considered a hallmark of Baptist identity, this tradition is most intelligible within the history of Baptists' struggles against established churches and within the Anglo cultural context. Outside that context, appropriate and inappropriate boundaries between government and Baptist churches is often more clouded. Baptist views about church-state relations derive from their concept of the nature of an individual's relationship with God. Believing that the relationship must always derive from a personal response to God's offer of salvation, they insist that the conscience must remain uncoerced. Legislation that seeks to privilege a particular church or set of beliefs is viewed as harmful to all true religion because it necessarily inhibits the consciences of some citizens. Therefore, Baptists have insisted that affairs of the church and those of civil government should remain distinct. In theory, this has meant that in the Baptist view no religion should be allowed to dictate its convictions on the rest of society through legislative acts, and no government should be permitted to use religious institutions as a means to enforce particular theological preferences. During the twentieth century, various developments among the global family of Baptists complicated their perspectives regarding applications of this doctrine. One such situation arose among Baptists in the Soviet Union. In 1944, the Soviet government allowed Baptists and Evangelical Christians to organize the All-Union Council of Evangelical Christians-Baptists. This council was intended to serve as a coordinating body for all churches in the Soviet Union that practiced believer's baptism. Only churches affiliated with the council could be registered with the government and thereby operate legally. In 1960, Nikita Khrushchev's administration forced the council to adopt statutes that limited the evangelistic activities of All-Union churches. Caught between the twin Baptist principles of showing respect for governing authorities and maintaining appropriate separation between the church and government, the council's compliance produced a schism. In 1962, a group of Baptists withdrew and later organized the Council of Churches of Evangelical Christians-Baptists, claiming that the All-Union Council was violating the principle of separation of church and state. The division continued even after the reforms of Mikhail Gorbachev. The tough questions Soviet Baptists had to negotiate was the degree to which should they be true to their Russianness and work within the existing political structure, and when should they draw the line on principles of conscience that demanded faithfulness to God above earthly government. Two different groups of Baptists answered that question in different ways. More troublesome than the differences of viewpoint, however, has been the fact that one group has not been able to allow the other to hold a differing position on the issue without harboring doubts about their identity as genuine followers of Christ.

In a different context, the Baptist Union of Southern Africa faced a somewhat similar dilemma in relation to government policies of apartheid. Amid struggles over issues of separation of church and state, Frederick Hale contends that the union became captive to "secular values and political rhetoric" and yielded its prophetic voice.[10] In this case, the principle of separation of church and state permitted many "white Baptists who were enjoying prosperous, comfortable lives in a society rent asunder by apartheid" largely to remain silent in the face of a great evil.[11] The union

---

[10] Frederick Hale, "The Baptist Union of Southern Africa and Apartheid," *Journal of Church and State* 48, no. 4 (Autumn 2006): 754.

[11] Ibid., 777.

confessed its negligence in the 1990s during the work of the Truth and Reconciliation Commission.

Another case arose in Hong Kong during the 1950s, 1960s, and 1970s regarding the possible use of government subsidies to support Baptist educational institutions, especially in the form of land grants. Tensions arose over different interpretations between some U.S. Baptist missionaries and leaders within the United Hong Kong Christian Baptist Churches Association over acceptance of subsidies, with survival of the institutions and their important ministries to refugee populations hanging in the balance.[12] Once again, complications arose over whether to favor actions that addressed urgent human needs or those that maintained a principle that might allow a socially disadvantaged group to continue in its suffering. Numerous African American Baptist churches in the United States have struggled with this tension as well, especially in relation to the government-supported faith-based initiatives of the early twenty-first century.[13]

The principle of separation of church and state also experienced challenges among many conservative Anglo-American Baptists late in the twentieth century. As cultural contexts began to shift in new directions, dominant Anglo Christian social, economic, and political traditions came under attack. Some U.S. Baptists joined with other Christian groups in attempts to legislate their religious values on all of society, thereby identifying their religious affiliations as a political force. Those actions exposed the difficulties endemic to identifying the lines of demarcation between church and state. Certain Baptists became convinced they should militantly endorse particular political parties and candidates as having been chosen by God and others as having been rejected by God on the basis of certain litmus-test issues. Many Anglo Baptists became convinced that Christianity was under siege by secular forces that had gained political advantage and needed to be defeated. A few Baptists even voiced the notion that separation of church and state was an invention of "liberals." These developments in many ways tested the resolve of countless Baptists in America who spoke from a threatened position of cultural privilege. They no longer identified with the position of their denominational ancestors, who had lived as a religious minority in a culture dominated by a privileged religious majority.

---

[12] See Chun-pang Vincent Lau, "Controversey over Public Funding to the Baptist Institutions in Colonial Hong Kong and the United States from the 1950s to the 1970s," *Baptist History and Heritage* 42, no. 2 (Spring 2007): 85–104.
[13] See, for example, Samuel K. Roberts, "Government Support of African American Church Faith-based Programs: A Call for Caution – A Challenge for Action," *American Baptist Quarterly* 21, no. 4 (December 2002): 432–45.

When viewed from a global Baptist perspective, commitment to complete religious freedom might be a better way to conceptualize this long-held Baptist principle. To the degree possible, and applied variously within different cultural, social, and political contexts, Baptists support the ideal of religious freedom for themselves and for others, regardless of their religious faith. This means that undue entanglement with government should be avoided because this, by nature, involves alliances with powers that tend to coerce the individual's conscience. In the early seventeenth century, the Baptist leader John Smyth stated the principle that has generally guided Baptists in this matter: "the magistrate is not by virtue of his office to meddle with religion, or matters of conscience, to force and compel men [and women] to this or that form of religion, or doctrine: but to leave Christian religion free, to every man's conscience, and to handle only civil transgressions."[14] Although this is an ideal that Baptists generally advocate, Baptist faith communities have and do live and flourish under forms of government that do not embrace this principle. Furthermore, Baptists also have struggled with when and under what conditions the endorsement of particular political parties and leaders as a faith community violates principles of complete religious freedom on the church's side of that equation.

BAPTIST SPIRITUALITY AND WORSHIP

Baptist Spirituality

For Baptists, spirituality engages both the inner and external life of the believer. Focus on the inner life begins with a process that produces cognizance of God's redemptive love. Baptists believe that all persons are born with an unavoidable tendency to sin (called original sin in Western Christian theology). Sin inherently involves choosing a course that goes against God and that ultimately proves to be destructive. Tempted by the "flesh," every human being who reaches physical, mental, and emotional maturity actually chooses sin and thereby becomes alienated from God. This means that each person needs to come to knowledge of God's redemptive love, which involves a process that might be described in several stages: encountering the gospel message, fearing God, repenting, and accepting God's justifying grace through faith in Jesus as the Christ.

---

[14] John Smyth, "Propositions and Conclusions" (1612), article 84 available in Lumpkin, *Confessions of Faith*, 140.

The gospel message about God's original intentions for creation, the human condition as a result of willful rebellion, and God's redemptive actions in Christ might be encountered in a variety of ways, including visual symbols, personal experiences, the spoken word, the printed word, and more. The most frequent method employed by Baptists is through verbal proclamation by a minister in a sermon or by some other church member through personal witness. The gospel message mystically communicates with an individual's inner life, thus creating awareness of her or his need for a change in relationship with God. This recognition of God's otherness and rightful claims on the life of each person is often referred to in the Bible as the fear of the Lord. Such fear or respect for God's claim is rooted in the perception that God is a living God who has promised redemption to those who believe, repent, and obey, and judgment for those who persevere in unbelief and disobedience. Recognizing God's rightful claim on one's life prompts the individual to acknowledge his or her condition of alienation from God and need for reconciling grace. When the repentant person recognizes that God's agent for effecting the power of this grace is Jesus Christ, and trusts in him as redeemer, that person is said to experience a new birth. This means that she or he has entered into a knowledge of God's truth – that is, has experienced a spiritual renewal through God's power, a transformed condition that opens the way for a life of discipleship. The appropriate responses to this reality include denoting it externally by baptism and nurturing the new life through active involvement in a Christian faith community.

Discipleship includes living in obedience to God, commitment to spiritual development, and engagement in Christian service that involves both inward and external dimensions, which are sometimes referred to as spiritual disciplines. The entire process of coming to know God in this way is an intricate work of God's Spirit. That same Spirit is also the instrument for a disciple's continued growth into holiness. Prayer, meditation, Bible study, and communal worship are among the spiritual disciplines emphasized by Baptists for nurturing inner holiness. Submission to God, moral living, witness, and benevolent service are among the disciplines taught for growing in external holiness.

Making Moral Decisions

Baptist beliefs and spiritual practices intersect functionally at the point of moral decision making. The magnitude of diversity among Baptists could lead the outside observer to conclude that they have no moral compass and that each person is free to act as he or she pleases; this is far from the case. For Baptists, moral decisions are grounded in the very nature of the triune God. Coming into the knowledge of God means that the believer is baptized into the life and mission of God. This life cannot be reduced to a set of rules or to intellectual assent toward a set of doctrines. Instead, the Christian life is dynamic, lived out in fellowship with God under God's guidance and power. Because moral living grows out of relationship rather than conformity to a set of humanly constructed standards, diversity is to be expected. But diversity does not excuse self-centered, biblically uninformed, or roguish behavior masking as discipleship. In the end, "the Christian life is not a moral achievement but a gift of grace. . . . So God can achieve in us, and even through us, what we could never do for ourselves."[15] Although the sincere and committed disciple will err in judgment and conduct, he or she remains responsible to God for his or her choices. This opens the possibility of freely joining in God's invitation to share in God's life and mission but also requires each person to bear responsibility for decision making.

Diversity among Baptists derives in part from the conviction that God does not create clones or robots but rather free moral agents capable of choosing. Therefore, discipleship includes both God's gracious call and our free response. No person can assume this responsibility for another individual. This means that life is lived in dynamic relationship with God, other persons, and the rest of creation. It would be easy to conclude that a moral decision reached by one individual through his or her faith interactions would mean that all other persons obedient to God would come to the same conclusion. If such consensus does not happen, it would be easy for that individual to conclude that the diverging other person is not listening to God. The historical Baptist conviction is that no person or institution has an infallible prehension of God's guidance. Therefore, individuals must always live humbly in the realization that they might be wrong. Such an attitude has the potential of producing moral paralysis and inaction. However, Baptists counter this through affirming that each believer must live faithfully according to the convictions of his or her conscience and the best light offered through the faith community. The confidence to live in that tension comes through realizing that God has promised both to forgive erroneous judgments when we seek it and to bring new life out of our disastrous choices. This assurance enables the

---

[15] Baptist World Alliance, *We Baptists* (Franklin, TN: Providence House Publishers, 1999), 36–7.

believer to live with openness toward the possibilities of growing into a better understanding.

Baptists believe that nurturing spiritual maturity entails several important qualities. The first is the leadership of Jesus the Christ over the life of the believer in the context of the believing community. Christian ethics essentially means living as Jesus Christ wishes the disciple to live. To choose a way of living that goes counter to Jesus' life and teachings would not be the way to live because that would deny his lordship. People confront many moral issues today that are not directly addressed in the Bible. Sometimes cultural traditions about certain practices are read into the Bible and presented as though they were biblical teachings. At times, individuals or groups reach conclusions on moral questions and present them as though they held the same force as the Scriptures themselves. Sometimes these conclusions play into popular prejudices, fears, or preferences. In no instance can the responsibility of the individual believer as a free moral agent under the leadership of Jesus Christ be relieved simply because some other voice of religious authority has offered its opinion. Baptists believe that the insights of responsible leaders should be carefully considered and assessed, and they often prove to be valuable aids in spiritual growth and moral decision making. However, those cannot substitute for the individual's responsibility in the matter.

A second quality that Baptists consider essential for growth in moral decision making is the Bible, God's written word. Because the leadership of Jesus Christ is very personal, Baptists also stress the importance of the Bible as a more objective standard for decision making. What a person concludes about Jesus' leadership in deciding a matter should have consistency with the biblical record about Jesus' teachings. Although differences exist among Baptists over the nature and composition of the biblical texts and over their interpretation, they still view the Bible as an appropriate source for God's guidance and the place to which the believer continually should turn for insight and direction as the standard for discerning God's truth.

A third important factor in moral decision making is the voice of the believing community. Baptists view the church as a gathering of those "called by God and held together in his covenant of love."[16] This fellowship of believers studies and listens to the Scriptures, prays for insight, shares individual and corporate experiences, and together seeks to discern God's leading. This offers the individual believer the benefit of corporate

---

[16] Ibid., 42.

experience and wisdom. But even this process may not result in a congregation's achieving a unanimous decision. Often differences of conviction emerge. When this happens, a congregation is sometimes able to allow the difference to stand as a matter of conscience. Other times, the differences cannot be tolerated and divisions result. As this study has shown, this solution has occurred with frequency in Baptists' history. A basic conviction among Baptists in moral decision making is that when believers seek to discern God's will "in the openness of faith and trust[,] . . . God is at work to guide his people by the Spirit. There are no guarantees that we will always get the right answer and do the right deeds, but at least we are trying to be alert to God and desire to live out his call in faithfulness."[17] Baptists believe that the essence of biblical faith is demonstrated through such pilgrimage, even when unanimity may not exist on important issues.

Finally, Baptist traditions generally acknowledge that sound moral decision making requires a broader knowledge of the basic facts associated with an issue. Frequently, those facts are complex, and the insight of experts is needed. Once again, the opinions of experts cannot replace the individual's responsibility in moral decision making, but they can assist. "Judging in willful ignorance of the facts does nothing to honor the Lord."[18] This means that secular wisdom can have value for the believer and the church and should not be ignored. On numerous occasions, matters of social justice, for example, have been raised first in the society at large before the church recognized them as justice concerns. In addition, secular sources of knowledge often furnish necessary information about issues that can present a new lens from which to view a moral concern. Baptist bodies vary in their willingness to admit such information into their processes of moral inquiry. However, individual Baptists as members of society seldom can avoid considering such data as they wrestle with the complex issues in the day-to-day matters of the world in which they live.

Worship

One author has quite succinctly summarized a major reality of Baptist worship: "Anyone attempting to identify practices which are universal to Baptists is either unusually courageous or simply uninformed."[19] Some diversity has existed from Baptists' earliest days, especially because of their emphasis on spontaneity. As the Baptist movement has become worldwide in scope, this diversity has increased exponentially. In addition, modern

[17] Ibid., 43.   [18] Ibid.   [19] Ibid., 52.

cultural shifts and generational differences have added to the mix. Still, amid great diversity, some generalities might be noted that can help inform inquirers regarding Baptist traditions of worship.

Early Anglo Baptist worship was shaped in significant ways by its reaction against the established Anglican Church, with its emphasis on liturgical formulas. This response ingrained certain values that persisted, especially among General Baptists. For them, worship was to be very free, liberating individuals to respond as the Spirit of God might lead at the moment. John Smyth expressed the extreme degree to which this reaction was taken in the 1608 treatise titled *Differences of the Churches of the Separation*. "Ther [sic] is no better warrant to bring translations of Scripture written into the church, & read them as partes or helps of worship, then to bring in expositions, resolutions, paraphrasts & sermons upon the Scripture seing al these are equally humane in respect of the work."[20] No liturgies were to be read, no set prayers (written prayers) to be offered, no sermon notes to be used, not even a translation of the Bible itself was to be used in worship. Over time, the extreme nature of this reaction was recognized and moderations made. Still, vestiges of those attitudes linger on within some Baptist circles today. In contrast, Particular Baptists tended to value order and reflection in worship. Their worship traditions were more heavily influenced by practices of the Reformed churches that emphasized decency and orderliness.

The contrast between spontaneity and order also surfaced among Baptists in America during the First Great Awakening. Regular Baptists modeled the value given to orderliness and reflection derived from the Particular Baptist tradition. Separate Baptists valued spontaneity and free expression in worship. Baptist denominations that emerged later in American history often reflected the Regular Baptist tradition, the Separate Baptist tradition, or varied mixtures of the two. In addition to those expressions, black Baptist traditions added the qualities and rhythms of African cultures to Baptist worship, eventually creating a distinctive style that was characterized in part by kinetic and group participation.

In a general sense, the Bible makes reference to at least five models of worship. In some fashion, Baptist worship formulas reflect one or a combination of these forms. The didactic model focuses on teaching or instruction and is reflected in worship styles that emphasize exposition.

---

[20] John Smyth, *Differences of the Churches of the Separation*, 1608, Chapter 12, reprinted in W. T. Whitley, ed., *The Works of John Smyth*, 2 vols. (Cambridge: Cambridge University Press, 1915): 269–92.

This worship style usually centers on a meticulous explanation of Bible texts in a methodical and prescriptive fashion. The liturgical model draws on formulas that give expression to key theological emphases and traditions of the Christian faith. In Baptist life, this style often centers on the cycles of the liturgical calendar and the use of litanies, confessions, and other formulas for remembering and affirming the great truths of Christian heritage. The sacramental model is less common in Baptist life but sometimes is combined with the liturgical style to focus worship around the Lord's Supper. This model is more commonly found among those Baptists who practice weekly observance of communion and make it the central act of worship. The charismatic model emphasizes exercise of the spiritual gifts of ministry, especially those that contribute to the worship experience. This style of worship is reminiscent of the early General and Separate Baptists and focuses on freedom of expression, spontaneity, and charismatic preaching. The festal model has become popular in those Baptist churches employing a so-called contemporary worship style. In the Hebrew Bible, this type of worship brought the people of God together in celebration, which is the atmosphere contemporary worship forms seek to re-create.[21]

Baptist churches can be found employing each of these worship models and combinations of them. Individual churches tend to employ the particular style that best fits the needs and inclinations of its members. They usually combine elements of more than one style as occasion demands and as a means of bringing variety to the worship experience. But no one model is considered *the* biblical form of worship, even though individual Baptists for varieties of reasons tend to adopt a personal preference and seek a church utilizing that style. In addition, Baptists at times develop strong resistance against or attractions toward particular models as a result of contextual influences. For example, Baptists in many Latin American cultures have tended to reject liturgical models of worship as too Catholic. When Pentecostal practices began to appear during the mid-twentieth century, many Baptist churches in Latin America also rejected the charismatic model as too emotional. Other Baptists, however, viewed Pentecostal worship styles as liberating and more accommodating to the worship needs of Latin American people. These differences caused bitter divisions between churches of the Brazilian Baptist Convention and those of the National Baptist Convention. In many ways, the divergences were reminiscent of earlier Baptist conflicts over spontaneity and order in worship.

[21] Ibid., 53.

Regardless of the worship style, Baptist services of worship typically include several elements: prayer, Scripture reading, singing, preaching, receiving the offering, an invitation to public response, and on occasion baptism and/or the Lord's Supper. These acts are conducted with orderliness and appropriate decorum, which varies according to culture, worship style, and occasion. Baptist worship is also congregational in nature, which means that focus is placed on every believer directly experiencing God's presence in worship and prayer without the intermediary role of a priest. Ministers plan, facilitate, and guide worship, but they do not mediate God's presence in any sacramental sense. The proclamation of biblically based messages assists believers in their reflection on and response to God's claims on their lives.

Music

Singing, preaching, and the invitation for public response have become hallmarks of Baptist worship in most cultures and traditions. However, the way these activities are conducted can and do vary greatly. In the early seventeenth century, Baptists joined many other groups derived from the Calvinist tradition in their opposition to hymn singing. Only chanting of biblical texts was permitted. The intent of this ban was to discourage congregants from focusing on the aesthetic appeal of the music itself rather than the message of the words. Nevertheless, hymn singing gradually was adopted by most Baptist churches and became a constituent part of almost every Baptist worship tradition. Wherever Baptist missionaries went, they introduced hymn singing as part of worship, often utilizing the familiar tunes from church services in England, the European continent, and North America, and substituting either translations of the existing lyrics into the languages of local peoples or creating altogether new lyrical messages. In many instances, this practice continued into the late twentieth century. As the twenty-first century approached, however, music reflective of local cultural traditions began to appear in Asian, African, and Latin American Baptist churches. This transition into music that was more culturally contextualized often ignited tensions between the musical traditionalists who preferred the "sacred" hymns of the missionaries and the innovators who wanted music that seemed more at home in their world.

Seventeenth-century Baptists also tended to reject the use of musical instruments to accompany congregational singing. The reasons for this varied but seem mostly connected to the Reformed Church tradition of unaccompanied singing and the fact that the instruments available to the less affluent Baptist congregations at the time generally were associated with secular settings. In the minds of many, such instruments contaminated worship with a worldly atmosphere. A distinctive style of singing referred to as the meter-hymn style or Dr. Watts's style became common among Baptists in the eighteenth century.[22] Typically, the song leader lined out the first line of the hymn melodically, and the congregation joined in near the end of the line, shaping a melody. This practice also became known as surge singing, as the congregation surged in at the end of the line. This style facilitated congregations through a gradual transition from psalter singing to continuous line singing. The method allowed the line to be spiritually massaged by the congregation, as members were able to identify with the ideas expressed according to their spiritual needs.[23] The second and subsequent lines would follow the same process. Thus, emphasis remained on the message of the song rather than the aesthetics of the music. Over time, most Baptist congregations abandoned the prohibition against use of musical instruments in worship, but a few Baptist bodies (mostly among the Primitivist Baptist traditions) continue the restriction, allowing only the human voice to be employed as a source of music in worship and following a style that emphasizes the message over the musicality.[24]

In the nineteenth and early twentieth centuries, pump organs, pianos, pipe organs, and later electric organs became a fixture in worship services of most Western Baptist congregations. Development of continuous line singing (i.e., hymn singing) made this type of accompaniment more important. As the specific instruments became more widely utilized by churches, they lost their secular associations and gained privileged status among Anglo Baptists for accompanying singing in worship. They became such standard features of worship that, after the mid-twentieth century, when other types of instruments were introduced, some Baptists resisted them as secular and regarded their sounds as detracting from the dignity of worship.

The emergence of contemporary styles of worship in the last quarter of the twentieth century added a much wider variety of instruments and more professional and entertainment qualities to the tenor of worship in a growing number of Baptist churches. Electronic pianos, electric guitars, horns, drums, synthesizers, soundtracks, and other innovations have

---

[22] A style developed by the British hymnodist Isaac Watts (1674–1748).

[23] Melva Wilson Costen, *In Spirit and in Truth: The Music of African American Worship* (Louisville, KY: Westminster/John Knox Press, 2004), 50.

[24] Beverly Bush Patterson, *The Sound of the Dove: Singing in Appalachian Primitive Baptist Churches* (Urbana: University of Illinois Press, 2001), 31–60.

become common not only in many Western Baptist churches but also in many other cultural contexts. Instruments indigenous to the many cultures of the world are increasingly utilized by Baptists in their particular contexts. For example, Native Baptists who once were pressured into worship styles characteristic of Anglo Baptist culture now more frequently utilize the drum, flute, traditional dances, and other accompaniments in tribally familiar patterns of worship. In Africa, missionaries initially banned the use of local instruments in worship, considering them part of pagan ritual traditions. Consequently, until the latter half of the twentieth century, African Baptists mostly employed vocal music in worship, except in rare instances where organs and a limited number of other "sacred" musical instruments were available. In the 1950s, guitars were introduced, along with the piano in some urban churches. In the 1980s, electric guitars, keyboards, synthesizers, soundtracks, and others instruments familiar to Western-style music became increasingly utilized. By the end of the century, many African melodic instruments like drums (among them the *tama* talking drums, the *bougarabou,* and the *djembe* in West Africa, the water drums in Central and West Africa, and the various types of *ngoma* drums in Central and Southern Africa), slit gongs, rattles (such as the *kosika* and rain sticks), double bells, a variety of harps (such as the Senufo one-string harp), flutes, and xylophone-like instruments (such as the *mbira*) were more frequently used in Baptist worship services. These locally familiar styles of music and musical instruments helped indigenize Baptist worship, making it more at home within the local contexts. Similar musical adaptations have occurred among Baptists in other cultural contexts as well. Overall, a major transformation has been occurring in the styles and varieties of music employed by Baptists globally.

Russian Baptists have a distinctive hymnody that is reflective of their cultural tradition. Reminiscent of the Orthodox style, their worship music characteristically has a slow and dramatic tempo and includes instrumental accompaniment. However, the range of instruments considered acceptable for worship is limited mostly to stringed instruments. The piano, organ, and guitar are usually considered acceptable; horns (like the saxophone) and drums are not deemed appropriate for worship. The electronic instruments and vocalizations familiar to Western-style contemporary worship are usually not permitted, as they contrast harshly with the dulcet sounds associated with Russian worship traditions. However, energetic younger generations of Baptists are increasingly attracted to Russian versions of this style of music, which suggests the possibility of greater variety of worship styles and music in the future.

African American music is also distinctive among Baptist traditions. With roots in American slave religion, black Baptist music draws on African conceptual approaches that "believe in the affective or transforming power of vocal music."[25] Singing helps ease the pain of work, transforms the environment, and unites the community. It is not intended for the ear alone, but also "for all the senses and faculties of the body."[26] It "reflects Africa's vision of the world on earth and the world beyond, a world of change and movement, a world in permanent search of betterment and perfection."[27] Consequently, African cultures use music to express every dimension of life, thus translating everyday feelings and experiences into meaningful sounds.[28] Such musical traditions and assumptions lie behind black Baptists' musical heritage.

As a distinctive musical tradition among Baptists, black Baptist music might be divided into three phases of development: the spirituals, African American hymnody, and gospel music. Uncertainty surrounds the origins of spirituals as a musical genre, although the context seems clearly to have been that of American slavery. "African chants, field hollers, work songs, and personal and communal cries of liberation" were the precursors for the style, form, and content of spirituals.[29] These traditions were united with the faith experiences of Christianity during the camp meetings of the First Great Awakening. This provided a religious environment in which many African Americans could hear and receive Baptist proclamations of the gospel and in which they could find a degree of freedom to express their faith convictions. "After the regular services, African Americans would continue the momentum in separate quarters with a preacher whom the community designated and a bottomless reservoir of biblical stories, faith expressions, and personal testimonies waiting to be shaped into spirituals."[30] In this milieu, spirituals as a distinctively African American form of musical expression spread among black Baptists, and that music began to permeate every part of worship.

As with Anglo and Anglo-American Baptists, meter-hymn singing became common among black Baptists during the eighteenth century, growing out of the call-and-response style of singing common to that heritage. This style of vocal music did not depend on the calculated metrical setting of the text that is characteristic of modern hymn singing. Instead,

---

[25] Melva Wilson Costen, *African American Worship*, 9.   [26] Ibid.
[27] Francis Bebey, "The Vibrant Intensity of Traditional African Music," *Black Perspective in Music* (Fall 1974): 117.
[28] Melva Wilson Costen, *African American Worship*, 9.   [29] Ibid., 36.   [30] Ibid., 38.

it depended on the song leader's melodic tuning of the line, which was followed by the congregation as it joined the leader. In that style, members of the congregation sang what they could remember of the melody, "creating and overlaying newly improvised melodies that were not only appropriate for the text but evoked a deeply spiritual worshiping ethos."[31] Black Baptists created and preserved a body of music that spoke to and communicated the African American experience. *Gospel Pearls*, published by the National Baptist Convention in 1921, preserved many hymns of this tradition and is considered by some "a milestone in the history of black church hymnody."[32]

African American gospel music is one of the musical genres that developed over time out of the experiences of black Americans. Its earliest roots are found in the preaching of black pastors whose message would be set to music. Later, and mostly out of the black Pentecostal tradition, this form of music was presented to audiences outside the church, initially as a way to proclaim good news to a larger public. In the secular environment, the biblical messages sometimes became distorted amid commercial interests, but the genre itself prospered. Thus, "taken out of the soulful context, reworked, [and] put on stage as paid entertainment," it was returned to the church as "music for worship."[33] In the process, this musical form gained wide public notoriety and acceptance. Edwin Hawkins's rendition of "O Happy Day," based on a hymn by Philip Doddridge, illustrates the continuing popularity and power of this music both inside the church and beyond.

Few activities have the ability to give expression to the egalitarian ideals of Baptist congregational church life like music. Through music everyone has the opportunity to participate regardless of skill level, to interpret through the individual emphases and inflections rendered while singing, and to contribute to a cause greater than self. People often are able to connect around music when they have little else in common, although shifting tastes in musical styles have regularly been a source of friction among Baptists. Notwithstanding their initial reluctance to embrace music in worship, this medium has become a major component of Baptists' life globally – through choirs, ensembles, bands, orchestras, soloists, congregations, and more.

---

[31] Ibid., 49.
[32] Eileen Southern, "Hymnals of the Black Church," in *The Black Christian Worship Experience*, rev. ed. (Atlanta: Interdenominational Theological Center, 1992), 136.
[33] Melva Wilson Costen, *African American Worship*, 75.

Proclamation

Given the centrality both of the Bible and of a personal faith experience in Baptist traditions, it is not surprising that preaching based on the biblical texts and appealing to individual religious experience should have the importance it does in Baptist worship. For most Baptist churches, the sermon is the focal point of worship and is given the greatest amount of time among the several elements of the service. Yet how this is done and the styles employed vary greatly. Some pastors utilize styles that are strongly reasoned with very modest display of emotional enthusiasm. Others place great value on emotional expression and interpret a worship service as devoid of God's Spirit if vocal and physical manifestations are not evident. Myriad stylistic variations can be found in between the two polarities.

Baptists closer to the Particular or Regular traditions have tended to prefer sermons that appeal to reason and the intellectual faculties. Some cultures, social classes, and personalities prefer more solemn and reflective approaches to worship that limit the display of emotion, although deep internal emotion might be experienced by the individual worshipper. In these traditions, the preacher's efforts focus on assisting the congregant to open his or her heart and mind to insights communicated through the Scriptures and on encouraging responses of increased commitment to faith in and obedience to God. Baptist pastors generally consider the sermon an awesome responsibility and the central duty of their ministries. The traditions inclined to more reasoned approaches tend to view poorly prepared sermons, ones that are inappropriately delivered, those lacking studied understanding of the biblical text, and sermons devoid of responsible applications to the life experiences of the hearers as violations of this high and holy office. Although a highly reasoned and less emotional preaching style today is often associated with urban Anglo Baptist worship traditions, such stereotyping often is misinformed, as no style is exclusive to any particular culture or ethnic group.

In African American Baptist traditions, the sermon typically is as much an art form as a method of communication. Lora-Ellen McKinney describes her impressions as a lifelong adherent of that heritage: "Something about African American lives and experience allows the creative proclamation of Christ's majesty in a unique and captivating way. The African American style of preaching celebrates the good news that Christ is Lord and that his redemption is available to all who believe in him."[34] Black Baptist

---

[34] Lora-Ellen McKinney, *Total Praise: An Orientation to Black Baptist Belief and Worship* (Valley Forge, PA: Judson Press, 2003), 70.

preaching varies widely in style, but typically it includes explanations and interpretations built around biblical texts intended to persuade (exhort) the hearer to act according to the explanations and to "bring souls to Christ." Usually the sermons are preached with great passion and elicit energetic emotional responses from the congregation, even as the sermon is being preached. As one black Baptist pastor noted,

Emotion is a gift from God. It provides a tool that helps us connect to one another through the shared experience of our African American history and our experience as we worship together on any given Sunday morning. We are thankful for, happy about, overwhelmed by, and amazed by God's mercies to us. In the context of preaching, emotion is also evidence that African Americans love God; because of the many challenges we have faced, it is impossible to talk about our love of God and his love for us without expressing emotion.[35]

As with most Baptist worship, preaching is the focal point of the African American church experience, and the manner in which the sermon is presented is critical. A pastor with a deep, resounding voice is especially appealing, and "those who sing beautifully and who present portions of their sermons in the ritualistic, syncopated, and rhythmic manner for which African American preachers are revered are viewed by their parishioners as being great orators."[36]

Eurasian Baptists also exhibit several distinctive features in their worship forms. One is the length of the service, which usually lasts no less than two hours and frequently may extend to three hours or more. Part of the reason for this is found in a unique feature of their preaching tradition. It is the custom for the church's several pastors (often four or five of them) to each deliver biblical sermons during the course of the service. Worship is marked by a remarkable reverence expressed by an intense and serious demeanor reminiscent of Orthodox congregations. The celebratory mood of the Western contemporary style of Baptist worship is apt to be interpreted as "Pentecostal" by these Baptists and considered somewhat aberrant. Several periods of spontaneous prayer are common in Russian Baptist worship when either a man or woman (the genders usually are segregated in worship) leads in prayer while the congregation prays with them in a whispered undertone.

Because of the prominence given to proclamation, Baptist ministers popularly have been titled "preachers" in many of their traditions. The preaching function more than any other has historically been the focus

---

[35] Ibid., 72–3.   [36] Ibid., 71.

of Baptist ministerial training. Courses in biblical interpretation, theology, church history, ethics, homiletics, and related subjects converge at the point of rightly proclaiming God's word. Although counseling, administration, visitation, and institutional development are indispensable for the success of most Baptist ministers, preaching is usually the litmus-test quality on which ministerial effectiveness is most heavily judged. As one Independent Baptist woman explained, "If [the preacher] don't sweat, we don't listen."[37] In other words, meeting congregational expectations in proclamation means everything.

Public Invitation   In many Baptist communions, especially those associated with and derived from Baptist traditions in the United States, an invitation for public response is offered at the end of the sermon. It is common in most Baptist traditions to have a time of private reflection and meditation following the message, but many Baptist traditions have a special time of appeal that focuses on a public decision for Christ. This practice evolved out of nineteenth-century American revivalistic practices derived from the new measures introduced by evangelist Charles G. Finney. Baptist incorporation of this practice in worship probably began as part of local church revival meetings, which became a regular feature of many Baptist churches in the United States after the Second Great Awakening and especially through the influence of Finney's techniques. Gradually, the practice became a part of each worship service. The invitation became a powerful and symbolic act that marked salvation for many Baptists, particularly Anglo-American Baptists in the Southern United States. Those Baptists often referred to the experience as walking the aisle, going forward, shaking the preacher's hand, and the sawdust trail. Over time, the public appeal was given for decisions other than salvation. Individuals went forward to rededicate their lives after a period of spiritual waywardness, to request membership in the church, to accept the call to full-time Christian vocation, and for other reasons as well.

Largely through the influence of missionaries, the practice of making an appeal for public response was introduced to and adopted by Baptist churches in many other parts of the world. But issuing an appeal of this type has not been universally practiced among Baptists. Strict and Particular Baptists, for example, have a tradition of emphasizing God's effective calling to the point that invitations are distrusted as human motivators that can interfere with the work of God's Spirit. The preacher's work is primarily

---

[37]   Bill J. Leonard, *Baptists in America* (Columbia University Press, 2007), ix.

that of confronting the sinner with his or her ruined condition. Once convinced of this condition, the individual must wait on God's Spirit to do the work of salvation and give him or her assurance of salvation. Article 35 of the Gospel Standard (1878 revision) explains:

When a man is quickened by the blessed Spirit, he has faith given him to know and feel he is a sinner against God. . . . And we further believe that such a man will be made to cry for mercy, to mourn over and on account of his sins, and, being made to feel that he has no righteousness of his own, to hunger and to thirst after Christ's righteousness; being led by the Spirit until, in the full assurance of faith, he has the Spirit's witness in his heart that his sins are put away. . . .

In some Primitive Baptist traditions, an invitation for public response is given but in a fashion that involves the entire congregation in the event. An observer describes the practice of one Primitive Baptist church:

When the congregation stands to sing the closing hymn, the pastor announces that the doors of the church are open to receive new members. He and any visiting elders [Primitive Baptists' title for pastor] stand facing the congregation to participate in the ritual hand of fellowship during the singing. Members of the congregation offer their right hands to those standing nearest them, sometimes engaging simultaneously in handshake and embrace, left arms lightly encircling the shoulders of the others with right hands clasped between them. Then they walk single file, singing from hymnbooks held in their left hands, to shake hands with the preachers and with all others at the meeting. Anyone who wants to join the church will make that wish known to the pastor during this time, usually in a tearful request, often moved to this step by the power of the strong, slow-paced, soulful singing. The pastor then informs the congregation of this person's desire for a "home in the church," and invites the person to tell briefly of the "travels" or experiences that gave a hope of salvation. The church receives the new member by baptism or by letter (referring to the transfer of membership from a "sister church" in which a letter is sent by the former church indicating that the person is a member in good standing of that congregation).[38]

Southern Baptists have a strong tradition of using evangelistic appeals to encourage hearers to respond by making public commitments of faith and life. Dotson M. Nelson Jr. offers a description of the invitation in a typical Southern Baptist worship service during the 1950s, a tradition that continues to be observed in many Southern Baptist churches:

The sermon generally is closed with an appeal to commitment and church membership. During the singing of a hymn of invitation, those responding make their

---

[38] Beverly Bush Patterson, *The Sound of the Dove: Singing in Appalachian Primitive Baptist Churches*, 5.

way to the front [of the sanctuary] where they are received for church membership. The sermons preached are characterized by emotional zeal. They are essentially evangelistic, aiming always at commitment.[39]

By the end of the twentieth century, some Baptist church leaders in the United States concluded that the unchurched people in their communities reacted very negatively to the traditional Baptist public appeal. Some of those churches developed an approach to worship called high-participation-seeker services. A band replaced the organ; vocal ensembles replaced the choir; an informal atmosphere replaced the formal churchy atmosphere; and sermons focused on practical life issues like dealing with stress, self-esteem, or finding purpose in life replaced those aimed at eliciting evangelistic and futuristic faith responses. Because postmodern hearers often need to try it on before they will trust it or commit to it, invitations for public commitments are not offered. Those who want to know more are invited to special classes where possibilities for greater commitment can be explored. Often these churches exclude the word *Baptist* from their names, as denominational labels tend to conjure negative images among many unchurched people. Saddleback Valley Community Church in Orange County, California, is illustrative of this approach. This diminished emphasis on denominational identity is a worrisome trend for some Baptist leaders, whereas others view it as a necessary accommodation to a changing culture.

BAPTIST COMMUNITY

Priesthood of All Believers

The foundation of Baptist community is located in the belief that Jesus Christ is head of the church and of each member. Baptists assert that all parts of the body of Christ are connected directly to the head and do not need any other human mediator to have relationship with God. Church government, ministry, polity, and education are all based on this simply stated but highly complex principle.

In its essence, this principle maintains that ministry belongs to the church as a whole, not just to an episcopal class of members. Thus, although every member has the privilege of approaching God directly, every member also has the priestly responsibility of ministering to the other. For Baptists,

---

[39] Dotson M. Nelson Jr., "Minister, the Southern Baptist," in *Encyclopedia of Southern Baptists*, 2 vols. (Nashville, TN: Broadman Press, 1958).

this means that every believer possesses some gift for ministering and is summoned to serve Christ and the world through exercising that gift in all parts of life. This ministry is carried out by people of each culture, ethnicity, gender, nationality, and profession. Those who help prepare, encourage, inspire, and organize the congregation of ministers for their individual and corporate ministries are called pastors. But although Baptist pastors are ordained and given special duties to perform on behalf of the congregation, they are not understood to possess special powers of access with God unavailable to all other believers. Pastors are gifted to guide the congregation of ministers in Bible study, worship, music, spiritual growth, and related activities. The congregation of ministers then scatters into the world, where the main work of ministry is done. In the world, each believer ministers in God's name regardless of life circumstance, and among various activities invites others to join him or her in the life of Christ.

Priesthood of all believers is sometimes misunderstood to mean that every believer is a church unto herself or himself, and that no one else can tell her or him what to believe or do. Although this statement bears some resemblance to the Baptist position, it deviates significantly from the historical Baptist understanding of this principle. Baptists traditionally have taught that every person is competent to interpret Scripture under the guidance of the Holy Spirit without some other priest determining the correct interpretation. When misapplied, however, this may lead an individual to assume that he or she has learned everything he or she needs to know theologically, spiritually, and otherwise. This can produce sterile orthodoxy, blind traditionalism, and even attitudes about the Christian life that have no basis in Scripture. The priesthood of all believers calls for each Christian to augment his or her skills in understanding and deciphering the teaching of the Bible for committed and communal Christian living.

Pastors and Deacons

Early Baptists spoke of a twofold ministry: the ministry of the word, which was the major responsibility of the pastor, and the ministry of daily necessity, the responsibility of the deacons. Today, in most Baptist traditions, deacons assist in spiritual leadership of the church as well as overseeing the mundane aspects of the church's life. Some Baptists appoint elders as well as deacons, with the elders sharing more closely the decision-making responsibilities of the pastor. Larger churches usually have multiple pastors, with each exercising vocational skills over defined areas of the congregation's life, such as music, youths, senior adults, or evangelism.

As this study has indicated, Baptist traditions have preferred men over women in their selection of pastors. This practice has been questioned and sometimes strongly challenged in Baptist circles, especially when the issue of cultural influences that masquerade as biblical teachings has been squarely faced. Occasionally in the past, a few congregations have accepted women as pastors but that has not been the general practice over the years. Today, the matter is much more strongly contested, and consequently, in some Baptist traditions, increasing numbers of women are being admitted into the pastorate. Still, the avenue for women into ordained pastoral leadership (especially as senior pastor) continues to be arduous and frustrating in most Baptist traditions. In many instances, the door remains closed altogether. Baptist congregations have been somewhat more willing to allow women to serve as deacons, but even that office has been prohibited to them (or at least not practiced) by most Baptist churches.

Some Baptist traditions place great importance on the benefits of ministerial education and will only consider candidates for ordination who have completed a prescribed degree in theological preparation. Many Baptist churches prefer a specified level of ministerial training but are willing to accept less qualified candidates on the basis of experience, giftedness, or other qualifications. A few Baptists, however, consider education to be a hindrance to ministry, believing that it interferes with the Spirit's work in the life of the minister. Consequently, they prefer an untrained ministry. Although each local church is free to choose as pastor whomever it wishes, in most traditions, congregations select only those persons "whose calling and gifts have been recognized by a wider representative body of churches."[40] Although most Baptists value congregational decision making, the nature of pastoral leadership can vary widely, from servant leaders to dictatorial rulers and chief executive officers.

The Autonomous Church and the Association Principle

Since their earliest days, Baptists customarily have valued the right of each local congregation to decide matters for themselves without intervention from a superior ecclesiastical authority. In 1611, the first Baptist congregation under the leadership of Thomas Helwys made the following declaration: "The Word of God cometh not from anie one, neither to anie one congregation in particular. . . . But unto everie particular Church. . . . And

---

[40] Baptist World Alliance, *We Baptists*, 30.

therefore no church ought to challeng anie prerogative over anie other."⁴¹
Explained more fully, Baptists globally have tended to insist that a congregation should be free from interference by both civil authorities and
other church bodies regarding matters of faith and internal operations.
Each church should be left to select its own leaders, manage its own discipline, and determine its own affairs. Just as individual believers live directly
under the lordship of Jesus Christ, each congregation of believers possessed
the same independent authority. Consequently, Baptist churches regularly
have resisted the creation of structures and offices that would compromise
the local church's autonomy.

Yet, although Baptists have affirmed the independence of each local
church, they also have tended to emphasize the need for individual congregations to relate (associate) with other like-minded congregations. Soon
after their creation, English Baptists began experimenting with ways that
would enable their independent congregations to connect cooperatively
with other congregations without violating the freedom of each church.
This led to the creation of associations. Known by a variety of names (such
as *unions, conventions, areas, regions,* and *districts*), Baptist associations are
considered not a superior body with authority over local churches but
an advisory body made up of representatives from those churches that
voluntarily choose to be part of that association. Member churches send
delegates (the maximum number is determined by the particular association) to periodic meetings of the association, where business germane to the
concerns of that body is treated. Decisions can be made by the association,
but they are not legally binding on the local churches. However, because
the decisions are made by representatives from the member churches, local
congregations usually are in agreement with the outcome. Should a congregation depart significantly from the advice of an association in which it is a
member, the association might choose to exclude that church from its list of
member churches by a vote of the delegates. Hence, although decisions of
associations have no legal force on the congregation, they do have force. In
the eighteenth and nineteenth centuries, Baptist churches in England and
the United States, for example, generally demonstrated reluctance toward
rejecting the advice of their associations because they valued membership
in those bodies. Usually when such breaks did occur, churches were quick
to form new associations with like-minded congregations.

⁴¹ Thomas Helwys, "A Declaration of Faith of the English People Remaining at Amsterdam in Holland," in *Baptist Confessions of Faith* (Philadelphia: Judson Press, 1959), 120 (article 12).

The earliest Baptist associations were formed in Britain in the 1640s and 1650s. As Dissenting churches, these Baptists wanted the freedom to decide matters for themselves, but they also needed the encouragement and strength that could be derived only from like-minded congregations who shared in persecution. In the United States, General Baptists formed the first association in the 1670s, although the Philadelphia Baptist Association organized in 1707 became the model for most associational life there. Other early American associations included the Charleston Association, the Warren Association, and the Sandy Creek Association. In Canada, missionaries from New England and New York helped organize early associations in Upper Canada (Ontario). In Nova Scotia, the Danbury Association of Connecticut furnished the model for associational development, and in Ottawa, the British pattern of association became the prototype. In Europe, Johann Oncken's influence helped establish a pattern of Baptist unions among the congregations he and his associates organized. Soon after missionaries and Baptist immigrants from North America, the Caribbean, and England established churches in Liberia, the Congo, and South Africa, those congregations organized themselves into associations. Likewise, Baptists in India began organizing associations in the early nineteenth century. In the 1860s and 1870s, Baptist churches in China and Japan also formed associations to strengthen their corporate ministries. Most associations in Latin America were developed according to models derived from the United States. Throughout the globe autonomous Baptist congregations have a history of developing appropriate structures that allow them to join in cooperative ventures without violating the decision-making authority of the local church.

In general, associations have served as a source of encouragement to member churches, a means for promoting some degree of unity in faith and practice, a resource offering guidance and assistance when needed, and a mechanism through which cooperative ventures among the churches can be advanced. For that reason, most Baptist churches participate in multiple associations. At the most basic and local level would be the district or area association consisting of several to a few dozen churches. Beyond that, many churches would also be part of a regional, provincial, or state association. These cover a larger geographic area and usually include churches from more than one local association. Often they are called unions or conventions, such as the Union of South Australia, the Baptist General Association of Virginia, or the United Baptist Convention of the Atlantic Provinces. Finally, most Baptist churches would also be members of a national association. This association does not have superior authority over the local and regional associations but coordinates the work of autonomous churches over a larger geographic area and includes churches participating in multitudes of local associations and perhaps several dozen regional associations. Among these associations are bodies such as the Baptist Union of Great Britain, the American Baptist Churches in the USA, the National Baptist Convention of the United States of America, Incorporated, the Communauté Baptiste du Fleuvre Zaire, A Convenção Batista Brasileira, and the Southern Baptist Convention. In some ways, the Baptists World Alliance serves a similar function at an international level. In addition, Baptist churches have frequently formed associations along ethnic lines, as illustrated by the Ukrainian Evangelical Baptist Convention of Canada, the Russian-Ukrainian Evangelical Baptist Union of the United States of America, Incorporated, and the Hispanic Baptist Convention of Texas.

Divisions have frequently erupted in Baptist life over conflicts between the autonomous principle and the associational principle in church matters. In the United States, for example, an antimission movement emerged among western frontier Baptists in the 1820s and 1830s, when some felt that the prerogatives of local congregations were being threatened. The Landmark movement carried local church independence to its extreme. J. R. Graves and J. M. Pendleton asserted that the local church was subject only to the authority of Christ and developed definitions and polity to ensure that. In the twentieth century, independent Baptist churches have strongly defended similar views. Such assertions have often come as a consequence of growing denominational machinery that seemed to be co-opting the rights of the local congregation.

BAPTISTS AND CULTURE

Many of the distinctives characterizing Baptists during the early centuries of their development put them at odds with other religious and political groups. Their emphasis on a believer's church in which they sought to maintain a regenerate membership by practicing believer's baptism and discipline placed them in opposition to those supporting an established church where baptism and citizenship were coterminous and where inhabitants of a geographical region were automatically part of the official church's parish. Such convictions automatically placed early Baptists among the ranks of Dissenters in their varied Anglo cultural contexts and consequently identified them as countercultural. In many other cultural contexts, Baptists also have originated as small minorities located in challenging or even hostile social environments. Factors such as social class, legal status, and theological identity in these situations have augmented Baptists' opposition to many of the prevalent values, religious assumptions, and practices of the world in which they have lived. As a consequence, it has not been uncommon for Baptists to develop distrustful and antagonistic attitudes toward their world. Such discrepancies inevitably have colored Baptists' understanding of the church, ecumenism, social engagement, soteriology, general education, and other areas.

Baptist theology has tended to draw sharp contrasts between God's kingdom and human culture. Mission engagement and evangelistic efforts have been motivated by intense desire to have persons reject the world and embrace a new community. Although the metaphors associated with this transformation usually have focused on a spiritual or inner change, cultural accoutrements usually are included as well. Among Baptists in the United States, for example, evidence of salvation has at times included rejection of all use of alcohol as a beverage, prohibition of dancing, not going to movie theaters, and keeping away from the company of persons of different religious affiliations. More recently, some Baptist denominations have taken rigid stands against scientific evidence supporting evolution, stem-cell research, homosexual identity, new roles for women in postmodern society, and similar concerns. Many non-Baptists seem to perceive such Baptists as idealistic, otherworldly, judgmental, and out of touch with reality when it comes to many basic concerns of everyday life. In many instances, Baptists have seemed exclusivist, self-absorbed, and aloof in regard to the pressing needs of the world around them. Their responses to uncomfortable cultural changes have tended to be negative rather than engaging. Although aversionist responses are not characteristic of all Baptists, and some individuals and organizations seek seriously to bring Baptist convictions and values into serious dialogue with rapidly developing scientific, cultural, and intellectual developments, multitudes of Baptists find those innovations overwhelming and seek the solace of religious tradition and familiarity as a respite from a world that seems confusing and threatening. Still, most Baptists find they cannot escape the hard questions posed by global, pluralist, diverse, and ever-changing cultures. Increasingly, Baptists are discovering that they need to develop new social and theological constructs through which to interpret and engage the many cultures of which they are part.

BAPTISTS AND THE "OTHER"

Baptists' cultural contexts today require the ability to relate to a rapidly changing world that is populated by diverse views, lifestyles, and religious beliefs, including many that stand in sharp contrast to those historically valued by the many Baptist traditions. One of the theological themes that has emerged with growing urgency in practically every locus of Baptist life has been the need for an adequate doctrine of the other. This study has noted that a frequent Baptist response to difference has been that of ill-considered reaction. However, the magnitude of change and discontinuity between Baptist traditions and twenty-first-century contexts cannot simultaneously sustain past patterns and a robust future. Baptists' divisive and blemished track record in dealing with discrepancies among viewpoints generated by medical, technological, political, social, and scientific innovations over the twentieth century betrays this challenge. Furthermore, as the pressures of varied and novel traditioning sources emerge more clearly in the twenty-first century, the demand for theological clarity at this point becomes more acute.

Earlier, this chapter noted that the starting point of Baptist theology has tended to be soteriology, which is couched in Baptist convictions about the Bible, God, and the nature of humanity. This point of departure has influenced Baptist values in numerous ways. For one thing, the character of Baptists' soteriological focus historically has placed heavy emphasis on a future life in ways that often have allowed the abuses and injustices suffered by the others in this life to go unaddressed. Baptists have a strong history of advocacy for religious liberty for all people, especially when Baptists themselves have been among those suffering the adverse effects of religious policies. A few Baptist bodies have remarkable records of social engagement – for which they often have faced heavy criticism from other Baptist communions and beyond. In many instances, however, saving souls for heaven has been allowed to substitute for the costly actions required to address the systemic suffering of others in the present. Furthermore, Baptists' understanding of soteriology has tended to encourage views that divide humanity into two camps – the saved and the lost – a categorical divide that easily has degenerated into insiders and outsiders along with certain concomitant social and political judgments. Consequently, clear parameters often been established to judge not only who and what belong inside and outside the Baptist camp but also who and what belong inside and outside of human society in general. With this, Baptists are confronted with the ethics and practices of exclusion. How should they view, relate to, and treat persons that are different from themselves? What would be an appropriate way of thinking about those categorized outside of Baptists' preferred theological, moral, and social values?

In some ways, Baptists face a situation similar to the one that confronted the returning Hebrew exiles in sixth-century BCE Israel. In that context, a small minority community faced the overwhelming challenges of establishing its identity amid larger populations with divergent views. The Old Testament books of Ezra and Nehemiah describe how that community's feelings of desperation led to brutal acts of fanaticism and exclusion in efforts to protect its purity, identity, and distinctness. Walter Brueggemann, in assessing those responses, observes that "when discipline is propelled primarily by anxiety that causes core commitments of the community to be surrendered for the sake of anxiety-assuaging disciplines . . . then the community asserts secondary matters at the cost of primary commitments. The question posed by the literature is how to maintain disciplines and boundaries without sacrificing core commitments in the process."[42] In a fashion somewhat parallel to the Hebrew exiles, a Baptist theology of the other must address two fundamental issues – the group's need somehow to preserve core values and identity and the fact that the manner in which a group does this can either enhance or destroy those very values and its treasured identity. In other words, mere exclusion may be just as deadly to a group as an uncritical absorption of strange, new values. Care must be given to how the other will be valued (or devalued) and included (or excluded).

Traditionally, Baptists have desired their churches to be communities of confessional formation. However, as the twenty-first century opens, that goal stands in contrast to the tendencies of postmodern people to ask their own questions and to follow them wherever they may lead. Many in contemporary society who confess to being spiritual also resist being labeled with a particular brand of church. There are indicators that such persons are open to joining others in spiritual pilgrimage but are not inclined to accept a predetermined confessional formation. A growing dimension of urban and postmodern experience seems to be disconnectedness – the tendency toward identity development that does not assume that persons are easily or automatically connected to others in intimate relationships or in larger communities.[43] David Tracy observes that "there is no longer a center with margins. There are many centers."[44] If these interpretations of twenty-first century trends are correct, then others cannot remain the objects or projections of Baptists' fears and hopes. They must become

[42] Walter Brueggemann, *An Introduction to the Old Testament: The Canon and Christian Imagination* (Louisville, KY: Westminster/John Knox Press, 2003), 371.
[43] Susan M. Simonaitis, "Teaching as Conversation," in *The Scope of Our Art*, ed. L. Gregory Jones and Stephanie Paulsell (Grand Rapids, MI: William B. Eerdmans Publishing, 2002), 109.
[44] David Tracy, *On Naming the Present: God, Hermeneutics, Church* (Maryknoll, NY: Orbis Books, 1994), 4.

genuine others in Baptists' consciousness. Whether the other might be of a different theological persuasion, a devotee of another religion, of a different sexual orientation, or simply a different Baptist, he or she cannot be approached simply as marginal to a particular Baptist adherent's center but must be recognized as having his or her own center. This runs counter to the traditions of interpretative intentionality, but it harmonizes with the historical inclinations of Baptist dreamers.

Biblical ethics is not indifferent concerning how the other should be treated. Baptists are challenged to decide not only whether the other can have status within their systems of belief but also whether the other has value as other totally apart from his or her willingness to conform to the expectations of Baptist traditions. Every community of any real significance has two ways of dealing with the other – assimilation or elimination. In the case of Ezra and Nehemiah, the strategy was elimination, thus the conclusion that the other was unacceptable. In the contemporary context, the other might be cultural, political, or theological. It might be anything that produces anxiety and threatens the dominance of the homogeneous Baptist population with which an adherent identifies. Although the clashes described in these chapters are real enough, what agendas will Baptists derive from the challenges they are facing? Will they plan and labor with stronger determination for exclusion, trying by every means to hold the center for themselves and their own groups while pushing others to the margins? Should they choose that response, how might that shape the future of their faith, communities, and understanding of God? Or, instead, might Baptists choose to dedicate themselves to helping the larger Baptist, Christian, religious, and human communities grasp the necessity of learning to live and work together – as centers of their own? What might it cost ultimately to give over to a cultural reality in which human relations become subservient to "the unbending insistence of forceful ideology"?[45]

In *An Introduction to the Old Testament*, Walter Brueggemann raises a haunting set of questions that the global families of Baptists are challenged to try to answer: "For Christians: How much Christianity is enough Christianity? And for whites, how much whiteness is enough? And for men, how much maleness is enough? And for Americans, how much patriotism is enough? And for Calvinists, how much Calvinism is enough? . . . For the insiders in any crisis over sameness, there is never enough . . . except for our own."[46] How such questions are addressed will seriously influence the shape

---

[45] Ibid., 372.   [46] Breuggemann, *Old Testament*, 373–4.

Figure 20. Kowloon City Baptist Church in Hong Kong (courtesy of Kowloon City Baptist Church).

Figure 21. Pleasant Valley Baptist Church near Kansas City, Missouri (author's photo). These churches are illustrative of the megachurch trend in the Baptist movement. By 2010, Kowloon City had more than twelve thousand members and Pleasant Valley more than eight thousand. Both churches have shopping-mall-sized campuses.

of the world in which all people, not just Baptists, will live. The culturally exclusivist approach advocated by varied interpretative intentionalities may address the concerns of specific Baptist communions for maintaining identities built on well-defined boundaries, but doing this in the end may destroy the very values and identities they are intended to protect.

A New Context for Baptist Identity

Baptists globally consist of a multitude of independent bodies that are sometimes connected formally through covenants of cooperation, sometimes bonded informally through common interests and goals, and sometimes not connected at all. Each Baptist entity, at any given time, usually is experiencing some combination of all three states of connectedness in relation to an array of other Baptist entities. Thus, with no centralized defining authority, how does one decide what is and is not Baptist? Some observers object that this is not even the correct question to be asking when exploring issues of identity in a postmodern context.

To a significant degree, *Baptist* is a self-designation. Over the past four centuries, individuals and groups have embraced the nomenclature for varied reasons, but most commonly they have done so on ecclesiological and soteriological grounds. As with many aspects of identity in a multiethnic, multicultural, and pluralistic society, blending can confuse the traditional lines of designation so thoroughly that for many people such identity becomes a matter of choice. Interpretative authorities try to offer what are usually very culturally biased attempts at definition, but there are no external powers capable of enforcing those designations on other Baptists. The product of such effort at best is capable only of defining or characterizing a specific body of Baptists in a particular way at a circumscribed period in time. Even then the designation would have validity only to the extent that significant numbers within that Baptist body agreed to accept the definitions.

When representatives of Baptist congregations meet in conventions, associations, or unions, they sometimes make decisions that carry authority for the churches that participate in their particular fellowship of Baptists. Churches that choose not to accept those decisions might be excluded from participation in the membership and activities of that association, but even that cannot deprive the dismembered church from being Baptist. The excommunicated church might afterward decide to become part of a different association of Baptist churches that would be willing to accept the dissenting congregation into its fellowship and common activities. The issues, goals, and qualifications around which a group of Baptist churches might fellowship are self-chosen. Thus, in a global setting, the beliefs, experiences, and goals capable of becoming the vehicles for Baptist church connection are almost infinite. Some of the most frequent ones are geographical proximity, ethnic identity, doctrinal connection, and common mission or ministries.

Despite this complexity of definition, it is possible to speak of a few attributes as characteristic of a large number of Baptists, even though these should be understood only as extrapolations and not as qualifying descriptions applicable to every Baptist body under all circumstances. Therefore, on the basis of the overviews and analyses presented in these chapters, it might be beneficial to note the following things about Baptists as a global movement. First, one of the core values of Baptists is the freedom of a local faith community to determine its own theological definitions – that is, to define itself, to determine for itself what shall be its significant beliefs and practices, and to do all of this under the guidance of the Bible and other sources of faith and theology without the control of any other human authority. Baptist history is replete with examples of churches that have failed to exercise that principle, abdicating this decision-making prerogative to external authorities, both ecclesial and civil. At times, dereliction in fulfilling the responsibilities of this much-touted badge of Baptist congregational distinction has been because of pressure from denominational powers, notions that they must conform to a set of unalterable Baptist rules or else lose their qualification for being Baptist, perceptions of being bound by certain immutable denominational traditions, prospective material benefits if they submit, inappropriate political allegiances, conformity to prevailing cultural expectations, or ignorance of Baptist heritage. While often better at stating the value than comprehending or practicing it, freedom remains one of the most widely self-chosen identifiers among Baptist people and congregations.

Second, the Baptist movement traditionally values the need for individuals to pursue truth in terms that are meaningful to them in their particular life contexts and also the need to have support from caring persons of faith in that pursuit. Frequently, the depth and quality of caring experienced by individuals have tended to accompany the extent of similarity and uniformity of shared values. In Baptist life, this has generally produced a high degree of ethnic, class, socioeconomic, and sometimes even political homogeneity within congregations and the focus of their ministries. It also has tended to color local Baptists' conceptions of God, resulting in very particularistic theologies of God's love, will, and work. When left unchallenged, this tendency has fueled expectations that all "others" would conform to the standards of "my" group or be judged as existing outside God's redemptive operations. A major challenge for Baptists in contemporary culture emerges at this juncture – how to value themselves in their great variety as particular people who play crucial roles in God's world-encompassing purposes while simultaneously recognizing that God's activities are far broader than their limited body of knowledge and experience.

Third, Baptist traditioning sources have an innate sense of the inadequacy of simply living a life of faith that is controlled by the rules and experiences of someone else's faith. This implies the inability to accept readily the definitions advanced by another individual, group, denomination, culture, or interpretive authority as an adequate basis for one's own relationship with God.

Fourth, a major source of tension for Baptists living under colonial conditions was the fact that once local Baptist faith communities truly comprehended what missionaries (i.e., representatives of Anglo and other Baptist communities) were teaching, they experienced within themselves the need to exercise faith for themselves and define its meaning within their own contexts. In other words, they needed to achieve full humanity. Sometimes this need did not correlate easily with certain values, definitions, or practices of sending Baptist communities. However, the principle of defining faith in terms that were relevant for a particular faith community was overriding. Some local faith communities found their identity by dissenting from the locally dominant cultures and embracing a counteridentity that Baptist missionaries or other representatives supplied. Others found it necessary to reinterpret the Baptist worldviews and values they had been offered and allow them to find meaning within new cultural contexts.

At the same time, some Baptists in the "mother" cultures discovered that certain long-held practices and definitions of Baptist identity could not adequately fit the new contexts that were evolving around them. Redefinitions were needed. Maintainers of the older interpretative traditions often considered such efforts at redefinition unacceptable and sought ways to protect the status quo. But ultimately, the voices of primal traditions managed to assert themselves in spite of the opposition. In each context, what it meant to be Baptist could not at the same time remain static and retain its value.

Finally, in the twenty-first century, the principle of local faith community decision making has taken on more than geographical dimensions as globalization has tended to shape group identities along other lines than

just (or even primarily) physical location or traditional confessional formulations. Sharon Welch is among the persons who see continued efforts
at community formation based on common experience as misguided. Not
only do they go against the grain of postmodern experience; they are inherently oppressive. In a polycentric world, communities that emerge amid
difference best express the ethos of global humanity.[1] Susan Simonaitis
describes the postmodern experience of "other" in terms of inscrutability
and inaccessibility. In a world that is filled with people, the others are
the unapproachable persons all around us who are part of the environment, wanting what we want, yet remaining distant and undiscoverable.
In this context, people are becoming skilled at connecting by utilizing
that distance between themselves and those in proximity as a vehicle for
linking. In this world, community emerges among persons who, though
not threatening, are not accessible.[2] A major challenge for Baptists, given
their movement's particular kind of ecclesiology, is to discover what – if
anything – is cohesive in this diversity. The chapters of this book have
portrayed the fact that Baptists are polycentric. Should they discover from
contemporary societies the art of forming communities derived in and
through difference, then many of their values might gain increased hearing
among today's cultures. Such communities will comprise real people who
risk themselves in bold experiments and are willing to be reshaped into
something that in the present is not clearly known. They will engage this
challenge in faith, trusting God to somehow guide them into lifestyles that
offer fulfillment for all members of society. That, indeed, is a world for
dreamers.

---

[1] Sharon Welch, *Feminist Ethic of Risk* (Minneapolis: Augsburg, 1990), 34.
[2] Susan M. Simonaitis, "Teaching as Conversation," in *The Scope of Our Art*, ed. L. Gregory Jones
and Stephanie Paulsell (Grand Rapids, MI: William B. Eerdmans Publishing, 2002), 110.

Index

Abbot, Elisha, 207
Abernathy, Ralph, 360
Aboriginal Baptists, 127, 128, 138, 283
Acadia University, 119, 337
ad fontes, 14, 15
Adorian, Constantin, 196
Adorian, Jegalia, 316
Africa Baptist Assembly, Malawi, 250
African American Baptist women, 181, 373
African American Baptists, 80, 96, 99, 137, 162, 200, 288, 411
African Baptist Association, Canada, 121
African Baptist Mission Society, 99, 136, 137, 162, 163
African Baptist women, 253
African Baptists, 133, 137, 202, 231, 232, 241, 242, 243, 245, 251, 255, 381, 391, 409
African Indigenous Churches, 243
African sacred cosmos, 11, 48, 80
Akiyama, Yoshigoro, 370
Alabama Baptists, general convention, 144, 147, 150, 353, 358
Albuquerque, Antônio Teixeira de, 166, 214, 216
Alf, Gottfried, 193
All Russian Union of Evangelical Christians, also see Paskovites, 323
Alliance of Baptists, U.S., 344, 348, 350, 372
Alline, Henry, 76, 119
All-Union Council of Evangelical Christians-Baptists, 398
Alves, José, 217
American Baptist Association, 278, 355
American Baptist Churches, USA, 298, 299, 347, 361, 367
American Baptist Convention, 164, 345, 347
American Baptist Education Society, 151, 152
American Baptist Foreign Mission Society, 136, 149, 173, 208, 351, 371, 386
American Baptist Free Mission Society, 149, 211, 222

American Baptist Home Mission Society, 149, 150, 151, 152, 169, 171, 172, 173, 174, 216, 223, 297, 298, 350, 371
American Baptist Missionary Convention, 163
American Baptist Missionary Union, 99, 151, 190, 192, 199, 201, 211, 240, 245, 247, 344
American Baptist Publication Society, 151, 153, 346, 385
American Baptist Tract Society, 151
American Baptist Women, ABC-USA, 292, 372, 377
American Baptist Women's Ministries, ABC-USA, 372
American Indian Mission Association, 158
Amherstburg Association, 122
Anabaptists, 57
Anderson, Johanna, 173
Andrews, Emery, 368
Anglican Church, also see Church of England, 10, 11, 17, 19, 20, 23, 24, 27, 32, 35, 39, 48, 56, 62, 72, 74, 76, 81, 102, 277, 280, 405
Anglo American Baptists, 37, 40, 41, 44, 71, 80, 141, 155, 156, 157, 162, 194, 196, 210, 212, 223, 228, 233, 234, 287, 342, 343, 364, 368, 369, 382, 391, 397, 399, 410, 414
Anglo Baptist Women, 175, 370
Anglo Baptists, also see British Baptists and English Baptists, 3, 19, 22, 23, 24, 40, 46, 49, 79, 111, 116, 124, 133, 141, 159, 204, 208, 219, 228, 259, 308, 342, 382, 393, 399, 408
Anglo-African Mutual Improvement and Aid Association, 121
Angus, George, 223
antimission controversy, 144, 145, 153, 361
antislavery controversy, 142, 148, 149
anti-Trinitarianism, 58
Argentine Baptists, 215, 217, 218, 287, 288, 289, 290
Arminianism, 18, 54, 59, 145
Armstrong, Annie, 172
Asian American Baptist women, 377